INTERNET CHILD PORNOGRAPHY AND THE LAW

Internet Child Pornography and the Law

National and International Responses

YAMAN AKDENIZ
University of Leeds, UK

ASHGATE

Published by
Ashgate Publishing Limited
Wey Court East,
Union Street,
Farnham,
Surrey,
GU9 7PT

Ashgate Publishing Company
Suite 420
101 Cherry Street
Burlington, VT 05401-4405
USA

Reprinted 2009

Ashgate website: http://www.ashgate.com

British Library Cataloguing in Publication Data
Akdeniz, Yaman
Internet child pornography and the law : national and international responses
1. Child pornography - Law and legislation 2. Internet pornography - Law and legislation
I. Title
344' .03276

Library of Congress Cataloging-in-Publication Data
Akdeniz, Yaman.
Internet child pornography and the law : national and international responses / by Yaman Akdeniz.
p. cm.
Includes bibliographical references and index.
ISBN 978-0-7546-2297-0
1. Child pornography--Law and legislation. 2. Internet pornography--Law and legislation. 3. Internet and children. 4. Child sexual abuse--United States--Prevention. I. Title.

K5293.A38 2008
344.05'47--dc22

2007030990

ISBN 978 0 7546 2297 0

Printed and bound in Great Britain by
TJ International Ltd, Padstow, Cornwall

Contents

List of Graphs and Tables

GRAPHS

TABLES

List of Cases

UK

Aston Cantlow and Wilmcote with Billesley Parochial Church Council v. Wallbank and another [2001] EWCA Civ 713; [2001] 3 All ER 393.
Atkins v. Director of Public Prosecutions; Goodland v. Director of Public Prosecutions [2000] 2 All ER 425; [2000] 1 WLR 1427 (QBD).
Attorney-General's Reference (No. 89 of 2004) [2004] EWCA Crim 3222.
Bunt v. Tilley and others [2006] EWHC 407 (QBD); [2006] 3 All ER 336.
Godfrey v. Demon Internet Ltd [1999] 4 All ER 342; [2000] 3 WLR 1020; [2001] QB 201 (QBD).
Harper v. The Information Commissioner and Royal Mail, Information Tribunal Appeal Case, No. EA/2005/0001, 15 November 2005.
Heather and others v. The Leonard Cheshire Foundation and another [2001] EWHC Admin 429, CO/4503/2000, CO/4727/00 (QBD).
R v. Allison [2001] EWCA Crim 1971, 17 September 2001.
R v. Avery [2004] EWCA Crim 2935.
R v. Barber [2002] 1 Cr App Rep (S) 548.
R v. Beaney [2004] Crim.L.R. 480.
R v. Bibby [2005] EWCA Crim 1859.
R v. Bishop [2005] EWCA Crim 829.
R v. Bolingbroke [2000] *The Times*, August 16 2000, (CA (Crim Div)).
R v. Bootland [2000] No. 00/5733/W2, 7 December 2000.
R v. Bowden [2000] 2 All ER 418.
R v. Canavan, Kidd and Shaw [1998] 1 Cr App R 79.
R v. Carr [2003] EWCA Crim 2416.
R v. Cawthorne [2004] All ER (D) 10 (Oct).
R v. Clark [2002] EWCA Crim 2925.
R v. Clarke [2005] EWCA Crim 948.
R v. Collard [2004] EWCA Crim 1664.
R v. Collier [2004] EWCA Crim 1411; [2004] All ER (D) 82 (Jun).
R v. Coutts [2005] 1 Cr App Rep 517.
R v. Coxon [2002] EWCA Crim 140 (No. 200105185/X4), 16 January 2002.
R v. Cruz [2002] EWCA Crim 1099 No. 01/6887/Y2, 8 May 2002.
R v. Edwards [2005] EWCA Crim 402.
R v. Evans [2005] All ER (D) 291 (Feb).
R v. Father Adrian McLeish (1996), unreported.
R v. Fellows and Arnold [1997] 1 Cr App R 244; [1997] 2 All E.R. 548; [1997] Crim. L.R. 524.

R v. Feuer [2005] EWCA Crim 948; [2005] EWCA Crim 2415.
R v. Fillary [2003] EWCA Crim 2682.
R v. Graham-Kerr [1988] 1 WLR 1098; (1989) 88 Cr App Rep 302.
R v. Grant [2003] EWCA Crim 2495 No. 03/3739/A5.
R v. Green [2004] EWCA Crim 2795.
R v. Grosvenor [2003] EWCA Crim 1627.
R v. Hardy [2005] EWCA Crim 1636.
R v. Hart [2003] EWCA Crim 2064.
R v. Hatchett [2003] EWCA Crim 426 No. 2002/03266/Y3.
R v. Healy [2003] EWCA Crim 551.
R v. Hill [2003] EWCA Crim 42 No. 2002/00327/Z3.
R v. Hopkinson [2001] EWCA Crim 84; [2001] WL 15091.
R v. Howe [2006] EWCA Crim 3147.
R v. Hughes [2002] EWCA Crim 3185.
R v. Humphreys [2006] EWCA Crim 640.
R v. Hyett [2001] EWCA Crim 669 No. 200004183/Z5, 14 March 2001.
R v. Jackson [2001] EWCA Crim 1990 No. 200104197/Y5, 17 August 2001.
R v. James [2000] 2 Cr App R(S) 258.
R v. Jefferson [2001] EWCA Crim 1278 (No. 200102455/W2), 14 May 2001.
R v. Jones [2003] EWCA Crim 2034.
R v. Kelly CA, [2004] EWCA Crim 256.
R v. Knights [2001] EWCA Crim 1694 (No. 2001/01858/X1), 13 July 2001.
R v. Koeller [2001] EWCA Crim 1854 (No. 200102718/Y1), 6 August 2001.
R v. Land [1999] QB 65; [1998] 1 All ER 403; [1998] 3 WLR 322.
R v. M.K. [2003] EWCA Crim 132.
R v. Makeham [2000] No. 200006484/Y5, 18 December 2000.
R v. Malone [2000] WL 1918630, 19 December 2000.
R v. Mansfield [2005] All ER (D) 195 (Apr) (15 April 2005).
R v. McInnes [2002] EWCA Crim 3193 No. 2002/06262/W2.
R v. Monument [2005] EWCA Crim 30; [2005] All ER (D) 189 (Jan).
R v. MS [2000] 2 Cr App R(S) 388.
R v. Nelson [2002] 1 Cr App Rep (S) 565.
R v. Nicholson [2004] EWCA Crim 2840.
R v. O'Carroll [2002] EWCA Civ 3190.
R v. Oliver and others (CA Criminal Division), [2002] EWCA Crim 2766; [2003] 2 Cr App R (S) 64; [2003] 1 Cr. App. R. 28; [2003] 2 Cr. App. R. (S.) 15; [2003] Crim. L.R. 127.
R v. Owen [1988] 1 WLR.
R v. Owens [2001] EWCA Crim 1370 No. 200101729/W1, 8 June 2001.
R v. Pardue [2003] EWCA Crim 1562; [2003] Crim. L.R. 641-642.
R v. Pepper; R v. Barber; R v. Lamont; R v. Gya; R v. Murray [2005] EWCA Crim 1181 (April 2005).
R v. Pittard [2002] EWCA Crim 415 (No. 02/475/X5), 11 February 2002.
R v. Poole [2003] EWCA Crim 222.
R v. Porter [2006] EWCA Crim 560; [2006] All ER (D) 236 (Mar).
R v. Proctor [2004] EWCA Crim 1932.

R v. Purcell [2003] EWCA Crim 723 No. 2002/05693/X2.
R v. Reast [2005] EWCA Crim 1957.
R v. Richards [2003] EWCA Crim 834.
R v. Rooke [2005] All ER (D) 08 (Apr); [2005] EWCA Crim 832.
R v. Russell [2003] EWCA Crim 1378.
R v. Saint CA, [2004] EWCA Crim 550.
R v. Sears [2003] EWCA Crim 367 No. 2002/06471/Y3.
R v. Skinner [2005] EWCA Crim 1439.
R v. Slinger [2003] EWCA Crim 2761.
R v. Smethurst [2001] EWCA Crim 772.
R v. Smith and R v. Jayson [2002] EWCA Crim 683; [2003] 1 Cr App R 13.
R v. Snelleman [2001] EWCA Crim 1530 (No. 200102539/Y5), 19 June 2001.
R v. Tatam [2004] EWCA Crim 1856.
R v. Thomas [2003] EWCA Crim 2681.
R v. Thompson [2001] EWCA Crim 1073 No. 01/1556/Y4, 26 April 2001.
R v. Thompson [2004] EWCA Crim 669; [2004] 2 Cr App R 262; [2005] 1 Cr App R (S) 1.
R v. Toomer, Powell, Mould [2001] Crim. L.R. 149; *The Times*, November 21 2000 (CA (Crim Div)).
R v. Turpin [2001] EWCA Crim 1600 (No. 2001/02905/W4), 3 July 2001.
R v. Wade [2003] EWCA Crim 12.
R v. Wakefield [2003] EWCA Crim 2624 No. 03/4086/A5.
R v. West [2001] EWCA Crim 811 No. 01/1117/Z3, 26 March 2001.
R v. West [2001] EWCA Crim 418 No. 200100133/Z5, 19 February 2000.
R v. White [2003] EWCA Crim 2035.
R v. Wild and Jefferson [2001] EWCA Crim 1433, QBD.
R v. Wild [2001] EWCA Crim 1272; [2002] 1 Cr App R (S) 37.
R v. Wright [2003] EWCA Crim 1672.
R v. Young [2005] EWCA Crim 1078.
Regina (O) v. Coventry Magistrates Court [2004] QBD, 5 April 2004.
Regina v. Clegg [2002] EWCA Crim 306 (No. 01/7067/W3), 7 February 2002.
Regina v. W [2005] EWCA Crim 1204.

USA

Ashcroft, Attorney General, et al. v. Free Speech Coalition et al. (US Supreme Court, 2002) 535 U.S. 234, 198 F3d 1083, 16 April 2002, No. 00–795, Argued October 30, 2001.
Austin v. CrystalTech Web Hosting (Ariz.App. 2005) 125 P.3d 389, 392–4.
Barrett v. Fonorow (Ill.App.Ct. 2003) 799 N.E.2d 916, 923–5.
Barrett v. Rosenthal, 112 Cal. App. 4th 1379, 1395 (1st Dist., Div. 2 2004); *Barrett v. Rosenthal*, 40 Cal.4th 33, 146 P.3d 510, 51 Cal.Rptr.3d 55 (Cal. Sup. Ct., Nov. 20, 2006).
Batzel v. Smith, 333 F3d 1018, 1027 n.10 (9th Cir. 2003).
Beauharnais v. Illinois, 343 U.S. 250, 266, 96 L. Ed. 919, 72 S. Ct. 725 (1952).

Ben Ezra, Weinstein, and Co. v. AOL, Inc., 206 F3d 980, 986 (10th Cir. 2000).
Blumenthal v. Drudge (D.D.C. 1998) 992 F.Supp. 44, 51.
Brandenburg v. Ohio, 395 U.S. 444 (1969).
Braun v. Soldier of Fortune Magazine, Inc., 968 F.2d 1110, 1118–19 (11th Cir. 1992). cert. denied, 506 U.S. 1071 (1993).
Broadrick v. Oklahoma, 413 U.S. 601 (1973).
Carafano v. Metrosplash.com, Inc. (9th Cir. 2003) 339 F3d 1119, 1123–4.
Chaplinsky v. New Hampshire, 315 U.S. 568, 571–3, 86 L. Ed. 1031, 62 S. Ct. 766 (1942).
Cubby, Inc. v. CompuServe Inc. 776 F. Supp. 135 (1991).
Doe One v. Oliver (Conn.Super.Ct. 2000) 755 A.2d 1000, 1003–4.
Doe v. America Online, Inc., 25 Media L. Rep. (BNA) 2112, 1997 WL 374223 (Fla. Cir. Ct. June 26, 1997); Case No. 97-2587 (Fourth District Court of Appeal, Fla., October 14 1998).
Doe v. America Online, Inc., 783 So. 2d 1010 (Fla. 2001), in approving the decision of *Doe v. America Online, Inc.*, 718 So. 2d 385, 27 Media L. Rep. (BNA) 1119 (Fla. Dist. Ct. App. 4th Dist. 1998), review granted, 729 So. 2d 390 (Fla. 1999) and decision approved, 2001 WL 228446 (Fla. 2001).
Doe v. GTE Corp. 347 F3d. 655 (7th Cir. 2003).
Donato v. Moldow (N.J. Super.Ct.App.Div. 2005) 865 A.2d 711, 720–27.
Free Speech Coalition v. Reno, 198 F3d 1083, 1092 (9th Cir. 1999), cert. granted sub nom. *Ashcroft v. Free Speech Coalition*, 148 L. Ed. 2d 788, 121 S. Ct. 876, 69 U.S.L.W. 3495 (U.S. 2001).
Ginzburg v. United States, 383 U.S. 463, 86 S. Ct. 942, 16 L. Ed. 2d 31 (1966).
Grayned v. City of Rockford, 408 U.S. 104, 108 (1972).
Green v. AOL, 318 F3d 465, 471 (3d Cir. 2003).
Heidemann v. U.S., 2004 WL 633241 (M.D. Ala. 2004).
Jane Doe v. America Online, Inc., Case No. CL 97-631 AE; Decision: 1997 WL 374223 (Fla. Cir. Ct. June 26, 1997).
Kingsley Int'l Pictures Corp. v. Regents of the Univ. of State of N.Y., 360 U.S. 684, 79 S. Ct. 1362, 3 L. Ed. 2d 1512 (1959).
Mento v. United States, 535 U.S. 1014, 152 L. Ed. 2d 617, 122 S. Ct. 1602 (2002).
Miller v. California, 413 U.S. 15 (1973).
Morrison v. America Online, Inc. (N.D.Ind. 2001) 153 F.Supp.2d 930, 933–4.
New York v. Ferber, 458 U.S. 747 (1982).
Osborne v. Ohio, 495 U.S. 103 (1990).
Padgett v. U.S., 302 F. Supp. 2d 593 (D.S.C. 2004), appeal dismissed, 119 Fed. Appx. 440 (4th Cir. 2005).
PatentWizard, Inc. v. Kinko's, Inc. (D.S.D. 2001) 163 F.Supp.2d 1069, 1071.
R.A.V. v. City of St. Paul, 505 U.S. 377, 382–3, 120 L. Ed. 2d 305, 112 S. Ct. 2538 (1992).
Religious Technology Center v. F.A.C.T.Net, Inc., 901 F. Supp. 1519 (D. Colo. 1995).
Religious Technology Center v. Netcom On-line Communication Services, Inc., 907 F. Supp. 1361 (N.D. Cal. 1995).
Roth v. United States, 354 U.S. 476, 484, 1 L. Ed. 2d 1498, 77 S. Ct. 1304 (1957).

Sable Communications of Cal., Inc. v. FCC, 492 U.S. 115 (1989).
Schneider v. Amazon.com, Inc. (Wn.App. 2001) 31 P.3d 37, 40–42.
Stanley v. Georgia, 394 U.S. 557 (1969).
Stratton Oakmont, Inc. v. Prodigy Servs., Co. 23 Media L. Rep. (BNA) 1794 (1995).
The Free Speech Coalition v. Reno, 1997 U.S. Dist. LEXIS 12212, No. C 97-0281 VSC, 1997 WL 487758, at *7 (N.D. Cal. Aug. 12, 1997).
U.S. v. Hilton, 363 F3d 58, 63–6 (1st Cir. 2004), *withdrawn by United States v. Hilton*, 2004 U.S. App. LEXIS 19528 (1st Cir. Sept. 20, 2004).
U.S. v. 12200 Ft. Reels, 413 U.S. 123 (1973).
U.S. v. Acheson, 195 F3d 645 (11th Cir. 1999).
U.S. v. Bach, 400 F3d 622 (8th Cir. 2005), cert. denied, 126 S. Ct. 243 (U.S. 2005).
U.S. v. Baker, 890 F. Supp. 1375 (1995).
U.S. v. Barbieri, 43 Fed. Appx. 367 (10th Cir. 2002).
U.S. v. Bender, 290 F3d 1279, 1282 n.2 (11th Cir.), cert. denied, 537 U.S. 1037, 154 L. Ed. 2d 457, 123 S. Ct. 571 (2002).
U.S. v. Cendejas, 2004 WL 388960 (A.F.C.C.A. 2004).
U.S. v. Cervini, 379 F3d 987, 993 n.4 (10th Cir. 2004).
U.S. v. Deaton, 328 F3d 454, 455 (8th Cir. 2003).
U.S. v. Detwiler, 338 F.Supp.2d 1166 D. Or., 2004.
U.S. v. Ellyson, 326 F3d 522 (4th Cir. 2003).
U.S. v. Farrelly, 389 F3d 649 (6th Cir. 2004).
U.S. v. Fox, 248 F3d 394 (5th Cir. 2001).
U.S. v. Fuller, 77 Fed. Appx. 371, 2003 WL 22331999 (6th Cir. 2003).
U.S. v. Grimes, 244 F3d 375, 56 Fed. R. Evid. Serv. 1048 (5th Cir. 2001).
U.S. v. Hall, 312 F3d 1250, 1260 (11th Cir. 2002), cert. denied, 155 L. Ed. 2d 502, 123 S. Ct. 1646 (2003).
U.S. v. Harms, 371 F3d 1208, 1213 (10th Cir. 2004).
U.S. v. Hersh, 297 F3d 1233, 1254 n.31 (11th Cir. 2002), cert. denied, 537 U.S. 1217, 154 L. Ed. 2d 1071, 123 S. Ct. 1319 (2003).
U.S. v. Hilton, 167 F3d 61, 68–9 (1st Cir. 1999), pet. for cert. filed, No. 98-9647 (U.S. May 28, 1999); *U.S. v. Hilton*, 363 F3d 58 (1st Cir.), vacated, 386 F3d 13 (1st Cir. 2004).
U.S. v. Honzik, 2003 WL 22862648 (A.F.C.C.A. 2003).
U.S. v. Irving, 452 F3d 110; (2nd Cir., 2006) U.S. App. LEXIS 16077.
U.S. v. James, 55 M.J. 297 (C.A.A.F. 2001).
U.S. v. Kelly, 314 F3d 908, 911 (7th Cir.), cert. denied, 155 L. Ed. 2d 829, 123 S. Ct. 1923 (2003).
U.S. v. Kimler, 335 F3d 1132, 1142 (10th Cir.), cert. denied, 157 L. Ed. 2d 759, 124 S. Ct. 945, 2003 U.S. LEXIS 9142, 72 U.S.L.W. 3392 (U.S. Dec. 8, 2003)(No. 03-7285).
U.S. v. Marchand, 308 F. Supp. 2d 498 (D.N.J. 2004).
U.S. v. Marcus (2001, ED NY) 193 F Supp 2d 552.
U.S. v. Matthews, 209 F3d 338, 28 Media L. Rep. (BNA) 1673 (4th Cir. 2000).
U.S. v. Mento, 231 F3d 912 (CA4 2000).
U.S. v. Morell, 429 F3d 1161 C.A.8 (Ark.), 2005.

U.S. v. Morgan, 2002 WL 975154 (D. Me. 2002).

U.S. v. Nolan, 818 F.2d 1015 (1st Cir. 1987).

U.S. v. Oakes, 224 F. Supp. 2d 296, 301–2 (D. Me. 2002).

U.S. v. Pearl, 89 F. Supp. 2d 1237 (D. Utah 2000); *U.S. v. Pearl*, 324 F3d 1210, 1213 (10th Cir. 2003), cert. denied, 156 L. Ed. 2d 616, 123 S. Ct. 2591, 2003 U.S. LEXIS 4722, 2003 WL 21184530 (U.S. June 16, 2003) (No. 02-10597).

U.S. v. Porter, 184 Fed. Appx. 112 (2d Cir. 2006).

U.S. v. Rearden, 349 F3d 608, 62 Fed. R. Evid. Serv. 1255, 2 *A.L.R. Fed.* 2d 765 (9th Cir. 2003), cert. denied, 125 S. Ct. 32, 160 L. Ed. 2d 32 (U.S. 2004).

U.S. v. Reedy, 119 Fed. Appx. 686; 2005 U.S. App. LEXIS 1474; *United States v. Reedy*, 304 F3d 358, 2002 U.S. App. LEXIS 17668 (5th Cir. Tex., 2002).

U.S. v. Reidel, 402 U.S. 351 (1971).

U.S. v. Rejkowski, 2003 WL 649089 (N.M.C.C.A. 2003).

U.S. v. Riccardi, 405 F3d 852, 870–71 (10th Cir. 2005).

U.S. v. Richardson, 304 [*1142] F3d 1061, 1063–4 (11th Cir. 2002), cert. denied, 537 U.S. 1138, 154 L. Ed. 2d 832, 123 S. Ct. 930 (2003).

U.S. v. Rodriguez-Pacheco, 475 F3d 434; (First Cir. 2007) U.S. App. LEXIS 2497.

U.S. v. Schmeltzer, 20 F3d 610 (5th Cir. 1994).

U.S. v. Sims, 220 F. Supp. 2d 1222 (D.N.M. 2002); 428 F3d 945; (Tenth Cir. 2005) U.S. App. LEXIS 24143.

U.S. v. Slanina, 359 F3d 356, 357 (5th Cir. 2004).

U.S. v. Stevens (1998, DC Alaska) 29 F Supp 2d 592.

U.S. v. Tucker (2002, CA10 Utah) 305 F3d 1193.

U.S. v. Vig, 167 F3d 443, 449–50 (8th Cir. 1999), cert. denied, 528 U.S. 859, 145 L. Ed. 2d 125, 120 S. Ct. 146, (1999).

U.S. v. Williams, 444 F3d 1286; 2006 U.S. App. LEXIS 8384; 19 Fla. L. Weekly Fed. C 418; Rehearing, *en banc*, denied by *United States v. Williams*, 186 Fed. Appx. 983, 2006 U.S. App. LEXIS 25218 (11th Cir. Fla., 2006); *United States v. Williams* (Supreme Court Docket No. 06-694) at <http://www.supremecourtus.gov/docket/06-694.htm>.

Yahoo!, Inc. v. La Ligue Contre Le Racisme Et L'Antisemitisme, Case Number C-00-21275 JF [Docket No. 17], United States District Court for the Northern District of California, San Jose Division, 169 F. Supp. 2d 1181; 2001 U.S. Dist. LEXIS 18378, November 7, 2001, Decided.

Yahoo! Inc. v. La Ligue Contre Le Racisme et L'Antisemitisme, 379 F3d 1120 (9th Cir. 2004).

Yahoo! Inc. v. La Ligue Contre Le Racisme et L'Antisemitisme, 399 F3d 1010 (9th Cir. 2005).

Yahoo! Inc. v. La Ligue Contre Le Racisme et L'Antisemitisme, 433 F3d 1199 (9th Cir. 2006).

Zeran v. America Online, Inc., U.S. District Court, E.D. Virginia, 958 F.Supp (1997); U.S Court of Appeals, 4th Circuit, CA-96-1564-A, 129 F.2d 327 (1997); U.S. Supreme Court, Certiorari denied, Pet. 97-1488.

CANADA

R v. Beattie [2005] CanLII 41352 (S.C.C.), 10 November 2005 Docket no 30999.
R v. Beattie [2005] 75 O.R. (3d) 117; 2005 Ont. Rep. LEXIS 69.
R v. Briere Ontario Superior Court of Justice, [2004] O.J. No. 5611; 2004 ON.C. LEXIS 6108.
R v. Brown [2006] W.C.B.J. LEXIS 1013; 2006 W.C.B.J. 23; 69 W.C.B. (2d) 780.
R v. Deck [2006] W.C.B.J. LEXIS 479; 2006 W.C.B.J. 62; 69 W.C.B. (2d) 88; 2006 ABCA 92.
R v. G.H.K. [2005] B.C.J. No. 2874; 2005 BCPC 618.
R v. M.H. [2002] B.C.J. No. 771; *R. v. E.O.* [2003] O.J. No. 563.
R v. Missions [2005] 196 C.C.C. (3d) 253; 2005 C.C.C. LEXIS 111.
R v. Pecchiarich [1995] 22 O.R. (3d) 748–766.
R v. Peterson [2006] A.J. No. 827; 2006 ABPC 177; 2006 AB.C. LEXIS 817 (Alberta Provincial Court).
R v. R.A.B. [2006] B.C.J. No. 1808; 2006 BCPC 367; 2006 BC.C. LEXIS 1858 (British Columbia Provincial Court).
R v. Sharpe [1999] 136 C.C.C. (3d) 97 (British Columbia Court of Appeal).
R v. Sharpe [1999] 22 C.R. (5th) 129 (British Columbia Supreme Court).
R v. Sharpe [2001] SCC 2. File No. 27376, 26 January 2001 (Supreme Court of Canada).
R v. Sharpe [2002] B.C.D. Crim. J. 2149; 2002 B.C.D. Crim. J. LEXIS 183; [2002] B.C.D. Crim. 250.90.60.00-01, decided on March 26, 2002.
R v. Sharpe [2004] B.C.J. No. 1565; 2004 BCSC 240; 2004 BC.C. LEXIS 1676, Judgment: February 20, 2004.

GERMANY

Criminal case of Somm, Felix Bruno, File No: 8340 Ds 465 JS 173158/95, Local Court (Amtsgericht) Munich. An English version of the decision is available at <http://www.cyber-rights.org/isps/somm-dec.htm>.

FRANCE

League Against Racism and Antisemitism (LICRA), French Union of Jewish Students v. Yahoo! Inc. (USA), Yahoo France, Tribunal de Grande Instance de Paris (The County Court of Paris), Interim Court Order, 20 November 2000.

EUROPEAN COURT OF HUMAN RIGHTS

Handyside v. UK, App. no. 5493/72, Ser A vol. 24 (1976).

Acknowledgements

I am indebted to Louise Ellison, my life partner, and Senior Lecturer in Law, School of Law, University of Leeds, for her invaluable support and assistance in helping me to finalize this book. Louise's assistance was instrumental especially during the editorial stage. I also thank my close friend, David Banisar, Director of the Freedom of Information Project of Privacy International in London and a long time visiting research fellow at the School of Law, University of Leeds for providing me with invaluable statistical data in relation to Chapter 3, obtained through the Transactional Records Access Clearinghouse (TRAC) based at Syracuse University (<http://trac.syr.edu/>).

Chapter 1
Introduction

The availability and distribution of child pornography through the Internet has become a social concern for society since the mid-1990s[1] when paedophiles started using this medium to share sexually explicit content. These activities take place within a 'subculture [that] operates beyond the boundaries of any particular state or legal jurisdiction and represents a new pattern of globalized crime and deviance'.[2] At the time of *Operation First-Out* in April 1994 it was acknowledged that the police in England and Wales knew 'nothing about the Internet or the strange world they were about to encounter'.[3] This personal ignorance was reinforced by the technological shortcoming that officers were only able to examine the UNIX computer machine confiscated in the operation with the help of US Customs officers. Following this 'enormous step into the unknown',[4] attempts at regulating the availability of child pornography on the Internet has taken centre stage because of its sensitive nature and its links to the sexual exploitation of children.

The impact and the role of the Internet in the production, dissemination and collection of child pornography have been assessed by a number of authors[5] in recent years and there is a general consensus that 'the Internet has increased the range, volume, and accessibility of sexually abusive imagery, including child pornography.'[6] This book takes as its theme child pornography law within the context of the Internet. It sets out to provide a critical assessment of the problem of Internet child pornography and its governance through legal and non-legal means, including a comparative assessment of laws and policy initiatives in England and

---

1 Akdeniz, Y., 'Child Pornography', in Y. Akdeniz, C. Walker and D. Wall (eds), *The Internet, Law and Society*, Harlow: Addison Wesley Longman, 2000, 231–49; Akdeniz, Y., 'Governing Pornography and Child Pornography on the Internet: The UK Approach', in Cyber-Rights, Protection, and Markets: A Symposium (2001), 32 *U. West. L.A. L. Rev.* 247–75.

2 Jenkins, P., *Beyond Tolerance: Child Pornography on the Internet*, New York: New York University Press, 2001, 5.

3 *R v. Fellows and Arnold* [1997] 1 Cr App R 244; [1997] 2 All E.R. 548; [1997] *Crim. L.R.*, 524.

4 Davis, D., *The Internet Detective: An Investigator's Guide*, Police Research Group, Home Office, 1998. See Appendix D.

5 Taylor, M. and E. Quayle, *Child Pornography: An Internet Crime*, Hove: Brunner-Routledge, 2003; Quayle, E. and M. Taylor (eds), *Viewing Child Pornography on the Internet: Understanding the Offence, Managing the Offender, Helping the Victims*, Lyme Regis: Russell House, 2005; Jenkins, P., *Beyond Tolerance: Child Pornography on the Internet*, New York: New York University Press, 2001.

6 Krone, T., 'A typology of online child pornography offending' (2004), *Trends and Issues in Crime and Criminal Justice*, 279, Australian Institute of Criminology Canberra, at <http://www.aic.gov.au/publications/tandi2/tandi279.html>.

Wales, the Unites States of America and Canada. In Part One, 'National Approaches to the Problem of Child Pornography', existing laws and regulations within these jurisdictions and the associated case law are examined to assess their effectiveness and limitations. Consideration is given to the emphasis placed upon core values such as freedom of expression in the treatment of computer-generated child pornography. In the United States and Canada recent government legislative action has faced constitutional challenge and this remains a 'deeply controversial area'.[7]

As one might expect, the legal situation as regards the Internet is far from clear and settled. The global, decentralized and borderless nature of the Internet creates a potentially infinite and unbreakable communications complex which cannot be readily bounded by one national government or even several or many acting in concert. The decentralized nature of the Internet moreover means that there is no unique solution for effective regulation at a national level.[8] In the words of Hirst and Thompson, 'nation-states have become the local authorities of the global system'[9] in fragmented postmodern states; this is certainly true for the control and policing of Internet child pornography. Criminal law is traditionally associated with nation-states and policing is a core activity of nation states. However, this legitimate activity is unsettled within a borderless medium such as the Internet.[10] The policing of Internet child pornography is possible at a national level only when the perpetrators are within the jurisdiction of the nation-state, or when extra-territorial policing activity and co-operation is possible.

Consequently, the governance of Internet child pornography requires a collective and 'multi-pronged response to a multifaceted problem'[11] in which both public and private bodies are involved at various levels. This pluralistic Internet governance approach as it is emerging may include several layers: the National (and the local), Supra National (for example, European Union), Regional (Council of Europe)

---

7 Jenkins, P., *Beyond Tolerance: Child Pornography on the Internet*, New York: New York University Press, 2001, 219.

8 See generally, MacLean, D., *Internet Governance: A Grand Collaboration*, New York: United Nations ICT Task Force, 2004; Gelbstein, E. and J. Kurbalija, *Internet Governance: Issues, Actors, and Divide*, DIPLO report, 2005, at <http://www.diplomacy.edu/isl/ig/>; Working Group on Internet Governance, *Background Report*, July 2005, at <http://www.wgig.org/docs/WGIGREPORT.pdf>; The Working Group on Internet Governance, *Final Report*, June 2005, at <http://www.wgig.org/docs/WGIGREPORT.doc>; Drake, W.J. (ed.), *Reforming Internet Governance: Perspectives from the Working Group on Internet Governance*, November 2005, at <http://www.wgig.org/docs/book/WGIG_book.pdf>.

9 Hirst, P. and G. Thompson, 'Globalization and the Future of the Nation State' (1995), *Economy and Society* 24(3), 408–42, at 414.

10 See generally, Wall, D., *Cybercrime: The Transformation of Crime in the Information Age*, Cambridge: Polity Press, 2007, 157–86; Wall, D., 'Policing and the Regulation of the Internet' (1998) *Crim. L.R.*, December Special Edition: *Crime, Criminal Justice and the Internet*, 79–91; Wall, D., 'Insecurity and the Policing of Cyberspace', in Crawford, A. (ed.), *Crime and Insecurity*, Cullompton: Willan, 2002, 186–209.

11 Report of the Special Rapporteur on the sale of children, child prostitution and child pornography (Mr Juan Miguel Petit), E/CN.4/2005/78, 23 December 2004, Commission on Human Rights, at <http://daccessdds.un.org/doc/UNDOC/GEN/G05/100/19/PDF/G0510019.pdf>, para. 121.

and International (United Nations). According to Healy, 'child pornography is a pressing problem on local, national, and international levels and...all nations have an important part to play in the solution.'[12] The effect of supranational, regional and international developments on nation-state governance cannot be underestimated, and the aligning of strategies and policies is necessary in the search for common solutions for Internet related problems. There are still many countries around the world that do not have specific legislation on child pornography. In the words of the UN Special Rapporteur on the sale of children, child prostitution and child pornography, 'this legal vacuum leaves a dangerous gap that exposes children to the risk of abuse, further increased by the impunity factor.'[13] For this reason efforts to harmonize laws at an international level constitute an important step in the fight against the sexual exploitation of children and child pornography. Part Two of this book, 'Supranational and International Approaches', details and assesses important developments in this area.

As technology advances, legal systems will inevitably often struggle to keep pace. This has proven true in relation to the issue of Internet child pornography.[14] Governing Internet child pornography may thus comprise not only regulatory action by governments but also self-regulation (by Internet Service Providers), co-operation with ISPs (notice and takedown provisions to remove illegal content), co-regulatory initiatives (creation of hotlines to report illegal content), and education and awareness campaigns. An assessment of the utility of additional and alternative methods of regulation, especially in the field of self-regulatory and co-regulatory initiatives for fighting Internet child pornography, is provided in Part Three, 'Internet Service Providers' Liability and Self-Regulation'.

PROBLEM OF PAEDOPHILIA AND CHILD PORNOGRAPHY

Paedophilia is commonly understood as a sexual preference or form of expression that involves fantasies and imaginings about sexual activity with children. A 1986 Report of the US Senate Permanent Subcommittee on Investigations on Child Pornography and Paedophilia stated, 'no single characteristic of paedophilia is more pervasive than the obsession with child pornography.'[15] While it is often argued that

---

12 Healy, M.A. (ECPAT), 'Child Pornography: An International Perspective', paper presented at the World Congress against Commercial Sexual Exploitation of Children, Sweden, 1996, at <http://www.crime-research.org/articles/536/>.

13 Report of the Special Rapporteur on the sale of children, child prostitution and child pornography (Mr Juan Miguel Petit), E/CN.4/2005/78, 23 December 2004, Commission on Human Rights, at <http://daccessdds.un.org/doc/UNDOC/GEN/G05/100/19/PDF/G0510019.pdf>, para. 112.

14 See generally, Quayle, E. and M. Taylor, *Viewing Child Pornography on the Internet: Understanding the Offence, Managing the Offender, Helping the Victims*, Lyme Regis: Russell House Publishing, 2005.

15 *Child Pornography and Paedophilia*: Report Made by the Permanent Subcommittee on Investigations, US Senate, 99th Cong. 2d Sess. 10–12 (1986): Quoted from US Department of Justice, Office of the Attorney General, *Project Safe Childhood: Protecting Children from*

pornography should not be proscribed on the basis of freedom of speech arguments, there is a general consensus that a line should be drawn with child pornography.[16] In most cases, child pornography is a permanent record of the sexual abuse of an actual child (except in the case of pseudo-photographs or computer generated images, drawings, cartoons and paintings). Child pornography involving sexual abuse and exploitation of children is undoubtedly 'linked to child prostitution, child sex tourism and the trafficking of children for sexual exploitation'.[17] Put simply, there is no 'acceptable "liberal" position when it comes to the sexual victimization of children',[18] and debate surrounding child pornography accordingly remains a deeply sensitive and emotive topic.[19]

At the outset it is necessary to take account of the ways in which child pornography can constitute child abuse. According to a US Senate Committee report, child pornography 'is a particularly pernicious evil, something that no civilized society can or should tolerate. It abuses, degrades, and exploits the weakest and most vulnerable members of our society, our children.'[20] Children are not and should not be seen as appropriate sexual partners, and the criminalization of child pornography not only aims to prevent 'the harm that flows from the use of children in pornography'[21] but also 'the harm that flows from the very existence of images and words which degrade and dehumanize children.'[22]

Child pornography involving real images of children is therefore a form of sexual abuse and exploitation in which the depiction of children engaging in sexually explicit conduct poses a serious threat to the physical and mental health, safety and well-being of children. Real images (as opposed to computer generated images, and drawings) of child pornography are seen as a permanent record of the victim's abuse, and its creation and distribution is considered a serious crime in most countries. It is often argued that child pornography can also be used for grooming children into

---

Online Exploitation and Abuse, May 2006, at <http://www.projectsafechildhood.gov/guide.htm>. See in particular Part II: The Need for a National Initiative to Protect Children, at <http://www.projectsafechildhood.gov/part2.pdf>.

16 See generally, Akdeniz, Y. and N. Strossen, 'Sexually Oriented Expression', in Y. Akdeniz, C. Walker and D. Wall (eds), *The Internet, Law and Society*, Harlow: Addison Wesley Longman, 2000, 207–31.

17 UN Commission on Human Rights, *Report of the Special Rapporteur on the sale of children, child prostitution and child pornography* (submitted by Mr Juan Miguel Petit), E/CN.4/2005/78, 23 December 2004, para. 18.

18 Adler, A., 'The Perverse Law of Child Pornography' (2001), 101 *Colum. L. Rev.* 209.

19 Taylor, M. and E. Quayle, *Child Pornography: An Internet Crime*, Hove: Brunner-Routledge, 2003, foreword.

20 See part IV of the US Senate Committee on the Judiciary Report on the Child Pornography Prevention Act of 1995, 104th Congress Report, Senate 2d Session 104–358, August 27, 1996. See further, Royal Commission into the New South Wales Police Service Final Report Volume IV: The Paedophile Inquiry Commissioner: The Hon Justice JRT Wood, August 1997, ISBN 07313 0916 2 (set), at <http://www.premiers.nsw.gov.au/publications/pubs_dload/police_rc/volume4.htm>.

21 *R v. Sharpe*, 2001 SCC 2. File No. 27376, 26 January 2001.

22 Ibid.

child pornography. In *Child Pornography*, Dr O'Brien explains what she terms the 'cycle' of child pornography:

> (1) child pornography is shown to a child for 'educational purposes'; (2) an attempt is made to convince a child that explicit sex is acceptable, even desirable; (3) the child is convinced that other children are sexually active and that such conduct is okay; (4) child pornography desensitizes the child, lowering the child's inhibitions; (5) some of these sessions progress to sexual activity involving the child; (6) photographs or films are taken of the sexual activity; and (7) this new material is used to attract and seduce yet more child victims.[23]

Additionally, the Williams Committee noted in the late 1970s:

> Few people would be prepared to take the risk where children are concerned and just as the law recognizes that children should be protected against sexual behaviour which they are too young to properly consent to, it is almost universally agreed that this should apply to participation in pornography.[24]

The possibility of such use for grooming purposes is often used as a justification for the criminalization of possession of child pornography as well as for the criminalization of the creation, making, distribution and the possession of computer generated pseudo-photographs and images of children in many jurisdictions. Pseudo-photographs or even videos can be created by computers by superimposing a child's facial image on an adult's body or on another child's body without using any real children during the process. Such images give rise to special concerns which are discussed at various points throughout this book.

PAEDOPHILIA, COMPUTER NETWORKS AND THE INTERNET

Neither paedophilia nor the use of computer networks to disseminate digital content involving child pornography are new phenomena. Paedophilia networks have been using computer networks for such purposes from as early as 1986.[25] References to digital content involving child pornography being exchanged within local computer bulletin board systems in Britain can be traced back to 1985.[26] The problem became

23 See O'Brien, S., *Child Pornography*, 2nd edn, Dubuque, IA: Kendall Hunt, 1992. See further, *Child Pornography and Paedophilia*: Report Made by the Permanent Subcommittee on Investigations, US Senate, 99th Cong. 2d Sess. 10–12 (1986).

24 Williams Committee Report, *Obscenity and Film Censorship*, Cmnd 7772, London: HMSO, 1979, p. 90, para. 6.68.

25 In 1986, the Meese Commission Report provided evidence that paedophile offenders and child pornographers had begun to use personal computers and computer networks for communication and distribution of materials. See Attorney General's Commission on Pornography: Final Report, 2 vols, Washington, DC: US Government Printing Office, July 1986 [The Meese Commission] at p. 629.

26 PBBS was an adult oriented Bulletin Board with at least 500 users in 1985. The Surrey based PBBS was closed down in June 1987 following allegations involving discussions of paedophilia and child pornography within the system. However, no charges were ever brought

more prominent in the 1990s, however, with the widespread use of the Internet. The increase in prosecutions and convictions involving child pornography since the mid-1990s is related to the exponential growth of Internet access from homes,[27] and the availability and circulation of child pornography over the Internet. The volume of abusive digital images and videos of children discovered by law enforcement agencies following successful operations suggest that paedophile networks, as well as individuals interested in such content, distribute and obtain these images and videos through a variety of public and private sources over the Internet.

Although largely developed as a non-commercial cottage industry, an explosion of commercial activity involving Internet child pornography has been witnessed in the last five years. The true scale of the problem is nevertheless unknown as the activities of paedophilia networks remain underground and hidden to some extent. According to a recent United Nations Special Rapporteur on the Rights of the Child report, the extent and seriousness of the problem of Internet child pornography 'are perceived unevenly across countries'.[28] The report observed that a 'technological divide is a determinant of the different perceptions',[29] and

> in countries with high rates of Internet access, the dimensions of child pornography on the Internet are bigger. Countries with a limited use of this technology do not see the dangers of the abusive use of the Internet as an immediate problem. If, on the one hand, it is true that the scale of use goes together with that of abuse, on the other hand, countries that do not have an adequate legislation and appropriate accompanying measures to prevent and combat this problem, expose their children to the risks of abuse and exploitation.[30]

In terms of its availability and modes of distribution on the Internet, the problem of child pornography appears to be one that exists mainly within newsgroups while the true nature of the same problem over the World Wide Web can only be speculated upon. A University College Cork study claimed in 1998 that the amount of child pornography accessible through the Internet is considerable, with the situation being fluid and dynamic with sites frequently changing addresses.[31] The Cork study suggested that 0.07 per cent of the 40,000 newsgroups carry 'child erotica' or 'pornography' (research carried out in January 1998), and that there are an additional

---

and the System Administrator traced the allegations to a single message involving one user's interest with 'young girl' material. For further information see Tate, T., *Child Pornography: An Investigation*, London: Methuen, 1990, 209–24.

27 While about 9 per cent of the population had access to the Internet from homes in 1998, this rose to 57 per cent in 2006, with an estimated 13.9 million households accessing the Internet. See The Office of National Statistics, Internet Access: 2006 First Release, 23 August 2006, at <http://www.statistics.gov.uk/pdfdir/inta0806.pdf>. See further, Cabinet Office, Prime Minister's Strategy Unit, *Connecting the UK: the Digital Strategy*, April 2005.

28 UN Commission on Human Rights, *Report of the Special Rapporteur on the sale of children, child prostitution and child pornography* (submitted by Mr Juan Miguel Petit), E/CN.4/2005/78, 23 December 2004, para. 15.

29 Ibid.

30 Ibid.

31 See a summary of the Cork Study in the Irish Department of Justice, Equality and Law Reform, *Illegal and Harmful Use of the Internet* (Pn.5231, Dublin, 1998), pp. 33–5.

238 'girl-related child pornography or erotica' web pages[32] (out of around 50 million web pages). Currently 211 newsgroups are listed as potentially illegal in the UK by the Internet Watch Foundation[33] and are known to carry child pornography. In the last few years the Internet Watch Foundation claims to have encountered increased numbers of websites carrying child pornography, including commercial Pay-Per-View websites hosted in Russia or the United States.[34]

While a search on 'child pornography' on a web search engine[35] would normally direct users towards sites campaigning against the availability of child pornography on the Internet,[36] the major problem for the future is the availability of channels devoted to child pornography within the Internet Relay Chat, ICQ environment[37] and on peer to peer (P2P) file sharing systems like Kazaa, and eDonkey.[38] On this front the Cork study concluded that 'due to the organized dynamic nature of paedophile activity it is not possible to estimate with accuracy the amount of traffic generated on IRC channels.'[39]

A study conducted by the United States General Accounting Office in 2003–2004 found that child pornography is easily found and downloaded from P2P networks.

> In one search, using 12 keywords known to be associated with child pornography on the Internet, GAO identified 1,286 titles and file names, determining that 543 (about 42 per cent) were associated with child pornography images.[40]

The wider dissemination and collection of child pornography in the Internet age bears no comparison to how it was obtained and disseminated prior to widespread

32 An unspecified larger number were boy-related according to the Cork Study.

33 See generally, the IWF Annual Report 2005, at <http://www.iwf.org.uk/documents/20060306_iwf_annual_report_2005_-_high_res.pdf>.

34 See IWF, Annual Report 2004 (January 2005) at <http://www.iwf.org.uk/documents/20050204_annual_report_2004.pdf>; the IWF Annual Report 2005, at <http://www.iwf.org.uk/documents/20060306_iwf_annual_report_2005_-_high_res.pdf>; and the IWF Annual Report 2006 at <http://www.iwf.org.uk/documents/20070412_iwf_annual_report 2006 (web).pdf>.

35 See, for example, Google at <http://www.google.co.uk>.

36 Report submitted by the Special Rapporteur of the Commission on Human Rights on the sale of children, child prostitution and child pornography to the General Assembly Sale of children, child prostitution and child pornography, Note by the Secretary-General, A/52/482, issued on 16 October 1997, para. 101.

37 See the Internet Crime Forum IRC sub-group, *Chat Wise, Street Wise: Children and Internet Chat Services*, March 2001, at <http://www.internetcrimeforum.org.uk>.

38 *Internet News*, Child Pornography Exchange Through Napster and Gnutella, 10 January 2001, at <http://www.internetnews.com/intl-news/article/0,,6_556161,00.html>.

39 Irish Department of Justice, Equality and Law Reform, *Illegal and Harmful Use of the Internet* (Pn.5231, Dublin, 1998), p. 34.

40 United States General Accounting Office, *File Sharing Programs: Users of Peer-to-Peer Networks can Readily Access Child Pornography*, Statement of Linda D. Koontz, Director, Information Management Issues, Testimony Before the Subcommittee on Commerce, Trade, and Consumer Protection, Committee on Energy and Commerce, House of Representatives, GAO-04-757T, May 2004.

use of the global communications network.[41] Ease of access, the partial anonymity[42] provided by the Internet, developments in digital photography,[43] issues surrounding the difficulty of policing international networks,[44] and the limited risk of detection have all contributed to the exponential growth in its availability. As Jenkins rightly observes, this has created a 'cosmopolitan "bandit culture" of suppliers and consumers of child pornography, which sustains a worldwide criminal market of unprecedented geographical scope.'[45]

It is also suggested that 'increased access to the Internet has greatly exacerbated the problem in this area by making pornographic images more easily accessible and increasing the likelihood of such material being found accidentally by others who may subsequently become corrupted by it.'[46] The risks are obvious and as Krone notes 'the Internet provides an environment for the proliferation of child pornography and the creation of an expanding market for its consumption.'[47] There is therefore potential for further growth of the problem especially if legal harmonization does not take place and countries do not address the problem of sexual exploitation of children and child pornography.

---

41 See further, US Department of Justice, Office of the Attorney General, *Project Safe Childhood: Protecting Children from Online Exploitation and Abuse*, May 2006, at <http://www.projectsafechildhood.gov/guide.htm>.

42 See generally, Akdeniz, Y., 'Anonymous Now', *Index on Censorship*, The Privacy Issue, 2000 (3), June, 57–62; Akdeniz, Y., 'Anonymity, Democracy, and Cyberspace' (2002), *Social Research* 69(1), Spring, 180–94; Wallace, J., 'Nameless in Cyberspace: Anonymity on the Internet', Cato Institute, December 1999, at <http://www.cato.org/pubs/briefs/bp-054es.html>.

43 Special Rapporteur (Ms Ofelia Calcetas-Santos) Report to the Commission on Human Rights on the sale of children, child prostitution and child pornography, A/52/482, 16 October 1997, presented at the fifty-second session of the General Assembly of the United Nations; Special Rapporteur (Ms Ofelia Calcetas-Santos) Report of the Commission on Human Rights on the sale of children, child prostitution and child pornography, E/CN.4/1998/101, 13 January 1998, presented at the fifty-fourth session of the General Assembly of the United Nations; Special Rapporteur (Ms Ofelia Calcetas-Santos) Report of the Commission on Human Rights on the sale of children, child prostitution and child pornography, E/CN.4/2001/78, 25 January 2001, presented at the fifty-seventh session of the General Assembly of the United Nations.

44 Note *Project Trawler: Crime on the Information Highways*, National Criminal Intelligence Service, June 1999, at <http://www.cyber-rights.org/documents/trawler.htm>.

45 Jenkins, P., *Beyond Tolerance: Child Pornography on the Internet*, New York: New York University Press, 2001, 7.

46 Rose LJ (V-P) in *R v. Oliver and others* (CA Criminal Division), [2002] EWCA Crim 2766; [2003] 2 Cr App R (S) 64; [2003] 1 Cr App R 28; [2003] 2 Cr App R (S.) 15; [2003] *Crim. L.R.*, 127.

47 Krone, T., 'A typology of online child pornography offending' (2004), *Trends and Issues in Crime and Criminal Justice*, 279, Australian Institute of Criminology Canberra, at <http://www.aic.gov.au/publications/tandi2/tandi279.html>.

DEFINING CHILD PORNOGRAPHY

Historically, the development of child pornography laws date back to the mid-1970s when the 'twin problems of child sexual abuse and child pornography'[48] became a huge concern. The Williams Committee inquiry[49] as well as the enactment of the Protection of Children Act 1978 in England and Wales responded to such concerns and provided the first 'specific' legal response to combat the problem of child pornography. Prior to this, sexually explicit content involving children (including photographs and videos) could be tackled under broader obscenity and indecency legislation such as the Obscene Publications Act 1959 and 1964 in England and Wales,[50] and under the *Miller*[51] obscenity standards in the United States. Since the late 1970s child pornography laws have been developed further and expanded continuously. The Marc Dutroux affair in Belgium[52] was a key factor in the European Union decision in the mid-1990s to take action with respect to the availability of illegal content on the Internet.[53] Yet, as Adler observes, 'the law's expansion has not solved the problem, but only presided over its escalation…Law is always a step behind the problem, racing to keep pace with a burgeoning social crisis.'[54]

In the fight against child pornography it is imperative from a legal point of view to define what constitutes child pornography. As will be seen in Chapter 2, in England and Wales, the Protection of Children Act 1978 concentrates on indecent

48 Adler, A., 'The Perverse Law of Child Pornography' (2001), 101 *Colum. L. Rev.* 209.

49 Williams Committee Report, 'Obscenity and Film Censorship', London: HMSO, 1979.

50 See generally, Akdeniz, Y., 'Governing Pornography and Child Pornography on the Internet: The UK Approach', in Cyber-Rights, Protection, and Markets: A Symposium (2001), *U. West. L.A. L. Rev.*, 247–75; Akdeniz, Y., *Sex on the Net? The Dilemma of Policing Cyberspace*, Reading: South Street Press, 1999; Akdeniz, Y. and N. Strossen, 'Sexually Oriented Expression', in Y. Akdeniz, C. Walker, D. Wall (eds), *The Internet, Law and Society*, Harlow: Addison Wesley Longman, 2000, 207–31; Akdeniz, Y., 'Governance of Pornography and Child Pornography on the Global Internet: A Multi-Layered Approach', in L. Edwards, L. and C. Waelde (eds), *Law and the Internet: Regulating Cyberspace*, Oxford: Hart, 1997, 223–41; 'Computer Pornography: A Comparative Study of the US and UK Obscenity Laws and Child Pornography Laws in Relation to the Internet' (1996), *International Review of Law, Computers and Technology* 10(2), 235–61.

51 *Miller v. California* (1973) 413 US 15, 37 L Ed 419, 93 S Ct 2607, 1 Media L R 1441, reh den 414 US 881, 38 L Ed 128, 94 S Ct 26. In *New York v. Ferber* (1982) 458 US 747, 73 L Ed 1113, 102 S Ct 3348, 8 Media L R 1809 the Supreme Court held that the Miller standards did not provide an adequate solution for the problem of child pornography.

52 See Walsh, J., 'The Terror and Pity', *Time International*, 148(11), 2 September 1996 and Millward, D., 'Belgian plea for help to crush child porn rings', *Daily Telegraph*, 20 August 1996; 'Belgium's trial of shame', *BBC News*, 17 June 2004; 'Belgium's Dutroux jailed for life', *BBC News*, 22 June 2004. See further, Dardenne, S., *I Choose to Live*, London: Virago, 1996.

53 European Commission Communication to the European Parliament, The Council, The Economic and Social Committee and the Committee of the Regions: Illegal and Harmful Content on the Internet, Com (96) 487, Brussels, 16 October 1996.

54 Adler, A., 'The Perverse Law of Child Pornography' (2001), 101 *Colum. L. Rev.* 209. See further, Adler, A., 'Inverting the First Amendment' (2001), 149 *U. Pa. L. Rev.* 921.

photographs and indecent pseudo-photographs of children, and there is no definition provided for 'child pornography' *per se*. Other common law jurisdictions such as the United States and Canada provide statutory legal definitions for child pornography (see Chapters 3 and 4). At the same time, during the past few years we have witnessed the development of supranational and international policy documents which set out to define 'child pornography'.

The European Union's Framework Decision on combating the sexual exploitation of children and child pornography,[55] which entered into force in January 2004, required member states to take necessary measures to comply with this Framework Decision by 20 January 2006.[56] The Council Framework Decision defines child pornography in article 1(b) as pornographic material that visually depicts or represents:

(i) a real child involved or engaged in sexually explicit conduct, including lascivious exhibition of the genitals or the pubic area of a child; or
(ii) a real person appearing to be a child involved or engaged in the conduct mentioned in (i); or
(iii) realistic images of a non-existent child involved or engaged in the conduct mentioned in (i).

The Council of Europe's Cybercrime Convention 2001,[57] which came into force on 1 July 2004, defines child pornography, under article 9(2), as pornographic material that visually depicts:

(a) a minor engaged in sexually explicit conduct;
(b) a person appearing to be a minor engaged in sexually explicit conduct;
(c) realistic images representing a minor engaged in sexually explicit conduct.

Finally, the United Nations' Optional Protocol to the Convention on the Rights of the Child on the Sale of Children, Child Prostitution and Child Pornography,[58] which came into force on 18 January 2002, defines child pornography in article 2(c) as 'any representation, by whatever means, of a child engaged in real or simulated explicit

---

55 Council Framework Decision 2004/68/JHA of 22 December 2003 on combating the sexual exploitation of children and child pornography (see OJ L 013 20 January 2004, pp. 44–8), at <http://register.consilium.europa.eu/pdf/en/03/st10/st10748en03.pdf>. For a summary of the Framework Decision see <http://europa.eu/scadplus/leg/en/lvb/l33138.htm>.

56 Article 12(1). Note European Parliament legislative resolution on the proposal for a Council Framework Decision on combating the sexual exploitation of children and child pornography (COM(2000) 854-C5-0043/2001–2000/0025(CNS)), 12 June 2001.

57 Convention on Cybercrime, ETS No. 185, at <http://conventions.coe.int/Treaty/EN/Treaties/Html/185.htm>.

58 Optional Protocol to the Convention on the Rights of the Child on the Sale of Children, Child Prostitution and Child Pornography, New York, 25 May 2000, Fifty-fourth session (97th plenary meeting), Agenda item 116 (a), Distr. General A/RES/54/263, 26 June 2000. See further, Special Rapporteur on the sale of children, child prostitution and child pornography, Thematic Report on child pornography on the Internet, E/CN.4/2005/78, Economic and Social Council, Commission on Human Rights, 23 December, 2004, at <http://daccessdds.un.org/doc/UNDOC/GEN/G05/100/19/PDF/G0510019.pdf>.

sexual activities or any representation of the sexual parts of a child for primarily sexual purposes'.

All three documents define a child as under the age of 18 and all three cover both real depictions as well as realistic and simulated representations within the definition of child pornography. Computer generated images as well as images of real persons above the age of 18 who appear to be a child under the age of 18 would therefore come under these definitions. While the EU and CoE definitions refer to visual depictions and representations, the UN definition is broader as it refers to 'any representation' and could also cover textual material including cartoons, and drawings. Written materials were deliberately left out[59] of the EU definition as there was no support or agreement for the inclusion of textual or written material in the definition of child pornography.

The inclusion of real images in the definition of child pornography is directly aimed at protecting children from sexual abuse and exploitation. However, the justification for the inclusion of simulated representations within the definition of child pornography is rather different. As mentioned above, there is concern that such simulated representations as well as computer generated or morphed images may be used by paedophiles to groom and lure children for sexual activity, or encourage children to participate in sexual activity. The Explanatory Memorandum of the Council of Europe's Cybercrime Convention 2001 states that 'it is widely believed that such material and on-line practices, such as the exchange of ideas, fantasies and advice among paedophiles, play a role in supporting, encouraging or facilitating sexual offences against children.'[60] The Council of Europe thus aims to criminalize not only abusive conduct involving real children but also abusive behaviour. Similar justifications were provided at the European Union and United Nations levels.

Finally, one should note the recent tendency to refer to sexually explicit images involving real children as 'abusive images'[61] rather than as child pornography as the use of the word 'pornography' is said to glorify the abusive content in question. Despite these reservations, the term 'child pornography' will be used throughout this book as the majority of the laws and international policy documents examined herein use this term.

---

59 See the European Parliament report on Sexual exploitation of Children (A5–0206/2001), European Parliament legislative resolution on the proposal for a Council Framework Decision on combating the sexual exploitation of children and child pornography (COM(2000) 854-C5-0043/2001–2001/0025(CNS)), 2002/C 53 E/108–113, vol. 45, 28 February 2002.

60 Explanatory Report of the Council of Europe Cybercrime Convention, 2001, at <http://conventions.coe.int/treaty/en/Reports/Html/185.htm>, para. 93.

61 Save the Children Europe argues 'The term "child pornography"...undermines the seriousness of the abuse. It also tends to oversimplify what is a very complex social problem.' See Save the Children Europe, *Visible Evidence – Forgotten Children*, 2006, at <http://www.childcentre.info/projects/internet/abusiveimage/dbaFile13904.pdf>, p. 4.

CHILD PORNOGRAPHY OFFENCES AND CHAIN OF LIABILITY

Although specific child pornography related offences will be discussed in detail later, it is important to mention the chain of liability in terms of offending behaviour. At the top of the chain of liability lie the 'creators' who produce abusive images or other types of abusive content involving children. This serious category of offenders could also be referred to as 'abusers' but not all child abusers produce child pornography. The second most serious category involves those who distribute child pornography over the Internet. The 'distributors' can be divided into 'commercial' (organized criminal activity) and 'non-commercial' distributors. Finally, 'possessors', or those who download and/or view child pornography, lie at the bottom of the chain of liability. Although generally recognized to be the least serious category of offenders, it is often acknowledged by courts that even 'the young inexperienced amateur who downloads one image for his or her personal gratification does a significant criminal act which adds to the scale of human misery because, if there was no market for these images children would not be degraded producing them.'[62] As noted above, the commercial market for child pornography has grown within the last few years, predominantly supplied through commercial websites based in Eastern Europe with organized crime involvement.[63] In many countries, as well as in international agreements and conventions, liability for Internet Service Providers (ISPs) is additionally provided for. As will be explained, in most cases liability is imposed only if there is 'knowledge and control' over the information which is transmitted or stored by an ISP.

With regards to penalties, child pornography laws provide strict sanctions, and imprisonment is almost guaranteed for the 'creators' as well as for 'commercial distributors' in almost all Western societies and provided for within international agreements and conventions. Imprisonment for 'non-commercial' distributors depends upon the nature and quantity of the distribution, but in most cases imprisonment is considered the appropriate penalty in England and Wales, the United States and Canada. As far as 'possessors' are concerned, the appropriate penalty depends upon the nature and extent of possession. In most cases, possession is also criminalized by prison sentences but non-custodial sentences are also imposed in many Western societies including in England and Wales and Canada for less serious offences committed by first-time offenders. In many countries, as well as in international agreements and conventions, liability for Internet Service Providers (ISPs) is additionally provided for. The role of the ISPs in terms of distribution and provision of child pornography (with or without knowledge) will be discussed in Chapter 8 where it is noted that in most cases liability is imposed only if there is 'knowledge and control' over the information which is transmitted or stored by an ISP.

---

62 *R v. Toomer, Powell, Mould* [2001] *Crim. L.R.*, 149; *The Times*, 21 November 2000 (CA (Crim Div)).

63 Note Report of the Special Rapporteur on the sale of children, child prostitution and child pornography (Mr Juan Miguel Petit), E/CN.4/2005/78, 23 December 2004, Commission on Human Rights, at <http://daccessdds.un.org/doc/UNDOC/GEN/G05/100/19/PDF/G0510019.pdf>, para. 25.

In terms of recent international agreements and conventions, the above-mentioned EU Framework Decision on combating the sexual exploitation of children and child pornography[64] required all EU member states to criminalize the production, distribution, dissemination or transmission of child pornography, and the supplying or making available of, and the acquisition or possession of child pornography. Some exceptions are provided, and member states may exclude from criminal liability certain conduct[65] relating to child pornography. The offences and the wording within article 3 are consistent with the Council of Europe's Cybercrime Convention (article 9). The Cybercrime Convention includes some additional offences such as offering and procuring child pornography in addition to the EU Framework Decision provisions. The above-mentioned UN Optional Protocol also includes the producing, distributing, disseminating, importing, exporting, offering, selling or possessing[66] of child pornography offences. While these international agreements provide up to ten years' imprisonment for the more serious offences of production and distribution, up to five years' imprisonment is generally provided for the relatively less serious offence of possession.

The provision and harmonization of these common legal standards by member states of the above-mentioned supranational, regional and international organizations would be a significant step towards fighting child pornography. However, all these agreements and conventions provide for reservations and the right not to apply certain provisions. The issue of harmonization will therefore ultimately depend upon how each member state implements these provisions. Part Two of this book provides an assessment of how these provisions have been implemented, shedding light on the extent of legal harmonization to date.

The total cleansing or elimination of Internet child pornography is an impossible task. A key message conveyed within this book is that effective implementation, enforcement and harmonization of child pornography laws could nevertheless help to reduce the availability and dissemination of child pornography on the Internet substantially. Panic-led policies must be avoided, however, and future policies should focus primarily on the wider problem of the sexual abuse and commercial sexual exploitation of children.

64 Council Framework Decision 2004/68/JHA of 22 December 2003 on combating the sexual exploitation of children and child pornography (see OJ L 013 20 January 2004, pp. 44–8), at <http://register.consilium.europa.eu/pdf/en/03/st10/st10748en03.pdf>. For a summary of the Framework Decision see <http://europa.eu/scadplus/leg/en/lvb/l33138.htm>.

65 Ibid., article 3(2).

66 Article 3(1)(c) of the Optional Protocol.

Part One
National Approaches

Recent years have witnessed a rapid growth in the availability of Internet access in the developed world. With this rise the availability of child pornography has become markedly more visible, prompting public concern verging on 'moral panic'. Governments have responded, in turn, with reforms designed to strengthen legal frameworks in the wake of technological advances accompanied by a drive towards the imposition of more punitive penalties.

At a national level, the availability of laws dealing with child pornography is the most important weapon to fight the creation, distribution and possession of child pornography. This part examines the crucial role that laws and the courts play in the fight against child pornography in England and Wales, the United States of America and Canada, demonstrating that priorities and approaches to common problems may well differ from country to country.

In England and Wales the move towards increasingly tougher and far-reaching legal sanctions has prompted limited critical debate to date despite the problematic nature of certain developments. In this regard useful contrasts can be made with the United States and Canada where government initiatives have faced vehement challenges on constitutional grounds. In the United States controversy has surrounded the criminalization of so-called virtual child pornography or pseudo-photographs, with free speech exponents and government supporters battling over the ultimate reach of Internet child pornography laws. In Canada debate has focused on the inclusion of text-based materials within the adopted definition of child pornography, and the potentially invasive outcomes in terms of privacy and freedom of expression of criminalizing the simple possession of child pornography.

The following three chapters provide a detailed overview of legal responses to Internet child pornography in these three jurisdictions: England and Wales (Chapter 2), the United States (Chapter 3) and Canada (Chapter 4). Contested aspects of legislative reforms are analysed against the backdrop of an ongoing debate regarding the best ways to protect vulnerable children from sexual exploitation without losing sight of basic civil liberties.

Chapter 2

Legal Approaches in England and Wales

> The area which most concerns me is the sickening trade in child pornography which both directly exploits and degrades the children involved ... and also encourages paedophiles to direct their perverted activities against other children. I firmly believe that society cannot tolerate this evil trade and that those who provide the market for child pornography must themselves face prison sentences. [*per* then Prime Minister John Major[1]]

In 1994 a House of Commons Home Affairs Committee Report described 'computer pornography' as a 'new horror'.[2] Although child pornography was the main concern of the Committee's inquiry, the impact of new communications technologies such as the Internet was not directly assessed. At the time the inquiry was conducted the real concern of the Committee was the circulation of obscene publications via floppy disks and CD-ROMs and publications in data format. The Internet was not yet seen to be a problem.

Following the publication of the Committee's report on computer pornography,[3] and the recommendations made by the Committee, the obscenity laws were amended by the Criminal Justice and Public Order Act 1994[4] to include publications in 'data format' in England and Wales. The definition of indecent photographs of children (child pornography) within the Protection of Children Act 1978 was also amended to include computer generated photographs and images of children in line with the 1994 legislation.

In subsequent years an exponential growth in Internet access[5] was witnessed world wide, and as the Internet proliferated during the 1990s, and paedophile networks started to use the Internet to circulate child pornography, public concern grew about the availability of illegal Internet content. A systematic growth in the number of child pornography prosecutions from 1995 (when child pornography became an issue of major public concern) is clearly visible from the official statistics set out within this chapter. The above-mentioned amendments to the 1978 legislation may thus be regarded as a timely intervention to counter the spread of child pornography over computer networks.

---

1 Duncan, G., 'Pledge of Action on Child Pornography', *The Scotsman*, 22 October 1993.

2 House of Commons, Home Affairs Committee: First Report on Computer Pornography, London: HMSO, 1994 p. V, para. 1.

3 Ibid.

4 See Part VII entitled 'Obscenity and Pornography and Videos of the 1994 Act'. Relevant sections are 84–6.

5 See The Office of National Statistics, Internet Access: 2006 First Release, 23 August 2006, at <http://www.statistics.gov.uk/pdfdir/inta0806.pdf>. See further, Cabinet Office, Prime Minister's Strategy Unit, *Connecting the UK: the Digital Strategy*, April 2005.

This chapter explores the current state of laws with respect to Internet child pornography in England and Wales. Individual offences are examined as well as related defences and the interpretation of these defences in cases involving Internet users. For example, particular consideration is given to the recent case of *R v. Porter*[6] and the meaning given to possession when a defendant has 'deleted' images from his or her computer. The public condemnation of those who commit offences related to child pornography resulted in the substantial increase of the penalties with the Criminal Justice and Court Services Act 2000. This in turn required the intervention of the Court of Appeal issuing a set of guidelines in *R v. Oliver*[7] to clarify the recommended sentencing in child pornography related convictions. The legal issues surrounding the sentencing debate are part of the debate examined in this chapter.

Legal controversy surrounding the making offence and the arguably problematic interpretation of the Court of Appeal in *R v. Bowden*[8] which blurred the distinction between making and possession offences is also analysed. Finally, the vexed issue of pseudo-photographs criminalized by the Criminal Justice and Public Order Act 1994 is addressed, and it will be argued that the justifications provided for criminalizing pseudo-photographs are clearly distinguishable from those underlying the criminalization of child pornography involving actual children where the making/creation almost certainly does involve the commission of sexual offences and direct harm to children.

PROTECTION OF CHILDREN ACT 1978

The main piece of legislation that deals with child pornography offences in England and Wales is the Protection of Children Act 1978. It has been amended and updated several times since 1978. In its amended form it covers the offences of taking, making and distributing child pornography. As will be explained below, the possession of indecent photographs of children was not criminalized until 1988. The 1978 Act was enacted in response to the problem of child pornography following calls by Mary Whitehouse, Chairwoman of the National Viewers and Listeners Association in 1977.[9] Whitehouse's campaign was successful despite the fact that the Williams Committee on Obscenity and Film Censorship found no evidence that child pornography was a growing problem at the time.[10] The overall aim of these provisions is the protection of children from sexual exploitation and degradation.[11]

---

6 *R v. Porter* [2006] EWCA Crim 560; [2006] All ER (D) 236 (Mar). See further, Ormerod, D., 'Commentary on *R v. Porter*' (2006), *Crim. L.R.*, 748.

7 *R v. Oliver* [2003] 1 Cr App R (S) 463.

8 *R v. Bowden* [2000] 2 All ER 418.

9 *Sunday Times*, 19 June 1977.

10 Williams Committee Report, *Obscenity and Film Censorship*, Cmnd 7772, London: HMSO, 1979. But note the criticism of the findings of the Williams Committee in Tate, T., *Child Pornography: An Investigation*, London: Methuen, 1990, 228–35.

11 See, for example, *R v. Collier (Edward John)* [2004] EWCA Crim 1411; *The Times*, July 13 2004 (CA (Crim Div)).

Since then the 1978 Act has been amended four times: by the Criminal Justice Act 1988 – to introduce the possession offence, as the original version of the 1978 Act only criminalized taking indecent photographs of children and distributing such photographs; by the Criminal Justice and Public Order Act 1994 ('CJPOA 1994') – to introduce the concept of computer generated pseudo-photographs; by the Criminal Justice and Court Services Act 2000 ('CJCSA 2000') – to extend the maximum imprisonment sentences for child pornography related offences; and by the Sexual Offences Act 2003 – to amend the definition of a child to bring it into line with international law.

Defining 'Child Pornography'

There is no legal definition of the term 'child pornography'. In fact, prior to the enactment of the Sexual Offences Act 2003,[12] the words 'child' and 'pornography' did not appear together in any legislation dealing with offences related to child pornography. The statutory provisions within the Protection of Children Act 1978 and section 160 of the Criminal Justice Act 1988 refer to offences related to indecent photographs and indecent pseudo-photographs (since 1994) of children.

As far as the definition of a child is concerned, for the purposes of the 1978 Act, a child was originally described as a person under the age of 16 by section 7(6) of the 1978 Act. However, this has been amended and changed to a person under the age of 18 by section 45(2) of the Sexual Offences Act 2003 which came into force in May 2004. The change was necessary to comply with international initiatives (by the European Union, Council of Europe and the United Nations) for the harmonization of laws in relation to child pornography.[13]

Section 45(3) of the Sexual Offences Act 2003 created a number of conditions which if satisfied provide that certain photographs of a child aged either 16 or 17 will not be regarded as indecent photographs for the purposes of both section 1 of the Protection of Children Act 1978[14] and section 160 of the Criminal Justice Act 1988.[15] The first exception provided in the newly introduced section 1A, entitled 'Marriage and other relationships', will apply in cases in which the defendant proves that the photograph in question was of a child aged 16 or over and that at the time of the taking or making of the photograph he and the child were married or living together as partners in an enduring family relationship.[16] The defendant must also show that

12 See sections 48–50 of the Sexual Offences Act 2003.

13 See further, Part II of this book.

14 Provided that the offence charged relates to a photograph and not to a pseudo-photograph. See Explanatory Notes to Sexual Offences Act 2003, at <http://www.legislation.hmso.gov.uk/acts/en2003/2003en42.htm>, para. 73. See further, Gillespie, A., 'The Sexual Offences Act 2003: (3) Tinkering with "Child Pornography"' (2004), *Crim. L.R.*, May, 361–8.

15 Similar conditions are set out in relation to the possession of indecent photograph of a child offence under section 160 of the Criminal Justice Act 1988. These are provided within the newly-introduced section 160A of the Criminal Justice Act 1988 entitled 'marriage and other relationships'.

16 See section 1A(1) of the Protection of Children Act 1978 as amended by the Sexual Offences Act 2003.

there is evidence to suggest that the child consented to the photograph being taken or made, or that the defendant reasonably believed that the child consented.[17] Finally, the photograph in question must not be one that shows a person other than the child and the defendant.[18] If these three conditions are satisfied the defendant commits no offence.

As far as the distributing or showing indecent photographs offences under section 1(1)(b) of the 1978 Act is concerned, the defendant will not be guilty of the offence unless it is proved that the showing or distributing was to a person other than the child.[19] In addition to the conditions set out above a person charged with 'being in possession of indecent photographs with a view to their being distributed or shown' offence as provided under section 1(1)(c) of the 1978 Act will be guilty if the prosecution can prove that he had the photograph in his possession with a view to distributing or showing it to a person other than the child.[20]

With regards to the content of photographs, under section 7(3) of the Protection of Children Act 1978, photographs and pseudo-photographs (including those comprised in a film) shall, if they show children and are indecent, be treated for all purposes of the 1978 Act as indecent photographs of children. References to a photograph include the negative as well as the positive version,[21] and data stored on a computer disc or by other electronic means which is capable of conversion into a photograph.[22] The definition of 'photograph' given in section 7(4) of the 1978 Act was extended to include photographs in electronic data format following the amendments made by section 84(4) of the CJPOA 1994. The circulation of digital images as well as computer generated images was becoming popular and available in the mid-1990s. The main purpose of the amendments was to close potential gaps in the measures available to police and prosecutors[23] at that time. References to an indecent photograph include an indecent film,[24] a copy of an indecent photograph or film, and an indecent photograph comprised in a film.[25]

Pseudo-photographs of Children

With the amendments made by the CJPOA 1994, both the 1978 and 1988 legislation criminalize a new form of child pornography known as computer generated child pornography. The amended version of the 1978 Act made it an offence 'to make'

17 Ibid., section 1A(4). See further, the Explanatory Notes to Sexual Offences Act 2003, at <http://www.legislation.hmso.gov.uk/acts/en2003/2003en42.htm>.

18 Ibid., section 1A(3).

19 Ibid., section 1A(5).

20 Ibid., section 1A(6).

21 Section 7(4)(a) of the Protection of Children Act 1978.

22 Section 7(4)(b) of the Protection of Children Act 1978.

23 Gibbons, T., 'Computer Generated Pornography' (1995), *International Yearbook of Law Computers and Technology* (9), 83–95, at 87.

24 'Film' includes any form of video-recording, see section 7(5) of the Protection of Children Act 1978.

25 See section 7(2) of the Protection of Children Act 1978.

indecent pseudo-photographs[26] of children. According to section 7(7) as introduced by the CJPOA 1994, pseudo-photograph means an image, whether made by computer-graphics or otherwise, which appears to be a photograph. According to section 7(8) of the 1978 Act:

> If the impression conveyed by a pseudo-photograph is that the person shown is a child, the pseudo-photograph shall be treated for all purposes of the 1978 Act as showing a child and so shall a pseudo-photograph where the predominant impression conveyed is that the person shown is a child notwithstanding that some of the physical characteristics shown are those of an adult.

Pseudo-photographs are technically photographs, but they are created by a variety of ways including by computers by the use of photo/image software. For example, a child's face can be superimposed on an adult body or to another child's body together with the alteration of the characteristics of the body.[27] A pseudo-photograph can also be created by taping together two photographs and then making a photocopy of that taped photograph.[28] The photograph on the photocopy could be regarded as a pseudo-photograph. Pseudo-photographs and images can also be created entirely by software without using any real images.[29]

In the evidence given to the 1994 Home Affairs Committee inquiry into computer pornography, the case of *Shakespeare* was mentioned.[30] This was the first known instance of a case in which the police encountered such a pseudo image. In that case, a young girl's head was superimposed on to a sexually explicit adult body on a photo. Prosecutors dealing with that case were unable to prosecute as the photographs involved were pseudo-photographs and not real indecent photographs of a child. Following the 1994 inquiry, it was the intention of the legislators to close this gap in the law with the 1994 CJPOA amendments mentioned above.

Why Criminalize Pseudo-photographs?

There is an argument for criminalizing the 'distribution' of computer generated images rather than their making, creation[31] and possession as there is no evident

---

26 See further, *Atkins v. DPP; Goodland v. DPP* [2000] 2 All ER 425; [2000] 1 WLR 1427 (QBD).

27 Such as removing clothes, pubic hair or the alteration of the size of breasts and face details.

28 See *Atkins v. DPP and Goodland v. DPP* [2000] 2 All ER 425.

29 For example, see the work of the Brazilian artist, Alceu Baptistao and his creation Kaya at <http://www.vetorzero.com.br/kaya/>. Note also art created by the French artist Sebastien Legrain at <http://sebleg.free.fr/>.

30 House of Commons, Home Affairs Committee, First Report on Computer Pornography, London: HMSO, 1994, Minutes of Evidence taken before the Home Affairs Committee, p. 2 para. 7.

31 A well known example is the Canadian case of *R v. Pecchiarich* [1995] 22 O.R. (3d) 748–66, in which Pecchiarich, aged 19, was convicted and sentenced to two years probation, and 150 hours of community service for distributing 'pseudo-photographs' of children over the Internet under section 163 (1) of the Canadian Criminal Code. Although Pecchiarich created

direct harm perpetrated upon any child(ren) at the point of creation or making of such pseudo-photographs. The children involved in child pornography may suffer physical and mental injuries, but with pseudo-photographs and computer generated images the situation is rather different. These pseudo images can be entirely created by the use of computers as explained above.[32] While there is no doubt that children are sexually abused in the creation process of content involving real indecent photographs of children (child pornography), there is no direct harm to children in the production of computer generated images or indecent pseudo-photographs as long as no real children are used for such production.

However, as explained by Richard Stone, the target of the CJPOA 1994 amendments was not the photographs themselves, which might or might not be obscene articles under the Obscene Publications Act 1959,[33] but the process by which the photographs were created.[34] It was also predicted that, in the future, in some cases it may be very difficult to separate or differentiate an indecent pseudo-photograph from a real indecent photograph. There are also other considerations that support the criminalization of pseudo-photographs. Certainly the British police believe that the creators or possessors of pseudo-photographs will end up abusing children at some stage, so the purpose of the 1994 amendments may be seen as a preparatory act being criminalized:[35] the prevention of child abuse.[36] The claimed justification for criminalizing making pseudo-photographs is that the picture itself may be associated with a danger that is distinct from the harms related to the original making of a picture. There is evidence to support the fact that photographs of children engaged in sexual activity are used as tools for 'grooming' children into child pornography and sexual activity,[37] and it is

---

these materials and they showed his paedophilic tendencies and fantasies, he did not commit any offences towards children. The case of Pecchiarich could be compared to the case of Jake Baker, who had fantasies about torturing, raping and murdering a female student at the University of Michigan. Baker's case was dismissed by a US District Court Judge ruling that he was protected by the First Amendment. Baker's case was tackled as a speech issue and although he had sick fantasies, they did not involve immediate danger or any criminal activity. See *U.S. v. Baker*, 890 F. Supp. 1375 (1995).

32 See further, Kleinhans, C., 'Virtual Child Porn: The Law and the Semiotics of the Image' (2004), *Journal of Visual Culture* 3(1), 17–34.

33 See generally, Akdeniz, Y., 'Computer Pornography: A Comparative Study of the US and UK Obscenity Laws and Child Pornography Laws in Relation to the Internet' (1996), *International Review of Law, Computers and Technology* 10(2), 235–61.

34 Stone, R., 'Extending the Labyrinth: Part VII of the CJPOA 1994' (1995) *MLR* 58(3) 389–94 at 389.

35 In March 1996 the author interviewed Detective Inspector David Davis, the former head of West Midlands Police Commercial Vice Unit, which deals with child pornography investigations. DI Davis clearly stated that the UK police believed that if somebody creates or posseses indecent pseudo-photographs of children, that person is a potential child abuser and will abuse children in the future. See also Explosive Substances Act 1883 as an example for preparatory acts being criminalized.

36 See Williams Committee Report, *Obscenity and Film Censorship*, Cmnd. 7772, London: HMSO, 1979, p. 90, para. 6.68.

37 See Attorney General's Commission on Pornography: Final Report, 2 vols, Washington, DC: US Government Printing Office, July 1986 (The Meese Commission) at p. 411.

argued[38] that photographs or pseudo-photographs will be used interchangeably for this purpose. This argument has also been raised in the United States and it is suggested by the findings of a US Senate Committee that paedophiles use any form of child pornography to stimulate and whet their own sexual appetites.[39] Policy makers intend to control and criminalize the market for such materials regardless of how such content may be created. The UN Special Rapporteur on the sale of children, child prostitution and child pornography also warned that 'although this kind of pornography does not involve the direct abuse of a child, its power to 'normalize' images of child sexual abuse and incite sexual exploitation of children should not be underestimated and must be adequately addressed.'[40]

There is also an anti-evasion aspect in that people accused of possessing or distributing child pornography may claim that the pictures they possess are not of real children but are pseudo-photographs. The making and availability of pseudo-photographs could in theory restrict prosecutors in their ability to obtain convictions because it could be impossible to prove that the content in question was produced using real children.

There has been international support for the criminalization of computer generated images as mentioned in Chapter 1. The criminalization of the making, possession and distribution of pseudo-photographs was supported by the Special Rapporteur of the Commission on Human Rights of the United Nations in October 1997. At the time it was proposed by the Special Rapporteur to include an absolute prohibition on 'pseudo-child pornography' including the 'morphing' of child and adult bodies to create virtual child pornographic images within the scope of article 34 of the Convention on the Rights of the Child.[41] The UN Optional Protocol on the Sale of Children, Child Prostitution and Child Pornography,[42] the Council of Europe's Cybercrime Convention 2001, as well as the EU Council Framework Decision on combating the sexual exploitation of children and child pornography[43]

38 See US Senate Committee on the Judiciary Report on the Child Pornography Prevention Act of 1995, 104th Congress Report, Senate 2d Session 104–358, 27 August 1996. Therefore, note the Child Pornography Prevention Act 1996 which includes provisions for pseudo child pornography. See further, the constitutional challenge involving the CPPA 1996: *Ashcroft, Attorney General, et al. v. Free Speech Coalition et al.* (US Supreme Court, 2002) 535 US 234, 198 F3d 1083, 16 April 2002, No. 00–795, Argued 30 October 2001.

39 See US Senate Committee on the Judiciary Report on the Child Pornography Prevention Act of 1995, 104th Congress Report, Senate 2d Session 104–358, 27 August 1996.

40 Report of the Special Rapporteur on the sale of children, child prostitution and child pornography (Mr Juan Miguel Petit), E/CN.4/2005/78, 23 December 2004, Commission on Human Rights, at <http://daccessdds.un.org/doc/UNDOC/GEN/G05/100/19/PDF/G0510019.pdf>, para. 22.

41 See Promotion and Protection of the Rights of Children: Sale of children, child prostitution and child pornography, Note by the Secretary-General, A/52/482, 16 October 1997, para. 53.

42 Optional Protocol to the Convention on the Rights of the Child on the Sale of Children, Child Prostitution and Child Pornography, New York, 25 May 2000, Fifty-fourth session (97th plenary meeting), Agenda item 116 (a), Distr. General A/RES/54/263, 26 June 2000.

43 Communication to the Council and the European Parliament COM(2000) 854–3, Brussels, 22 January 2001. Proposal for a Council Framework Decision on combating the

include provisions criminalizing various offences in relation to pseudo-photographs as well as real indecent photographs of children (discussed in Chapters 5, 6 and 7).

PROTECTION OF CHILDREN LEGISLATION IN ACTION

Both the Protection of Children Act 1978 and section 160 of the Criminal Justice Act 1988 have been successfully used in many cases involving the making, distribution and possession of child pornography.

There have been 4,771 prosecutions involving 3,789 convictions for offences involving taking, making, distributing, showing, possessing with intent to distribute or show, or publishing any advertisement conveying the distribution of indecent photographs (or pseudo-photographs since the CJPOA 1994 amendments) under the Protection of Children Act 1978 according to official statistics and research conducted by the author. These statistics obtained from the Home Office refer to the period 1980–2004. In addition to these prosecutions, a total of 732 persons were cautioned for a section 1 offence in the same period.

According to official statistics,[44] there have been 1,831 possession prosecutions involving 1,267 convictions[45] under section 160 of the Criminal Justice Act 1988 between 1988 and 2004, and a total of 624 persons have been cautioned for a possession offence in the same period.

A grand total of 6,602 prosecutions have resulted in 5,056 convictions from the early 1980s until the end of 2004. The number of cautions involving all child pornography related offences within England and Wales reached 1,356 by the end of 2004.

A sharp increase in prosecutions involving child pornography related offences is visible in the mid-1990s (see Table 2.1). The official figures do not provide specific information on how child pornography is made, distributed or possessed by the offenders, but the increase is more evident after the 1978 and 1988 Acts were amended by the Criminal Justice and Public Order Act 1994 to cover images in computer data format. One might therefore reasonably assume that the increase in prosecutions in the 1990s is related to the exponential growth of Internet access from

---

sexual exploitation of children and child pornography, OJ C E/2001/62/E/25 327, pp. 327–30, 27 February 2001. Council Framework Decision 2004/68/JHA of 22 December 2003 on combating the sexual exploitation of children and child pornography (see OJ L 013 20 January 2004, pp. 44–8), at <http://register.consilium.europa.eu/pdf/en/03/st10/st10748en03.pdf>.

44 Main source for these statistics is the Crime and Criminal Justice Unit (RDS), Home Office, October 2001–2006. See Hansard for further statistics, for example, House of Commons Hansard, Commons Written Answers, 22 December 1988; House of Commons Written Answers on Child Pornography, 15 July 1998, column 191; House of Commons, Hansard, Written Answers, 8 December 1999, pt 1; Home Department, Child Pornography Prosecutions; House of Lords Written Answers, Indecent and Obscene Material on the Internet, 15 January 2001; House of Commons Written Answers, 'Child Pornography', 19 January 2006 (Paul Goggins).

45 Note that the conviction (but not prosecution) statistics were made available in January 2006: House of Commons Written Answers, 'Child Pornography', 19 January 2006 (Paul Goggins).

Table 2.1 Child pornography prosecution and conviction statistics (1980–2004)

Year	S.1 Prosecutions	S.1 Convictions	Possession Prosecutions	Possession Convictions	S.1 Cautions	S.160 Cautions
1980	13	13				
1981	13	14				
1982	9	12				
1983	12	12				
1984	18	19			2	
1985	22	24			1	
1986	10	11			1	
1987	23	29				
1988	32	31	1	2		
1989	44	39	21	16	5	2
1990	44	35	36	32	10	5
1991	40	39	53	43	10	3
1992	46	44	43	30	10	13
1993	42	37	48	35	7	4
1994	40	27	53	36	6	7
1995	53	44	60	37	18	11
1996	80	69	125	79	15	16
1997	111	103	124	81	14	17
1998	116	82	167	105	26	19
1999	175	139	163	99	31	34
2000	287	217	129	77	35	25
2001	398	289	126	75	38	32
2002	582	434	156	97	63	69
2003	1,464	1,048	326	239	239	205
2004	1,097	978	200	184	201	162
Total	**4,771**	**3,789**	**1,831**	**1,267**	**732**	**624**

homes,[46] and the availability and circulation of child pornography over the Internet. The statistics also indicate a systematic growth in the number of prosecutions from 1995 when child pornography became an issue of major public concern.

However, in the absence of detailed statistics it is not possible to say how many of the prosecutions under the 1978 and 1988 legislation involved child pornography

46 See The Office of National Statistics, Internet Access: 2006 First Release, 23 August 2006, at <http://www.statistics.gov.uk/pdfdir/inta0806.pdf>. See further, Cabinet Office, Prime Minister's Strategy Unit, *Connecting the UK: the Digital Strategy*, April 2005.

obtained through the Internet or child pornography possessed or distributed in data format. It also remains unclear why there is a huge gap between prosecution and conviction statistics considering the fact that in most cases the defendants plead guilty to such crimes.

Operation Ore

It may be noted from Table 2.1 that compared to 2002, statistics almost tripled in 2003. While there were a total of 738 prosecutions resulting in 531 convictions and 132 cautions in 2002, there were a total of 1,790 prosecutions resulting in 1,374 convictions and 444 cautions in 2003. The sharp increase in prosecutions in 2003 stems directly from the ongoing 'Operation Ore', the biggest Internet child pornography operation of recent times. Operation Ore was launched in the UK after the FBI passed credit card details of 7,250 alleged British subscribers to a child pornography portal operated in Texas called Landslide.[47] This massive operation resulted in approximately 3,750 arrests which included teachers, care workers, social workers, soldiers, surgeons and 50 police officers. Although the police have been reportedly struggling to deal with such a huge number of cases,[48] approximately 6,500 of the British Landslide subscribers have been subjected to investigation. The highest priority group of suspects, featuring approximately 1,200 names including convicted paedophiles and those who work and have access to children, were investigated first. It was reported in June 2005 that these investigations had resulted in 1,670 prosecutions,[49] 1,451 convictions and 500 cautions.[50] As of April 2005, 1,300 investigations were still ongoing and 879 were pending.[51] The noticeable rise in the cautions statistics since 2002 could also be related to the huge number of investigations conducted in relation to Operation Ore. One hundred and nine children were rescued from abusive homes[52] during the investigations.

The conduct of police has been criticized by experts who allege to have revealed serious flaws in the handling of evidence obtained from the United States which triggered the investigation.[53] Campbell claims that 'many of the Britons who have

47 'FBI Investigation into child porn sites spans the world; Internet Crackdown: Dozens of British arrests have followed an international inquiry launched into three websites based in Houston', *Independent*, 14 September 2002. See generally, Oswell, D., 'When Images Matter: Internet Child Pornography, Forms of Observation and an Ethics of the Virtual' (2006), *Information, Communication and Society* 9(2), 244–65.

48 'Sex offenders slip the net: Thousands escape with cautions because police cannot cope with the flood of child porn offences', *Guardian*, 28 September 2003.

49 See, 'Paedophile crackdown rescues 102 children', *Press Association*, 14 April 2004; 'Police rescue 100 child porn victims', *The Times*, 15 April 2004.

50 '1,400 are in the clear as child-porn inquiry ends', *Daily Mail*, 26 November 2006.

51 Warren, P., 'UK police tackle mounting Internet porn caseload', *Register*, 22 April 2005, at <http://www.theregister.co.uk/2005/04/22/uk_police_internet/>. No further statistical update is available in relation to Operation Ore prosecutions as of this writing.

52 'Paedophile crackdown rescues 102 children', *Press Association*, 14 April 2004.

53 Campbell, D., 'Operation Ore Exposed', *PC Pro*, 1 July 2005.

been publicly branded dangerous paedophiles'[54] were victims of systematic credit card fraud and their credit cards, unknown to the suspects, were fraudulently used on the Landslide portal website. Evidence revealed by Campbell and Bates[55] indicates that many British suspects had never subscribed to the Landslide websites. Experts maintain that the police did not find any child pornographic content on computers belonging to these suspects, and as a result decided to charge them with an 'incitement' to distribute indecent photographs of children,[56] and/or attempted incitement to distribute indecent photographs offences contrary to common law and section 1 of the Criminal Attempts Act 1981 based solely upon the credit card transaction evidence. Thirty-nine suspects caught up in the Operation Ore investigations have committed suicide[57] rather than face public humiliation, including commander of British forces in Gibraltar, Commodore David White, who allegedly downloaded child pornography from the Landslide websites.[58] An inquest into his death revealed that 'computer equipment and a camera memory chip belonging to Commodore White had yielded no evidence that he downloaded child pornography',[59] and a Ministry of Defence police-written confirmation indicates 'there were no substantive criminal offences to warrant pressing charges.'[60] Such cases[61] cast a dark shadow over the true success of Operation Ore,[62] and raise serious questions about police handling of these inevitably sensitive investigations.

A detailed examination of the provisions and application of the Protection of Children Act 1978 and section 160 of the Criminal Justice Act 1988 will now follow, beginning with the possession offence.

---

54 Campbell, D., 'Sex, Lies and the Missing Videotape', *PC Pro*, 1 April 2007. Note also Campbell, D., 'Operation Ore flawed by fraud', *Guardian*, 19 April 2007.

55 Bates, J., *The Ore Reports*, at <http://www.computer-investigations.com/index3.html>.

56 Note for example 'Former school caretaker jailed in child porn case; Crown Court: Judge sentences Coventry father-of-two on incitement', *Coventry Evening Telegraph*, 16 November 2005. See further, *Regina (O) v. Coventry Magistrates Court* [2004] QBD, 5 April 2004.

57 Ibid. Note also Leppard. D., 'Child porn suspects set to be cleared in evidence "shambles"', *Sunday Times*, 3 July 2005; Campbell, D., 'Sex, Lies and the Missing Videotape', *PC Pro*, 1 April 2007.

58 'Navy man's death puts spotlight on child porn inquiry', *Daily Telegraph*, 12 January 2005.

59 'No evidence against man in child porn inquiry who "killed himself"', *Independent*, 1 October 2005; 'Officer "cracked" after porn claims', *The Times*, 14 April 2006.

60 Ibid.

61 See, for example, 'My hell over false child porn charges – doctor', *Yorkshire Post*, 4 October 2004; 'Cases may be dropped after suspects fell victim to disguised link on legal sites', *Sunday Life (Belfast Telegraph)*, 18 May 2003.

62 See Arthur, C., 'Is Operation Ore the UK's worst-ever policing scandal?', *Guardian*, 26 April 2007. See further, Operation Ore Exposed, <http://www.ore-exposed.co.uk/>.

Criminalizing Possession

Simple possession of indecent photographs and/or pseudo-photographs of a child is criminalized under section 160 of the Criminal Justice Act 1988.[63] As mentioned above, the possession of indecent photographs of children was not originally criminalized by the provisions of the Protection of Children Act 1978. The reason behind the criminalization of possession of indecent photographs was outlined in *R v. Land*,[64] in which it was stated:

> the object is to protect children from exploitation and degradation. Potential damage to the child occurs when he or she is posed or pictured indecently, and whenever such an event occurs the child is exploited. It is the demand for such material which leads to the exploitation of children and the purpose of the Act is to reduce, indeed as far as possible to eliminate, trade in or possession of it.

Although possession is considered to be a less serious crime,[65] the courts have consistently taken the view that those who demand and possess child pornography contribute to the sexual exploitation of children and the trade in child pornography.[66]

Necessity of Possession Offence

The possession prosecution examples that will be mentioned later in this chapter[67] show that many of the defendants are first time offenders and that most reported cases do not involve any actual child abuse. This conclusion appears to challenge the necessity of possession offences and whether the existence of such an offence in fact protects children or acts as a preventative measure for child sexual abuse. An important question of where to draw the line between permissible and impermissible material needs to be answered. Many would argue that society and the government have a responsibility to protect children from the 'evils associated with the possession of child pornography'.[68] But what are these risks?

---

63 As amended by section 84(4) of the CJPOA 1994. See generally, Edwards, S.M., 'Prosecuting "Child Pornography": Possession and Taking of Indecent Photographs' (2000), *Journal of Social Welfare and Family Law* 22(1), 1–21.

64 *R v. Land* [1999] QB 65.

65 Note also *R v. O'Carroll* [2002] EWCA Civ 3190 which involved a conviction of the defendant being knowingly concerned in the importation of indecent photographs of children. O'Carroll, T. is the author of *Paedophilia: The Radical Case* (Contemporary Issues Series, Peter Owen Publishers, 1980) which pushed for the normalization of adult–child sexual relationships in the early 1980s.

66 See generally, Ost, S., 'Children at Risk: Legal and Societal Perceptions of the Potential Threat that the Possession of Child Pornography Poses to Society' (2002), *Journal of Law and Society* 29(3), September, 436–60.

67 See further, Akdeniz, Y., 'Child Pornography', in Y. Akdeniz, C. Walker and D. Wall (eds), *The Internet, Law and Society*, Harlow: Addison Wesley Longman, 2000, 231–49 for an overview of earlier possession cases.

68 *R v. Sharpe*, 2001 SCC 2. File No. 27376, 26 January 2001.

The Courts believe that 'even the young inexperienced amateur who downloads one image for his or her personal gratification does a significant criminal act which adds to the scale of human misery because, if there was no market for these images children would not be degraded producing them.'[69] The official response is that although those who download and possess child pornography are not 'directly responsible for corrupting children so as to obtain pictures of this kind',[70] it is obvious that because they are inclined to obtain them, they are contributing to a market for such material which encourages the production and dissemination of such images without which the trade would not flourish.[71] According to judicial opinion, 'children somewhere at some time were being most shamefully abused in order to produce such material'[72] for this sort of market. It is also claimed that a person who only downloads and views images also 'contributes to the risk of psychological harm suffered by the children forced to pose or to participate in sexual conduct captured by the images'.[73] The images themselves are a record of the abuse.[74] The serious psychological injury to which the children would be at risk arises 'from their knowledge that what they were to do would be viewed by others and their awareness that there were people getting a perverted thrill from watching them forced to pose and behave in this way.'[75] As Taylor and Quayle rightly state, 'at worst it is a permanent record of crime, and serves to perpetuate the images and memory of that abuse for as long as it exists.'[76] The downloading, possession as well as distribution and further circulation of these images 'ensures the continued and even increased availability of the record of the abuse'.[77]

At the same time, it may be argued that privately kept and possessed material may do less harm or no harm if there is no substantial link to the furtherance of other crimes. The matter may be even more complicated when the creation of such content does not involve direct harm to children at all, as in the case of written materials, drawings,[78] and as in the case of computer generated images of children.[79] Those who commit

---

69 *R v. Toomer and others* [2001] 2 Cr App R(S) 30, Lexis UK CS 1705, para. 6.

70 *R v. Koeller* [2001] EWCA Crim 1854, para. 11.

71 See *Beaney* [2004] Crim.L.R. 480; *R v. Monument* [2005] EWCA CRIM 30; [2005] All ER (D) 189 (Jan); *R v. Knights* [2001] EWCA Crim 1694.

72 Ibid.

73 Ibid.

74 See generally, Taylor, M. and E. Quayle, *Child Pornography: An Internet Crime*, Hove: Brunner-Routledge, 2003, chapter 2 entitled 'The Nature of Child Pornography', pp. 21–47.

75 Ibid.

76 Ibid., 194.

77 Ibid.

78 The Canadian Supreme Court case of *R v. Sharpe*, 2001 SCC 2. File No. 27376, 26 January 2001, shows that there may be challenges on privacy and free speech grounds as far as 'private possession only' of such content is concerned. This case and the Canadian law and policy will be discussed in Chapter 4.

79 Note the contrasting decisions in the US cases involving the Child Pornography Prevention Act 1996 which criminalizes computer generated images: *Free Speech Coalition v. Reno* 198 F3d 1083, 1092 (9th Cir. 1999), cert. granted sub nom., and *Ashcroft v. Free Speech Coalition*, 148 L. Ed. 2d 788, 121 S. Ct. 876, 69 U.S.L.W. 3495 (U.S. 2001). The

the possession offence may solely download such indecent images from the Internet rather than distribute such images, trade in them or, more importantly, produce them.

There is, as yet, no conclusive correlation between individuals who access, view and possess child pornography and offences of sexual abuse of children in the United Kingdom or elsewhere. According to a statement made by Baroness Scotland of Asthal in the House of Lords,

> People who sexually abuse children are often found to be in possession of indecent images of children. There is evidence to suggest that child pornography can be used in an attempt to legitimize their sexual activities with children and to 'groom' or encourage compliance from their victims. However, we are not currently aware of any evidence to support a direct causal link between access to child pornography and the commission of sexual offences against children.[80]

It may be recalled that in 1990 Home Office research conducted by Howitt and Cumberbatch relating to pornography concluded that there was no evidence of any causal links between pornography and sexual violence.[81] Howitt and Cumberbatch's research concluded that pornography's contribution to the development of pathological or criminal sexuality is far from clear.[82] The authors accordingly caution that 'it is important to distinguish between the use of pornography by "deviant" persons and the effects of pornography in creating that deviancy.'[83]

Recent research in the United States seems to suggest that about 40 per cent of arrested child pornography possessors were 'dual offenders', who sexually victimized children and possessed child pornography at the same time.[84] The authors of the 2005 *Child-Pornography Possessors Arrested in Internet-Related Crimes: Findings from the National Juvenile Online Victimization Study* accept that their research does not 'explain how possessing child pornography is related to child sexual victimization or whether it causes or encourages such victimization'.[85] They nevertheless claim, 'it is reasonable to view and treat arrested child pornography possessors as at high risk for victimizing children.'[86] Michael Briere, who kidnapped, raped and murdered a ten-year-old girl, Holly Jones, in Canada confessed to police that child pornography obtained through the Internet pushed him over the edge. During his murder trial, the

---

cases involving the CPPA 1996 were resolved at the Supreme Court level: *Ashcroft, Attorney General, et al. v. Free Speech Coalition et al.* (16 April 2002). The CPPA 1996 and the Supreme Court decision will be discussed in Chapter 3.

80 Baroness Scotland of Asthal, HL Hansard, Written Answers: 'Child Pornography and Sexual Offences', 11 March 2004.

81 Howitt, D. and G. Cumberbatch, *Pornography: Impacts and Influences*, London: HMSO, 1990.

82 Ibid., 83.

83 Ibid.

84 See Wolak, J., D. Finkelhor and K.J. Mitchell, *Child-Pornography Possessors Arrested in Internet-Related Crimes: Findings From the National Juvenile Online Victimization Study*, National Center for Missing and Exploited Children, 2005, at <http://www.missingkids.com/en_US/publications/NC144.pdf>.

85 Ibid.

86 Ibid.

prosecution argued that 'it was the presence of child pornography, his accessing of it, that immediately motivated him to go out on the street and snatch Holly Jones and eventually murder and rape her.'[87] The prosecution also stated, 'this case of all cases is, in any event, functionally an indication of the cancer and impact that child pornography can have on our society.'[88]

Cases such as *Briere* are rare[89] but provide further justification for those who argue that those who possess child pornography should be treated as high risk. However other researchers, such as Seto, argue that a history of viewing child pornography is not necessarily itself a strong indicator of who is going to sexually abuse children.[90] A study conducted by Seto and Eke on 201 Canadian child pornography offenders[91] listed on the Ontario Sex Offender Registry concluded that the likelihood of later offending by child pornography offenders is unknown.[92] According to their research, 'child pornography offenders with prior criminal records were significantly more likely to offend again in any way during the follow-up period.'[93] Consistent with current theories of sexual offending, the authors argue that child pornography offenders 'who had committed a prior or concurrent contact sexual offence were the most likely to offend again, either generally or sexually'.[94]

A study[95] involving 202 child pornography related convictions between 1996 and 2005 in New Zealand conducted by the Department of Internal Affairs was also

87 See *R v. Briere* [2004] O.J. No. 5611; 2004 ON.C. LEXIS 6108 (Ontario Superior Court of Justice).

88 Ibid.

89 Note the case of *R v. Coutts* [2005] 1 Cr App R 517 within the context of possession and viewing of extreme violent pornography and its possible link to the commission of violent offences such as murder. Note also the Home Office Consultation Paper, *Possession of Extreme Pornographic Material*, August 2005 at <http://www.scotland.gov.uk/Publications/2005/08/30112423/24254>, as well as Cyber-Rights.Org's Response, December 2005 at <http://www.cyber-rights.org/cyber-rights.org_response.pdf>, and Rowbottom, J., 'Obscenity Laws and the Internet: Targeting the Supply and Demand' (2006), *Crim. L.R.*, February, 97–109.

90 See Aster, A.Z., 'New study examines risk factors for child sexual offences', CrossCurrents, The Centre for Addiction and Mental Health (CAMH), at <http://www.camh.net/Publications/Cross_Currents/Autumn_2005/sexualoffences_crcuautumn05.html>.

91 Persons convicted for possession, distribution, or production of child pornography, as defined by Canadian criminal law.

92 Seto M.C. and A.W. Eke, 'The Criminal Histories and Later Offending of Child Pornography Offenders' (2005), *Sexual Abuse: A Journal of Research and Treatment* 17, 201–10.

93 Ibid.

94 Ibid. Note further Seto, M.C., J.M. Cantor, and R. Blanchard, 'Validation of Child Pornography Possession as a Diagnostic Indicator of Pedophilia' (2006), *Journal of Abnormal Psychology* 115, 610–15.

95 Sullivan, C., *Internet Traders of Child Pornography: Profiling Research*, Department of Internal Affairs, New Zealand (November 2005), at <http://www.dia.govt.nz/pubforms.nsf/URL/Profilingupdate2.pdf/$file/Profilingupdate2.pdf>. This is an updated version of the same named more comprehensive version of the report written by A. Carr and first published in April 2004: <http://www.dia.govt.nz/Pubforms.nsf/URL/entirereport.pdf/$file/entirereport.

inconclusive in terms of whether it is possible to draw a causal link between viewing child pornography and offending against children, even though the study concluded that an association between the two offences is suggested by the findings of the study. 74.51 per cent of the 202 offenders did not have a prior criminal history and only 14 per cent had convictions for offences of a sexual nature.[96] The study called for further research into viewing objectionable material and committing physical offences to understand better the nature of the association.

The Offence of Possession under Section 160

It is an offence under section 160(1) of the 1988 Act for a person to have an indecent[97] photograph[98] or pseudo-photograph[99] of a child under the age of 18[100] in his or her possession.[101]

Under section 160(2A) of the 1988 Act[102] a person shall be liable on conviction on indictment of an offence of possession of an indecent photograph or a pseudo-

pdf>. Note also the November 2004 update at <http://www.dia.govt.nz/pubforms.nsf/URL/profilingupdate.pdf/$file/profilingupdate.pdf>.

96 See ibid. Note that 12 offenders were convicted for a non-violent, non-sexual crime (5.88 per cent), 3 for minor offence of a sexual nature (1.47 per cent), 9 for a sexual offence against a female aged under 16 years (4.41 per cent), 5 for a sexual offence with a male aged under 16 years (2.45 per cent), and 1 for a sexual offence against an adult (0.49 per cent).

97 In terms of what amounts to indecent see *R v. Graham-Kerr* [1988] 1 WLR 1098; (1989) 88 Cr App R 302; *R v. Land* [1999] QB 65; [1998] 1 All ER 403; [1998] 3 WLR 322; and *R v. Smethurst* [2001] EWCA Crim 772.

98 Section 7(4)(a) of the Protection of Children Act 1978.

99 There is no statutory definition of the term 'child pornography'. In fact, prior to the enactment of the Sexual Offences Act 2003 (sections 48–50 of the Sexual Offences Act 200) the words 'child' and 'pornography' did not even appear together in any legislation dealing with offences related to child pornography. The statutory provisions within the Protection of Children Act 1978, and section 160 of the Criminal Justice Act 1988 refer to the criminalization of offences related to indecent photographs and indecent pseudo-photographs (since 1994) of children.

100 A child was originally described as a person under the age of 16 by section 7(6) of the 1978 Act. However, this has been amended and changed to a person under the age of 18 by section 45(2) of the Sexual Offences Act 2003 which came into force in May 2004. The change was necessary mainly to comply with international initiatives for the harmonization of laws in relation to child pornography. Note the European Union's Council Framework Decision 2004/68/JHA of 22 December 2003 on combating the sexual exploitation of children and child pornography. See OJ L 13, 20 January 2004; the Council of Europe's Cybercrime Convention 2001 (ETS no.185), article 9; and the United Nations' Optional Protocol to the Convention on the Rights of the Child on the Sale of Children, Child Prostitution and Child Pornography (General Assembly resolution A/RES/54/263 of 25 May 2000): Entered into force on 18 January 2002).

101 Note the case of *R v. Owen* [1988] 1 WLR. 134 in relation to the relevancy of the age of a child in terms of establishing whether the photographs in question are indecent or not. Note also Gillespie, A., 'The Sexual Offences Act 2003: (3) Tinkering with "Child Pornography"' (2004), *Crim. L.R.*, May, 361–8.

102 As amended by the Criminal Justice and Court Services Act 2000. The previous maximum penalty was six months' imprisonment.

photograph of a child to imprisonment for a term not exceeding five years or a fine subject to the sentencing guidelines set out by the Court of Appeal in *R v. Oliver*[103] (see later discussion). A person shall be liable on summary conviction of an offence under this section to imprisonment for a term not exceeding six months or a fine not exceeding level 5 on the standard scale, or both.

Many cases of simple possession offences have been brought before the courts in England and Wales. As mentioned above, between 1988 and 2004 there were a total of 1,831 possession prosecutions involving 1,267 convictions.[104] During the same period 624 people were also cautioned in England and Wales (see Table 2.2; Graph 2.1).

Table 2.2 Statistics for section 160, 1988 Act, 1988–2004

Possession Prosecutions	Possession Convictions	S.160 Cautions
1,831	1,267	624

The courts' attitude towards those who are prosecuted and convicted of possession of child pornography and related sentencing issues is examined later within this chapter. A few noteworthy cases are, however, worth mentioning at this stage.

The first person to be convicted of possession of child pornography obtained through the Internet was Christopher Sharp, who was fined £9,000 in October 1995.[105] Sharp admitted two charges of possessing indecent photographs of children under the age of 16 contrary to section 160 of the Criminal Justice Act 1988. The Sharp prosecution was followed by the prosecution of Martin Crumpton in 1996. Crumpton also admitted possession of indecent pictures of children and was the first person to be jailed in the UK for an offence concerning child pornography and the Internet. He was sentenced to three months' imprisonment at a Birmingham magistrates' court.[106] The most publicized possession of child pornography case is arguably that of Paul Gadd (better known as Gary Glitter), who was sentenced to four months' imprisonment following conviction for a possession offence involving 4,000 images downloaded from the Internet[107] in November 1999.[108]

103 *R v. Oliver and others* [2002] EWCA Crim 2766; [2003] 2 Cr App R (S) 64; [2003] 1 Cr App R 28; [2003] 2 Cr App R (S.) 15; *The Times*, 6 December 2002; 2002 WL 31599711.

104 As was previously mentioned, the conviction (but not prosecution) statistics for 2004 were made available in January 2006: See House of Commons Written Answers, 'Child Pornography', 19 January 2006 (Paul Goggins).

105 Bunyan, N., 'Man fined £9,000 for Internet porn', *Daily Telegraph*, 27 October 1995.

106 'Man jailed over child pornography on Internet', *Daily Telegraph*, 5 January 1996.

107 The judge at Bristol Crown Court said the 4,000 images downloaded from the Internet were of the 'very, very worst possible type'. See further, 'Glitter jailed for worst type of child pornography', *The Scotsman*, 13 November 1999.

108 (1999) *The Times* 13 November, p. 1. The crime was reportedly detected when the defendant's personal computer was taken for repair to a retailer who alerted the police. See further, 'Gary Glitter arrested in child porn inquiry', *The Times*, 20 November 1997.

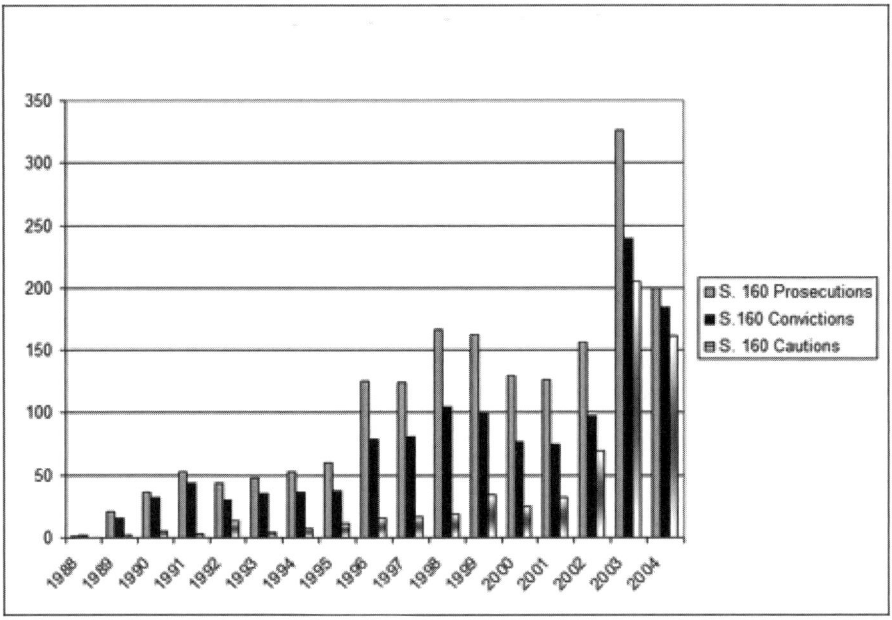

Graph 2.1 Section 160, Criminal Justice Act 1988 statistics

Available Defences under Section 160

Specific defences associated with the possession offence are set out in section 160(2) of the 1988 Act which provides that:

> (2) Where a person is charged with an offence under subsection (1), it shall be a defence for him to prove –
> (a) that he had a legitimate reason for having the photograph or pseudo-photograph in his possession; or
> (b) that he had not himself seen the photograph or pseudo-photograph and did not know, nor had any cause to suspect, it to be indecent; or
> (c) that the photograph or pseudo-photograph was sent to him without any prior request made by him or on his behalf and that he did not keep it for an unreasonable time.[109]

These three defences, namely, legitimate reason, knowing possession, and unsolicited photographs or pseudo-photographs are examined in turn below.

109 Note also that some further defences were introduced by the Sexual Offences Act 2003 in the form of exceptions for 'marriage and other relationships' through section 160A under the Criminal Justice Act 1988. The exception provided under section 160A(1) will apply in cases in which the defendant proves that the photograph in question was of a child aged 16 or over and that at the time of possession he and the child were married or living together as partners in an enduring family relationship. Under section 160A(4), the

Legitimate Reason Defence

A defendant will be able to claim that he had a legitimate reason for having photographs or pseudo-photographs in his possession only in limited circumstances where there is evidence to support his claim. The defence is available to police and to prosecutors involved in the investigation and prosecution of child pornography related offences. Organizations such as the Internet Watch Foundation, which acts as a government supported hotline to report Internet child pornography, may also claim this defence since it is officially recognized as a quasi-governmental body which receives complaints from the public and works with the police and the Internet Service Providers.[110]

There have been a number of recent cases where defendants have claimed that they had a 'legitimate reason' to possess child pornography as part of their 'academic research'. In *Atkins v. Director of Public Prosecutions* and *Goodland v. Director of Public Prosecutions*,[111] Dr Atkins, a lecturer at the Department of English at Bristol University, argued in his defence that he had a legitimate reason for having photographs in his possession for the purpose of legitimate academic research under section 160(2)(a). Ultimately the Magistrates' Court found, and the High Court (Queen's Bench Division) agreed, that Atkins was not conducting 'honest and straightforward research into child pornography'. According to the Queen's Bench Division, the question of what constitutes 'a legitimate reason'[112] is a pure question of fact (for the magistrate or jury) in each case. The central question when the defence is raised will be whether the defendant is essentially a person of unhealthy interests in possession of indecent photographs in the pretence of undertaking research, or by contrast a genuine researcher with no alternative but to have this sort of unpleasant material in his possession. The Queen's Bench Division emphasized that this would depend upon the facts of an individual case but at the same time stated that the courts 'are plainly entitled to bring a measure of scepticism to bear upon such an enquiry: they should not too readily conclude that the defence has been made out.'[113]

---

defendant must also show that there is evidence to suggest that the child consented to the photograph being in possession, or that the defendant reasonably believed that the child consented. Finally, under section 160A(3) the photograph in question must not be one that shows a person other than the child and the defendant. If these three conditions are satisfied, the defendant would have a defence for possessing such images.

110 See <http://www.internetwatch.org.uk/hotline/>. See further, the *IWF Half Yearly Report 2006*, at <http://www.iwf.org.uk/documents/20060719_2006_half_yearly_report.pdf>. Note also the Memorandum of Understanding Between Crown Prosecution Service (CPS) and the Association of Chief Police Officers (ACPO) concerning section 46 Sexual Offences Act 2003, October 2004, at <http://www.cps.gov.uk/publications/docs/mousexoffences.pdf>.

111 *Atkins v. DPP* and *Goodland v. DPP* [2000] 2 All ER 425; [2000] 1 WLR 1427.

112 For the purposes of both section 160(2)(a) of the 1988 Act and section 1(4)(a) of the 1978 Act.

113 *Atkins v. DPP* and *Goodland v. DPP* [2000] 2 All ER 425; [2000] 1 WLR 1427.

In *R v. Wrigley*,[114] the defendant, a graduate of the Keele University, was convicted of one offence of distributing indecent photographs of children under section 1(1)(b) of the Act, and one offence of possessing indecent photographs of children for distribution under section 1(1)(c) of the 1978 Act. He was sentenced to three months' imprisonment for the first offence, and to six months' imprisonment for the second offence – these to run concurrently. The police, acting on information received, found 32 disks containing 677 indecent images of young boys. There was evidence to suggest that Wrigley downloaded the images and was swapping these images through the Internet with two American paedophiles. On appeal, the appellant admitted the possession of indecent photographs, but claimed that 'he had a legitimate reason for possessing the indecent material, namely genuine academic research'. Wrigley argued that he was conducting an informal pilot study as to whether there was material for a PhD research project. This, he claimed, required him to pose as a paedophile while he evaluated the different responses to specific indecent pictures of two different sorts of paedophiles. The Court, however, noted several evidential difficulties in the academic research defence. For example, the appellant had not discussed his research programme with any of his tutors. Moreover, following his initial arrest, despite the advice by a number of his tutors to take his research material to the police, he did not do so.

The prosecution agreed that genuine academic research could be a legitimate reason and a defence in such cases, but maintained that Wrigley's research was for 'his personal gratification and/or his sexual orientation' and pointed to the absence of any supporting evidence and specifically to Wrigley's failure to inform any of his tutors about his research programme. The appeal was dismissed.

Knowing Possession

In *Atkins v. DPP*,[115] it was established that a person is not guilty of the offence of possession under section 160(1) unless he *knows* that he has the indecent photographs in possession. In the words of Simon Brown LJ:

> ... knowledge is an essential element in the offence of possession under section 160 so that an accused cannot be convicted where, ... he cannot be shown to be aware of the existence of a cache of photographs in the first place ... Returning to section 160(2)(b), it seems to me indeed that the very fact that Parliament created a defence for those possessing photographs reasonably not known to be indecent, strongly suggests that there was no intention to criminalize unknowing possession of photographs in the first place.[116]

---

114 CA, Case No. 99/01497/Z5, 26 May 2000.

115 *Atkins v. DPP* [2002] 2 1040 Cr App R 248. When applying this proposition it must be borne in mind that the test for indecency is an objective one: see *R v. Smethurst* [2001] EWCA Crim 772; [2002] 1 Cr App R 6. See further, Gillespie, A., 'Child Pornography: Balancing Substantive and Evidential Law to Safeguard Children Effectively from Abuse' (2005), *International Journal of Evidence and Proof* 9(1), 29–50.

116 Ibid.

Further clarification was provided in *R. v. Collier (Edward John)*[117] where the defendant had in his possession tapes and CD-ROMs containing indecent images but maintained that he never suspected that the material would include indecent images of children. It was acknowledged by the Court of Appeal that subsections (a) and (c) proceed on the assumption that the defendant is aware that the photograph is an indecent photograph of a child and that he has either a legitimate reason for possessing it or it has been sent to him without prior request and he did not keep it for an unreasonable time.[118] On this basis, the Court of Appeal stated that it would seem wrong to penalize a person for having images which he proves that he has not seen when he also proves that he did not know or have reason to suspect that they were indecent[119] images of a child.[120] If the defendant, on balance of probabilities, proves that he had not seen the photograph and did not know and had no cause to suspect that it was an indecent photograph of a child, he must be acquitted of the possession offence under section 160.[121] It was further agreed in *R v. Smith and Jayson*[122] that a person is not guilty of an offence of 'making' or 'being in possession' of an indecent pseudo-photograph contained in an email attachment if, before he opens the attachment, 'he is unaware that it contains or is likely to contain an indecent image'.

Unsolicited Photographs and Pseudo-photographs

The section 160(2)(c) defence is available where a photograph or pseudo-photograph is sent to the defendant without any prior request by him or on his behalf, provided the defendant does not keep it for an unreasonable time. The issue of reasonableness is a matter for the jury to decide on the facts of any individual case. Within the context of the Internet, presumably, the courts would treat pop-up websites as unsolicited,

---

117 *R. v. Collier (Edward John)* [2004] EWCA Crim 1411; *The Times*, 13 July 2004 (CA (Crim Div)). See further, Rees, T. and D. Ormerod, 'Possession of Indecent Pseudo-photographs of Children' (2004), *Crim. L.R.*, December, 1039–41.

118 *R. v. Collier (Edward John)* [2004] EWCA Crim 1411; para. 22.

119 Ibid., para. 22. See further, section 7 and 2(3) of the Protection of Children Act 1978.

120 The Court also referred to *R v. Smith and R v. Jayson* [2002] EWCA Crim 683; [2003] 1 Cr App R 13 and thought that this interpretation receives some support from that judgment. A discussion of this case is provided later in this article. See further, Akdeniz, Y., Case Report: Court of Appeal Clarifies the Law on Downloading Child Pornography from the Web (2002), *Computer Law and Security Report* 18(6), 433–5. An online copy of this report is available through <http://www.cyber-rights.org/documents/smith_jayson.pdf>.

121 Compare with *R v. Land* [1999] QB 65 in relation to section 1(1)(c) of the 1978 Act. Note also the recent case of *R v. Skinner* [2005] EWCA Crim 1439, and Ormerod, D., 'Case Commentary on *R v. Skinner*' (2006), *Crim. L.R.*, January, 56–60.

122 *R v. Graham Westgarth Smith and Mike Jayson* [2002] EWCA Crim 683 (No. 2001/00251/Y1), 7 March 2002, and note Akdeniz, Y., Case Report: Court of Appeal Clarifies the Law on Downloading Child Pornography from the Web (2002), *Computer Law and Security Report* 18(6), 433–5. See further, Ormerod, D.C., 'Case Comment on *R v. Smith (Graham Westgarth)*' (2002), *Crim. L.R.*, August, 659–63.

and if certain websites trigger pop-up advertisements involving indecent images of children then this could be treated as unsolicited if there was no further intention to store the advertisement images by the suspect.[123] The circumstances in which a defendant may be said to have divested himself of possession are discussed below.

Possession of Deleted Images and R v. Porter

Digital evidence-gathering, retrieval of information, and data analysis from suspect computers to prosecute offenders are standard procedures nowadays to the extent that retrieval of deleted files from computers is also possible in most cases.[124] In *R v. Porter*[125] the Court of Appeal considered the issue of 'deleted images' from computers where a person is no longer able himself to retrieve or gain access to deleted indecent material. The defendant in *Porter* was charged with possessing indecent photographs of children contrary to section 160(1) of the Criminal Justice Act 1988 after police raided his home and seized two computers found to contain 3,575 still images and 40 movie files of child pornography in the hard disk drives.

The case is noteworthy as police discovered that 875 of the still images were deleted from the two computers in the sense that they had been placed in the 'recycle bin'[126] of the computer which had then been emptied. Officers were nevertheless able to recover these images by means of special forensic software. Of the 40 movie files, police were able to recover seven which had been placed in the recycle bin. The remaining 33 movie files were recovered from the cache (temporary Internet files) record of the two hard disk drives.

The remaining 2,700 images were deleted from the two computers but the 'thumbnail' images of these were viewable through an ACDSee software programme that the defendant used on his Microsoft Windows based PC. ACDSee is commercial photo management software[127] designed for viewing graphical images. As with most software of this kind, ACDSee creates thumbnail images[128] of pictures viewed or loaded into its image database, and then makes them available for viewing through

123 Note *R v. Humphreys* [2006] EWCA Crim 640.

124 See for example Casey, E., *Digital Evidence and Computer Crime*, London: Academic Press, 2004; and Marcella, A.J., *Cyber Forensics: A Field Manual for Collecting, Examining and Preserving Evidence of Computer Crimes*, Boca Raton, FL: Auerbach, 2002.

125 *R v. Porter* [2006] EWCA Crim 560; [2006] All ER (D) 236 (Mar). See further, Akdeniz, Y., 'Possession and Dispossession: A Critical Assessment of Defences in Possession of Indecent Photographs of Children Cases' (2007), *Crim. L.R.*, April, 274–88.

126 Known as 'Trash' in Mac OS X and Linux based systems.

127 See <http://www.acdsee.com/>. There are a number of similar software available nowadays in the age of digital cameras and digital photography including the popular free alternative IrfanView. See <http://www.irfanview.com/>.

128 Thumbnail images are basically a smaller reduced size snapshot version of the images that are retained on the image database of the programme. Thumbnails enable easy viewing of all the images within the gallery view, and each thumbnail image would be associated to the original image stored in the computer and the database of the ACDSee programme. If one had clicked on the thumbnail, the larger image could be viewed in full through such galleries and databases that are created by such photo and image management software.

its 'gallery view' function. Although the defendant deleted the 2,700 original images, their thumbnails remained in the ACDSee database. It was conceded by the Crown that the thumbnail images were only retrievable with the use of specialist forensic techniques and equipment provided by the US Federal Government which would not have been available to the public. It was further accepted that the defendant did not have the software to retrieve or view the deleted still or movie files although such software could be readily downloaded from the Internet or otherwise purchased.

At trial, the defendant argued that he was no longer in possession of images he had deleted since he had done all that he could do to divest himself of possession by placing them in the recycle bin which he had then emptied. This submission was rejected by the trial judge who ruled that Porter had possessed all the files within his computer regardless of whether they were in an active category or a deleted category:

> … files may be active or deleted, recovered, lost or unallocated and the mere fact that an image is on a deleted file, rather than an active file, does not mean that the user is not in possession, because the file deleted or not, is one of the files he had on a hard disk which was in his possession, was his computer and his hard disk. The issue in this case, is whether he knew that the images were indecent, or likely to be indecent.[129]

Court of Appeal in R v. Porter

The appeal raised an important point as to the meaning of 'possession' in section 160(1) of the 1988 Act. It was argued on behalf of the appellant that a person does not commit the offence of possession of indecent images on the hard drive of his computer unless the images are 'readily accessible to him at the time when they were said to be possessed, or capable of being made so accessible without the need to obtain additional specialist software'. It was further submitted that a person who has at some time in the past been in possession of such images, but who has taken all the reasonable steps to destroy them or make them irretrievable by deleting such images is no longer in possession of them. On this basis, the appellant accepted that he had been in possession of the 33 movie files in the cache. The defendant conceded that the 33 movie files in the cache were retrievable within his technical knowledge and were, therefore, in his possession. Offering a rival interpretation, the Crown submitted that a defendant in control of a hard disk drive continues to possess all images on that hard disk that are recoverable and capable of being viewed. Applying this approach, the Crown conceded that the defendant was not in possession of the 2,700 still images which had been saved by the ACDSee programme. The Crown nevertheless maintained that Porter had been in possession of the seven movie files and the 875 still images which had been emptied from the recycle bin and recovered during the police investigation.

Allowing the appellant's appeal, the Court of Appeal ruled that possession in the context of photographs or pseudo-photographs on the hard drive of a computer refers to a defendant's control or custody of the images. In the special case of deleted

129 *R v. Porter* [2006] EWCA Crim 560, para. 8.

computer images, the Court expressed the view that a person cannot be said to have control or custody of images if he cannot retrieve or gain access to them, even if those images remain on the hard disk of a computer in the defendant's possession. The first question for the jury in such a case is whether the defendant had possession of the image at the relevant time, in the sense of custody or control of the image. If, at the alleged time of possession, the image had been beyond his control then he would not possess it. If, however, at the alleged time of possession, the image is within his control, in that, for example, he had had the ability to produce it on his screen, to make a copy of it, or to send it to another, he would possess it. It would be a matter for the jury in each case, the Court argued, to decide whether images on a hard disk drive were within the control of the defendant, and accordingly within his possession having regard to all the factors in the case, including his knowledge and particular circumstances. The outcome of a case may thus hinge on a defendant's computer literacy and access to relevant software:[130]

> … images which had been emptied from the recycle bin might be considered to be within the control of a defendant who was skilled in the use of computers and who owned the software necessary to retrieve such images; whereas such images might be considered not to be within the control of a defendant who did not possess these skills and did not own such software.

The Court further stipulated, in line with section 160(2)(c), that it would be sufficient for a person to delete unsolicited images of child pornography on receipt through email.

Interpretation of R v. Porter

The Court of Appeal's judgment in *Porter* introduces a subjective element into the concept of physical possession in the context of computer images. It follows that in the scenario of A receiving unsolicited indecent images via email and deleting them, A would have a defence to a possession charge even if the images may be retrievable by specialist software, provided A does not have such software or there is no evidence to suggest that A tried to recover the deleted indecent images by using such software. Equally, where A accidentally downloaded indecent images and decided to delete them within a reasonable period with no intention to undelete or recover them, then A would avoid possession if he does not have recovery software in his possession or, if he did, there is no evidence to suggest that A tried to recover the deleted images using such software.

Following *Collier*,[131] A would also have a defence if he possessed photographs not known to be indecent, either because he did not himself see the photographs or pseudo-photographs (for example, an unsolicited and unopened email message

---

130 Note Ormerod, D., 'Commentary on *R v. Porter*' (2006), *Crim. L.R.*, 748. See further, Akdeniz, Y., 'Possession and Dispossession: A Critical Assessment of Defences in Possession of Indecent Photographs of Children Cases' (2007), *Crim. L.R.*, April, 274–88.

131 *R v. Collier* [2004] EWCA CRIM 1411; [2005] Cr App R 129; [2004] All ER (D) 82 (Jun).

containing an indecent photograph automatically moved into a SPAM folder but not deleted from the computer), or because he had no cause to suspect it to be indecent (for example, a bulk of images intentionally downloaded in an unopened compressed zip file on the assumption that they did contain indecent photographs of adults over the age of 18).

In the scenario of A knowingly downloading indecent images but deciding to delete them with no intention to undelete or recover them, A would expect to avoid possession and could also have a defence, if the images were in deleted state and unrecoverable by A at the alleged time of possession and A does not have such software or there is no evidence to suggest that A tried to recover the deleted images by such software.

This clear demarcation contrasts with the situation of an application under the Freedom of Information Act 2000. The Information Tribunal recently considered[132] whether information which has been deleted but which can be recovered by various technical means is still held by a public authority. The Tribunal concluded that the answer to this question will be a 'matter of fact and degree, depending on the circumstances of the individual case, whether potentially recoverable information is still held'.[133] The Tribunal acknowledged that information may be deleted and emptied from a computer but this may not actually mean that it is eliminated from the system at that point, and that there is a distinction between 'merely deleted' and 'eliminated' information. In the case of 'merely deleted' data the Tribunal considered such information to be still held under the Freedom of Information Act.[134] It follows that 'merely deleted' data could be subject to a Freedom of Information request and depending upon the circumstances could be argued to be possessed by a public authority. This decision is encouraging in the context of open government but is wholly distinguishable from section 160 wherein one is seeking to show culpable behaviour.

But in this complex scenario, following *Porter*, it would be a matter for the jury to decide whether the deleted indecent images were within the control of A having regard to all the factors in the case, including his knowledge and particular circumstances and the available evidence. Alternatively, based upon the available evidence, a Court may reach the conclusion that A could claim no defence to a possession charge and that he did knowingly possess the indecent images for a period of time prior to deleting them. A consideration of this possible outcome was not considered by the Court of Appeal in *Porter*, but future possession cases may depart from the *Porter* view if there is evidence to suggest that an accused did knowingly possess indecent photographs for a period of time prior to eliminating them from his computer.

It is also worth noting in relation to this scenario that in *Attorney-General's Reference* (No.89 of 2004),[135] the Court of Appeal discussed the issue of software designed to erase material from the hard disks of computers. The Court of Appeal

---

132 *Harper v. The Information Commissioner and Royal Mail*, Information Tribunal Appeal Case No. EA/2005/0001, 15 November 2005, at <http://www.informationtribunal.gov.uk/our_decisions/documents/harper_v_information_commissioner.pdf>.

133 Ibid., paras 20–21.

134 Ibid., para. 27.

135 *Attorney-General's Reference* (No.89 Of 2004) [2004] EWCA Crim 3222.

stated that in 'an appropriate case the use of some programmes may well assist a court to draw the inference that the material erased was illegal and that the reason for erasing it was to thwart the criminal investigation', adding that this would have to be based upon an assessment of the evidence available to that effect. It follows that the mere possession of very specialist recovery programs might likewise provoke suspicions that the user is seeking to hide the evidence by sophisticated technological ruses even though such software is commonly available for users for the deletion or removal of sensitive personal information from home computers. Thus, in the final scenario of A knowingly downloading indecent images and deleting them but intending to recover them at a later time with special software, it may be argued, following *Porter*, that the images are still within the control of A leading into him committing the possession offence.

Offences under Section 1 of the Protection of Children Act 1978

Section 1 of the 1978 Act contains a number of offences. These include the offences of taking, permitting to be taken, and making any indecent photograph or pseudo-photograph of a child under section 1(a); distributing or showing such indecent photographs or pseudo-photographs under section 1(b); to have in possession such indecent photographs or pseudo-photographs, with a view to their being distributed or shown under section 1(c); and publishing or causing to be published any advertisement likely to be understood as conveying that the advertiser distributes or shows such indecent photographs or pseudo-photographs, or intends to do so under section 1(d).

As mentioned above, there have been 4,771 prosecutions involving 3,789 convictions under section 1 of the Protection of Children Act 1978 according to official statistics and research conducted by the author. These statistics refer to the period 1980–2004.[136] In addition to these prosecutions, a total of 732 persons were cautioned for a section 1 offence during the same period (see Table 2.3; Graph 2.2). The prosecution and conviction statistics for section 1 do not differentiate between these offences but section 1(a), and section 1(b) are the provisions most likely to be used during prosecutions involving indecent photographs or pseudo-photographs of children.

Table 2.3 Statistics for Protection of Children Act 1978, 1980–2004

S.1 Prosecutions	S.1 Convictions	S.1 Cautions
4,771	3,789	732

136 Note that the conviction (but not prosecution) statistics were made available in January 2006: House of Commons Written Answers, 'Child Pornography', 19 January 2006 (Paul Goggins).

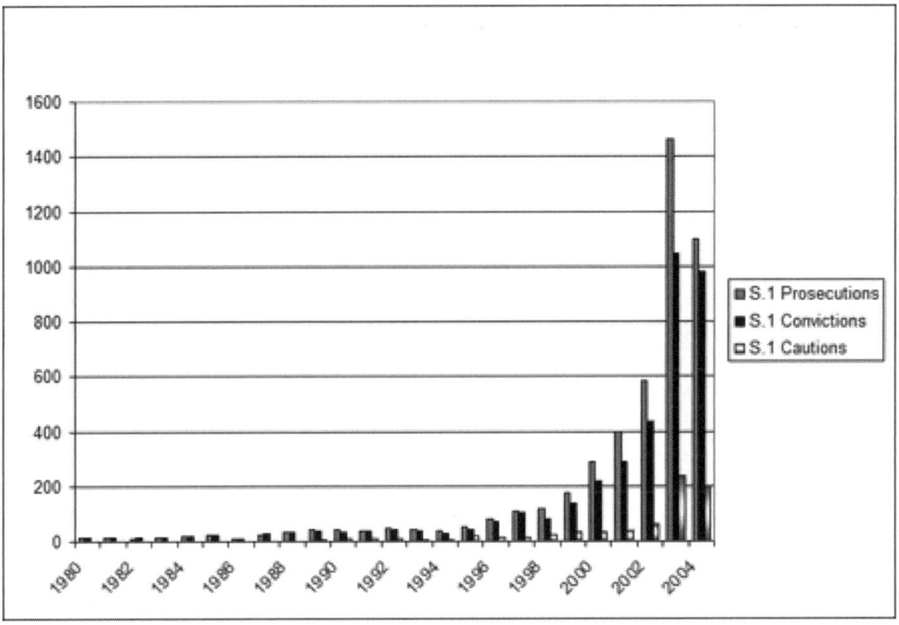

Graph 2.2 Section 1, Protection of Children Act 1978 statistics

Defences and exceptions introduced by section 45 of the Sexual Offences Act 2003[137] were described in previous sections.[138] Section 46 of the Sexual Offences Act 2003 creates a limited defence to the offence of 'making' an indecent photograph or pseudo-photograph of a child, under section 1(1)(a) of the 1978 Act. The defence will apply where a person 'making' such a photograph or pseudo-photograph can prove that it was necessary for him to do so for the purposes of the prevention, detection or investigation of crime, or for the purposes of criminal proceedings.[139]

An analysis of the distribution offence and its application is set out below and is followed by an examination of offences of taking, permitting to be taken, and making any indecent photograph or pseudo-photograph of a child under section 1(a) of the 1978 Act.

137 Date in force: 1 May 2004, see SI 2004/874, art. 2.

138 Section 45 of the Sexual Offences Act 2003 created a number of conditions which if satisfied will mean that certain photographs of a child aged either 16 or 17 will not be regarded as indecent photographs for the purposes of both section 1 of the Protection of Children Act 1978 and section 160 of the Criminal Justice Act 1988. This defence is provided within section 1A of the 1978 Act.

139 See section 1B of the 1978 Act.

Distribution Offence – Section 1(1)(b) and 1(1)(c) of the 1978 Act

Under section 1(1)(b), it is an offence to distribute or show indecent photographs or pseudo-photographs. According to section 1(2) of the 1978 Act, a person is to be regarded as distributing an indecent photograph or pseudo-photograph if he parts with possession of it to, or exposes or offers it for acquisition by, another person. If a person sends an indecent photograph as an attachment to an email message, or posts the same indecent photograph to a newsgroup, or publishes that photograph (or image) on a website, or makes it available for sharing or download through a P2P (peer to peer) network, that would qualify as distribution under section 1(1)(b) of the 1978 Act.[140] Under section 1(1)(c) of the 1978 Act,[141] it is also an offence to have in possession indecent photographs or pseudo-photographs with a view to these being distributed or shown.

The penalties under section 1 of the Protection of Children Act 1978 were increased by the Criminal Justice and Court Services Act ('CJCSA') 2000.[142] In its latest amended incarnation, section 6(1) of the 1978 Act provides that offences under section 1 shall be punishable either on conviction on indictment or on summary conviction. Section 6(2) provides that a person convicted on indictment of any offence under the 1978 Act shall be liable to imprisonment for a term of not more than ten years,[143] or to a fine or to both. A person convicted summarily of any offence under section 6(3) of the 1978 Act shall be liable to imprisonment for a term not exceeding six months; or to a fine not exceeding the prescribed sum for the purposes of section 32 of the Magistrates' Courts Act 1980 (punishment on summary conviction of offences triable either way: £1,000 or other sum substituted by order under that Act), or to both.

Limited defences to the above-mentioned offences are provided under section 1(4) of the 1978 Act which states:

> (4) Where a person is charged with an offence under subsection (1)(b) or (c), it shall be a defence for him to prove –
> (a) that he had a legitimate reason for distributing or showing the photographs or pseudo-photographs or (as the case may be) having them in his possession; or
> (b) that he had not himself seen the photographs or pseudo-photographs and did not know, nor had any cause to suspect, them to be indecent.

140 It is also possible to bring forward a charge of incitement to distribute or show indecent photographs or pseudo-photographs of children: *R v. Thomas* [2003] EWCA Crim 2681.

141 Note that it is also an offence to publish or cause to be published any advertisement likely to be understood as conveying that the advertiser distributes or shows indecent photographs or pseudo-photographs, or intends to do so under section 1(1)(d) of the 1978 Act.

142 See section 41, Indecent photographs of children: increase of maximum penalties. Criminal Justice and Court Services Act 2000.

143 Date in force: 11 January 2001: see SI 2000 No.3302, art. 2(a).

These statutory defences only apply to the offences of distribution and having such indecent images in possession with a view to their distribution under subsection (1)(b) or (c); they do not apply to the taking and making offences under subsection 1(a) as noted below.[144]

Research conducted by the author suggests that the number of distribution cases falls well short of simple possession cases. However, distribution through the Internet is becoming increasingly common and more prosecutions involving the section 1(1)(b) offence have taken place in recent years.

R v. Arnold and Fellows,[145] the 'Birmingham University case', is the most famous distribution case and the first of its kind pre-dating the amendments made by the Criminal Justice and Public Order Act 1994. Arnold and Fellows faced a total of 18 charges (involving both section 1(1)(b) and 1(1)(c) under the Protection of Children Act 1978, and the Obscene Publications Act 1959). West Midlands Police Commercial Vice Squad swooped on the Department of Metallurgy at the University of Birmingham following a referral from Jefferson County Police, in Kentucky USA via US Customs.[146] The Vice Squad discovered thousands of pictures of youngsters engaged in obscene acts stored in the computer system. Fellows had compiled an extensive library of explicit images called 'The Archive', featuring children as young as three, on a computer within the Department of Metallurgy where he worked, and the material could be accessed through the Internet across the world by those issued with a password.

After the trial judge ruled that computerized images could be legally regarded as photographs, Fellows admitted to four charges of possessing indecent photographs of children with a view to distributing them and one of possessing obscene photographs of adults for publication. Arnold also admitted distributing indecent photographs of children. Fellows was jailed for three years, and Arnold for six months for providing Fellows with up to thirty pornographic pictures of children. Passing sentence, Owen J. stated, 'the pictures could fuel the fantasies of those with perverted attitudes towards the young and they might incite sexual abuse on innocent children.'[147]

On appeal, Evans LJ upheld the ruling of the trial judge, that images stored on computer disc constituted photographs.[148] His Lordship reviewed the terms of the 1978 Act and decided that although the computer disk was not a photograph in itself, it was 'a copy of an indecent photograph'. According to the Court, 'on their true construction the definitions of "indecent photograph" set out in sections 1 and 7 of the 1978 Act were wide enough to include a form of technology which was either not anticipated or was in its infancy when the Act was passed and therefore to include later as well as contemporary forms of copies of photographs.'[149]

---

144 See generally, *R v. Land* [1999] QB 65.

145 *R v. Fellows and Arnold* [1997] 1 Cr App R 244; [1997] 2 All E.R. 548; [1997] *Crim. L.R.*, 524; Manchester, C., 'More About Computer Pornography' (1995), *Crim. L.R.*, 645.

146 See Davis, D., *The Internet Detective: An Investigator's Guide*, Police Research Group, Home Office, 1998, Appendix D.

147 *R v. Fellows and Arnold* [1997] 1 Cr App R 244; [1997] 2 All E.R. 548.

148 See *R v. Fellows and Arnold* [1997] 1 Cr App R 244.

149 *R v. Fellows; R v. Arnold* [1997] 2 All ER 548; [1997] 1 Cr App R 244; [1997] *Crim. L.R.*, 524.

Another interesting distribution case involved the prosecution of Father Adrian McLeish,[150] a Roman Catholic priest from Durham. Police officers seized four computers that he had built himself and began examining a huge library of disks, many of which had been erased. McLeish had two hard disks which he referred to as his 'nice disk' and his 'naughty disk'. His activities were exposed a year before during 'Operation Starburst'.[151] Alerted by their counterparts in Germany, Durham Police launched their own 'Operation Modem', which led to a raid on St Joseph's presbytery.[152] The police discovered that McLeish was linked to the Internet through at least four different companies and used encryption software. Prosecutors showed that the correspondence from his computer demonstrated that he was involved in an international paedophile ring on the Internet in which he connected regularly with at least nine people in Sweden, Germany, France, New Zealand and the United States.

McLeish admitted corresponding with a German paedophile to whom he had sent indecent photographs of 14-year-old boys. There was also evidence that McLeish had sent pictures of at least one boy he had abused and talked on the Internet of 'grooming' the boy for use in later life. This is the first time a direct link between child abuse and the use of the Internet was established. McLeish admitted 12 specimen charges of indecent assaults against two boys of ten, one aged 12 and another aged 18. He also admitted distributing indecent photographs, possessing them with intent to distribute them, and being involved in the importation of pornographic videos of children. Mr Justice Moses told McLeish:

> You corrupted those children and damaged them emotionally. You, and other paedophiles like you, dangerously delude yourselves if you think there is one iota of care, affection or even thought for those children. There is none.[153]

Father McLeish was sentenced to six years' imprisonment at the Newcastle upon Tyne Crown Court in November 1996 but served only two.[154]

In *R v. Fitchie*,[155] the defendant, aged 37, had 10,751 pictures, 81 films and more than five hundred pages of stories about child sex stored on computer hard disks and CD drives. Fitchie pleaded guilty to sending indecent photographs and films via the Internet. He also pleaded guilty to indecently assaulting an 11-year-old boy in one of the films. He was jailed for three years in July 1997 after Judge John Bull told him there was 'growing international revulsion' at the use of the Internet by paedophiles.[156]

---

150 *R v. Father Adrian McLeish* (1996), unreported.

151 See further, Akdeniz, Y., 'The Regulation of Pornography and Child Pornography on the Internet' (1997) (1), *The Journal of Information, Law and Technology*.

152 Stokes, P., 'Six years for priest who broadcast abuse of boys to Internet paedophiles', *Daily Telegraph*, 13 November 1996.

153 Wilkinson, P. and R. Gledhill, 'Paedophile priest circulated porn on the Internet', *The Times*, 13 November 1996.

154 'Paedophile Priest Says Church Knew', *Northern Echo*, 30 April 2001, p. 10; 'Sick Paedophile Priest Adrian McLeish's Child Porn Network', *Evening Chronicle*, 25 April 2001, p. 2.

155 Unreported.

156 Fleet, M., 'Pornographer is trapped by paedophile', *Daily Telegraph*, 26 July 1997.

In *R v. Fiona Hyett*,[157] the defendant, 42 years of age, and one of the few women to be prosecuted for offences involving child pornography, was convicted of distributing indecent photographs of a child, and sentenced to four months' imprisonment at Northampton Crown Court in June 2000.[158] Hyett admitted that she encouraged and instructed her daughter of 13 years of age to accede to the requests of a man to see her breasts through a chatroom conversation despite her protest that 'it was disgusting and seriously gross'.

There are many other cases which may be cited, but the application of the distribution offence has not in itself given rise to much debate. This may be contrasted with the associated impact upon the punishment of offenders in light of sentencing guidelines set out by the Court of Appeal in *R v. Oliver*,[159] discussed later in this chapter.

Creation (Taking and Making) Offence under Section 1(1)(a) of the 1978 Act

Under section 1(1)(a) of the 1978 Act, it is an offence for a person to take, or permit to be taken or to make, any indecent photographs or pseudo-photographs of a child. The wording of section 1(4) of the 1978 Act suggests that the limited defences provided under that sub-section are not available to the taking and making offences provided under section 1(1)(a) of the 1978 Act. Technically, there are no statutory defences available to the offences provided under section 1(1)(a). This is a deliberate omission as explained in *R v. Land*:[160]

> no statutory defence is available for the individual who creates the material or advertises its availability. The defence is limited to persons who distribute or are in possession of such material either for legitimate reason, or for an individual who was ignorant of and had no reason to believe that he was in possession of or distributing indecent material or in the case of simple possession, those who receive it unsolicited and get rid of it with reasonable promptness.

Although this explanation and the reasoning behind such exclusion are clear, the defences provided under section 1(4) should arguably be available to those who are charged with 'making indecent pseudo-photographs of children' as it is possible that no actual children are involved with the creation of such images as previously explained. The provisions under section 1 of the 1978 Act do not differentiate between the two separate crimes of 'taking indecent photographs of (real) children',[161] and 'making

157 *R v. Hyett* [2001] EWCA CRIM 669, No. 200004183/Z5, 14 March 2001.

158 Ibid. The applicant stood trial with her partner, Philip Faber, who was jointly charged with and convicted of distributing an indecent photograph of a child. Faber was convicted of further offences against the applicant's children and offences of taking and making indecent photographs, indecent assault on a female and indecent assault on a male. He was sentenced to a total period of 5 years' imprisonment.

159 *R v. Oliver and others* (CA Criminal Division) [2002] EWCA Crim 2766; [2003] 2 Cr App R (S) 64; [2003] 1 Cr App R 28; [2003] 2 Cr App R (S.) 15.

160 *R v. Land* [1999] QB 65. See further, *R. v. Collier (Edward John)* [2004] EWCA Crim 1411.

161 See cases such as *R v. Wade* [2003] EWCA Crim 12; and *R v. M.K.* [2003] EWCA Crim 132; *R v. Healy* [2003] EWCA Crim 551; *R v. Wright* [2003] EWCA Crim 1672; *R v.*

indecent pseudo-photographs of children'. As will be seen below, the inclusion of the 'making offence' under section 1(1)(a) has created significant difficulties of legal interpretation as well as sentencing problems.

Since the enactment of the Sexual Offences Act 2003, there are now some limited exceptions to the general rule that 'no statutory defence is available for the individual who creates the material'. As mentioned above, the Sexual Offences Act 2003 introduced a new defence dealing with marriage and other relationships. If the defendant proves that the photograph was of a child aged 16 or over, and that at the time of the offence charged the child and the defendant (a) were married, or (b) lived together as partners in an enduring family relationship, a defence under the new section 1A of the 1978 Act could be maintained.[162]

Another new exception is created by section 46 of the Sexual Offences Act 2003.[163] This introduced a new section, 1B, entitled 'exception for criminal proceedings, investigations etc.' under the Protection of Children Act 1978. This newly created section provides a limited defence to the offence of 'making'[164] an indecent photograph or pseudo-photograph of a child, under section 1(1)(a) of the Protection of Children Act 1978. The defence will apply if the defendant can prove that it was necessary to do so for the purposes of the prevention, detection or investigation of crime, or for the purposes of criminal proceedings. The defence will also apply to a member of the Security Service or GCHQ (Government Communications Headquarters) who can prove that it was necessary to 'make' the photograph or pseudo-photograph for the exercise of the functions of the Security Service or GCHQ.

Leaving apart defence related issues, perhaps the most problematic application of the Protection of Children Act 1978 has been in relation to the 'making' offence. It was held by the Court of Appeal in *R v. Bowden*[165] that the downloading and/or printing out of computer data of indecent images of children from the Internet was capable of amounting to a 'making' offence within the meaning of section 1(1)(a) Protection of Children Act 1978. As explained below, this ruling blurred the distinction between 'making offence' and the 'simple possession offence' under section 160 of the Criminal Justice Act 1988, with the former rather than the latter offence being used to prosecute those who downloaded child pornography from the Internet.

Hart [2003] EWCA Crim 2064; *R v. Clark* [2002] EWCA Crim 2925 involving taking indecent photographs of children.

162 Amendment made by section 45(3) of the Sexual Offences Act 2003. A similar amendment is also made to section 160 of the 1988 Act in relation to possession offences. Section 45(4) of the Sexual Offences Act 2003 added section 160A to the 1988 Act.

163 Note also the Memorandum of Understanding Between Crown Prosecution Service and the Association of Chief Police Officers concerning section 46 Sexual Offences Act 2003 at <http://www.iwf.org.uk/documents/20041015_mou_final_oct_2004.pdf>.

164 'Making' covers, for example, the situation where a person downloads an image from the Internet or copies a computer hard drive. See further, the Explanatory Notes to Sexual Offences Act 2003, at <http://www.legislation.hmso.gov.uk/acts/en2003/2003en42.htm>, para. 93. Note the discussion in this chapter involving *R v. Bowden* (2000) 2 All ER 418.

165 *R v. Bowden* [2000] 2 All ER 418.

R v. Bowden

Jonathan Bowden, a schoolteacher, downloaded photographs containing indecent images of young boys from the Internet and either printed them out or stored them on computer discs for his own personal use. During the police investigation of his computer, Bowden did not contest that all the photographs were indecent and involved children under the age of 16. He admitted that he had printed out some of the photographs that he had downloaded from web pages over the Internet. Bowden was charged with 12 counts of having 'made an indecent photograph' contrary to section 1(1)(a) Protection of Children Act 1978, and nine other offences of possession. Initially, Bowden pleaded not guilty to the making offences under the 1978 Act, but changed his plea after a ruling from the judge that his behaviour had amounted to taking or making an indecent photograph and that he was not merely in possession of them.

Bowden was sentenced to four months' imprisonment for the offences involving 'making an indecent photograph' and three months' concurrent for the possession of indecent photograph offences. Bowden appealed on the ground that he possessed the images but did not *make* them under the 1978 Act.

The Court of Appeal held that section 1 of the 1978 Act remains clear and unambiguous in its true construction. Lord Justice Otton stated that the 1978 Act rendered unlawful the making of a photograph or a pseudo-photograph. The words 'to make' had to be given their natural and ordinary meaning. In this context it is: 'to cause to exist; to produce by action, to bring about' (Oxford English Dictionary). According to the Court of Appeal, such a meaning applies as a matter of construction, not only to original photographs but also to negatives, copies of photographs and data stored on computer disc by virtue of section 7 of the 1978 Act. The Court of Appeal preferred a submission made on behalf of the Crown:[166]

> … a person who either downloaded images on to disc or who printed them is making them. The Act is not only concerned with the original creation of images, but also their proliferation … To download or print the images within the jurisdiction was to create new material.

The Court of Appeal concluded,[167]

> … despite the fact that he made the photographs and the pseudo-photographs for his 'own use', his conduct is clearly caught by the Act. The judge's ruling was correct, … the convictions must stand and we dismiss the appeal.

It was accepted that Bowden was of good character and he did not cause any 'risk to the public'.[168] His good character was taken into account, and the Court of Appeal

---

166 Ibid. at p. 422.

167 Ibid. at p.423. However, a conditional discharge of 12 months for all counts was substituted because the appellant was of good character and there was no breach of trust nor any evidence of risk to the public.

168 Ibid.

ruled that the sentences of imprisonment were wrong in principle and manifestly excessive. The Court of Appeal imposed a conditional discharge for 12 months in respect of each count in the indictment.

The 'making approach' adopted by the Court of Appeal is problematic. This is due to the fact that Bowden did not 'create' the images himself, and his actions resulted in 'copying' and/or downloading existing images from the Internet. Bowden did not take the pictures, he was merely accessing or making copies of existing images. Therefore, it is very questionable whether Bowden could be regarded as the original creator of the images or even as a child abuser. It is also doubtful whether it was the intention of Parliament to regard 'downloading' or 'copying' from the Internet as a 'making' offence rather than a simple possession (or, where appropriate, distribution) offence.

As the box below indicates, the original version of the 1978 Act only included the verb 'take' and only with the amendments provided by section 84 of the Criminal Justice and Public Order Act 1994 was the verb 'to make' added to the section 1 offence, together with the words 'pseudo-photographs'.

Section 1(1)(a) of protection of Children Act 1978 states:

It is an offence for a person –

(a) to take, or permit to be taken [or to make], any indecent photograph [or pseudo-photograph] of a child;

Note: the words in square brackets were added by the Criminal Justice and Public Order Act 1994, ss. 84(2)(a), (b), 168(3), Sch 11.

It was clearly the intention of Parliament to criminalize the 'making of pseudo-photographs' during the passage of the Criminal Justice and Public Order Act 1994.[169] During the Parliamentary discussions, the amendment to section 1 and the introduction of the words 'or to make' and 'or pseudo-photographs' were explained as follows:

> It simply provides that a pseudo-photograph is an image, whether *made* by computer graphics or by any other means of technology that *make it* appear to be a photograph [emphasis added].[170]

There was no discussion to suggest that making a copy of an existing indecent photograph or an indecent pseudo-photograph by means of downloading such a photograph from the Internet would be regarded as a section 1 offence.

However, the Court of Appeal in *Bowden* saw no 'necessity to refer to Parliamentary material for assistance in interpretation' of the legislation in question,

169 See generally, House of Commons, Standing Committee B, Criminal Justice and Public Order Bill, 1993–1994, vol. II, Sixteenth Sitting, 15 February 1994, at cols. 741–2.

170 Ibid. at col. 733, *per* Mr David Maclean.

ignoring the fact that Bowden was not the person who originally 'took' or 'made' those photographs and pseudo-photographs. Bowden made copies by printing the photographs downloaded from the Internet but was not responsible for bringing those images to life. The two actions, as well as the level of offence, are quite distinct.

This was a case which could and arguably should have been treated as a case of possession. The Court of Appeal's approach has resulted in the unfortunate blurring of the distinction between simple possession offences and the much more serious offence of making under section 1 of the 1978 Act.

The approach in *Bowden* was subsequently followed in the cases of *Atkins v. Director of Public Prosecutions* and *Goodland v. Director of Public Prosecutions*,[171] in which the Court of Appeal stated that *R v. Bowden*[172] was rightly decided and that 'making' photographs included copying, provided it was done with knowledge.[173] For example, there was no 'making' involved in images stored in computer caches according to the Court.[174]

In the author's view, the verb 'make' is used in the sense of 'create', and should not be understood to encompass mere downloading or printing out of computer data. There was support for this line of view at least by the Magistrate's ruling in *Atkins*:[175]

> Since biblical times, the maker has been the creator, that is he has fashioned something new. I have read Hansard and the Reports of the Committee Stages and I accept that Parliament has tried steadfastly to counter a rising tide of child pornography. It has firstly added the concept of 'making' to prohibited activities, and has later defined the pseudo-photograph. It has sought to extend the possible net of manufacture as wide as is possible. All that has, to an extent, been achieved. There is no doubt that indecent pictures 'made' in any creative way are caught. It has not however in my judgment altered the basic principle of manufacture. 'Made' still means 'created', 'novated', 'fabricated' – all definitions from the Oxford English Dictionary. It does not mean 'stored', 'isolated', or 'reserved' in whatever form. For those reasons I say now that I find the concept of 'making' in this case difficult in relation to [the 'making' charges] and I say that there is no case to answer in respect of them.

However, this view was rejected by the High Court (Queen's Bench Division) in *Atkins v. Director of Public Prosecutions* and *Goodland v. Director of Public Prosecutions*[176] together with the argument raised by the defence in the *Atkins* case, that

> the amended section 1(1)(a) should be construed as if it read: 'It is an offence for a person to take, or permit to be taken, any indecent photograph of a child, or to make any pseudo-photograph of a child.' What paragraph (a) is aimed at is the creation of indecent child pornography, not its proliferation.

---

171 [2000] 2 All ER 425; [2000] 1 WLR 1427.
172 [2000] 2 All ER 418.
173 Ibid., at p. 436.
174 Ibid.
175 [2000] 2 All ER 425.
176 Ibid.

This interpretation was subsequently confirmed in *Smith and Jayson*[177] and has led prosecutors to opt for the more serious 'making charge' rather than 'simple possession charge' in cases where Internet downloading is involved.[178]

R v. Smith and Jayson

Within the context of the 'making offence' debate, it is also worth discussing the appeal cases involving *R v. Smith and Jayson*,[179] in which the appellants were convicted of the offence of making an indecent photograph or pseudo-photograph of a child contrary to section 1(1) of the 1978 Act. In the case of *Smith*, the image in question was received as an attachment to an email message. In the case of *Jayson*, the images were downloaded by the appellant from the Internet. In each case the image in question was saved in the temporary Internet cache as a result of the automatic function of the computer.

Smith was convicted of one count of making indecent pseudo-photographs of a child and was sentenced to two years' probation in December 2000. Police found an email with attachments in Smith's computer which showed images of a naked girl called Eva, apparently taken by her mother, an internationally renowned photographer. According to the appeal decision, the attachments had been sent to the appellant in July 1998 by someone calling herself 'Yvonne Nystrom', whose email address was 'smallthings@hotmail.com'. An important fact of the case was that the images were not sent unsolicited to Smith, but according to the case report, were sent after Smith asked this person to send him the Eva images. The images in question had not been deleted and remained as an attachment to an email in Smith's mailbox. The defence on behalf of Smith suggested that 'upon the proper construction of section 1(1)(a) of the Act the appellant had not "made" a pseudo-photograph within the meaning of that provision by simply opening an attachment to an e-mail and looking at the images, without doing more.'

However, the Crown submitted that the appellant had effectively solicited the photographs by email, had shown an interest in receiving them and in opening them, and in failing to delete them, he had 'made' the photographs in question. Following the interpretation of this issue in the above-mentioned cases of *Bowden*,[180] and *Atkins v. DPP*,[181] the trial judge ruled that Smith 'has sought to "make" photographs, in effect by proliferating them rather than taking the option, which was otherwise available to him, which was to delete them altogether'.

---

177 *R v. Graham Westgarth Smith and Mike Jayson* [2002] EWCA Crim 683 (No. 2001/00251/Y1), 7 March 2002; [2003] 1 Cr App R 21; and note Akdeniz, Y., Case Report: Court of Appeal Clarifies the Law on Downloading Child Pornography from the Web (2002), *Computer Law and Security Report*, 18(6), 433–5.

178 At the time *Bowden* was decided, the defendants faced a maximum penalty of six months' imprisonment (summary offence only) for a possession charge, while the defendants charged with a making offence under section 1 faced a more serious penalty of maximum three years' imprisonment.

179 *R v. Graham Westgarth Smith and Mike Jayson* [2002] EWCA Crim 683.

180 *R v. Bowden* [2000] 2 All ER 418.

181 *Atkins v. DPP and Goodland v. DPP* [2000] 2 All ER 425.

The defence argued, 'section 1(1)(a) of the Act should be construed as narrowly as is reasonably possible, and it should not be construed so as to apply to a case such as the present.' The defence's argument was essentially that Smith's actions should be distinguished 'from that of a conscious and deliberate downloading of an image from the Internet'.

The Court of Appeal agreed that a person is not guilty of an offence of 'making' or 'being in possession' of an indecent pseudo-photograph contained in an email attachment if, before opening the attachment, 'he is unaware that it contains or is likely to contain an indecent image'. This would mean that liability would not arise if the indecent photographs are received unsolicited, and that the receiver is not aware of the contents of that particular message. Such a defence would have been available under section 160(2)(c) of the Criminal Justice Act 1988 if Smith had been charged with a simple possession offence. Obviously the courts and prosecutors would also look into the behaviour and actions of an accused following the unsolicited receipt of such images via email. It is very much doubted that liability would arise if the images and the message in question were immediately deleted upon the realization of their nature. However, it may be a completely different scenario if the images were viewed and the message containing the attachment was moved into a folder named hypothetically 'my naughty folder'. At that point the unsolicited nature of the message in question may not be as relevant for the purposes of a prosecution under section 1(1) of the 1978 Act.

When charged with a section 1(1)(a) offence of making an indecent photograph or a pseudo-photograph, it is not open to the defendant to argue, 'the photograph [or pseudo-photograph] was sent to him without any prior request made by him or on his behalf and that he did not keep it for an unreasonable time.' As mentioned above, the defences which are available under section 1(4) of the 1978 Act[182] are not available to charges under section 1(1)(a) of the 1978 Act. Although the provisions of section 1(1)(a) seem to create absolute offences, this is not the case on its true construction according to the judgment of the High Court (Queen's Bench Division) in *Atkins v. Director of Public Prosecutions*; *Goodland v. Director of Public Prosecutions*.[183]

The Court of Appeal concluded that Smith's case came 'nowhere near the paradigm case of the innocent person who, wholly unsuspecting, opens an unsolicited e-mail or attachment quite unaware of what it contains'. There is no doubt that Smith was guilty of an offence involving possession under section 160 of the Criminal Justice Act 1988. It remains doubtful, however, whether Smith should have been found guilty of the making offence under section 1(1)(a) of the 1978 Act for reasons discussed above.

In *Jayson*, the defendant pleaded guilty to seven counts of making an indecent photograph of a child in October 2001. In August 2000 the police found images of child pornography on Jayson's computer. The images found were stored in the cache directory rather than in a specific folder in his hard disk. All of the images had been

182 This subsection does not include a similar defence to which has been provided for possession offences under section 160(2)(c) of the Criminal Justice Act 1988.

183 [2000] 2 All ER 425; [2000] 1 WLR 1427. According to Simon Brown LJ, 'whilst "making" includes intentional copying (*R v. Bowden*), it does not include unintentional copying.'

automatically emptied from the cache directory before the computer was seized by the police. The images were retrieved and undeleted by a special process undertaken by prosecution computer experts. Jayson was sentenced to concurrent sentences of 12 months' imprisonment. His plea of guilty followed a ruling by the trial judge on the definition of 'making' for the purposes of section 1(1)(a) of the 1978 Act. The trial judge ruled that the browsing of the Internet for child pornography amounted to the offence of making an indecent photograph if it resulted (a) in an image being displayed on the computer screen of the browser, or (b) the automatic downloading of the image to a temporary Internet cache, provided that there was the requisite *mens rea*.

The prosecution had argued that Jayson, having had thirty years' experience with computers, must have been aware of the fact that images called up on to his screen would be automatically downloaded into the temporary cache.

On appeal, the defence argued that Jayson did not intend subsequent retrieval of the images even though he viewed them. The defence further submitted that 'in order to be guilty of the offence of making a photograph or pseudo-photograph by causing data to be stored on a computer disc, the necessary mens rea is that an offender must intend to store and intend to retrieve the material subsequently.'

The Court of Appeal ruled that 'the act of voluntarily downloading an indecent image from a web page on to a computer screen is an act of making a photograph or pseudo-photograph.'[184] The Court of Appeal reached its conclusion by referring to the ordinary use of language, and giving to the word 'make' its ordinary and natural meaning in line with *Bowden*.

> By downloading the image, the operator is creating or causing the image to exist on the computer screen. The image may remain on the screen for a second or for a much longer period. Whether its creation amounts to an act of making cannot be determined by the length of time that the image remains on the screen.

The Court of Appeal took the view that the question of retrieval was irrelevant to the issue of whether the downloading of the image on to the screen amounted to an act of making.[185] It was explained that the *mens rea* for the act of making should be 'a deliberate and intentional act with knowledge that the image made is, or is likely to be an indecent photograph or pseudo-photograph of a child',[186] and this 'did not require an intention on the part of the maker to store the images with a view to future retrieval.'[187]

The Court of Appeal also clarified the requirement in section 7(4)(b) of the 1978 Act, stating that 'data stored on a computer disc or by other electronic means 'should be capable of conversion into a photograph. It is not a requirement that the data should be retrievable.'[188]

---

184 [2002] EWCA Crim 683 (No. 2001/00251/Y1), 7 March 2002, para. 33.

185 Ibid., para. 34.

186 Ibid.

187 Ibid., para. 36.

188 It was hinted that there may be an appeal to the House of Lords following the decision of the Court of Appeal in *Jayson*, but as of June 2007 there has been no such appeal.

Problems Arising from the Bowden Interpretation

Since Bowden, the Court of Appeal has been reluctant to re-consider the meaning of 'making'. A sharp increase in prosecutions for taking, making and distribution offences under the 1978 Act for the years 2000–2003 (see Graph 2.3) suggests the 'making offence' may have been preferred to the simple possession offences by the prosecutors following the decision in the *Bowden* case.

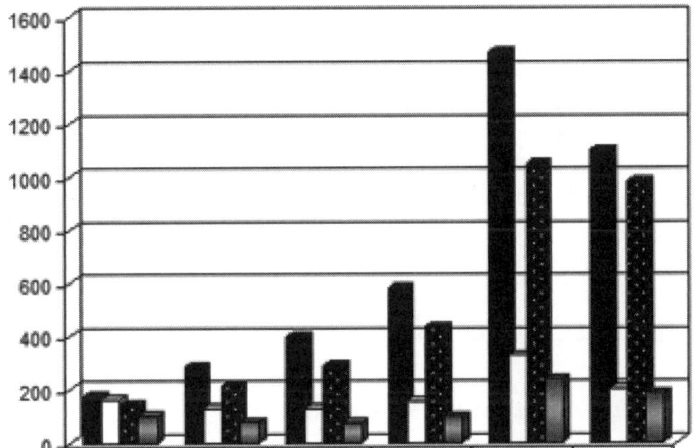

	1999	2000	2001	2002	2003	2004
Prosecutions for section 1	175	287	390	502	1464	1097
Prosections for section 160	163	129	126	156	326	200
Convictions for section 1	139	217	289	434	1048	978
Convictions for section 160	99	77	75	97	239	184

Graph 2.3 Statistical comparison for prosecutions and convictions (1999–2004)

Evidence is provided by the fact that the number of prosecutions for possession offences started to decrease sharply after 2000, even more so between 2001 and 2003 (see Graph 2.4). Compared to 167 possession prosecutions in 1998, there were only 88 prosecutions in 2001. On the other hand, compared to 116 section 1 prosecutions in 1998, there were 398 such prosecutions in 2001. One possible reason for the decrease in numbers for simple possession offences may be related to the use of the 'making offence' in relation to downloading child pornography from the Internet.[189]

189 However, note that it is not possible to prove this conclusion in the absence of specific statistics.

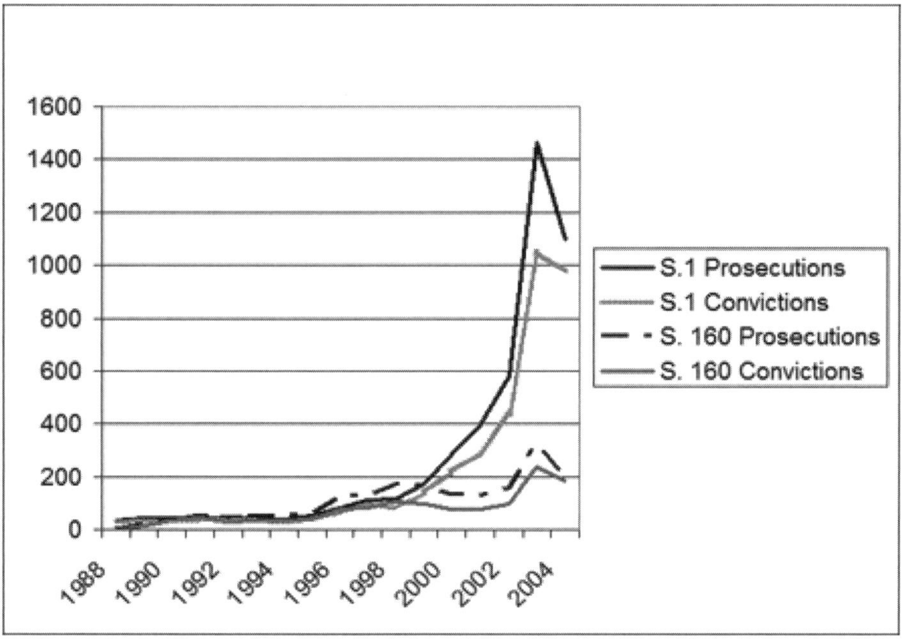

Graph 2.4 Comparison of section 1 statistics with section 2 statistics

Following *Bowden*, the distinction between 'making' and 'possession' offences has certainly become blurred, and there seems to be limited scope for possession offences as far as the downloading of such images from the Internet is concerned. The application of the 1978 Act in this way by prosecutors casts a dark shadow given the real purpose of section 1(1)(a) – the punishment of those who take indecent photographs of children.

This author has no doubt that the appropriate offence should be one of possession under section 160 of the Criminal Justice Act 1988 in cases involving 'downloading' of child pornography from the Internet (unless of course there was further distribution). In such cases, the offenders download and possess the images in their computers rather than 'take' or 'make' the images.

At present, an offender, A, who 'takes' his own photographs with a digital camera while sexually abusing a child and then circulates these images over the Internet is placed in the same category under the 1978 Act[190] as offender B who 'downloads' the same images created by offender A and stores (possesses) those images in his computer (at least as far as for wrongdoing if not for sentencing purposes). Although the offence committed by offender A is of a different order to the offence committed by offender B, following *Bowden*, both offenders could be charged with the same offence under section 1(1)(a) of the 1978 Act. This is surely wrong in principle.

190 Of course the offender would face further sexual abuse charges, for example, under the Sexual Offences Act 2003.

It may be noted that the Court of Appeal has since established sentencing guidelines in child pornography cases. In *R v. Oliver*[191] (discussed in detail below), the Court specifically opined that 'merely locating an image on the Internet will generally be less serious than downloading it. Downloading will generally be less serious than taking an original film or photograph of indecent posing or activity.'[192] This clarification is welcome but unsatisfactorily leaves the problems surrounding the interpretation of 'making' unresolved. These are offences carrying incredible stigma and should be interpreted so as to avoid such mislabelling. Although the 'theme' of the 1978 Act is compatible with article 10(2) of the European Convention on Human Rights, clarity and precision in relation to the meaning of making under section 1(1)(a) of the 1978 Act is still needed.[193]

Deleted Images and the Making Offence

An interesting question raised by the Court of Appeal's above-mentioned decision in *Porter*[194] is what approach prosecutors will adopt in the future when confronted with a case involving 'deleted images' which were originally downloaded from the Internet. Will prosecutors opt for a possession charge as in Porter, or will they opt for the making charge under section 1 of the 1978 Act?

The Court of Appeal's decision in *Smith and Jayson*[195] is instructive in this regard. In *Jayson*, images were deleted from the cache directory by the defendant but were retrieved and undeleted by a special process undertaken by prosecution computer experts. In contrast to Porter, Jayson was charged with a making offence under section 1(1)(a) of the Protection of Children Act 1978 rather than with a possession offence, and on appeal, the defence argued that Jayson did not intend subsequent retrieval of the images even though he viewed them initially. *Jayson* suggests that 'it is not a requirement that the data should be retrievable'. *Porter* on the other hand suggests that this will depend upon whether the images were within the defendant's control or not (which remains a matter for the jury to decide). *Porter* could have clarified *Jayson* but unfortunately the Court did not refer to *Jayson* in its decision.

---

191 (CA Criminal Division), [2002] EWCA Crim 2766; [2003] 2 Cr App R (S) 64; [2003] 1 Cr App R 28; [2003] 2 Cr App R (S.) 15. See further, Gillespie, A., 'Sentences for Offences Involving Child Pornography' (2003), *Crim. L.R.*, February, 81–92; and Thomas, D.A., 'Sentencing: Making Indecent Photographs or Pseudo Photographs of Children: Sentencing Guidelines' (2003), *Crim. L.R.*, February, 127–33.

192 *Per* Rose LJ (V-P), ibid.

193 Within this context note the case of *R v. Smethurst* [2001] EWCA Crim 772 (No. 2000/03467/Z2), 20 March 2001.

194 *R v. Porter* [2006] EWCA Crim 560; [2006] All ER (D) 236 (Mar). See further, Ormerod, D., 'Commentary on *R v. Porter*' (2006), *Crim. L.R.*, 748; Akdeniz, Y., 'Possession and Dispossession: A Critical Assessment of Defences in Possession of Indecent Photographs of Children Cases' (2007), *Crim. L.R.*, April, 274–88.

195 *R v. Graham Westgarth Smith and Mike Jayson* [2002] EWCA Crim 683; [2003] 1 Cr App R 21; and note Akdeniz, Y., Case Report: Court of Appeal Clarifies the Law on Downloading Child Pornography from the Web (2002), *Computer Law and Security Report*, 18(6), 433–5.

Considering the fact that no statutory defences are available for the making offence, one might expect prosecutors to bring forward a 'making charge' when they encounter deleted images relying on the *Smith and Jayson*[196] interpretation if they can establish the elements of a making charge rather than bringing forward a possession charge in which the defendant can claim the *Porter* defence.

Jayson to some extent clarifies issues surrounding Internet cache and images stored in cache directories, but does not clarify the issue of deleted images. In fact, it serves to complicate matters further.

Sentencing Problems

Inconsistent sentencing in cases such as *Bowden*, *James*,[197] *Owens*[198] and *Bolingbroke*[199] add to the controversy surrounding section 1(1)(a) of the 1978 Act in relation to making offences.

In response to criticism, the Court of Appeal issued guidelines in the case of *R v. Toomer*[200] in November 2000, but these were to prove insufficient to clarify the sentencing problems triggered by the *Bowden* interpretation of section 1(1)(a) offences. The Court of Appeal sought the views of the Sentencing Advisory Panel in relation to offences involving indecent photographs and pseudo-photographs of children, particularly in relation to the question as to when the custody threshold should be regarded as having been passed in the case of *R v. Wild (No.1)*.[201] Sentencing guidelines based on the Sentencing Advisory Panel's consultation and proposals were issued by the Court of Appeal on 21 November 2002 in *Oliver and others*.[202] The following sections chart these significant developments.

The Toomer Guidelines

In the case of *Toomer*,[203] the defendant pleaded guilty to 30 offences of taking indecent photographs or pseudo-photographs of children, contrary to section 1(1)(a) of the 1978 Act. Toomer obtained a large number of images involving children aged between three and 13 through chat rooms and logging on to the ICQ system during the course of two years. He was downloading and trading at the same time.

---

196 Ibid.

197 *R v. James* [2000] 2 Cr App R(S) 258.

198 [2001] EWCA Crim 1370, CA (Criminal Division), 8 June 2001, para. 8 of the judgment.

199 *R. v. Bolingbroke* (Leslie John) [2001] 1 Cr App R (S) 277; (2000) *The Times*, 16 August (CA (Crim Div)).

200 *R v. Toomer, Powell, Mould* [2001] *Crim. L.R.*, 149; *The Times*, 21 November 2000; 2000 WL 1675175 (CA (Crim Div)).

201 [2001] EWCA Crim 1272; [2002] 1 Cr App R (S) 157.

202 [2003] 1 Cr App R (S) 463.

203 *R v. Toomer, Powell, Mould* [2001] 2 Cr App R (S) 30. It should be noted that at the time the Court of Appeal issued the sentencing guidelines in the case of *R v. Toomer, Powell, Mould*, the maximum penalty provided by the 1978 Act for section 1 offences was 3 years' imprisonment.

He was sentenced to 12 months' imprisonment on each count to run concurrently in July 2000. Toomer also pleaded guilty to two offences of distributing indecent photographs or pseudo-photographs, contrary to section 1(1)(b) of the 1978 Act. He was sentenced to 24 months' imprisonment on each count to run concurrently.

On appeal, it was argued by the defence that the distribution was on a relatively minor scale, that there was no commercial element in Toomer's activities, and that the trial judge had recognized his previously good character. The Court of Appeal in *Toomer*[204] agreed that this was not a contested case, and 'some allowance does have to be made for cases worse than this one'.[205] His prison sentence was subsequently reduced to one of 18 months from the initial sentence of 24 months for the distribution offence.

The Court of Appeal emphasized that within the statutory maximum it is clear that the 'most severe sentences will be imposed on those who make and distribute such photographs on a substantial scale for commercial ends, especially if they have previous convictions for offences of this nature.'[206] The Court, however, acknowledged that there may not always have been an entirely structured approach to sentencing in this field and issued the following guidelines:

> Firstly, sentences up to statutory maximum should be imposed where there is a contested case, and there is evidence of commercial or large scale exploitation, and the amount of material is significant, especially if the offender has previous convictions.
>
> Secondly, non-custodial disposals should normally be reserved for isolated offences where the amount of material is very small, and it is for personal use, or use within a very restricted circle, as for example by passing it to one other recipient, when there is no commercial element and the defendant has pleaded guilty and is a first offender.
>
> Thirdly, where between those two extremes a particular case falls, will depend on the circumstances, and in particular on, first of all, the quality and nature of the material and the quantity thereof. Secondly, whether there is any element of exploitation or commercial gain.[207]
>
> Fourthly, whether the offence is simply one of making; that is to say, in most cases downloading and saving or also involves distribution and, if so, to what extent there has been distribution, whether it has been by email to a single specified recipient, or whether the distribution has been significantly more widespread.
>
> Fifthly, the character of the defendant is an important factor, and also the effect of the conviction upon the individual.
>
> Finally, it is of great importance to consider whether there has been a plea of guilty coupled with co-operation from the outset in the investigation.

---

204 Ibid.

205 Ibid.

206 Ibid.

207 Note also the case of *R v. Michael Keith Wild* [2001] EWCA Crim 1272 (CA No.2001/02292/Y5, 14 May 2001) which discusses this issue further.

While developing the guidelines, the Court of Appeal noted the decision in *R. v. Bolingbroke*[208] which concluded that 'in offences of this kind a very firm line would be taken even if the defendant was of good character and no profit had been made, since the material could be made available to an extremely wide audience and might have a corrupting effect.'[209]

The Toomer guidelines in action Application of the Toomer guidelines resulted in a reduction in sentences in a number of appeal cases[210] where the applicants were first time offenders who had pleaded guilty and co-operated with the prosecution. In some cases the issue of whether the applicant was a danger to children had also been a consideration. In *R v. Toomer*[211] itself, the absence of any involvement in abuse or incitement of children was taken into account by the Court. In *Mould*,[212] a custodial sentence was reduced to a conditional discharge for a period of 12 months from a custodial sentence. Mould was prosecuted for the making of a single photograph, 'not of the most degrading sort', which had to be taken into consideration by the Court.[213]

In *R v. Makeham*,[214] the defendant pleaded guilty to three offences of making an indecent photograph or pseudo-photograph of a child. The police found a number of pictures involving young children either posing naked or committing sexual acts with one another in Makeham's computer following a discovery by his girlfriend. The children appeared to be aged from five to 13 or 14, and amongst other things there was an image of a young girl in manacles and blindfolded. Makeham was sentenced to serve nine months' imprisonment concurrently on each of the three offences at Exmouth Magistrates' Court in September 2000.

On appeal the defence argued that the sentence was manifestly excessive because 'it failed sufficiently to take into account the fact that there was no evidence of distribution.'[215] Moreover, according to the defence, his good character, the remorse he

---

208 *R. v. Bolingbroke* (Leslie John) [2001] 1 Cr App R (S) 277; (2000) *The Times*, 16 August (CA (Crim Div)).

209 Ibid.

210 Note also the following cases reviewed by the Court of Appeal after the Toomer guidelines were introduced: *R v. Peter John Jefferson* [2001] EWCA Crim 1278 (No. 200102455/W2), 14 May 2001; *R v. Vincent Knights* [2001] EWCA Crim 1694 (No. 2001/01858/X1), 13 July 2001; *R v. Anthony Martin Koeller* [2001] EWCA Crim 1854 (No. 200102718/Y1), 6 August 2001; *R v. John Bootland* [2000] No. 00/5733/W2, 7; *R v. Christopher Alexander Malone* [2000] No. 00/6721/Y1, 19 December 2000; *R v. David Charles West* [2001] EWCA Crim 811, No. 01/1117/Z3, 26 March 2001; *R v. John Makenzie Owens* [2001] EWCA Crim 1370, No. 200101729/W1, 8 June 2001; *R v. Nicholas Victor Turpin* [2001] EWCA Crim 1600 (No. 2001/02905/W4), 3 July 2001; *R v. David John Thompson* [2001] EWCA Crim 1073, No. 01/1556/Y4, 26 April 2001; *R v. Daniel William West* [2001] EWCA Crim 418, No. 200100133/Z5, 19 February 2001; *R v. Antonio Augustus Cruz* [2002] EWCA Crim 1099, No. 01/6887/Y2, 8 May 2002.

211 *R v. Toomer, Powell, Mould* [2001] 2 Cr App R (S) 30.

212 *R v. Toomer, Powell, Mould* [2001] *Crim. L.R.*, 149.

213 Ibid. Note also the similar case of *R v. Malone* (Christopher Alexander) (2000) WL 1918630 (CA (Crim Div)), 19 December 2000.

214 *R v. Makeham* [2000] No. 200006484/Y5, 18 December 2000.

215 Ibid.

had expressed, his plea of guilty and the fact that he had obtained therapeutic help was not taken into account during sentencing. The Court stated that it was concerned that

> the Internet provides a ready market for those who distribute such material. Images can be downloaded easily and in private. It is people such as this appellant who constitute the market and who, in our view, can properly be said to perpetuate the child abuse recorded in the images concerned. In the circumstances, there is no doubt that a custodial sentence was justified.[216]

The Court also stated that 'the making of child pornography necessarily involves the serious abuse of children and sometimes, as here, very young children. Indeed it is self evident that the children involved in the images in the current case must have suffered in different combinations and degrees, fear, distress and a corruption of their values and morals. The learned judge rightly described this as a "vile activity".'[217] However, the Court took into account the Toomer guidelines and quashed the sentences of nine months and substituted concurrent sentences of six months. This is a case similar to *Bowden* in the sense that downloading activity resulted in the possession of child pornography rather than Makeham creating or taking the indecent photographs himself.

Makeham may be contrasted with that of *R v. West*,[218] where the Court of Appeal declined to reduce the sentence of 12 months' detention in a young offenders institution[219] despite the special circumstances of the applicant's young age (20 years old), and his suffering from agoraphobia.[220]

In the case of *R v. Coxon*,[221] the defendant, who had previous convictions for gross indecency and indecent assault on a female under 16, pleaded guilty to 17 counts of making an indecent pseudo-photograph of a child. He was sentenced to 18 months' imprisonment concurrent on each count in August 2001. He was also ordered to register under the Sex Offenders Act 1997 for ten years. The pre-sentence report included the comments of a probationer officer who stated that Coxon 'displayed typical traits of a paedophile, with no remorse or victim empathy and described the risk of offending as high'.[222]

On appeal the defence relied upon the Toomer guidelines and argued that there was no commercial gain or distribution involved in Coxon's activities, and very young children were not involved within the images. Although the Court of Appeal

216 Ibid.

217 Ibid.

218 *R v. West* (Daniel William) [2001] EWCA Crim 418; 2001 WL 239632.

219 But note also *R. v. Hopkinson* (Frank) [2001] EWCA Crim 84; 2001 WL 15091 (CA (Crim Div)), 16 January 2001 in which the sentence was appropriate given the large quantity of images involved and applicant's previous conviction for a similar offence.

220 Agoraphobia is the intense fear of situations that may be difficult or embarrassing to leave. People with this phobia worry that they will not be able to get somewhere safe. They often worry about having a panic attack or panic symptoms like dizziness, vomiting, loss of control or difficulty breathing. See <http://www.health-center.com/mentalhealth/agoraphobia/default.htm>.

221 *R v. Coxon* [2002] EWCA Crim 140 (No. 200105185/X4), 16 January 2002.

222 Ibid.

distinguished Coxon's case from both *Toomer* and *Makeham* on the ground that those did not have 'the antecedents that Coxon had',[223] the overall sentencing was reduced to 12 months' imprisonment.

In *R v. Pittard*,[224] the defendant was convicted of five counts of distributing indecent photographs of children,[225] and five counts of making indecent photographs of a child. On each of these counts he was sentenced to four months' imprisonment, all of them to run concurrently. Pittard was arrested following an investigation by the Obscene Publications Unit in London into the users of an Internet newsgroup called 'alt.tinygirls' in November 2000. The officers obtained copies of 11 entries which had been made by Pittard using one of two email addresses which belonged to him. Five of the entries were images of naked girls under the age of 16.[226] Pittard's computer was seized in February 2001 and this revealed approximately 100 images of children, some of which involved explicit sexual activity. Pittard admitted that he had posted the five photographs originally obtained on the newsgroup. The pre-sentence report before the court recommended a community rehabilitation order, as Pittard was of previous good character possessing many good qualities, but the trial judge recommended a short custodial sentence of four months' imprisonment, as 'the seriousness of the charges crossed the custody threshold, albeit only just'.[227]

The Court of Appeal, with some hesitation, reached a different conclusion from that of the trial court. The custodial sentence was substituted with a conditional discharge for a period of one year as the 'degree of distribution was minimal',[228] the material distributed 'did not depict sexual activity',[229] and the 'degree of distribution fell close to the lowest end of that activity.'[230] This case fell 'just short of the custody threshold'[231] following the Toomer guidelines. However, it was emphasized that relatively minor involvement in conduct of this type could lead 'to the very real risk of a custodial sentence'[232] and that the 'courts should view cases of this sort extremely seriously from the public point of view.'[233]

In *R v. Hopkinson*,[234] the defendant pleaded guilty to six offences of making indecent photographs or pseudo-photographs of a child, and was sentenced to 12 months' imprisonment. The police found about 550 images of males, the majority of which were under the age of 16, 'in candid nude poses or depicted sexual activity

223 Ibid.

224 *R v. Pittard* [2002] EWCA Crim 415 (No. 02/475/X5), 11 February 2002.

225 They are not specimen counts but rather reflect the entirety of the appellant's offending in that respect.

226 None of these young girls were shown to be engaging in any form of sexual activity.

227 *R v. Pittard* [2002] EWCA Crim 415 (No. 02/475/X5), 11 February 2002.

228 Ibid.

229 Ibid.

230 Ibid. See further, 'Internet child porn sentence quashed', *Sentinel (Stoke)*, 13 February 2002.

231 Ibid.

232 Ibid.

233 Ibid.

234 *R v. Hopkinson* [2001] EWCA CRIM 84 (No. 200006466/Y4), 16 January 2001.

between children and an adult or with other children'.[235] He was a member of an organization called 'Gay Teen Boys'. According to the judgment, the defendant stated that he 'had received an unsolicited email from a member of the club which had about a dozen attachments of what looked like younger people. After that he received two further emails from this person. He accepted that the boys in some of the images looked under 16.'[236]

Hopkinson had a previous conviction (in 1990) for offences, including taking indecent photographs of children, two offences of buggery, and one of gross indecency. The Court of Appeal considered the Toomer guidelines but dismissed Hopkinson's appeal by agreeing with the judgment of the trial judge who stated:

> Just as it is said that if there were no receivers there would be no burglars, similarly it seems to me that it may be said that if there were no end users then the chronic and widescale abuse of children would be diminished and you are an end user and it seems to me that in the circumstances which I have outlined the court must do what it can to discourage this sort of activity both in you, because you plainly have not learnt your lesson from the last conviction, and in others.[237]

In *R v. Allison*,[238] the defendant, with no previous convictions, pleaded guilty to a count of distributing indecent photographs of children, contrary to section 1(1)(b) of the Protection of Children Act 1978. He was sentenced to nine months' imprisonment in June 2001. The photographs in question were sent by email to a friend who pleaded guilty at the South Durham Magistrates' Court to one count of possessing indecent photographs and was fined £100, with £55 costs. This case involved 15 pictures involving eight children between the ages of 7 and early teens. The pictures included images of the children posing naked, performing oral sex upon adult males, and having sexual intercourse with adult males.

On appeal, Allison argued relying on the Toomer guidelines that 'the sentence of nine months' imprisonment was wrong in principle and excessive in circumstances where the court was faced with a single offence committed some time before, by a man with no relevant previous convictions, where the quantity of material transmitted was relatively limited and there was no commercial element involved.'[239] The Court, in turn, stated that they did not understand anything said in the case of *Toomer* to suggest that a non-custodial sentence is necessarily appropriate where those mitigating characteristics appear. The Court also referred to the decision of the appeal court in the case of *R v. Wild*[240] and stated that the degree of obscenity and corruption in a number of the images involved was high. This factor did not provide any alternative but to impose a custodial sentence in this case. The Court nevertheless took into account the other above-mentioned factors and reduced the imprisonment to six months from nine months.

235 Ibid.

236 Ibid.

237 Ibid.

238 *R v. Allison* [2001] EWCA Crim 1971, 17 September 2001.

239 Ibid.

240 *R v. Wild* [2001] EWCA Crim 1272, No. 200102292/Y5, 14 May 2001.

Toomer guidelines as interpreted in Wild In *R v. Wild*,[241] the defendant pleaded guilty to 15 offences of making an indecent photograph or pseudo-photograph contrary to section 1(1)(a) of the Protection of Children Act 1978. He was arrested on suspicion of making indecent images of children. When asked about the images he told the police that he had deleted them and that the images in question were 'sent to him unsolicited'. The police experts managed to recover 15 indecent images from the hard drive of Wild's computer even though these were deleted by the defendant. These involved children of both sexes, aged between approximately two to three months and 13 years old. Many of the pictures showed the children engaged in sexual activity with adults. Wild was sentenced to four months' imprisonment for each count to run concurrently in March 2001.

On appeal, Wild argued that he had been sent the images unsolicited, and that the images were automatically downloaded to the hard drive of his computer. The Court of Appeal noted the remarks of the Crown Court judge in terms of the conflicting approaches to an offence of this kind by differently constituted divisions of the Court of Appeal.[242] However, at the time the Crown Court issued its judgment in *Wild*, the Crown Court did not have access to the decision of the Court of Appeal in *Toomer* and the related guidelines. The defence on appeal argued by relying on *Toomer* that there were a comparatively small number of images with no question of commercial profit, and the use of the images made by this appellant was personal. However, the Court described the images of a grave kind including fellatio, ejaculation over the face and body of a child and apparent intercourse.

The Court in *Wild* expanded upon the principles laid down in *Toomer*, especially in relation to the *second* (quantity of the material and the non-custodial sentences) and *third principles* (quality and nature of the material) there set out. The Court expressed the view that distribution or further dissemination of obscene material is almost inevitably likely to be an 'aggravating factor'. Whether the penalty will be custodial will depend upon the extent of the distribution in addition to the factors laid down in *Toomer*.[243]

In relation to the quality of the images involved, the Court in *Wild* considered that the aspects of the images which give rise to aggravating features are the age and number of children involved, whether the children are of one or both sexes, and the nature of the conduct to which they are subjected or in which they are depicted as taking part. This will, in the view of the Court, reflect upon the gravity of the offence as it necessarily reflects the degree of corruption to which the unfortunate child was in the first place exposed. According to the Court:

> Those who acquire images of this kind do not, of course, have a direct responsibility for that corruption, but they do have an indirect responsibility because, unless there were

---

241 Ibid.

242 *R v. Bowden* [2000] 2 Cr App R(S) 26; *R v. James* [2000] 2 Cr App R(S) 258; and *R v. MS* [2000] 2 Cr App R(S) 388.

243 Rose LJ in *Wild*, CA, QBD, [2001] EWCA Crim 1433 (No. 200102292/Y5, No. 200102454/W2), 15 June 2001.

> people willing to take into their possession images of this kind, they would not be created in the first place.[244]

Having laid down these additional principles, the Court stated that the conduct of Wild did not cross that threshold even though it came close. The Court thought this was an offence which could properly have been dealt with by a substantial fine. As Wild had already served two months' imprisonment, the initial sentence of four months' imprisonment was substituted with a conditional discharge for a period of 12 months.[245]

The Court of Appeal reemphasized that 'when this class of offence occurs, even if they are committed by persons of good character without any desire for profit, a very firm line will be taken',[246] at the same time acknowledging that the previous cases had not clarified where to draw the line in terms of the custody threshold. In *R v. Knights*,[247] the Court of Appeal explained further the principles laid down in *Wild*:

> In *R v. Wild* (CA 14.5.01), and also in *R v. Jefferson* (CA 14.5.01), another division of this court felt able to hold that in such cases, provided there had been no distribution or dissemination of obscene material, that it had been kept wholly under the control of the offender, that in the case of a man of good character who had pleaded guilty and co-operated with the prosecution and had done no more than download such material for his own private purposes, then such an offence did not pass the custody threshold but could properly be dealt with by a substantial fine.[248]

In *Wild* the Court stated that it 'would derive great assistance if the Sentencing Advisory Panel were to consider the matter and to give this Court the benefit of its advice.'[249] It is important to re-emphasize the fact that the approach taken by the Court of Appeal in the *Bowden* case had a significant impact upon how the Courts dealt with offenders who downloaded child pornography from the Internet. Many of the appeal cases mentioned prior to and after *Toomer* and *Wild* would have been avoided if the offenders in those cases had been charged with possession offences under section 160 of the Criminal Justice Act 1988.

Cases following the Toomer guidelines as interpreted in Wild It is important to note some of the cases following *Wild* before examining the recommendations of the Sentencing Advisory Panel. In *Regina v. Clegg*,[250] the defendant pleaded guilty to 30 contraventions of section 1(1)(a) of the Protection of Children Act 1978. The police found approximately 12,000 images in Clegg's computer involving both adult

---

244 *R v. Wild* [2001] EWCA Crim 1272.

245 But note also the decision of the Court of Appeal in *R v. Michael Keith Wild and Peter John Jefferson*, CA, QBD, [2001] EWCA Crim 1433 (No. 200102292/Y5, No: 200102454/W2), 15 June 2001 involving issues of jurisdiction. Note also the similarities with the judgment in *R v. Vincent Knights* [2001] EWCA Crim 1694 (No. 2001/01858/X1), 13 July 2001.

246 *R v. Bolingbroke* [2001] Cr App R 277, *per* the Lord Chief Justice.

247 [2001] EWCA Crim 1694, CA Criminal Division, 13 July 2001.

248 Paragraph 11 of the judgment.

249 *R v. Wild* [2001] EWCA Crim 1272.

250 In *Regina v. Clegg* [2002] EWCA Crim 306 (No. 01/7067/W3), 7 February 2002.

and child pornography. The 30 photographs which were the subject matter of his prosecution depicted young girls, some of which originated from a website known as Lolita Child Sex. Clegg was sentenced to 30 concurrent terms of 12 months' imprisonment. He was registered for ten years with the sex offenders register, and was also disqualified from working with children.

On appeal it was argued that Clegg was a man of good character, who pleaded guilty at an early stage. The risk of his re-offending was regarded as low according to the pre-sentence report, and 'his remorse for what he had done appeared to be genuine.'[251] Clegg had to retire early due to ill-health and 'circumstances of his premature retirement contributed to his somewhat depressed state during the period these offences were committed'.[252] Although the sentencing judge regarded prison as unavoidable, the defence referred to *Toomer* and also to the case of *Wild*[253] as this was not a case involving wide-scale or commercial distribution. The Court of Appeal referred to the second[254] and third principles[255] in *Toomer*. The Court also referred to Rose LJ in *Wild*[256] in relation to the custody threshold as well as to his identification of different degrees of obscenity where images of children were involved:

> An image of a child's genitalia may be significantly less serious than an image of a child being subjected to sexual abuse by an adult, or an image of the child participating in sexual behaviour with an adult. There is little doubt that the images in the present case, which included fellatio, ejaculation over the face and body of a child and apparent intercourse, were of a grave kind. It is also a feature of the present case that children of both sexes were involved and the age of the children was, as we have indicated, from a few months old in the case of one of the children, up to prepubescent years in the case of other children. There were also a considerable number of different children involved. Those features, in our judgment, are rightly accepted by [counsel] as aggravating the degree of obscenity.

However, the Court in *Clegg* thought that the amount of material that Clegg had in his computer could not be regarded as 'very small', and although these images appeared to have been of the same order of gravity as those in *Wild*, the Court concluded that the custody threshold had been crossed. Nevertheless the Court thought that the sentence of 12 months was manifestly excessive. The sentence was quashed and substituted with a sentence of six months.

---

251 Ibid.

252 Ibid.

253 CA, QBD, [2001] EWCA Crim 1433 (No: 200102292/Y5, No: 200102454/W2), 15 June 2001.

254 'Non-custodial disposals should normally be reserved for isolated offences where the amount of material is very small, and it is for personal use, or use within a very restricted circle, as for example by passing it to one other recipient, when there is no commercial element and the defendant has pleaded guilty and is a first offender.'

255 'Where between the two extremes a particular case falls will depend on the circumstances, and in particular on, first of all, the quality and nature of material and the quantity thereof. Also, whether there is any other element of exploitation or gain.'

256 CA, QBD, [2001] EWCA Crim 1433 (No: 200102292/Y5, No: 200102454/W2), 15 June 2001.

In *R v. Jackson*,[257] the defendant, a residential social worker who worked at children's homes, pleaded guilty to 19 offences of making indecent photographs or pseudo-photographs of children. He was sentenced to three months' imprisonment on each count to be served concurrently. Jackson downloaded the images from the Internet, and four of the pictures involved girls aged between five and eight performing fellatio on young men, one showed an eight-year-old performing a similar act. Five pictures showed young boys engaged in acts of buggery.

On appeal, the defence argued that the Crown Court did not follow the *Toomer* and *Wild* guidelines, and if these were followed the custody threshold had not been passed. The defence argued that Jackson was a man of good character and the quantity of the material was relatively small (a total of 35 images) and that there had been no commercial element. It was also argued that the pictures he downloaded were less obscene than those described in the judgment of *Wild*. The Court considered the difference to be marginal and regarded Jackson's work with children 'in particular, with damaged children as a residential care worker'[258] an aggravating feature. A custodial sentence was deemed appropriate and the appeal dismissed. Mr Justice Grigson stated:

> He cannot have failed to appreciate the corrupting effect that the activities depicted in the pictures are almost certain to have had upon the children involved.[259]

In *R v. Snelleman*,[260] the appellant was sentenced to six months' imprisonment for possession of indecent photographs contrary to section 160 of the Criminal Justice Act 1988. He was also sentenced to nine months' imprisonment on eight counts of making indecent photographs of children contrary to section 1(1)A of the Protection of Children Act 1978, to be served concurrently with each other and concurrent with the six months making a total of nine months.

On appeal, it was argued that the appellant pleaded guilty and was of good character. The amount of material was comparatively small and there was no suggestion that the material was for anything other than his own purposes. The defence argued that considering these factors, the nine months' imprisonment sentence was manifestly excessive. The Court of Appeal referred to the second and third principles as laid down in *Toomer*, and confirmed and extended in *Wild*. Applying these principles, it was decided that the sentences imposed were manifestly excessive. The Court substituted the sentences imposed with a sentence of three months on each offence, all those to be served concurrently.[261]

---

257 *R v. Jackson* [2001] EWCA Crim 1990 No. 200104197/Y5, 17 August 2001.

258 Ibid.

259 Ibid.

260 *R v. Leslie Snelleman* [2001] EWCA Crim 1530 (No. 200102539/Y5), 19 June 2001.

261 For a similar decision see *R v. Anthony Martin Koeller* [2001] EWCA Crim 1854 (No. 200102718/Y1), 6 August 2001 resulting in a reduction of sentence. Note also *R v. Christopher Alexander Malone* [2000] No. 00/6721/Y1, 19 December 2000: Conditional discharge was deemed appropriate compared to custody as there were no images found on the applicant's computer itself, but seven images of a thoroughly indecent nature were recovered

As mentioned above, the Court of Appeal in *Wild* sought the views of the Sentencing Advisory Panel in relation to offences involving indecent photographs and pseudo-photographs of children, particularly in relation to the question as to when the custody threshold should be regarded as having been passed. Although the Court of Appeal issued its own guidelines in *Toomer* and extended these in *Wild*, the maximum penalties for the relevant offences had been substantially increased with the Criminal Justice and Court Services Act 2000, and the increase in penalties suggested a need for a new set of sentencing guidelines.

Sentencing Advisory Board Report and Recommendations

Following the call for assistance by the Court of Appeal in *Wild*,[262] the Sentencing Advisory Panel (which reports annually to the Home Secretary and the Lord Chancellor) issued a consultation paper on the sentencing of offences involving child pornography in January 2002.

Following the consultation, the Panel published its advice involving sentencing guidelines on offences involving the making, possession and distribution of child pornography in August 2002.[263] The Panel took the view that sentencing for these offences should reflect the harm suffered by children who are abused and exploited. Consistent with various judgments of the Court of Appeal, the Sentencing Advisory Panel report acknowledged that even an offender who has simply downloaded images from the Internet for his own use, without showing or distributing them to others, must bear some responsibility for the child abuse involved in making the images.

The Panel recommended a structured approach to assess the seriousness of an individual offence and selecting the appropriate penalty, proposing that the two primary factors determining the seriousness of an offence should be:

- the *nature of the indecent material* (from images of nudity or erotic posing to those depicting gross assault of children by adults, sadism or bestiality); and
- the *extent of the offender's involvement* with the material (from possession for the offender's personal use to the original production of images or wide scale commercial distribution).

---

from one of the back-up cartridges. The images showed young girls, mostly aged between 13 and 14, either naked or partially dressed, and one image in particular showed a girl of 8 or 9 performing an act of oral sex on an adult male. See further, *R v. Nicholas Victor Turpin* [2001] EWCA Crim 1600 (No. 2001/02905/W4), 3 July 2001 in which a sentence of eight months' imprisonment was quashed and substituted with concurrent community rehabilitation orders of one year. Contrast and compare *Turpin* with the decision in *R v. Antonio Augustus Cruz* [2002] EWCA Crim 1099, No. 01/6887/Y2, 8 May 2002.

262 [2002] 1 Cr App R (S) 37.

263 See the report of the Sentencing Advisory Panel entitled Offences Involving Child Pornography, August 2002 at, <http://www.sentencing-advisory-panel.gov.uk/c_and_a/advice/child_offences/page1.htm>, and <http://www.sentencing-advisory-panel.gov.uk/c_and_a/advice/child_offences/advice_child_porn.pdf>. Note further Press Notice SAP 7/02, 15 August 2002 at <http://www.sentencing-advisory-panel.gov.uk/press/press_15_aug_2002.htm>.

The Panel accepted that in cases of showing or distributing indecent photographs a prison sentence is normally the only option. Nevertheless, the Panel pointed out that community penalties requiring attendance at a sex offender treatment programme could be effective in preventing some offenders from committing further offences. Accordingly, the Panel advised that, when the offence is less serious, the offender's suitability for treatment should be assessed.

The nature of the material As far as the nature of the indecent material is concerned, the Panel strongly recommended that sentencing courts should always view for themselves the images involved in a particular case, in order to reach their own judgment on the nature of the material. A modified version of the COPINE[264] (Combating Paedophile Information Networks in Europe, at the University of Cork) typology was adopted by the Panel to assist the sentencing courts (see Table 2.4):

Table 2.4 The Sentencing Advisory Panel image description scale

Level	Description	COPINE typology
1	Images depicting nudity or erotic posing, with no sexual activity	2. Nudist (naked or semi-naked in legitimate settings/sources) 3. Erotica (surreptitious photographs showing underwear/nakedness) 4. Posing (deliberate posing suggesting sexual content) 5. Erotic posing (deliberate sexual or provocative poses) 6. Explicit erotic posing (emphasis on genital area)
2	Sexual activity between children, or solo masturbation by a child	7. Explicit sexual activity not involving an adult
3	Non-penetrative sexual activity between adult(s) and child(ren)	8. Assault (sexual assault involving adult)
4	Penetrative sexual activity between child(ren) and adult(s)	9. Gross assault (penetrative assault involving adult)
5	Sadism or bestiality	10. Sadistic/bestiality (sexual images involving pain or animal)

According to the Panel, the nature of the material involved based upon the typology outlined in Table 2.4 should be taken into consideration during sentencing. The nature of the material involved should be assessed alongside the nature of the offender's involvement with the material in question.

264 For further information see <http://www.copine.ie/>. The Panel did not include COPINE category 1 (Indicative (non-erotic/nonsexualisedpictures)) in its scale because images of this nature would not be classed as indecent.

The nature of the offender's activity The Panel reported that there was broad agreement among respondents to the Panel's consultation paper, that the seriousness of an individual offence increases with the offender's proximity to and responsibility for the original abuse, and that any element of commercial gain will place an offence at a high level of seriousness. It was also suggested that non commercial swapping of images should in itself be regarded as a commercial activity, because it fuels the demand for the material.

The Panel also tried to clarify for sentencing purposes the issue of making indecent photographs following the controversial decision of the Court of Appeal in *Bowden*. The Panel stated that 'downloading of indecent images onto a computer for personal use should be treated, *for sentencing purposes*, as equivalent to possession, despite the Court of Appeal's decision in *Bowden* that someone who has downloaded such an image may properly be convicted of 'making' an indecent photograph under section 1(1)(a) of the 1978 Act.'[265] The panel provided the following explanation:

> 'making' in the sense of making or taking an original indecent film or photograph of a child is clearly a more serious matter than downloading an image from the Internet, which is more akin to buying a pornographic magazine from a shop or mail order service.[266]

This was a sensible and welcome interpretation, but is no substitute for judicial clarity. The Sentencing Advisory Panel report also referred to the decision of the Court of Appeal in *R v. Smith and Jayson*,[267] which extended the interpretation of 'making', to include a simple request for the downloading of an indecent image so that it is displayed on screen.[268] Therefore,

> It is no longer necessary for the offender to take any further action to 'save' the image, although the prosecution does have to prove that the accused knew what sort of image he was calling for. The effect of this judgment is that a conviction of 'making' can be based solely on the locating by a computer expert of an image in the Internet browser 'cache', provided there is additional evidence to show that the offender was seeking such material.[269]

The Panel suggested that the starting point for sentence should be lower in such a 'making' (website visiting/viewing) case than in one where the offender has actively saved (actively downloaded) the material.

Aggravating and mitigating factors such as the quantity of material, the age of the children, the defendant's good character, a timely guilty plea and co-operation with the investigation, and the problem of young offenders were also considered within the Panel's report. Sentencing guidelines based on the Sentencing Advisory Panel's report were issued by the Court of Appeal on 21 November 2002 in *Oliver and others*.[270]

---

265 Paragraph 23 of the Sentencing Advisory Panel report.

266 Ibid.

267 *Times Law Report* 23 April 2002; [2002] EWCA Crim 683.

268 Ibid., para. 24.

269 Ibid.

270 [2003] 1 Cr App R (S) 463.

R v. Oliver and Others

In *R v. Oliver and others*,[271] the Court of Appeal considered the advice of the Sentencing Advisory Panel published in August 2002 in relation to offences involving child pornography, particularly in relation to the question as to when the custody threshold should be regarded as having been passed. The Court of Appeal largely adopted the Panel's advice. The Court of Appeal agreed with the Panel that 'the two primary factors determinative of the seriousness of a particular offence are the nature of the indecent material and the extent of the offender's involvement with it.'[272]

The nature of the material Rose LJ (V-P), delivering the judgment of the court, stated, in line with the Sentencing Advisory Panel's recommendations, that 'as to the nature of the material, it will usually be desirable for sentencers to view for themselves the images involved, unless there is an agreed description of what those images depict.'[273] Subject to one matter, the Court of Appeal accepted the Panel's analysis of increasing seriousness by reference to five different levels of activity, derived from the COPINE Project's description of images. The Court of Appeal categorized the relevant levels as in Table 2.5.

Table 2.5 Oliver image description scale

(1)	images depicting erotic posing with no sexual activity
(2)	sexual activity between children, or solo masturbation by a child
(3)	non-penetrative sexual activity between adults and children
(4)	penetrative sexual activity between children and adults
(5)	sadism or bestiality

The Court of Appeal disagreed with the Sentencing Advisory Panel that COPINE typologies 2 and 3 (see Table 2.4)[274] are properly within Level 1.[275] The Court thought that 'neither nakedness in a legitimate setting, nor the surreptitious procuring of an image, gives rise, of itself, to a pornographic image',[276] and hence excluded these typologies from the Oliver image description scale.

271 *R v. Oliver and others* (CA Criminal Division), [2002] EWCA Crim 2766; [2003] 2 Cr App R (S) 64; [2003] 1 Cr App R 28; [2003] 2 Cr App R (S.) 15. See further, Gillespie, A., 'Sentences for Offences Involving Child Pornography' (2003), *Crim. L.R.*, February, 81–92; and Thomas, D.A., 'Sentencing: Making Indecent Photographs or Pseudo Photographs of Children: Sentencing Guidelines' (2003), *Crim. L.R.*, February, 127–33.

272 Ibid.

273 Ibid.

274 2. Nudist (naked or semi-naked in legitimate settings/sources) 3. Erotica (surreptitious photographs showing underwear/nakedness).

275 Note further The Sentencing Advisory Panel, *Sexual Offences 2 Consultation Paper*, 22 April 2004, para. 21, at <http://www.sentencing-guidelines.gov.uk/docs/consult_sexualoffences2.pdf>.

276 *R v. Oliver and others* [2002] EWCA Crim 2766; [2003] 2 Cr App R (S) 64.

The nature of the offender's activity As to the nature of the offender's activity, Rose LJ (V-P) stated:

> ... the seriousness of an individual offence increases with the offender's proximity to, and responsibility for, the original abuse. Any element of commercial gain will place an offence at a high level of seriousness. In our judgment, swapping of images can properly be regarded as a commercial activity, albeit without financial gain, because it fuels demand for such material. Wide-scale distribution, even without financial profit, is intrinsically more harmful than a transaction limited to two or three individuals, both by reference to the potential use of the images by active paedophiles, and by reference to the shame and degradation to the original victims.[277]

On the issue of downloading child pornography from the Internet, Rose LJ (V-P) noted 'merely locating an image on the Internet will generally be less serious than downloading it. Downloading will generally be less serious than taking an original film or photograph of indecent posing or activity.'[278]

Despite this clarification, the Court's previous decision in *Bowden* was not overruled. The Court agreed with the Sentencing Advisory Panel and judgments in previous cases that the choice between a custodial and non-custodial sentence was a particularly difficult one to make, stating,

> On the one hand, there is considerable pressure, demonstrated by Parliament increasing the maximum permissible sentence, to mark society's abhorrence of child sexual abuse and child pornography by the use of custody. On the other hand, there is evidence that sex offender treatment programmes can be effective in controlling offenders' behaviour and thus preventing the commission of further offences.[279]

The Court expressed support for the Sentencing Advisory Panel's recommendation that 'in any case which is close to the custody threshold, the offender's suitability for treatment should be assessed with a view to imposing a community rehabilitation order with a requirement to attend a sex offender treatment programme',[280] observing that the appropriate sentence should not be determined by the availability of additional orders, or by the availability of treatment programmes for offenders in custody.

In setting out these guidelines the Court of Appeal stressed that they 'are not to be construed as providing sentencers with a straightjacket from which they cannot escape',[281] bearing in mind 'the current state of overcrowding in prisons, and that a custodial sentence should only be imposed when necessary.'[282] That said, the Court also duly noted the public concern in this area, which in many cases demand long prison sentences for those who commit child pornography related crimes.

---

277 Ibid.
278 Ibid.
279 Ibid.
280 Ibid.
281 Ibid.
282 Ibid.

Oliver Guidelines

Under the new guidelines of the Court of Appeal, a *fine* will normally be appropriate in a case where the offender was merely in possession of material solely for his own use, including cases where material was downloaded from the Internet but was not further distributed, and either the material consisted entirely of pseudo-photographs, the making of which had involved no abuse or exploitation of children, or there was no more than a small quantity of material at Level 1 as described above. A *conditional discharge*, on the other hand, may be appropriate in such a case if the defendant pleads guilty and has no previous convictions but should not be granted for the purpose of avoiding the requirement of registration under the Sex Offenders Act 1997.

According to the Court, possession, including downloading, of artificially created pseudo-photographs and the making of pseudo-photographs, should generally be treated as being at a lower level of seriousness than possessing or making photographic images of 'real children'. However, there may be exceptional cases in which the possession of a pseudo-photograph is as serious as the possession of a photograph of a real child in the view of the Court of Appeal.[283] This could include,

> for example, where the pseudo-photograph provides a particularly grotesque image generally beyond the scope of a photograph. It is also to be borne in mind that, although pseudo-photographs lack the historical element of likely corruption of real children depicted in photographs, pseudo-photographs may be as likely as real photographs to fall into the hands of, or to be shown to, the vulnerable, and there to have equally corrupting effect. It will usually be desirable that a charge or count in an indictment specifies whether photographs or pseudo-photographs are involved.[284]

A *community sentence* may be appropriate in a case where the offender was in possession of a large amount of material at Level 1 and/or no more than a small number of images at Level 2, provided the material had not been distributed or shown to others. For an offender with the necessary level of motivation and co-operation, the appropriate sentence would be a *community rehabilitation order* with a sex offender programme.

Custody threshold In agreement with the Sentencing Advisory Panel the custody threshold will usually be passed where any of the material has been shown or distributed to others, or, in cases of possession, where there is a large amount of material at Level 2, or a small amount at Level 3 or above.

---

283 See further, The Sentencing Advisory Panel, *Sexual Offences 2 Consultation Paper*, 22 April 2004, para. 23, at <http://www.sentencing-guidelines.gov.uk/docs/consult_sexualoffences2.pdf>.

284 *R v. Oliver and others* [2002] EWCA Crim 2766; [2003] 2 Cr App R (S) 64.

A custodial sentence of up to six months will generally be appropriate in a case where (a) the offender was in possession of a large amount of material at Level 2 or a small amount at Level 3; or (b) the offender has shown, distributed or exchanged indecent material at Level 1 or 2 on a limited scale, without financial gain. A custodial sentence of between six and 12 months will generally be appropriate for (a) showing or distributing a large number of images at Level 2 or 3; or (b) possessing a small number of images at Levels 4 or 5. In relation to more serious offences, a custodial sentence between 12 months and three years will generally be appropriate for (a) possessing a large quantity of material at Levels 4 or 5, even if there was no showing or distribution of it to others; or (b) showing or distributing a large number of images at Level 3; or (c) producing or trading in material at Levels 1 to 3.

Sentences *longer than three years* should be reserved for cases where (a) images at Levels 4 or 5 have been shown or distributed; or (b) the offender was actively involved in the production of images at Levels 4 or 5, especially where that involvement included a breach of trust, and whether or not there was an element of commercial gain; or (c) the offender had commissioned or encouraged the production of such images. An offender whose conduct merits more than three years will merit a higher sentence if his conduct is within more than one of categories (a), (b) and (c) than one where conduct is within only one such category.

Sentences approaching the *ten-year maximum* will be appropriate in very serious cases where the defendant has a previous conviction either for dealing in child pornography, or for abusing children sexually or with violence. Previous such convictions in less serious cases may result in the custody threshold being passed and will be likely to give rise to a higher sentence where the custody threshold has been passed,[285] (the sentencing guidelines are summarized in Table 2.6).

Finally, the Court of Appeal argued that these offences should very rarely result in the prosecution or cautioning of offenders under the age of 18. When such a person has to be sentenced, the appropriate sentence is likely to be a supervision order with a relevant treatment programme despite the shortage of such treatment programmes for young sex offenders. This is a welcome conclusion as a number of children under the age of 18, including a boy aged 13, were arrested for offences relating to child pornography during Operation Appal in 2001.[286] However, despite the Court of Appeal's warning, official statistics revealed that a total of 11 children under the age of 18 were convicted of child pornography offences in 2005.[287]

---

285 An extended sentence may be appropriate in some cases, even where the custodial term is quite short: see *R v. Nelson* [2002] 1 Cr App R (S) 565.

286 See, for example, N. Mackay, 'Slipping through the net', *Sunday Herald*, 19 January 2003; 'Children in crisis: boy, 17 held in paedos swoop', *Scottish Daily Record*, 25 April 2002. Note also 'Boy, 13, put on sex offenders register; youth had child sex porn on computer', *Birmingham Evening Mail*, 15 May 2001; '13-year-old trawled web for penpals but was lured into seedy world of child sex abuse; net porn snared boy', *Express*, 15 May 2001; 'Judge places boy, 13, on sex offenders' register', *The Scotsman*, 15 May 2001.

287 14 children aged ten to 17 were convicted for a child pornography related offence during 2004. See Internet Pornography, House of Commons, Hansard Written Answers for 7 November 2006. Three children aged ten to 15, and six children aged 16 to 17 were found guilty of a section 1 offence in 2005. At the same time two children aged 16 to 17 were

Table 2.6 Oliver sentencing guidelines

Recommended Sentencing	Reason for Sentence
Fine	If the offender was merely in possession of material solely for own use, including cases where material was downloaded from the Internet but was not further distributed, and either the material consisted entirely of pseudo-photographs, the making of which had involved no abuse or exploitation of children, or there was no more than a small quantity of material at Level 1.
Conditional discharge	If the defendant pleads guilty and has no previous convictions. But a discharge should not be granted, for the purpose of avoiding the requirement of registration under the Sex Offenders Act 1997.
Community sentence	The offender was in possession of a large amount of material at Level 1 and/or no more than a small number of images at Level 2, provided the material had not been distributed or shown to others. For an offender with the necessary level of motivation and co-operation, the appropriate sentence would be a community rehabilitation order with a sex offender programme.
Custody threshold	If any of the material has been shown or distributed to others, or, in cases of possession, where there is a large amount of material at Level 2, or a small amount at Level 3 or above.
A custodial sentence of up to six months	This would generally be appropriate in a case where (a) the offender was in possession of a large amount of material at Level 2 or a small amount at Level 3; or (b) the offender has shown, distributed or exchanged indecent material at Level 1 or 2 on a limited scale, without financial gain.
A custodial sentence of between six and 12 months	This would generally be appropriate for (a) showing or distributing a large number of images at Level 2 or 3; or (b) possessing a small number of images at Levels 4 or 5.
A custodial sentence between 12 months and three years	This would generally be appropriate for (a) possessing a large quantity of material at Levels 4 or 5, even if there was no showing or distribution of it to others; or (b) showing or distributing a large number of images at Level 3; or (c) producing or trading in material at Levels 1 to 3.

convicted for a possession offence. See Pornography: Children, House of Commons, Hansard Written Answers for 19 February 2007.

Table 2.6 Continued Oliver sentencing guidelines

Recommended Sentencing	Reason for Sentence
Sentences longer than three years	These should be reserved for cases where (a) images at Levels 4 or 5 have been shown or distributed; or (b) the offender was actively involved in the production of images at Levels 4 or 5, especially where that involvement included a breach of trust, and whether or not there was an element of commercial gain; or (c) the offender had commissioned or encouraged the production of such images. An offender whose conduct merits more than three years will merit a higher sentence if his conduct is within more than one of categories (a), (b) and (c) than one where conduct is within only one such category.
Sentences approaching the ten-year maximum	These will be appropriate in very serious cases where the defendant has a previous conviction either for dealing in child pornography, or for abusing children sexually or with violence. Previous such convictions in less serious cases may result in the custody threshold being passed and will be likely to give rise to a higher sentence where the custody threshold has been passed.

Aggravating factors The above-mentioned guidelines are more of a general nature and are appropriate for adult offenders after a contested trial and without previous convictions. There are specific factors which are capable of aggravating the seriousness of a particular offence. These are identified as follows by the Court of Appeal:

(i) If the images have been shown or distributed to a child.
(ii) If there are a large number of images. It is impossible to specify precision as to numbers.[288] Sentencers must make their own assessment of whether the numbers are small or large.[289]
(iii) The way in which a collection of images is organized on a computer may indicate a more or less sophisticated approach on the part of the offender to trading, or a higher level of personal interest in the material. An offence will be less serious if images have been viewed but not stored.
(iv) Images posted on a public area of the Internet, or distributed in a way making it more likely they will be found accidentally by computer users not looking for pornographic material, will aggravate the seriousness of the offence.

288 For example, 28 images did not amount to 'large quantities of material of level 4' sufficient to have taken the instant case into the 12-month to three-year bracket identified in the guidelines: See *R v. Evans* [2005] All ER (D) 291 (Feb).

289 Within this context note *R v. Canavan, Kidd and Shaw* [1998] 1 Cr App R 79.

(v) The offence will be aggravated if the offender was responsible for the original production of the images, particularly if the child or children involved were members of the offender's own family, or were drawn from particularly vulnerable groups, such as those who have left or have been taken from their home or normal environment, whether for the purposes of exploitation or otherwise, or if the offender has abused a position of trust, as in the case of a teacher, friend of the family, social worker, or youth group leader.

(vi) The age of the children involved may be an aggravating feature. In many cases it will be difficult to quantify the effect of age by reference to the impact on the child. But in some cases that impact may be apparent. For example, assaults on babies or very young children attract particular repugnance and may, by the conduct depicted in the image, indicate the likelihood of physical injury to the private parts of the victim. Some conduct may manifestly (that is to say, apparently from the image) have induced fear or distress in the victim, and some conduct which might not cause fear or distress to an adolescent child, might cause fear or distress to a child of, say, 6 or 7.[290]

If present, and applicable, these aggravating factors should also be taken into account by the sentencers during sentencing. As far as mitigation is concerned, the Court agreed with the Panel that some, but not much, weight should be attached to the 'good character' of a defendant. On the issue of a plea of guilty, the Court reminded that by virtue of section 152 of the Powers of Criminal Courts (Sentencing) Act 2000, there is a statutory mitigating factor. Section 152 states that a court shall take into account,

(a) the stage in the proceedings for the offence at which the offender indicated his intention to plead guilty; and

(b) the circumstances in which this indication was given while determining what sentence to pass on an offender who has pleaded guilty to an offence.[291]

The extent of the sentencing discount to be allowed for a plea of guilty will vary according to the timing and circumstances of the plea. The sooner it is tendered, the greater is likely to be the discount.[292] An analysis of a number of appeal cases reveal that many defendants plead guilty at an early stage, and many do seem to have a previous good character. This has a considerable impact upon the reduction of overall sentencing in relation to offences involving child pornography.

In *R v. Kelly*,[293] and in other recent cases, the Court of Appeal has emphasized that the age of the children involved in such indecent photographs will be taken as an 'aggravating feature'.[294] This contrasts with the view of the Sentencing Advisory Panel which in its 2002 report stated that 'the age of the child(ren) portrayed should not *in itself* be taken to aggravate or mitigate the seriousness of an offence, since it is

---

290 *R v. Oliver and others* [2002] EWCA Crim 2766; [2003] 2 Cr App R (S) 64.

291 See further, Ashworth, A., 'Sentencing', in M. Maguire, R. Morgan and R. Reiner (eds), *The Oxford Handbook of Criminology*, Oxford: Oxford University Press, 2002, 1076–112, at 1095.

292 *R v. Barber* [2002] 1 Cr App R (S) 548.

293 *R v. Kelly* [2004] EWCA Crim 256.

294 See further, *R v. Rooke* [2005] EWCA Crim 832; [2005] All ER (D) 08 (Apr); and *R v. Grosvenor* [2003] EWCA Crim 1627.

very difficult to quantify the effect of age in terms of aggravation of the offence.'[295] However, the Panel has itself acknowledged that 'where the nature of the material indicates that the victim is likely to have suffered particularly serious harm (for example, with an image showing genital abuse of a baby)',[296] that should be reflected in the sentence.

Thompson Guidelines

A related and important case that requires attention is *R v. Thompson*,[297] in which the Court of Appeal considered the question of assessing the 'quantity of images' for the purposes of the Oliver guidelines. In this case, the Court stated that 'the prosecution had not provided any schedule listing the 3,735 images and no question was raised by the [trial] Judge as to the deficiency in the information provided in respect of these images.'[298] According to the Court of Appeal, 'the Judge allowed himself to be placed in a very difficult position in this case by not requiring to be told of the approximate number of images at each level contained in the count relating to the 3,735 images, so that he could properly proceed to sentence in accordance with the guidelines set out in Oliver.'[299]

The Court of Appeal in *Thompson* emphasized that this sort of situation is not 'uncommon',[300] and accordingly suggested that in each case of this kind the following good practice guideline should be adopted in the drafting of indictments, and the same practices might also be adopted in the selection of images for presentation in summary proceedings:[301]

> (i) In cases where there are significant numbers of photographs, in addition to the specific counts, the inclusion of a comprehensive count covering the remainder is a practice that should be followed.
> (ii) The photographs used in the specific counts should, if it is practicable, be selected so as to be broadly representative of the images in the comprehensive count. If agreement can then be reached between the parties that (say) 5 images at level 2, 10 at level 3, and 2 at level 4 represent 500 level 2, 100 level 3 and 200 level 4 images in the comprehensive count of 800 images, the need for the judge to view the entirety of the offending material may be avoided.

---

295 Sentencing Advisory Panel report, *Offences Involving Child Pornography*, August 2002, para. 44.

296 Ibid.

297 *R v. Thompson* [2004] EWCA Crim 669; [2004] 2 Cr App R 262; [2005] 1 Cr App R (S) 1.

298 Ibid.

299 See ibid., para. 10 of the judgment.

300 Note also the Sentencing Advisory Panel report, *Offences Involving Child Pornography*, August 2002, para. 42.

301 See *R v. Thompson* [2004] EWCA Crim 669, para. 11 of the judgment.

(iii) Where it is impractical to present the court with specific counts that are agreed to be representative of the comprehensive count there must be available to the court an approximate breakdown of the number of images at each of the levels. This may best be achieved by the prosecution providing the defence with a schedule setting out the information and ensuring that the defence have an opportunity, well in advance of the sentencing hearing, of viewing the images and checking the accuracy of the schedule.

(iv) Each of the specific counts should in accordance with what was stated by this court in *Oliver* make it clear whether the image in question is a real image or a pseudo-image; the same count should not charge both. As this Court pointed out in *Oliver*, there may be a significant difference between the two and where there is a dispute, then there should be alternative counts. In the majority of cases there will be no doubt as to whether the image in question should be dealt with either as a real image or a pseudo-image.

(v) Each image charged in a specific count should be identified by reference to its 'jpg' or other reference so that it is clear with which image the specific count is dealing.

(vi) The estimated age range of the child shown in each of the images should where possible be provided to the Court.

These additional guidelines as laid down in *Thompson* should help to improve the quality of prosecutions.[302] The submission of a *Thompson schedule* during trial may, to some extent, specifically avoid the considerable number of appeals that the Court of Appeal is currently facing in this area.[303]

In terms of the impact of the 'quantity' issue on sentencing, it was acknowledged in *Thompson* that the Court was 'conscious that quantity is only one factor, albeit an important one.'[304] But, as rightly stated by the Sentencing Advisory Panel report, 'it is not easy to be precise about what constitutes a "small" or a "large" amount, especially given that collections of hundreds or even thousands of images do not appear to be uncommon among Internet users.'[305] While a small number of images at levels 4 or 5 under the Oliver guidelines would trigger a custodial sentence of between six and 12 months, a larger quantity in level 4 or 5 would result in a sentence of 12 months to three years. Considering these circumstances, the Court in *Thompson* is right to state that the quantity issue is an important, if not a 'crucial' factor.

What specifically constitutes a 'large quantity' has been a matter of some dispute. The Court of Appeal, by reference to the Oliver guidelines in *R v. Thompson*,[306] did not regard 88 images at level 4 as a large quantity, nor were 28 images at level 4 in *R v. Evans*,[307] and nor were 21 in *R v. Hardy*.[308] Even 397 images at level 4 in *R*

302 Note the case of *R v. Feuer* [2005] EWCA Crim 2415.

303 See further, the case of *R v. Clarke* [2005] EWCA Crim 948 in which the same problem was faced.

304 *R v. Hardy* [2005] EWCA Crim 1636.

305 Sentencing Advisory Panel report, *Offences Involving Child Pornography*, August 2002, para. 41.

306 *R v. Thompson* [2004] EWCA Crim 503.

307 *R v. Evans* [2005] EWCA Crim 439.

308 *R v. Hardy* [2005] EWCA Crim 1636. The Court quashed a sentence of two years' imprisonment and substituted for it one of nine months.

v. Edwards[309] was not considered to be a large quantity by the Court of Appeal. A collection of 1,693 images were regarded as a small collection in *R v. Edwards*,[310] even though this case was regarded as a more serious case than *Thompson* in terms of the quality of the collection in question as will be discussed below. Similarly, in *R v. Bishop*[311] a collection of 2,482 images were regarded (regrettably) not to be exceptional, nor unusually large for cases of this sort. In *R v. Hardy*,[312] the Court of Appeal stated that they were 'quite sure that in none of those cases did this court purport to lay down any rules',[313] and that 'what is a large quantity at a particular level may depend on what exactly the practice of the particular defendant was.'[314] The Court of Appeal also stated that they 'do not wish to be thought to be attempting any such definition'[315] in terms of what constitutes a 'large number of images at whatever level'.[316]

In terms of overall quantity of images possessed by defendants, it was noted in *Hardy* that 'collections of many thousands of images are commonly encountered.'[317] For example, in *R v. Tatam*[318] a total of 495,524 indecent photographs and video images of children possessed by the defendant was regarded as 'the biggest seizure of child pornography as part of Operation Ore in the United Kingdom'.[319] In *R v. Tatam*,[320] the defendant was in the possession of 3,140 images at level 4 (showing penetrative sexual activity between children and adults), and 336 images at level 5 (including sadism involving adults and children and bestiality). Even though this was not a contested case, the appeal court stated that this was a case of exceptional gravity, and had certain aggravating features set out in the Oliver guidelines to an exceptional degree, including the large number of images possessed, as well as the exceptionally high number of images at levels 4 and 5. The Court stated:

> The way in which the appellant's collection of images was organized demonstrated to our mind a high level of interest in the material. There were a significant number of

309 *R v. Edwards* [2005] EWCA Crim 402.

310 Ibid.

311 *R v. Bishop* [2005] EWCA Crim 829.

312 *R v. Hardy* [2005] EWCA Crim 1636.

313 Ibid.

314 Ibid.

315 Ibid.

316 Ibid. Note also *R v. Purcell* [2003] EWCA Crim 723, No. 2002/05693/X2. See further, *R v. Slinger* [2003] EWCA Crim 2761. The defendant had 200 indecent images of children; 197 belonged in category 1, and three images belonged in category 4 and depicted sexual activity between children and adults. The Court, having regard to the Oliver guidelines, and the subsequent cases of *R v. Russell* [2003] EWCA Crim 1378, *R v. Purcell* [2000] EWCA Crim 723 and *R v. Sears* [2003] EWCA Crim 367 thought that a sentence of 12 months' imprisonment for charges of making indecent photographs or pseudo-photographs of children was too long. This was substituted with an eight months' imprisonment sentence.

317 *R v. Hardy* [2005] EWCA Crim 1636.

318 *R v. Tatam* [2004] EWCA Crim 1856.

319 Ibid.

320 Ibid.

particularly young children who had been abused for the purposes of the original making of the images.[321]

The Court concluded that the sentence of five years' imprisonment and an extension period of one year for the making offences, and a concurrent sentence of four years' imprisonment for the possession offences were not excessive individually or in their totality.

Although not conclusive, it appears that a 'large quantity' will be regarded as thousands rather than hundreds of images at level 4 or 5 by reference to the Oliver guidelines. However, as the Court in Oliver noted, 'it is impossible to specify precision as to numbers', and sentencers 'must make their own assessment of whether the numbers are small or large.'[322]

Application of the Oliver Guidelines

A number of subsequent sentencing cases are examined below to assess how the sentencing and appeal courts have interpreted the Oliver guidelines starting with the *Oliver* case itself.

In *R v. Oliver and others*,[323] the first defendant, Oliver, pleaded guilty to six offences of making indecent photographs or pseudo-photographs of a child in May 2002. He was sentenced to eight months' imprisonment and an extended licence period of 28 months. The police found about 20 thousand images of children, some as young as six or seven, performing oral sex on adult males in some instances, and in others being anally raped. These images were judged to be at levels 3 and 4 on the Oliver scale by the Court. Oliver argued that his interest was an addiction. Rose LJ (V-P) stated, 'the sentence passed was entirely appropriate and in accordance with the guidelines'[324] which the Court of Appeal set out. However, according to the Court, the judge erroneously purported to order that the applicant register indefinitely under the Sex Offenders Act 1997.

The second applicant, Hartrey, pleaded guilty to one charge of distributing an indecent photograph or pseudo-photograph of a child, and one charge of making an indecent photograph or pseudo-photograph of a child in April 2002. Hartrey was arrested as part of Operation Round Table, the UK leg of an international operation conducted in ten countries worldwide.[325] In June 2002, at Oxford Crown Court, he was sentenced to concurrent terms of three years' and one year's imprisonment

321 Ibid.

322 According to the Court, regard must be had for the principles presently applying by virtue of *R v. Canavan, Kidd and Shaw* [1998] 1 Cr App R 79. It was held that the practice of sentencing for offences that had neither been admitted nor proved by verdict was incorrect, contrary to fundamental principle. See further, Thomas, D.A., 'Sample Counts and Specimen Charges' (2005), *Crim. L.R.*, 575–9. Note also *R. v. Pardue* [2003] EWCA Crim 1562; [2003] *Crim. L.R.*, 641–2; and *R v. Proctor* [2004] EWCA Crim 1932.

323 *R v. Oliver and others* [2002] EWCA Crim 2766; [2003] 2 Cr App R (S) 64; [2003] 1 Cr App R 28; [2003] 2 Cr App R (S.) 15; [2003] *Crim. L.R.*, 127.

324 Ibid.

325 'Police in 10 countries hold paedophile ring suspects', *Independent*, 21 March 2002.

respectively. As in the case of Oliver, the police found a total of 20,000 indecent images and 500 computer movie files of child abuse in two computers owned by Hartrey. The Court described the material as a clear level 4 category as these included images of naked children of both sexes from the age of about six and upwards, performing sexual acts on other children and adults.[326] The Court concluded that this was a case of distribution of a large number of level 4 images of victims, some of whom displayed obvious distress, and some of whom were apparently unconscious or semi-conscious by virtue of drugs. In the judgment of the Court, a sentence of three years on a guilty plea was the minimum appropriate in accordance with the Oliver guidelines.

In *R v. Grant*,[327] the appellant, with previous convictions for indecent assault, pleaded guilty to a total of four counts of making and possessing indecent photographs of a child. He was sentenced to six months' imprisonment to run concurrently for each count in June 2003. The police found a number of videos at the defendant's home and one of these included zoomed-in images of a baby girl's genitalia and upper thighs, those images lasting for some 13 minutes. A further search at the defendant's home revealed zoomed-in images of a baby's genitalia for some ten minutes in an 8mm camcorder cassette. The police also found photographs of a naked baby girl. The sentencing judge stated:

> Some of the aggravating features normally present in this sort of offending were plainly absent – there was no harm to the child; but it did amount to exploitation of a child, it was said, even though the child could not be aware and was not aware of the particular situation. It was accepted that the photographs were taken for his own personal use. But he had a history of previous convictions for indecent assault. Those previous convictions for indecent assault, the last, as I say, being in 1991, were serious convictions and had involved prison sentences of some length. They included, for example, the attempted buggery of a 3-year-old boy. That history could not be overlooked. The appellant was in poor health. He had been assessed as at very high risk of re-offending in some form in relation to sexual offending and a danger to young children.[328]

The appeal court followed the Oliver guidelines, and took the view that this case fell within the lowest category of seriousness of this type of offending and that there were no aggravating features. The Court stated:

> … the judge was wrong to impose an immediate custodial sentence when other options were available and too much weight was given to his previous convictions for sexual offences, particularly in circumstances where it was made plain in the reports that he suffered from angina and asthma and had other medical problems. Because of this defendant's previous convictions for sexual offences it is a matter for considerable concern that his perverted sexual inclinations are still apparent. On the other hand, as these sort of cases go, this was an offence very much at the lower end of the scale and it cannot be said, as is usually

326 *R v. Oliver and others* [2002] EWCA Crim 2766; [2003] 2 Cr App R (S) 64.

327 *R v. Grant* [2003] EWCA Crim 2495, No. 03/3739/A5.

328 Ibid.

> the case in these offences, that this was a case where the taking of the photographs had involved exploitation of the child.[329]

The Court quashed the sentence and substituted a community rehabilitation order for two years, stating that the appellant's activities would be kept under review by the probation service.

In *R v. Sears*,[330] the defendant pleaded guilty to ten charges of making an indecent photograph of a child. He was sentenced to a term of 15 months' imprisonment on each count concurrent in October 2002. His computer contained 12,000 meticulously indexed indecent images. This collection included 98 indecent photographs of children. Of these 98 photographs, ten formed the basis of the charges. Sears kept these images for his own use and there was no evidence of distribution.

On appeal, it was stated that Sears was married, and has no previous convictions, and that he suffered from an obsessive compulsive disorder and also from habit disorder. The habit disorder took the form of collecting all manner of items for the sheer pleasure of possession. This habit was confirmed by members of his family and it was argued that his downloading of indecent images was a continuation of this habit. It also appeared from psychiatric reports that he found some of the images disgusting. On the evidence, it was argued that Sears was not a paedophile and he did not pose a risk to the public. The Oliver guidelines were adopted by the Court but it was also stated that 'guidelines are not intended to be applied mechanistically. They exist to assist the sentencing judge in doing what is right on all the evidence before him.'[331]

The Court noted that the sentencing judge did not have the benefit of relying on the Oliver guidelines as the sentencing pre-dated the *Oliver* decision. According to the Court, the appellant downloaded and possessed nine images at level 4 or level 5 but did not distribute them, disputing the defence's argument that the images were at level 3 but acknowledging that the precise classification of the images was a matter which could be debated. Having made a one-third discount for the plea of guilty, the Court ruled that an appropriate starting point for sentencing in such a case would be a prison sentence ordinarily in the region of eight months. However, it was decided that the imposition of a community rehabilitation order lasting for two years, with conditions of treatment as set out in the pre-sentence report, was more likely to prevent the appellant from collecting child pornography in the future. The Oliver guidelines were not 'mechanistically' followed, and the special circumstances surrounding the appellant, namely, suffering from obsessive compulsive disorder and habit disorder, were taken into account.

In *R v. Hatchett*,[332] the defendant pleaded guilty to having in his possession indecent photographs of children in November 2001. He also pleaded guilty to 12 counts of indecent assault on a female, six counts of taking indecent photographs of a child, and one count of showing an indecent photograph to a child in February

---

329 Ibid.

330 *R v. Sears* [2003] EWCA Crim 367, No. 2002/06471/Y3.

331 Ibid.

332 *R v. Hatchett* [2003] EWCA Crim 426, No. 2002/03266/Y3.

2002. The police not only found indecent photographs of children downloaded from the Internet (a total of 9), but also found indecent photographs of six girls (a total of about 260) for whom the appellant had acted as a babysitter. Three of the girls were aged three, seven and four respectively, and the images involved, among other things, the defendant performing oral sex upon one of the girls. It was stated during his trial that his character was such that there was a high risk of re-offending. The probation officer in the case recommended a community rehabilitation order with a condition of treatment, but this option was rejected by the trial judge who imposed an 18 months' imprisonment for each of the offences of taking or showing indecent photographs; those sentences were to be concurrent with one another, but consecutive to those for the indecent assaults. A further five years' imprisonment sentence was imposed for the indecent assault charges bringing the total to six-and-a-half years of imprisonment.

On appeal, in relation to the child pornography offences, the Court referred to the Oliver guidelines and stated that 'one of the evils of these offences is that the offender is likely to go on to commit indecent assaults against actual children, as has happened in this case.'[333]

The Court thought that in terms of the indecent photographs offences, a substantial prison sentence was appropriate, stating that the 'term of 18 months cannot be faulted in the light of the recent guideline decision of this court and in the light of the Sentencing Advisory Panel's report.'[334] However, the Court considered that the total sentence of six-and-a-half years' imprisonment was too long and that a more appropriate total sentence to reflect the whole of the appellant's criminality was imprisonment of five-and-a-half years.

In *R v. Hill*,[335] the defendant was convicted of four counts of making indecent photographs of children in September 2001. He was also convicted of taking indecent photographs of a child in November 2001. He had taken 67 indecent photographs of an unidentified boy who had attended his flat. The boy had seen an advertisement asking for photographic models which had been placed by the applicant in local newspapers. The images taken were considered to be at level 1 of the Oliver scale depicting erotic posing with no sexual activity. The defendant was convicted to 18 months' imprisonment for the taking offence, and nine months' imprisonment for the making offences, all these sentences to run concurrently. On appeal, the Court stated that this was an approach which

> … the trial judge was not only entitled to take, but was right to take in the circumstances of a case such as the present … The mitigation put forward on behalf of the applicant, such as his health and the fact that he had no previous convictions for offences of this kind, in no way leads us to the conclusion that the sentence on count 1 [taking offence][336] was either wrong in principle or manifestly excessive, or indeed in any way excessive.[337]

333 Ibid.

334 Ibid.

335 *R v. Hill* [2003] EWCA Crim 42, No. 2002/00327/Z3.

336 Parentheses added by the author.

337 *R v. Hill* [2003] EWCA Crim 42, No. 2002/00327/Z3.

The decision is consistent with the former decisions of the Court of Appeal and is in line with the Oliver guidelines. Although the images in question were considered to be at level 1, the proximity of the appellant to the original abuse, by taking the images in question, resulted in a higher prison sentence. If the defendant had only possessed or made the images in question, for example, by downloading them from the Internet, then a lesser sentence would have been more appropriate considering the nature of the images (images depicting erotic posing with no sexual activity). His responsibility for taking the images distinguished this case from making or possession cases.

R v. McInnes,[338] bears similarities to *R v. Hill*.[339] However, although the defendant in *McInnes* appeared in the images in question himself, he was only charged with making indecent photographs of a child. He was sentenced to 12 months' imprisonment in October 2002. The offences related to seven photographs of a child known as 'P', who was aged between nine and 11 years when the offending photographs were taken. The images showed the defendant unclothed, but P dressed. These were part of a large number of photographs the police found at his home. The judge, in sentencing the appellant, explained that to subject a young person to the taking of photographs of this nature could only result in a prison sentence. On appeal it was argued that the offence was not serious enough to cross the custody threshold, and that the trial judge failed to give proper credit for the guilty plea, the appellant's mitigating circumstances, and to the particular value of the benefits that would accrue to the appellant by having a community rehabilitation order imposed upon him. The Court stated that the photographs in this case fell at the bottom of level 1 on the Oliver scale:

> Bearing in mind the mitigating circumstances of this appellant, which comprise not only the plea that he entered, but also his particular personal mitigating factors, we take the view that the appropriate sentence that ought to have been imposed in this case was one of four months' imprisonment.[340]

McInnes received a more lenient sentence compared to *Hill* as the Court considered the images in question to be of substantially less erotic acts. However, it is not clear from the facts of the case why McInnes was not charged with taking rather than making.

In *R v. W*,[341] the defendant pleaded guilty to 65 offences of distributing indecent photographs or pseudo-photographs of children contrary to section 1 of the Protection of Children Act 1978. The defendant's computer was seized following a tip off from the German police. The defendant placed notices in chat rooms, indicating that he was to be the premier supplier of indecent images of young children up to the age of five. He was found in possession of approximately 25,754 images of children, of which 80 per cent were indecent, and the images were at levels 4 and 5 involving penetrative sexual activity between children and adults, or acts of sadism and bestiality. The

338 *R v. McInnes* [2002] EWCA Crim 3193, No. 2002/06262/W2.

339 [2003] EWCA Crim 42, No. 2002/00327/Z3.

340 *R v. McInnes* [2002] EWCA Crim 3193, No. 2002/06262/W2.

341 *Regina v. W (David Lutz)* [2005] EWCA Crim 1204.

defendant was involved in distributing over 30,000 images covering 57 countries, and distributing about 3,000 images each day and receiving approximately 600 in return. He received a term of nine years' imprisonment concurrent on each of the 65 counts of distribution.

The police also discovered 61 encrypted files in W's computer and when these files were eventually decrypted they revealed the defendant sexually assaulting a nine-month-old baby girl. He was sentenced to ten years' imprisonment concurrent on each count of indecent assault and on the count of attempted rape, consecutive to the nine year term on the distribution offence. He also received seven years' imprisonment for two offences of taking indecent photographs concurrent with each other and with the other terms of imprisonment on the second indictment, but consecutive to the first indictment involving the distribution charges. The total term imposed was therefore 19 years' imprisonment.

On appeal it was stated that the images were distributed on a very large scale around the world. The Court of Appeal stated that this Court made it clear in *Oliver* that:

> the seriousness of a particular offence or offences is determined by the nature of the indecent material and the extent of the offender's involvement in it. In this case the material depicted images of the most serious levels of activity, namely levels 4 and 5, and the judge rightly described the appellant as being involved in a sophisticated and large-scale supply globally of child pornography.[342]

The Court also noted that the appellant had expressed the aim of being the premier supplier of such abusive images internationally and he had specifically requested and encouraged images of babies, bondage, sadism and child rape to be sent to him. His conduct therefore fell within two of the three categories identified by the court in *Oliver* each meriting a higher sentence for an offender whose crimes required a sentence of longer than three years. There were also several aggravating features present in this case which resulted in a higher sentence including the exceptionally high number of images he possessed, the very young age of the children in the images and the scale of the distribution. The Court also noted that although there was no element of commercial gain,

> the trading of images such as occurred in this case is properly to be regarded as a commercial activity, albeit without financial gain, because it fuelled demand for such material. Further, widespread distribution even without financial profit is intrinsically more harmful than a transaction limited to two or three individuals, both by reference to the potential use of the images by active paedophiles, and by reference to the degradation to the original victims.[343]

Despite these aggravating factors, and despite the serious nature of distribution, as well as the quality of the images involving very young children, the Court held that nine years' imprisonment which is close to the maximum sentence of ten years' imprisonment, was too harsh. The Court noted that the defendant was not in any way connected to the original production of the images that he distributed and

342 Ibid.

343 Ibid.

did not have any previous convictions for offences of this nature. In *Oliver* it was stated that if such factors were present, a substantially higher sentence would be required. Having considered the absence of these other serious aggravating features which would merit a higher sentence, in particular the proximity of the appellant to the original abuse, the Court quashed the sentences of nine years' imprisonment imposed on each count, and substituted sentences of seven years on each count to run concurrently with each other, the total sentence being reduced from 19 years' imprisonment to 15 years' imprisonment.[344]

Many would argue that the taking charge involving the defendant 'sexually assaulting a nine-month-old baby girl' and photographing himself warranted more than seven years' imprisonment. Under the Oliver guidelines, sentences approaching the ten years maximum imprisonment are appropriate for cases involving sexual abuse of children, and the defendant was responsible for the original production of the images in question. The Court of Appeal in *Oliver*, and later cases such as *R v. Kelly*,[345] has emphasized that the age of the children involved in the images could be seen an aggravating feature, and the Court in *Oliver* referred to assaults on babies as in *W* as an example of such an aggravating feature. As one of the worst offenders involving section 1 charges under the 1978 Act, it is submitted that W's[346] punishment should have been closer to the maximum penalty of ten years' imprisonment in relation to the taking charges.

Summary

In *R v. Kelly*,[347] the Court of Appeal emphasized that the Oliver guidelines 'are intended to help sentencers',[348] and they are 'not to be construed as providing sentencers with a straitjacket from which they cannot escape'.[349] Similarly, in *Sears*,[350] it was stated by the Court of Appeal that guidelines are guidelines, and they are not to be applied 'mechanistically'. As a result, sentencing may not always be consistent, and the courts from time to time show mercy towards certain defendants as in *Wakefield*.[351] An examination of the above post-*Oliver* cases demonstrates that the aggravating factors have an impact upon the final sentence. The nature of the offender's activity, and his proximity to the original offences of taking and producing the images have been taken on board by the sentencing courts as aggravating factors.

344 Note also the cases of *R v. Hughes* [2002] EWCA Crim 3185; *R v. Richards* [2003] EWCA Crim 834; *R v. Jones* [2003] EWCA Crim 2034; *R v. Carr* [2003] EWCA Crim 2416; *R v. Poole* [2003] EWCA Crim 222.

345 *R v. Kelly* [2004] EWCA Crim 256.

346 *Regina v. W (David Lutz)* [2005] EWCA Crim 1204.

347 *R v. Kelly* [2004] EWCA Crim 256. Note further *R v. Bishop* [2005] EWCA Crim 829 in which the Court of Appeal stated in relation to *Oliver* that 'the sentencing brackets are guidelines and not a straitjacket', and that the 'suggested levels of sentence set out in the judgment relate to contested trials'.

348 Ibid.

349 Ibid.

350 [2003] EWCA Crim 367, No. 2002/06471/Y3.

351 *R v. Wakefield* [2003] EWCA Crim 2624, No. 03/4086/A5.

It should be noted that further complications in relation to sentencing could also result following the enactment of the Criminal Justice Act 2003,[352] which came into force in April 2005. The 2003 Act provides a new regime of public protection sentences for specified violent or sexual offences committed by dangerous offenders of any age. The new provisions provided within the 2003 Act replace those provided in section 85 of the Powers of Criminal Courts (Sentencing) Act 2000.[353] Offences under section 1 of the Protection of Children Act 1978, as well as section 160 of the Criminal Justice Act 1988, are included within the list of 'sexual offences' provided in the 2003 Act.[354] Unlike section 1 offences under the 1978 Act, the possession offence provided under section 160 of the 1988 Act was not included under section 161 of the Powers of Criminal Courts (Sentencing) Act 2000 as a 'sexual offence'.[355] From now on, all those who commit child pornography related offences will be treated as dangerous offenders.

> Under the new scheme, dangerous offenders who have been convicted of a trigger sexual or violent offence for which the maximum penalty is between two and ten years will be given an extended sentence.[356] This sentence will be a determinate sentence served in custody to the half way point.[357]

It remains to be seen how this will be applied by the sentencing Courts and whether this will have an impact upon sentencing involving child pornography related offences and whether possession offences will be seen as more serious than they are at present.[358]

CONCLUSION

The law enforcement response in the fight against eliminating the market for child pornography has been energetic as witnessed by the cases assessed and prosecution statistics provided in this chapter. Long term operations such as Operation Ore show the determination of the law enforcement agencies, prosecutors and the courts to combat the problem of child pornography.[359] However, nearly 20 years on, the impact of technology including Internet distribution and complex computer operation

---

352 Note section 226–36 of the Criminal Justice Act 2003.

353 This section is entitled 'Sexual and violent offences: licences etc.'.

354 See Schedule 15 of the Criminal Justice Act 2003.

355 Note *R v. Nicholson* [2004] EWCA Crim 2840 and *R v. Pepper*; *R v. Barber*; *R v. Lamont*; *R v. Gya*; *R v. Murray* [2005] EWCA Crim 1181 (April 2005).

356 Note section 227 of the Criminal Justice Act 2003.

357 See the Explanatory Notes to Criminal Justice Act 2003, at <http://www.opsi.gov.uk/acts/en2003/2003en44.htm>.

358 Note for example *R v. Howe* [2006] EWCA Crim 3147.

359 However, note the criticism related to the unreliability of evidence in certain Operation Ore related cases: Campbell, D., 'A flaw in the child porn witch-hunt', *Sunday Times*, 26 June 2005; Campbell, D., 'Operation Ore Exposed', *PC Pro*, 1 July 2005; Leppard. D., 'Child porn suspects set to be cleared in evidence "shambles"', *Sunday Times*, 3 July 2005; Campbell, D., 'Sex, Lies and the Missing Videotape', *PC Pro*, 1 April 2007; Campbell, D.,

systems and the developments in digital evidence gathering continue to unsettle the application of laws related to child pornography.

The Protection of Children Act has a 27-year history and it has been amended and updated several times to take into account new offences (such as possession) as well as the impact of new technologies (making of pseudo-photographs). The government has also responded to public condemnation of those who commit offences related to child pornography, and amended the penalties for child pornography related offences with the Criminal Justice and Court Services Act 2000, as well as tackling the problem of grooming children[360] by criminalizing this activity under section 15 of the Sexual Offences Act 2003.[361] This latter development followed proposals which were included within the White Paper on *Protecting the Public: strengthening protection against sex offenders and reforming the law on sexual offences*[362] published in November 2002. The Sexual Offences Act 2003 came into force in May 2004.[363]

In terms of judicial action and the application of child pornography laws, the Court of Appeal has attempted to clarify the sentencing problems created initially by the *Bowden*[364] interpretation of the 'making offence' with not one but two guidelines. The initial set of guidelines developed in *Toomer*[365] were considered too broad and required the intervention of the Sentencing Advisory Board following *Wild*.[366] The Court of Appeal finally adopted the Oliver[367] guidelines and the Oliver image description scale based upon the report of the Sentencing Advisory Board to help and assist the sentencing courts in relation to child pornography related cases. The

'Operation Ore flawed by fraud', *Guardian*, 19 April 2007; Arthur, C., 'Is Operation Ore the UK's worst-ever policing scandal?', *Guardian*, 26 April 2007.

360 See generally, Ost, S., 'Getting to Grips with Sexual Grooming? The New Offence under the Sexual Offences Act 2003' (2004), *Journal of Social Welfare and Family Law* 26(2), 147–59.

361 Section 15 of the Sexual Offences Act 2003 is entitled 'Meeting a child following sexual grooming etc.', and makes it an offence for a person (A) aged 18 or over to meet intentionally, or to travel with the intention of meeting, a child aged under 16 in any part of the world, if he has met or communicated with that child on at least two earlier occasions, and intends to commit a 'relevant offence' against that child either at the time of the meeting or on a subsequent occasion. An offence is not committed if A reasonably believes the child to be 16 or over. A person guilty of an offence under this section is liable – (a) on summary conviction, to imprisonment for a term not exceeding 6 months or a fine not exceeding the statutory maximum or both; (b) on conviction on indictment, to imprisonment for a term not exceeding ten years.

362 Cm 5668.

363 First known prosecution is *R v. Mansfield* [2005] All ER (D) 195 (Apr) (15 April 2005) in which the defendant pleaded guilty to one count of meeting a child following sexual grooming, three counts of sexual activity with a child and causing a child to engage in sexual activity. He was imprisoned for six years. In each case, the extended licence period was three years. The defendant also pleaded guilty to possession of indecent photographs of a child, for which he was sentenced to nine months' imprisonment to run consecutively.

364 [2000] 2 All ER 418; [2000] 2 WLR 1083; [2000] *Crim. L.R.*, 381.

365 [2001] 2 Cr App R(S) 30.

366 [2001] EWCA Crim 1272; [2002] 1 Cr App R (S) 157.

367 [2003] 1 Cr App R (S) 463.

guidelines issued in *Oliver* were necessary to clarify the recommended sentencing after the Criminal Justice and Court Services Act 2000 came into force in 2001.[368] The Act increased the maximum penalties for the child pornography related offences substantially. Under the Oliver guidelines sentences approaching the five-year and 10-year maximum will only be appropriate in very serious cases where the defendant has a previous conviction either for dealing in child pornography, or for abusing children sexually or with violence.

Prior to the increase in maximum penalties,[369] the problematic interpretation of the making offence in *Bowden*[370] resulted in a vast number of section 1 making charges being brought forward by prosecutors. This was obviously a tactical victory for the Crown Prosecution Service as offenders faced harsher penalties under section 1 compared to a maximum of 6 months' imprisonment for possession charges until the provisions of the Criminal Justice and Court Services Act 2000 came into force in January 2001. Prosecutorial success is evident in the official statistics discussed earlier in this chapter. Following publication of the Oliver guidelines, and the increase in the maximum penalty for possession charges to five years' imprisonment, charges for possession have increased.[371]

In terms of legal controversies, the Court of Appeal in *Porter*[372] had the opportunity to clarify the defences in respect of possession of offences but the decision raised more questions than answers. Although the Court of Appeal's continuous efforts to send a very strong message to those who possess indecent photographs of children is admirable, *Porter* lacks certainty as the outcome of a possession case involving deleted images may hinge on a defendant's computer literacy and access to relevant software. Such uncertainty could in the future lead to mislabelling and prosecutors opting for a making offence rather than a possession offence as this chapter has

368 The 2000 Act was enacted on 30 November 2000 and came into force on 11 January 2001.

369 *R v. Bowden* [2000] 2 All ER 418; [2000] 2 WLR 1083; [2000] *Crim. L.R.*, 381 was decided on 10 November 1999. The *Toomer* [2001] 2 Cr App R(S) 30 guidelines were issued on 6 November 2000. The Court of Appeal issued its sentencing guidelines in *R v. Oliver* [2003] 1 Cr App R (S) 463 on 21 November 2002.

370 [2000] 2 All ER 418; [2000] 2 WLR 1083; [2000] *Crim. L.R.*, 381.

371 See for example *R v. Reast* [2005] EWCA Crim 1957; *R v. Feuer* [2005] EWCA Crim 948; *R v. Young* [2005] EWCA Crim 1078; *R v. Bibby* [2005] EWCA Crim 1859; *R v. Rooke* [2005] All ER (D) 8 (Apr), [2005] EWCA Crim 832; *R v. Evans* [2005] All ER (D) 291 (Feb); *R v. Avery* [2004] EWCA Crim 2935; *R v. Green* [2004] EWCA Crim 2795; *R v. Cawthorne* [2004] All ER (D) 10 (Oct); *R v. Collier* [2004] EWCA CRIM 1411, [2004] All ER (D) 82 (Jun); *R v. Collard* [2004] EWCA Crim 1664; *R v. Thompson* [2004] EWCA Crim 669, [2004] 2 Cr App R 262, [2005] 1 Cr App R (S) 1; *R v. Saint* [2004] EWCA Crim 550; *R v. Grosvenor* [2003] EWCA Crim 1627; *R v. White* [2003] EWCA Crim 2035; *R v. Fillary* [2003] EWCA Crim 2682.

372 [2006] EWCA Crim 560; [2006] All ER (D) 236 (Mar). See further, Ormerod, D., 'Commentary on *R v. Porter*' (2006), *Crim. L.R.*, 748.

sought to argue. As cases such as *Bowden*,[373] *Atkins v. DPP*[374] and *Smith and Jayson*[375] blurred the distinction between making and possession offences, it was also rather unsatisfactory that the Court of Appeal did not contrast the possession offence with the making offence in terms of the treatment of the deleted images. Further consideration and judicial clarification of the complex issue of deleted images in terms of both the possession and the making offences will be needed to avoid legal uncertainties. As Ormerod rightly states, 'the time is surely ripe for Parliament to re-examine the scope of these offences with the aim of creating a rational and coherent scheme.'[376]

Limited Rights Arguments?

In addition to the guidelines as set out in *Oliver*, one might consider that a limited consideration should be given to privacy and free-speech rights as in the Canadian case of *R v. Sharpe*,[377] which will be discussed in detail in Chapter 4. The obvious question would be whether the offences in relation to possession, making and distribution of indecent photographs under the Protection of Children Act 1978 (as well as under the Criminal Justice Act 1988) are compatible with articles 8 and 10 of the European Convention on Human Rights, as well as with the Human Rights Act 1998.

To some extent Lord Woolf CJ considered these issues in the case of *R v. Smethurst*,[378] which involved a prosecution for making indecent photographs of children, contrary to section 1(1)(a) of the Protection of Children Act 1978. According to Lord Woolf CJ, the exceptions in article 10(2) cover the 1978 legislation:

> the requirement to protect children justifies the terms of the offence as understood by this court in *Graham-Kerr*.[379] It is there for the prevention of crime, for the protection of morals, and in particular for the protection of children from being exploited, which is undoubtedly a matter which is necessary in a democratic society.[380]

The court concluded that the 1978 Act is 'designed to protect children from being exploited',[381] and that 'unless there is a prohibition against the taking of indecent photographs, then there is no way in which children can be protected from being exploited. The balance has been drawn by Parliament in the way indicated in section

373 *R v. Bowden* [2000] 2 All ER 418.

374 *Atkins v. DPP* [2002] 2 1040 Cr App R 248.

375 *R v. Graham Westgarth Smith and Mike Jayson* [2002] EWCA Crim 683 (No. 2001/00251/Y1), 7 March 2002; [2003] 1 Cr App R 21; and note Akdeniz, Y., Case Report: Court of Appeal Clarifies the Law on Downloading Child Pornography from the Web (2002), *Computer Law and Security Report* 18(6), 433–5.

376 Ormerod, D., 'Commentary on *R v. Porter*' (2006), *Crim. L.R.*, 748.

377 *R v. Sharpe* (2001) SCC 2. File No. 27376, 26 January 2001. Note also Ross, J., 'R v. Sharpe and Private Possession of Child Pornography' (2000), *Constitutional Forum* (11)50.

378 *R v. Smethurst* [2001] EWCA Crim 772, CA (Criminal Division), 20 March 2001.

379 *R v. Graham-Kerr* [1988] 1 WLR 1098; (1989) 88 Cr App R 302.

380 *R v. Smethurst* [2001] EWCA Crim 772, para. 24.

381 Ibid., at para. 22.

1 of the Protection of Children Act 1978.'[382] The question of the necessity of the 1978 Act and whether its provisions are proportionate under article 8 were also raised in *R v. Bowden*.[383] Here the Court held that section 1 offences under the 1978 Act were not inconsistent with the European Convention.[384]

Although the 1978 Act seems broadly compatible with articles 8(2) and 10(2) of the European Convention on Human Rights, clarity and precision in relation to the meaning of 'to make' under section 1(1)(a) is still required. Despite public condemnation of the subject, there may also be a limited privacy argument as far as pseudo-photographs are concerned regardless of how distasteful or shocking and disgusting such content may be. It could be argued that as long as children are not abused in the process leading to the creation of such content (as in the case of written material and computer generated images), and there is no further distribution of such images, there is no direct harm to children. Although it is often argued that paedophiles could make use of such images to lure children into the commitment of sexual activity, the law already provides tough penalties for sexual offences as well as for grooming and causing or inciting a child to be involved in pornography.[385]

The Oliver guidelines draw a distinction between crimes involving indecent photographs of real children and those created by computers (pseudo-photographs), and for sentencing purposes, possession, including downloading, of artificially created pseudo-photographs and the making of such images should generally be treated as being at a lower level of seriousness. Some commentators have gone further and challenged the necessity of the possession offence, questioning whether the existence of such an offence protects children or acts as a preventative measure against child abuse.[386] Such arguments notwithstanding, there is little prospect of a relaxation of child pornography law. As forthcoming chapters will demonstrate, child pornography has been condemned globally over the last ten years; existing laws have been strengthened and new laws introduced as countries battle to stem the tide of material available through the Internet.

---

382 Ibid.

383 [2000] 2 All ER 418; [2000] 2 WLR 1083; [2000] *Crim. L.R.*, 381.

384 Ibid., at 423.

385 Section 48 of the Sexual Offences Act 2003 makes it an offence for a person intentionally to cause or incite a child under 18 to be involved in pornography anywhere in the world. Note also section 49 of the Sexual Offences Act 2003 entitled 'Controlling a child prostitute or a child involved in pornography' as well as section 50 entitled 'Arranging or facilitating child prostitution or pornography'. According to section 51(1), for the purposes of sections 48 to 50, a person is involved in pornography if an indecent image of that person is recorded; and similar expressions, and 'pornography', are to be interpreted accordingly.

386 See generally, Williams, K.S., 'Child Pornography Law: Does It Protect Children?' (2004), *Journal of Social Welfare and Family Law* 26(3), 245–61.

Chapter 3

Legal Approaches in the United States of America

> I would like to use the law of the land to do everything I possibly can to protect America's children from abuse and violence ...[1]

Child pornography has been a serious concern in the United States, as in England and Wales and other Western societies. The United States has, however, witnessed a major constitutional challenge to child pornography laws at the Supreme Court level following the amendments introduced by the Child Pornography Prevention Act 1996. The Act introduced the concept of computer-generated images and criminalized content that depicts children engaging in sexually explicit conduct whether or not the content in question involved real children. The Constitutional challenge involved these provisions and, as will be detailed below, the Supreme Court[2] struck down two of the three provisions of the 1996 Act relating to virtual child pornography in a seven to two decision in April 2002.

Following the Supreme Court decision, US prosecutors were concerned by the fact that defendants in child pornography related prosecutions would frequently raise the theoretical possibility that rapidly advancing computer imaging technology was involved in the production of the materials, rather than real children, in order to avoid conviction, and it was asserted that the Supreme Court decision would make it 'immeasurably more difficult'[3] to prosecute offenders. There was also concern that in any trial prosecutors would have the 'burden of proving beyond a reasonable doubt that the visual depictions at issue involved real children'.[4] This chapter will demonstrate by reference to several subsequent appeal judgments[5] that

---

1 Janet Reno, the former A-G for the United States, at the White House, 11 February 1993.

2 *Ashcroft, Attorney General, et al. v. Free Speech Coalition et al.*, 535 U.S. 234 (US Supreme Court, 2002) 198 F3d 1083, 16 April 2002, No. 00–795, Argued 30 October 2001, at <http://supct.law.cornell.edu/supct/html/00-795.ZS.html>.

3 See Attorney General Transcript, Response to Supreme Court Decision in *Free Speech Coalition v. Ashcroft*, Tuesday, 16 April 2002, at <http://www.usdoj.gov/archive/ag/speeches/2002/041602newsconferenceresponse.htm>.

4 *U.S. v. Sims*, 220 F. Supp.2d 1222, 1226–7 (D.N.M. 2002); *U.S. v. Ellyson*, 326 F3d 522 (2003), U.S. App. LEXIS 4720, F3d, 2003 WL 1194332 (4th Cir. Mar. 17, 2003): Note also *U.S. v. David Hilton*, Crim. No. 97-78-P-C, Civil No. 02-235-P-C, US District Court for the District of Maine (2003), U.S. Dist. LEXIS 4208, March 20, 2003, Decided.

5 See *U.S. v. Kimler*, 335 F3d 1132, 1142 (10th Cir., 2003), cert. denied, 157 L. Ed. 2d 759, 124 S. Ct. 945, 2003 U.S. LEXIS 9142, 72 U.S.L.W. 3392 (U.S. Dec. 8, 2003) (No. 03-7285); *U.S. v. Deaton*, 328 F3d 454, 455 (8th Cir. 2003) (*per curiam*) (citing *U.S. v. Vig*, 167 F3d 443,

prosecutors witnessed minor rather than substantial problems in a small number of cases,[6] and that that the Supreme Court decision did not have a visible detrimental impact upon prosecutions and conviction rates as the government predicted. It will be argued that the courts demonstrated their readiness to deal appropriately with defence claims that contested images were computer-generated images rather than depictions of real children.

This chapter additionally provides a critical overview of the Protect Act 2003 amendments which were introduced by the US government as a response to the Supreme Court decision. There are both similarities and significant differences evident in legal responses to Internet child pornography in the United States and England and Wales and these are highlighted throughout the chapter.

DEVELOPMENT OF CHILD PORNOGRAPHY LAWS IN THE UNITED STATES

There are both federal laws and state laws dealing with child pornography. Many states passed laws following the unanimous decision of the Supreme Court in *New York v. Ferber*[7] in 1982, which held that states can prohibit the depiction of minors engaged in sexual conduct. In this case, the Supreme Court acknowledged that 'the exploitive use of children in the production of pornography ha[d] become a serious national problem'.[8] The Supreme Court ruled that the usual obscenity standard

449–50 (8th Cir. 1999)); *U.S. v. Hall*, 312 F3d 1250, 1260 (11th Cir. 2002), cert. denied, 155 L. Ed. 2d 502, 123 S. Ct. 1646 (2003); *U.S. v. Slanina*, 359 F3d 356, 357 (5th Cir. 2004); *U.S. v. Fuller*, 77 Fed. Appx. 371, 2003 WL 22331999 (6th Cir. 2003). Note further that in an opinion that was subsequently withdrawn, the First Circuit held that expert evidence was required to show that downloaded images of child pornography are images of real children. *U.S. v. Hilton*, 363 F3d 58, 63–6 (1st Cir. 2004), *withdrawn by U.S. v. Hilton*, 2004 U.S. App. LEXIS 19528 (1st Cir. Sept. 20, 2004). See further, *U.S. v. Farrelly*, 389 F3d 649, 653–4 (6th Cir. 2004).

6 Within this context note the cases of *U.S. v. Hilton*, 363 F3d 58 (1st Cir.), vacated, 386 F3d 13 (1st Cir. 2004); *U.S. v. Ellyson*, 326 F3d 522 (4th Cir. 2003); *U.S. v. Pearl*, 324 F3d 1210 (10th Cir. 2003), cert. denied, 539 U.S. 934, 123 S. Ct. 2591, 156 L. Ed. 2d 616 (2003); *U.S. v. Barbieri*, 43 Fed. Appx. 367 (10th Cir. 2002).

7 *New York v. Ferber* 458 U.S. 747 (1982). Note Schauer, F., 'Codifying the First Amendment: *New York v. Ferber*' (1982), *Sup. Ct. Rev* 285, 317.

8 The Supreme Court referred to the *Sexual Exploitation of Children*, Hearings before the Subcommittee on Select Education of the House Committee on Education and Labor, 95th Cong., 1st Sess. (1977), as well as to a Senate Report on the same subject, No. 95-438 (1977).

established in *Miller*[9] did not apply to child pornography on the grounds that child pornography is *per se* obscene.[10] The Court gave five reasons for its decision:

(1) Using children as subjects of pornography could be harmful to their physical and psychological well-being and child pornography does not fall within the protection of the First Amendment.[11]
(2) Application of the *Miller* standard for obscenity is not a satisfactory solution to the problem of child pornography.[12]
(3) The financial gain involved in selling and advertising child pornography provides incentive to produce such material – and such activity is prohibited throughout the US.[13]
(4) The value of permitting minors to perform / appear in lewd exhibitions is negligible at best.[14]
(5) The distribution of photographs and films depicting sexual activity by juveniles is intrinsically related to sexual abuse of children[15] and is therefore within the state's interest and power to prohibit.

Following *Ferber*, child pornography joined the category of speech that lacks any protection under the First Amendment. The Supreme Court ruled that the value of speech in content involving child pornography was outweighed by other significant considerations, including the prevention of sexual exploitation and abuse of children.

The *Ferber* approach was later extended when the Supreme Court upheld a statute making it illegal to possess child pornography in 1990 in *Osborne v. Ohio*.[16] Although the decision in *Osborne* went against the earlier decision of the Court in *Stanley v. Georgia*[17] (which held that neither the states nor the federal government may prohibit possession of obscene material in the privacy of one's home), the Court in *Osborne* argued, consistent with the *Ferber* approach, that the legislation sought not to 'control men's minds' but rather to protect children from exploitation

---

9 *Miller v. California* 413 U.S. 15 (1973). The *Miller* test for obscenity is a three part test and all parts must be satisfied before the material in question can be considered obscene: (1) Whether 'the average person, applying contemporary community standards', would find that the work, taken as a whole, appeals primarily to the prurient interest; (2) Whether the work depicts or describes, in a patently offensive way, sexual conduct specifically defined by the applicable state law; (3) Whether the work, taken as a whole, lacks serious literary, artistic, political or scientific value.

10 458 U.S. 747 (1982) at 764. See also Scheller, J.C., 'PC Peep Show: Computers, Privacy and Child Pornography' (1994) *John Marshall Law Review* 27, Summer, 989–1016 at 997.

11 458 U.S. 747 (1982) at 762.

12 Ibid. 759.

13 Ibid. 761.

14 Ibid. 762.

15 Ibid. 759.

16 495 U.S. 103 (1990). Note Smith, L.S., 'Private Possession of Child Pornography: Narrowing At-Home Privacy Rights' (1991), *Ann. Surv Am. L.* 1011; and Quigley, J., 'Child Pornography and the Right to Privacy' (1991), 43 *Fla. L. Rev* 347.

17 394 U.S. 557 (1969). But the Court has refused to recognize a privacy right to receive such material by post in *U.S. v. Reidel* 402 U.S. 351 (1971) or to import it for personal use in *U.S. v. 12200 Ft. Reels* 413 U.S. 123 (1973).

and harm involved in the production of child pornography.[18] According to the State of Ohio, the additional provisions criminalizing possession were necessary as a direct result of the *Ferber* decision. The Court argued that it was difficult 'if not impossible, to solve the child pornography problem by only attacking production and distribution'.[19] In fact, at the time of the constitutional challenge, Ohio was one of many states that had elected to criminalize the possession of child pornography.

As noted, in *Ferber* the Supreme Court recognized other interests to support the criminalization of possession, including the fact that the materials produced by child pornographers permanently record the child victim's abuse. This continued existence, in the view of the Supreme Court, could cause child victims continuing harm by haunting them in years to come.[20] It was envisaged that a ban on possession could usefully encourage 'the possessors of these materials to destroy them'.[21] According to the Supreme Court in *Osborne*, the ban on possession was necessary as evidence suggested that paedophiles use child pornography to groom children into sexual activity. This view was based upon the findings of the Meese Commission on Pornography which argued that child abusers would not merely keep materials for themselves, but would frequently give or trade the materials with other child abusers or paedophiles,[22] or use child pornography as part of a method of seducing child victims.[23]

In addition to case law laying down principles for criminalizing content involving real children in sexual context, the US government also introduced Federal laws to combat child pornography. Chapter 10 of the US Federal Code, entitled *Sexual exploitation and other abuse of children*, includes child pornography related offences, and these are similar to the offences of creation, distribution and possession under the Protection of Children Act 1978 in England and Wales. These Federal laws dealing with child pornography in the United States will be discussed later in the chapter. However, it is first necessary to examine constitutional challenges to the Child Pornography Prevention Act 1996 which expanded the definition of child pornography provided in federal statutes to include 'pseudo-photographs' and/or computer-generated images of children. The 1996 law, the legal challenges to the 1996 law at the Supreme Court level, and the subsequent policy initiatives as a response to the Supreme Court decision have significantly shaped US child pornography laws in the recent years as detailed below.

18 Susan Dwyer, *The Problem of Pornography*, Belmont, CA: Wadsworth, 1995, 246.

19 Ibid.

20 458 U.S., at 759.

21 *Osborne v. Ohio*, 495 U.S. 103 (1990).

22 See Attorney General's Commission on Pornography: Final Report, 2 vols, Washington, DC: US Government Printing Office, July 1986 (The Meese Commission) at p. 407.

23 Ibid., at 649.

CHILD PORNOGRAPHY PREVENTION ACT 1996

Sexually explicit pseudo-photographs as well as computer-generated images involving children were not covered by US legislation until October 1996. Such indecent pseudo-photographs were subject to the *Miller*[24] obscenity test and other federal laws dealing with obscenity but not regarded as child pornography.

> Up until 1996 the actual participation and abuse of children in the production or dissemination of pornography involving minors was the *sine qua non* of the regulating scheme.[25]

The Child Pornography Prevention Act 1996 ('CPPA')[26] was introduced to criminalize material that depicts children engaging in sexually explicit conduct whether or not the content in question involved real children. The new approach 'shifted from defining child pornography in terms of the harm inflicted upon real children to a determination that child pornography was evil in and of itself, whether it involved real children or not.'[27] Senator Hatch introduced the CPPA by arguing that Federal law had failed to keep pace with technology, unlike the purveyors of child pornography who had kept in line with it. The CPPA was intended to address this gap. In the words of Senator Hatch:

> Even more shocking than the occurrence of this type of repulsive conduct is the fact that, under current Federal law, those pictures, depicting naked children involved in sex with other children, adults, and even animals, would not be prosecutable as child pornography. That is because current Federal child pornography and sexual exploitation of children laws, USC 18, sections 2251, 2251A, and 2252, cover only visual depictions of children engaging in sexually explicit conduct whose production involved the use of a minor engaging in such conduct; materials such as photographs, films and videotapes.[28]

In June 1996 the Bill was the subject of intense debate,[29] and it was included as part of a broad-spending Omnibus Consolidated Appropriations Act 1996 which was signed into law by President Bill Clinton. It passed the US Senate on 30 September 1996 just hours before the midnight deadline for the start of the fiscal year 1997.

---

24 *Miller v. California* 413 U.S. 15 (1973).

25 *Free Speech Coalition v. Reno*, 198 F3d 1083, 1097 (9th Cir. 1999), striking down part of the CPPA, cert. granted sub nom. *Ashcroft v. Free Speech Coalition*, 148 L. Ed. 2d 788, 121 S. Ct. 876 (22 January 2001).

26 HR n.a., section 1237 sponsored by Sen. Hatch (R-UT), Abraham (R-MI), Grassley (R-IA) and Thurmond (R-SC).

27 This shift would form the basis of the constitutional challenge to the 1996 Act. See *Free Speech Coalition v. Reno*, 198 F3d 1083, 1097 (9th Cir. 1999), striking down part of the CPPA, cert. granted sub nom. *Ashcroft v. Free Speech Coalition*, 148 L. Ed. 2d 788, 121 S. Ct. 876 (22 January 2001).

28 The Child Pornography Prevention Act 1995, Statements of Introduced Bills and Joint Resolutions, US Senate, 13 September 1995 (104th Congress, 2nd Session).

29 See US Senate Committe Report 104-358 – Child Pornography Prevention Act of 1996.

Congressional Findings

The 1996 Act reflected important findings by the US Judiciary Committee:

> The effect of [computer generated pornography] on a child molester or paedophile using the material to whet his sexual appetites, or on a child shown such material as a means of seducing the child into sexual activity, is the same whether the material is photographic or computer-generated depictions of child sexual activity.[30]

It was emphasized, as in *Osborne v. Ohio*[31] and the Meese Commission report, that paedophiles might use the materials to encourage children to participate in sexual activity. According to the US Judiciary Committee, a child who is reluctant to engage in sexual activity with an adult, or to pose for sexually explicit photographs, can sometimes be convinced by viewing depictions of other children 'having fun' participating in such activity.[32] Additionally, as mentioned in Chapter 2, with the advancement in new technologies, including in imaging technology, it is becoming more and more difficult for law enforcement agencies and prosecutors to prove that a particular picture was produced using actual children. The US Congress extended the ban to virtual child pornography to ensure that defendants possessing child pornography involving real children could not evade prosecution.[33]

The Congress also re-emphasized the fact that the elimination of child pornography and the protection of children from sexual exploitation provide a

> compelling governmental interest for prohibiting the production, distribution, possession, sale, or viewing of visual depictions of children engaging in sexually explicit conduct, including both photographic images of actual children engaging in such conduct and depictions produced by computer or other means which are virtually indistinguishable to the unsuspecting viewer from photographic images of actual children engaging in such conduct.[34]

The CPPA 1996 provisions set mandatory prison sentences of 15 years for the production of child pornography, five years for the possession of child pornography, and life imprisonment for repeat offenders convicted of sexual abuse of a minor.[35] Section 18 U.S.C. 2256(8) defined the term 'child pornography' as:

> any visual depiction, including any photograph, film, video, picture, drawing or computer or computer-generated image or picture, which is produced by electronic, mechanical or other means, of sexually explicit conduct, where: (1) its production involved the use of a minor engaging in sexually explicit conduct, or; (2) such visual depiction is,

---

30 Dr Victor Cline gave evidence on 4 June 1996 and stated that seeing a computer-created depiction would be extremely traumatic for the depicted child. See US Senate Committee Report 104–358 – Child Pornography Prevention Act of 1996, Congressional Findings, note (8).

31 495 U.S. 103 (1990).

32 Congressional Findings, note (3) following §2251.

33 Note (6)(A).

34 Congressional Findings, note (13).

35 See the new 18 U.S.C. 2252A.

> or appears to be, of a minor engaging in sexually explicit conduct; (3) such visual depiction has been created, adapted or modified to appear that an 'identifiable minor'[36] is engaging in sexually explicit conduct …

The CPPA 1996 expanded the federal prohibition on child pornography to include not only pornographic images made using actual children as in 18 U.S.C. §2256(8)(A), but also to 'any visual depiction, including any photograph, film, video, picture, or computer or computer-generated image or picture' that 'is, or appears to be, of a minor engaging in sexually explicit conduct', through the newly introduced section 2256(8)(B).

The CPPA 1996 also added section 2256(8)(D) which states that any sexually explicit image that is 'advertised, promoted, presented, described, or distributed in such a manner that conveys the impression' depicts 'a minor engaging in sexually explicit conduct'. Thus section 2256(8)(B) banned a range of sexually explicit images, referred to as 'virtual child pornography' or 'indecent pseudo-photographs' that appear to depict minors but were produced by means other than using real (actual) children, such as through the use of youthful-looking adults or computer-imaging technology.

The American Civil Liberties Union (ACLU) criticized the 1996 Act arguing that the new definitions and provisions were clearly unconstitutional because they criminalized images produced without the involvement of an actual child.[37] The ACLU argued that its view was supported by the decision in *Ferber*,[38] where the Supreme Court made clear that restrictions on child pornography were justifiable because the government had a compelling interest in preventing the physical and psychological abuse of children who are forced to engage in sexual activity for commercial purposes. The ACLU referred specifically to the view expressed by the Supreme Court that child pornography lacks First Amendment protection because actual depictions of child exploitation and abuse affect 'the welfare of children engaged in its production'. On this basis, the ACLU argued that it was clear from *Ferber* that the government's interest was based on protecting children from actual harm, and not shielding the general public from such images. Moreover, it claimed that 'the bill would have a severe chilling effect on constitutionally protected expression'.[39]

The US Judiciary Committee rejected the arguments raised by the ACLU and stated that the Government had an interest in prohibiting computer-generated child pornographic depictions because of the actual or possible future harm to children.

---

36 Under 18 U.S.C. 2256 (9) a prosecutor will not be required to prove the minor's actual identity.

37 See *ACLU Cyber-Liberties Update*, 'Senate Ready to Hatch "Virtual" Child Porn Bill', 10 July 1996 at <http://www.aclu.org>.

38 458 U.S. 747 (1982).

39 See *ACLU Cyber-Liberties Update*, 'Senate Ready to Hatch "Virtual" Child Porn Bill', 10 July 1996 at <http://www.aclu.org>.

CONSTITUTIONAL CHALLENGE TO THE CPPA 1996

Soon after the enactment of the 1996 Act, the Free Speech Coalition[40] challenged the CPPA and argued that it was unconstitutionally overbroad and vague in violation of the First Amendment. Until this challenge, child pornography laws were the 'least contested area of First Amendment jurisprudence'.[41] The court challenge to CPPA 1996 was resolved after a long battle at the US Supreme Court. In a seven to two decision, the Supreme Court[42] struck down two of the three provisions of CPPA relating to virtual child pornography.

District Court Decision

The initial case, *The Free Speech Coalition v. Reno*,[43] took place at the United States District Court for the Northern District of California. The Coalition sought declaratory and injunctive relief by a pre-enforcement challenge to certain provisions of the CPPA 1996. The Coalition alleged that the 'appears to be' and 'conveys the impression' provisions of the CPPA 1996 were overbroad and vague, chilling them from producing works protected by the First Amendment. The plaintiffs based their overbreadth argument on the assertion that the CPPA 'impermissibly suppresses material that is protected under the First Amendment'[44] by defining child pornography as including visual depictions of adults that appear to be minors. According to the plaintiffs, this resulted in the CPPA 1996 provisions banning 'a wide array of sexually-explicit, non-obscene material that has serious literary, artistic, political, and scientific value'.[45]

However, the District Court disagreed with the Free Speech Coalition and granted the Government summary judgment. The District Court found that the CPPA was content-neutral, was neither unconstitutionally vague nor overbroad, and did not constitute an improper prior restraint of speech. The District Court reasoned that the law was passed to prevent the secondary effects of the child pornography industry, specifically the exploitation and degradation of children. The District Court also found that the CPPA addressed the need to control child pornography because virtual pornography led to the encouragement of paedophilia and the molestation of children. This reasoning was based on a finding that the CPPA is intended 'to counteract the effect that [real or virtual child pornography]

---

40 The Coalition involved a trade association that defends First Amendment rights against censorship, the publisher of a book dedicated to the education and expression of the ideals and philosophy associated with nudism, and individual artists whose works include nude and erotic photographs and paintings; see <http://www.freespeechcoalition.com/>.

41 Adler, A., 'The Perverse Law of Child Pornography' (2001), 101 *Colum. L. Rev* 209.

42 *Ashcroft, Attorney General, et al. v. Free Speech Coalition et al.*, 535 U.S. 234, US Supreme Court (2002) 198 F3d 1083, 16 April 2002, No. 00–795, Argued 30 October 2001, at <http://supct.law.cornell.edu/supct/html/00-795.ZS.html>.

43 See *The Free Speech Coalition v. Reno*, 1997 U.S. Dist. LEXIS 12212, No. C 97-0281 VSC, 1997 WL 487758, at *7 (N.D. Cal. 12 August 1997).

44 Ibid.

45 Ibid.

has on its viewers, on children, and to society as a whole'.[46] The District Court reasoned that it was highly unlikely that the types of valuable works plaintiffs feared would be outlawed under the CPPA would be treated as 'criminal contraband'. These included, for example, depictions used by the medical profession to treat adolescent disorders, adaptations of sexual works like 'Romeo and Juliet', and artistically-valued drawings and sketches of young adults engaging in passionate behaviour. The District Court concluded:

> As long as a work does not depict children, or what appears to be children, engaged in sexually explicit conduct as defined by the statute, and the work is not marketed as child pornography or in such a way that exploits its sexual nature as child pornography, then there is no likelihood that the work will be prohibited by the CPPA. The CPPA is not overbroad because it prohibits only those works necessary to prevent the secondary pernicious effects of child pornography from reaching minors.[47]

The plaintiffs had contended that the CPPA was unconstitutionally vague as it did not give a person of ordinary intelligence a reasonable opportunity to know what was prohibited so that he may act accordingly.[48] The District Court disagreed, stating that the CPPA does exactly what the Supreme Court had required of child pornography legislation as set out in *Ferber*:

> it must (1) adequately define the prohibited conduct; (2) be limited to visual depictions of children below a specific age; and (3) suitably limit and describe the category of forbidden 'sexual conduct'.[49]

The District Court argued that the CPPA clearly and specifically defined the prohibited conduct as the depiction of children engaged in sexually explicit conduct.

> This is limited to visual depictions of minors, but simply redefines the term 'depiction' to include images of children that were produced using computers or other artificial means.[50]

In terms of the category of forbidden conduct, the District Court ruled that the CPPA suitably limits and describes what is permissible and not permissible.

The Free Speech Coalition appealed.

---

46 Ibid.

47 Ibid.

48 This issue was based upon the principles laid down in *Grayned v. City of Rockford* 408 U.S. 104, 108 (1972).

49 458 U.S. at 764.

50 *The Free Speech Coalition v. Reno*, 1997 U.S. Dist. LEXIS 12212, No. C 97-0281 VSC, 1997 WL 487758, at *7 (N.D. Cal. 12 August 1997).

Decision of the Ninth Circuit US Court of Appeals

The decision of the District Court was reversed in *The Free Speech Coalition v. Reno*[51] by the Ninth Circuit US Court of Appeals. The Ninth Circuit held that the First Amendment prohibits the US Congress from enacting a statute that makes criminal the generation of images of fictitious children engaged in imaginary but explicit sexual conduct. The Court reasoned that the Government could not prohibit speech[52] because of its tendency to persuade viewers to commit illegal acts. Unlike the District Court, the Ninth Circuit held the CPPA to be substantially overbroad because it banned materials that were neither obscene under *Miller v. California*,[53] nor produced by the exploitation of real children as in *New York v. Ferber*.[54] According to the Court:

> The new law sought to stifle the use of technology for evil purposes. This of course was a marked change in the criminal regulatory scheme. Congress had always acted to prevent harm to real children. In the new law, Congress shifted the paradigm from the illegality of child pornography that involved the use of real children in its creation to forbid a 'visual depiction' that 'is, or appears to be, of a minor engaging in sexually explicit conduct.'[55]

Unlike the District Court, the Ninth Circuit found that the phrases 'appears to be a minor' and 'conveys the impression that the depiction portrays a minor' were vague and overbroad and thus did not meet the requirements of the First Amendment:

> The two phrases in question are highly subjective. There is no explicit standard as to what the phrases mean. The phrases provide no measure to guide an ordinarily intelligent person about prohibited conduct and any such person could not be reasonably certain about whose perspective defines the appearance of a minor, or whose impression that a minor is involved leads to criminal prosecution … In the same light, the absence of definitions for these key phrases in the CPPA allows law enforcement officials to exercise their discretion, subjectively, about what 'appears to be' or what 'conveys the impression' of prohibited material. Thus, the vagueness of the statute's key phrases regarding computer images permits enforcement in an arbitrary and discriminatory fashion.[56]

It was also emphasized by the Court that the balance of the CPPA was constitutional when these two phrases were removed. Moreover, the Ninth Circuit referred to the

51 See *Free Speech Coalition v. Reno*, 198 F3d 1083, 1097 (9th Cir. 1999), striking down part of the CPPA, cert. granted sub nom. *Ashcroft v. Free Speech Coalition*, 148 L. Ed. 2d 788, 121 S. Ct. 876 (22 January 2001).

52 In *U.S. v. Hilton*, 167 F3d 61, 68–9 (1st Cir. 1999), pet. for cert. filed, No. 98-9647 (U.S. 28 May 1999), the First Circuit found that the Act at issue was content-based because it expressly aimed to curb a particular category of expression, child pornography, by singling out the type of expression based on its content and then banning it.

53 *Miller v. California* 413 U.S. 15 (1973).

54 458 U.S. 747 (1982).

55 *Free Speech Coalition v. Reno*, 198 F3d 1083, 1097 (9th Cir. 1999).

56 Ibid.

relationship between the dissemination of fabricated images of child pornography and additional acts of sexual abuse as the critical ingredient of their analysis and stated:

> Factual studies that establish the link between computer-generated child pornography and the subsequent sexual abuse of children apparently do not yet exist.[57] … The legislative justification for the proposition was based upon the Final Report of the Attorney General's Commission on Pornography,[58] a report that predates the existing technology. The Final Report emphasized the victimization of real children by adult distribution of the pornographic material. The report shows that the use of sexually explicit photos or films of actual children to lure other children played a small part in the overall problem involving harm to children.[59] Thus, while such images are unquestionably morally repugnant, they do not involve real children nor is there a demonstrated basis to link computer-generated images with harm to real children. Absent this nexus, the law does not withstand constitutional scrutiny.[60]

The Court also dismissed the case put forward regarding secondary effects which assumed that 'children will be enticed by paedophiles to illicit sexual behaviour, and consequent injury, if they look at pictures of other kids engaged in sexually explicit conduct.'[61] The Court stated, 'many innocent things can entice children into immoral or offensive behaviour, but that reality does not create a constitutional power in the Congress to regulate otherwise innocent behaviour.'[62]

In a dissenting judgment, Judge Ferguson agreed with the District Court on the ground that virtual images, like obscenity and real child pornography, should be treated as a category of speech unprotected by the First Amendment.[63] He argued that the US Congress was not attempting to regulate 'evil ideas'. On the contrary,

---

57 See Adelman, R.W., 'The Constitutionality of Congressional Efforts to Ban Computer-Generated Child Pornography: A First Amendment Assessment of S. 1237' (1996), 14 *J. Marshall J. Computer and Info. L.* 483, 488, 490.

58 See Attorney General's Commission on Pornography: Final Report, 2 vols, Washington, DC: US Government Printing Office, July 1986 (The Meese Commission).

59 *See Free Speech Coalition v. Reno*, 198 F3d 1083, 1097 (9th Cir. 1999) citing A-G Report at 649–50.

60 Ibid.

61 Ibid.

62 Ibid.

63 See 198 F3d, at 1097. In 1999, in a previous judgment, the First Circuit held that the CPPA survives constitutional challenge as it is neither vague, nor a substantial infringement on protected expression. See *U.S. v. Hilton*, 167 F3d 61 (1st Cir. 1999), at 65. In 1997 a federal grand jury indicted Hilton for criminal possession of computer disks containing three or more images of child pornography in violation of 18 U.S.C. § 2252A(a)(5)(B). The district court granted the defendant's motion to dismiss the indictment, finding the language 'appears to be a minor' was overbroad and vague. *U.S. v. Hilton*, 999 F. Supp. 131, 137 (D. Me. 1998). On appeal, the First Circuit reversed, finding no reason to strike down the CPPA as unconstitutionally vague. *Hilton*, 167 F3d at 76. See generally, Mota, S.A., 'The US Supreme Court Addresses the Child Pornography Prevention Act and Child Online Protection Act in *Ashcroft v. Free Speech Coalition* and *Ashcroft v. American Civil Liberties Union*' (2002), *Federal Communications Law Journal* 55(1), 85–98.

Judge Ferguson stated that Congress had provided compelling evidence that virtual child pornography causes real harm to real children:

> As a result, virtual child pornography should join the ranks of real child pornography as a class of speech outside the protection of the First Amendment.[64]

According to Judge Ferguson, the majority had ignored the fact that child pornography, real or virtual, has little or no social value,[65] stating, 'the First Amendment, does not protect certain limited categories of speech that are utterly without redeeming social importance'.[66] There was no valid reason to treat virtual child pornography differently from real child pornography, he declared:

> While this distinction is noteworthy, it does not somehow transform virtual child pornography into meaningful speech. Virtual child pornography, like its counterpart real child pornography, is of 'slight social value' and constitutes 'no essential part of the exposition of ideas.'[67] Therefore, the majority is wrong to accord virtual child pornography the full protection of the First Amendment.[68]

As a final point, Judge Ferguson observed that the CPPA merely extended the existing prohibitions on real child pornography to a narrow class of computer-generated pictures easily mistaken for real photographs of real children.[69]

---

64 *Free Speech Coalition v. Reno*, 198 F3d 1083, 1097 (9th Cir. 1999).

65 *See Ferber*, 458 U.S. at 762 stating that the value of child pornography is 'exceedingly modest, if not *de minimis*'.

66 See *R.A.V v. City of St. Paul*, 505 U.S. 377, 382–3, 120 L. Ed. 2d 305, 112 S. Ct. 2538 (1992); *Roth v. United States*, 354 U.S. 476, 484, 1 L. Ed. 2d 1498, 77 S. Ct. 1304 (1957). These categories include 'obscenity', *Roth*, 354 U.S. at 483, 'libel', *Beauharnais v. Illinois*, 343 U.S. 250, 266, 96 L. Ed. 919, 72 S. Ct. 725 (1952), and 'fighting words', *Chaplinsky v. New Hampshire*, 315 U.S. 568, 571–3, 86 L. Ed. 1031, 62 S. Ct. 766 (1942). See further, Strossen, N., *Defending Pornography: Free Speech, Sex and the Fight for Women's Rights*, New York: Abacus, 1996; and Walker, S., *Hate Speech: The History of an American Controversy*, University of Nebraska Press, 1994.

67 *See Chaplinsky*, 315 U.S. at 572.

68 *Free Speech Coalition v. Reno*, 198 F3d 1083, 1097 (9th Cir. 1999).

69 See the above mentioned *Congressional Findings* of the US Senate Committe Report 104–358 – Child Pornography Prevention Act of 1996.

While the Ninth Circuit found the CPPA invalid on its face, four other appeal courts have sustained it:[70] the First,[71] Eleventh,[72] Fourth[73] and Fifth Circuit.[74]

---

70 See *U.S. v. Acheson*, 195 F3d 645 (11th Cir. 1999) (rejecting First Amendment challenge to CPPA on grounds of vagueness, overbreadth and facial invalidity); *U.S. v. Hilton*, 167 F3d 61 (1st Cir. 1999) (same), cert. denied, 528 U.S. 844 (1999); see also *U.S. v. Pearl*, 89 F. Supp. 2d 1237 (D. Utah 2000) (holding CPPA survives strict scrutiny review and expressly rejecting the panel's analysis). See further, *U.S. v. Fox*, 248 F3d 394 (CA5 2001); *U.S. v. Mento*, 231 F3d 912 (CA4 2000).

71 *U.S. v. Hilton*, 167 F3d 61 (1st Cir. 1999).

72 *U.S. v. Acheson*, 195 F3d 645 (11th Cir. 1999): In a subsequent decision, the Eleventh Circuit upheld a conviction under the CPPA, affirming a District Court's decision that the statute is constitutional. The defendant pleaded guilty to knowingly receiving visual depictions of minors engaged in sexually explicit conduct that had been transported in interstate commerce. The Eleventh Circuit found the CPPA was neither overbroad nor impermissibly vague. Note that there is no post-*Free Speech Coalition* docket activity and there was nothing pending before the Supreme Court at the time of its *Free Speech Coalition* decision to warrant a remand.

73 *U.S. v. Mento*, 231 F3d 912 (4th Cir. 2000): While stating that 'the First Amendment is the bedrock upon which our political system is founded', the court noted, 'Congress may regulate protected speech to promote a compelling governmental interest.' Ibid. at 918, 920. Since Congress found that pornography involving those who *appear* to be minors has the same effects on child molesters as pornography involving *actual* minors, the government's interest in banning this material is equally as compelling. Ibid. at 921. Finding the CPPA to be 'bold and innovative in its attempt to combat the sexual exploitation of minors', the Fourth Circuit held the CPPA does not offend the First Amendment. Ibid. at 923. See generally, Mota, S.A., 'The US Supreme Court Addresses the Child Pornography Prevention Act and Child Online Protection Act in *Ashcroft v. Free Speech Coalition* and *Ashcroft v. American Civil Liberties Union*' (2002), *Federal Communications Law Journal* 55(1), 85–98. With regards to Mento, a defendant whose petition for certiorari review was pending at the issuance of Free Speech Coalition, the Supreme Court vacated and remanded his case to the Fourth Circuit immediately. *Mento v. United States*, 535 U.S. 1014, 152 L. Ed. 2d 617, 122 S. Ct. 1602 (2002). Mento was on supervised release at the time the Supreme Court vacated his judgment and the docket shows that on 13 May 2002 he was discharged from his supervised release. The order from the Fourth Circuit vacating and remanding the judgment for dismissal of the indictment or for such other further proceeding was entered on the docket on 2 August 2002. See *U.S. v. David Hilton*, Crim. No. 97-78-P-C, Civil No. 02-235-P-C, United States District Court for the District of Maine, 2003 U.S. Dist. LEXIS 4208, March 20, 2003, Decided.

74 *U.S. v. Fox*, 248 F3d 394 (5th Cir. 2001): The Fifth Circuit confirmed the defendant's sentence and conviction, finding that virtual child pornography, like 'real' child pornography, is not entitled to First Amendment protection, and that the CPPA is not overbroad. Ibid. at 404. In the immediate aftermath of *Free Speech Coalition*, on 25 April 2002, Fox filed a successful motion for release pursuant to 18 U.S.C. §3143(b). On 31 May 2002 the Fifth Circuit, having received the order vacating and remanding from the Supreme Court, entered an order remanding the case to the District Court for further proceedings and disposition consistent with *Free Speech Coalition*. *U.S. v. Fox*, 293 F3d 237 (2002). Fox's motion for release was granted on 29 July 2002. Trial was set, but Fox eventually pleaded guilty to time served. See further, Mota, S.A., 'The US Supreme Court Addresses the Child Pornography Prevention Act and Child Online Protection Act in *Ashcroft v. Free Speech Coalition* and *Ashcroft v. American Civil Liberties Union*' (2002), *Federal Communications Law Journal* 55(1), 85–98.

An appeal was ultimately lodged with the Supreme Court by the US Attorney General.[75]

The Supreme Court Decision Involving the CPPA 1996

The Supreme Court in *Ashcroft, Attorney General, et al. v. Free Speech Coalition et al.*[76] held in a 6–3 opinion[77] that the prohibitions provided in section 2256(8)(B) and 2256(8)(D) were overbroad and unconstitutional. The Supreme Court ruled that section 2256(8)(B) as introduced by the 1996 Act covered materials beyond the categories recognized in *Ferber* and *Miller* and the reasons the Government offered in support of limiting freedom of expression had no justification in the Supreme Court's precedents or First Amendment law.

The Supreme Court rejected the Government's argument that speech prohibited by the CPPA was virtually indistinguishable from material that may be banned under *Ferber*. The Supreme Court stated that *Ferber* upheld a prohibition on the distribution and sale of child pornography, as well as its production, because these acts were 'intrinsically related' to the sexual abuse of children in two ways:[78]

> First, as a permanent record of a child's abuse, the continued circulation itself would harm the child who had participated.[79] Second, because the traffic in child pornography was an economic motive for its production, the State had an interest in closing the distribution network.[80]

In contrast to the speech in *Ferber* (speech that was itself the record of sexual abuse), the CPPA prohibited speech that records no crime (as the images are, for example, computer-generated) and creates no real victims by its production. There was no actual abuse and there was therefore no permanent record of a child's abuse present under the CPPA provisions. According to the Supreme Court, virtual or computer-generated child pornography is not 'intrinsically related' to the sexual abuse of children. While the Government asserted that the images can lead to actual instances of child abuse, the causal link was contingent and indirect in the view of the Supreme Court. It was decided that the harm did not necessarily follow from the speech, but depended upon some unquantified potential for subsequent

---

75 For a detailed pre-Supreme Court decision assessment of US child pornography laws see Klain, E.J., H.J. Davies and M.A. Hicks, *Child Pornography: The Criminal-Justice-System Response*, 2001, ICMEC, at <http://www.missingkids.com/en_US/publications/NC81.pdf>.

76 *Ashcroft, Attorney General, et al. v. Free Speech Coalition et al.* 535 U.S. 234 (US Supreme Court, 2002), 198 F3d 1083, 16 April 2002, No. 00–795, Argued 30 October 2001, at <http://supct.law.cornell.edu/supct/html/00-795.ZS.html>.

77 Kennedy J, delivered the opinion of the Court, in which Stevens, Souter, Ginsburg and Breyer JJ, joined. Thomas J, filed an opinion concurring in the judgment. O'Connor J, filed an opinion concurring in the judgment in part and dissenting in part, in which Rehnquist CJ, and Scalia J, joined as to Part II. Rehnquist CJ, filed a dissenting opinion, in which Scalia J, joined except for the paragraph discussing legislative history.

78 *New York v. Ferber* 458 U.S. 747 (1982), at 759.

79 Ibid.

80 Ibid., at 760.

criminal acts in the case of virtual or computer-generated child pornography. The Supreme Court stated that the Government's argument that these indirect harms were sufficient because, as *Ferber* acknowledged, child pornography rarely can be valuable speech[81] suffered from two flaws:

> First, *Ferber*'s judgment about child pornography was based upon how it was made, not on what it communicated. The case reaffirmed that where the speech is neither obscene nor the product of sexual abuse, it does not fall outside the First Amendment's protection.[82] Second, *Ferber* did not hold that child pornography is by definition without value. It recognized some works in this category might have significant value,[83] but relied on virtual images – the very images prohibited by the CPPA – as an alternative and permissible means of expression.[84] Because *Ferber* relied on the distinction between actual and virtual child pornography as supporting its holding, it provides no support for a statute that eliminates the distinction and makes the alternative mode criminal as well.[85]

The Supreme Court also rejected other arguments offered by the Government to justify the CPPA's prohibitions. It challenged the Government's justification of the CPPA based upon the possibility that paedophiles may use virtual child pornography to seduce children and held that the speech in question should not be silenced completely in an attempt to shield children from it.[86] The Court explained:

> the evil in question depends upon the actor's unlawful conduct, defined as criminal quite apart from any link to the speech in question, establishes that the speech ban is not narrowly drawn. The argument that virtual child pornography whets paedophiles' appetites and encourages them to engage in illegal conduct is unavailing because the mere tendency of speech to encourage unlawful acts is not a sufficient reason for banning it,[87] absent some showing of a direct connection between the speech and imminent illegal conduct.[88]

The Court refuted the market deterrence theory as there was no crime involved in the creation of such virtual images. Finally, the Supreme Court stated that the First Amendment was 'turned upside down by the argument that, because it is difficult to distinguish between images made using real children and those produced by computer imaging, both kinds of images must be prohibited. The overbreadth

81 Ibid., at 762.

82 Ibid., at 764–5.

83 Ibid., at 761.

84 Ibid., at 763.

85 *Ashcroft, Attorney General, et al. v. Free Speech Coalition et al.* 535 U.S. 234 (US Supreme Court, 2002), 198 F3d 1083, 16 April 2002, No. 00–795.

86 See for example *Sable Communications of Cal., Inc. v. FCC*, 492 U.S. 115 (1989), 130–31.

87 *Stanley v. Georgia*, 394 U.S. 557 (1969), 566.

88 See for example *Brandenburg v. Ohio*, 395 U.S. 444 (1969), 447 (*per curiam*).

doctrine prohibits the Government from banning unprotected speech if a substantial amount of protected speech is prohibited or chilled in the process.'[89]

The Supreme Court held that the CPPA was inconsistent with the *Miller* standard on obscenity which requires the Government to prove that the work in question, taken as a whole, appeals to the prurient interest, is patently offensive in light of community standards, and lacks serious literary, artistic, political or scientific value.[90] On this issue, the Supreme Court argued:

> Materials need not appeal to the prurient interest under the CPPA, which proscribes any depiction of sexually explicit activity, no matter how it is presented. It is not necessary, moreover, that the image be patently offensive. Pictures of what appear to be 17-year-olds engaging in sexually explicit activity do not in every case contravene community standards.[91]

The Supreme Court concluded that the government had failed to show a causal link between computer-generated images of child pornography and harm to actual children. Supreme Court Justice Anthony M. Kennedy, delivering the judgment of the Supreme Court, stated:

> First Amendment freedoms are most in danger when the government seeks to control thought or to justify its laws for that impermissible end. The right to think is the beginning of freedom, and speech must be protected from the government because speech is the beginning of thought.[92]

Lord Justice Kennedy gave the example of a Renaissance painting depicting a scene from classical mythology, a 'picture' that 'appears to be, of a minor engaging in sexually explicit conduct' being covered by the wording used in section 2256. According to Justice Kennedy, the statute would also prohibit Hollywood movies, filmed without any child actors, if a jury believes an actor 'appears to be' a minor engaging in 'actual or simulated … sexual intercourse' under section 2256(2).[93]

Rehnquist CJ, dissenting stated:

> The aim of ensuring the enforceability of our Nation's child pornography laws is a compelling one. The CPPA is targeted to this aim by extending the definition of child pornography to reach computer-generated images that are virtually indistinguishable

---

89 *Ashcroft, Attorney General, et al. v. Free Speech Coalition et al.* 535 U.S. 234 (US Supreme Court, 2002), 198 F3d 1083, 16 April 2002, No. 00–795. See further, *Broadrick v. Oklahoma*, 413 U.S. 601 (1973), 612.

90 *Miller v. California* (1973) 413 U.S. 15, at 24.

91 *Ashcroft v. Free Speech Coalition* (00-795) 198 F3d 1083, affirmed.

92 Ibid.

93 But note S.Rep. No. 104–358, pt. IV(C), at 21 '[The CPPA] does not, and is not intended to, apply to a depiction produced using *adults* engaging i[n] sexually explicit conduct, even where a depicted individual may appear to be a minor.'

> from real children engaged in sexually explicit conduct.[94] The statute need not be read to do any more than precisely this, which is not offensive to the First Amendment.[95]

To reinforce his view, Rehnquist CJ referred to Judge Ferguson's dissenting judgment at the Ninth Circuit that 'the CPPA merely extends the existing prohibitions on "real" child pornography to a narrow class of computer-generated pictures easily mistaken for real photographs of real children.'[96]

It should be stressed that the decision of the Supreme Court is limited to the constitutionality of §§ 2256(8)(B) and 2256(8)(D); the CPPA definitions which prohibit possessing and distributing images which were not produced using real children.[97] The ruling does not affect other provisions dealing with child pornography. These are addressed later in this chapter.

POST-FREE SPEECH COALITION CASES AND POLICY

> At risk are the prosecutions against child pornographers who are frequently child molesters ... How can we protect our children when the prosecution will have to prove beyond a reasonable doubt that a child pornographer possesses a picture of a real child and not a computer generated picture.[98]

---

94 He quoted the decision of the Court of Appeals for the First Circuit to support this point: '[T]he legislative record, which makes plain that the [CPPA] was intended to target only a narrow class of images–visual depictions "which are virtually indistinguishable to unsuspecting viewers from unretouched photographs of actual children engaging in identical sexual conduct".' *U.S. v. Hilton*, 167 F3d 61, 72 (1999) (quoting S. Rep. No. 104–358, pt. I, p. 7 (1996)). Rehnquist CJ also quoted Judge Ferguson who similarly dissented: 'From reading the legislative history, it becomes clear that the CPPA merely extends the existing prohibitions on "real" child pornography to a narrow class of computer-generated pictures easily mistaken for real photographs of real children.' *Free Speech Coalition v. Reno*, 198 F3d 1083, 1102 (9th Circuit 1999).

95 *Ashcroft v. Free Speech Coalition* (00-795) 198 F3d 1083, affirmed.

96 *Free Speech Coalition v. Reno*, 198 F3d 1083, 1102 (9th Circuit 1999).

97 See, for example, *U.S. v. Pearl*, 324 F3d 1210, 1213 (10th Cir. 2003) (noting that 18 U.S.C. § 2256 contained both constitutional and unconstitutional definitions of 'child pornography'), cert. denied, 156 L. Ed. 2d 616, 123 S. Ct. 2591, 2003 U.S. LEXIS 4722, 2003 WL 21184530 (U.S. June 16, 2003) (No. 02-10597); *U.S. v. Kelly*, 314 F3d 908, 911 (7th Cir.), cert. denied, 155 L. Ed. 2d 829, 123 S. Ct. 1923 (2003); *U.S. v. Richardson*, 304 [*1142] F3d 1061, 1063–4 (11th Cir. 2002), cert. denied, 537 U.S. 1138, 154 L. Ed. 2d 832, 123 S. Ct. 930 (2003); *U.S. v. Hersh*, 297 F3d 1233, 1254 n.31 (11th Cir. 2002), cert. denied, 537 U.S. 1217, 154 L. Ed. 2d 1071, 123 S. Ct. 1319 (2003); *U.S. v. Bender*, 290 F3d 1279, 1282 n.2 (11th Cir.), cert. denied, 537 U.S. 1037, 154 L. Ed. 2d 457, 123 S. Ct. 571 (2002).

98 Hon. Lamar S. Smith, Chairman of the Subcommittee, Enhancing Child Protection Laws after the April 16, 2002 Supreme Court Decision, *Ashcroft v. Free Speech Coalition*. Hearing Before the Subcommittee on Crime, Terrorism, and Homeland Security of the Committee on the Judiciary House of Representatives, One Hundred Seventh Congress Second Session, 1 May 2002, Serial No. 75, at <http://commdocs.house.gov/committees/judiciary/hju79366.000/hju79366_0.HTM>.

Many thought the Supreme Court decision sent out a disturbing message. The US Attorney-General John Ashcroft was the first to criticize the Supreme Court judgment stating at the time that 'the United States Supreme Court has made our ability to prosecute those who produce and possess child pornography immeasurably more difficult.'[99] He accused the Supreme Court of creating a dangerous window of opportunity for child abusers to escape prosecution.[100] US prosecutors were concerned by the prospect that defendants in child pornography related prosecutions would frequently raise the theoretical possibility that rapidly advancing computer imaging technology was involved in the production of the materials, rather than real children, in order to avoid conviction. There was also concern that in any trial prosecutors would have the 'burden of proving beyond a reasonable doubt that the visual depictions at issue involved real children'.[101]

The above-mentioned arguments were raised by a number of defendants in various appeal cases following the Supreme Court decision. However, several appeal courts have considered this issue and concluded that the Supreme Court decision did not establish a broad requirement that the Government present expert testimony to establish that the sexually explicit images in consideration depict real children.[102]

---

99 See Attorney General Transcript, Response to Supreme Court Decision in *Free Speech Coalition v. Ashcroft*, Tuesday, 16 April 2002, at <http://www.usdoj.gov/archive/ag/speeches/2002/041602newsconferenceresponse.htm>.

100 Attorney General Transcript, News Conference with Attorney General John Ashcroft, Topic: Supreme Court decision on child pornography, Justice Department, Washington, DC, 1 May 2002, at <http://www.usdoj.gov/archive/ag/speeches/2002/050102ag-transcriptschildpornography.htm>.

101 *U.S. v. Sims*, 220 F. Supp.2d 1222, 1226–7 (D.N.M. 2002); *U.S. v. Ellyson*, 326 F3d 522, 2003 U.S. App. LEXIS 4720, F3d, 2003 WL 1194332 (4th Cir. Mar. 17, 2003): While there was evidence before Ellyson's jury that some of the depictions in question involved actual children, many of the images that were introduced were not accompanied by testimony concerning the use of actual minors and the jury instructions were given based on the pre-*Free Speech Coalition* definition of child pornography. Had the jury found Ellyson guilty based on these images because they 'appeared to be' a depiction of child pornography, the verdict could not stand under *Free Speech Coalition*. Note also *U.S. v. David Hilton*, Crim. No. 97-78-P-C, Civil No. 02-235-P-C, United States District Court for the District of Maine, 2003 U.S. Dist. LEXIS 4208, 20 March, 2003, Decided.

102 See *U.S. v. Kimler*, 335 F3d 1132, 1142 (10th Cir.), cert. denied, 157 L. Ed. 2d 759, 124 S. Ct. 945, 2003 U.S. LEXIS 9142, 72 U.S.L.W. 3392 (U.S. Dec. 8, 2003)(No. 03-7285); *U.S. v. Deaton*, 328 F3d 454, 455 (8th Cir. 2003) (*per curiam*) (citing *U.S. v. Vig*, 167 F3d 443, 449–50 (8th Cir. 1999)); *U.S. v. Hall*, 312 F3d 1250, 1260 (11th Cir. 2002), cert. denied, 155 L. Ed. 2d 502, 123 S. Ct. 1646 (2003); *U.S. v. Slanina*, 359 F3d 356, 357 (5th Cir. 2004); *U.S. v. Fuller*, 77 Fed. Appx. 371, 2003 WL 22331999 (6th Cir. 2003). Note also that in an opinion that was subsequently withdrawn, the First Circuit held that expert evidence was required to show that downloaded images of child pornography are images of real children. *U.S. v. Hilton*, 363 F3d 58, 63–6 (1st Cir. 2004), withdrawn by *U.S. v. Hilton*, 2004 U.S. App. LEXIS 19528 (1st Cir. Sept. 20, 2004). Note further *U.S. v. Farrelly*, 389 F3d 649, 653–4 (6th Cir. 2004).

In *U.S. v. Kimler*,[103] the defendant was convicted of one count of receiving or distributing, by computer, images of minors engaged in sexually explicit conduct in violation of 18 U.S.C. §2252(a)(2), one count of possession of such images in violation of 18 U.S.C. §2252(a)(4)(B), and four counts of distribution of such images in violation of 18 U.S.C. §2252(a)(2). Kimler was sentenced to 87 months' imprisonment and three years of supervised release. In his defence, Kimler argued that the Supreme Court decision required either direct evidence of the identity of children in the proscribed images or expert testimony that the images depicted are those of real children rather than computer-generated 'virtual' children. There was no evidence in this case identifying the children depicted in the images who were the subject of the charges. The issue for the Tenth Circuit was whether the Supreme Court decision in *Free Speech Coalition* 'laid down a categorical rule of evidence applicable to cases such as this, requiring expert testimony in all instances to prove that proscribed depictions of children are actually those of real rather than virtual children'.[104]

Kimler's defence cited no authority for this argument, other than *Congressional Findings* that technological advances had made it 'possible to create realistic images of children who do not exist'.[105] Kimler's defence also relied upon the representations made by the government to the Supreme Court that it has become difficult to meet the burden of proof in cases involving prohibited images because of such technological advances. The Tenth Circuit disputed this argument and found this hypothesis implausible by stating:

> What Kimler does not note, however, is direct language by the Court that imaging technology might be good and getting better, but it is implausible to conclude that it has actually arrived at the point of indistinguishability … If virtual images were identical to illegal child pornography, the illegal images would be driven from the market by the indistinguishable substitutes. Few pornographers would risk prosecution by abusing real children if fictional, computerized images would suffice.[106]

Dismissing the appeal, the Tenth Circuit concluded:

> *Free Speech Coalition*, did not establish a broad, categorical requirement that, in every case on the subject, absent direct evidence of identity, an expert must testify that the unlawful image is of a real child. Juries are still capable of distinguishing between real and virtual images; and admissibility remains within the province of the sound discretion of the trial judge.[107]

103 *U.S. v. Kimler*, 335 F3d 1132, 1142 (10th Cir. 2003), cert. denied, 157 L. Ed. 2d 759, 124 S. Ct. 945, 2003 U.S. LEXIS 9142, 72 U.S.L.W. 3392 (U.S. Dec. 8, 2003)(No. 03-7285).

104 Ibid.

105 *Free Speech Coalition*, 535 U.S. at 240.

106 *U.S. v. Kimler*, 335 F3d 1132, 1142 (10th Cir. 2003), cert. denied, 157 L. Ed. 2d 759.

107 Ibid.

Subsequently, it was agreed by the Fifth Circuit in *U.S. v. Slanina*[108] that the Government was not required to present any additional evidence or expert testimony to meet its burden of proof to show that the images downloaded by the defendant depicted real children, and not virtual children. The Fifth Circuit in *Slanina* argued that the District Court, as the trier of fact, was capable of reviewing the evidence to determine whether the Government met its burden to show that the images depicted real children.

A similar position was taken by the Eight Circuit in *U.S. v. Deaton*,[109] in which the defendant argued on appeal that the District Court committed plain error in failing to consider the Supreme Court's decision in *Ashcroft v. Free Speech Coalition*, as there was no proof offered at trial that the images on his computer depicted actual children. In line with *Kimler*, the Eighth Circuit concluded:

> In this case, the jury was not instructed that it could find Deaton guilty if the images found on his computer 'appeared' to be child pornography. Instead, the jury was instructed that it needed to find that production of the images involved the use of a minor. Further, we have previously upheld a jury's conclusion that real children were depicted even where the images themselves were the only evidence the government presented on the subject.[110]

The Eleventh Circuit agreed with *Kimler* and *Deaton* in its ruling in *U.S. v. Hall*,[111] in which the defendant was sentenced to 97 months' imprisonment for possession and distribution of child pornography offences, and three years' supervised release. On appeal, Hall claimed the District Court's jury instructions were erroneous in the light of *Ashcroft v. Free Speech Coalition*. The prosecution conceded that the jury instruction was erroneous because it included the words 'or appears to be', and that the error was plain. However, it was also submitted that the error did not affect Hall's substantial rights, and that affirming Hall's convictions would not 'seriously affect the fairness, integrity or public reputation of judicial proceedings'.[112] The Eleventh Circuit agreed as

108 *U.S. v. Slanina*, No. 03-20181 c/w 03-20447, United States Court of Appeals for the Fifth Circuit, 2004 U.S. App. LEXIS 1246, 28 January 2004, Filed; Appeals from the United States District Court for the Southern District of Texas. USDC No. H-00-CR-75-1. Sam R Cummings, US District Judge. *U.S. v. Slanina*, 313 F3d 891, 2002 U.S. App. LEXIS 24271 (5th Cir. Tex., 2002).

109 *U.S. v. Deaton*, 328 F3d 454, 2003 U.S. App. LEXIS 8751 (8th Cir. 2003) (*per curiam*).

110 Ibid. See further, *U.S. v. Vig*, 167 F3d 443, 449–50 (8th Cir.) (Government, as part of affirmative case, was not required to negate unsupported speculation that images may have been computer-generated or other than what they appeared to be), cert. denied, 528 U.S. 859, 145 L. Ed. 2d 125, 120 S. Ct. 146 (1999).

111 *U.S. v. Hall*, 312 F3d 1250, 1260 (11th Cir. 2002), cert. denied, 155 L. Ed. 2d 502, 123 S. Ct. 1646 (2003).

112 Ibid.

> (1) the evidence established that the children depicted in the pictures introduced at trial were actual children and (2) no one ever claimed, or even hinted, that the images were of virtual children.[113]

The Court concluded that a reasonable jury could not have found that the images were of virtual children created by computer imaging technology as opposed to actual children.[114] Furthermore, in *U.S. v. Farrelly*[115] the Sixth Circuit explicitly rejected 'the suggestion of a heavier burden of proof and held that the presentation of photographs sufficiently demonstrated that pornographic images received by a defendant were of real children to support a conviction.'[116] In this case the government expert could not clearly state whether the sexually explicit images involved real or virtual children. Nevertheless the court thought that the government provided 'sufficient evidence' by showing the images in question to the jury.

A defendant's claim that the government must present extrinsic evidence was more recently rejected in *U.S. v. Irving*[117] as the defendant provided 'no evidence suggesting that the images were not created using actual children'.[118] The Second Circuit stated, 'it does not appear that video technology is so far advanced that a jury is incapable of determining whether a real child was used to make a video.'[119] The Second Circuit therefore ruled that the government did not need to 'present expert testimony proving the children in the unlawful images are in fact real children'.[120] The Court stated:

> Although the Supreme Court noted the possible evidentiary difficulty of distinguishing virtual and actual child pornography, it did not establish a bright-line rule requiring that the government proffer a specific type of proof to show the use of an actual child.[121]

---

113 Ibid. *Kimler* was confirmed in *U.S. v. Sims*, 428 F3d 945; (Tenth Cir. 2005) U.S. App. LEXIS 24143, and also in *U.S. v. Riccardi*, 405 F3d 852; (Tenth Cir. 2005) U.S. App. LEXIS 6631.

114 Note also the above-mentioned case of *U.S. v. Vig*, 167 F3d 443, 449 (8th Cir. 1999) which held that 'the images were viewed by the jury which was in a position to draw its own independent conclusion as to whether real children were depicted'; and *U.S. v. Oakes*, 224 F. Supp. 2d 296, 301–2 (D. Me. 2002) which held based on an examination of the images by the court that the defendant did not meet the standard of establishing 'actual innocence'. See further, Slocum, B.G., 'Virtual Child Pornography: Does It Mean the End of the Child Pornography Exception to the First Amendment?' (2004), 14 *Alb. L.J. Sci. and Tech.* 637.

115 *U.S. v. Farrelly*, 389 F3d 649, 2004 FED App. 0362P (6th Cir. 2004).

116 Buckman, D.F., 'Validity, Construction, and Application of 18 U.S.C.A. § 2252A(a), Proscribing Certain Activities Relating to Material Constituting or Containing Child Pornography', 2 *A.L.R. Fed.* 2d 533.

117 *U.S. v. Irving*, 452 F3d 110; (2nd Cir., 2006) U.S. App. LEXIS 16077.

118 Ibid.

119 Ibid.

120 Ibid.

121 Ibid.

However, the court restricted its decision to cases that present facts similar to that of *Irving*; that is, cases involving video images rather than still images or photographs.

Finally, in *U.S. v. Rodriguez-Pacheco*[122] the First Circuit in agreement with the decision of its sister circuit courts emphasized that the Supreme Court in *Free Speech Coalition* 'did not rule on the nature of the proof the government must produce to demonstrate that an image of a child was of a real child. That argument was not before the Court, which had before it only the issue of the facial constitutionality of the statute.'[123]

US prosecutors are required to prove that the images under consideration are created using real rather than virtual children. However, following from the above-mentioned rulings neither expert testimony nor the identification of actual child victims is required in order to sustain a conviction.[124] Prosecutors can prove that the images involved actual children by examining the images themselves 'where no evidence suggests that the images are anything other than real',[125] or by non-expert testimony. As explained above, the images themselves could be sufficient to support a jury finding[126] that actual children were involved, but in some cases the prosecutors may also rely on expert testimony.[127] Although not obliged to do so, defendants are free to present evidence of their own to the effect that the images involved virtual rather than real children, including expert testimony.[128]

POLICY AND LEGAL DEVELOPMENTS FOLLOWING *ASHCROFT V. FREE SPEECH COALITION*

As a result of the Supreme Court decision, several legislative proposals were introduced[129] to address the issues of child pornography, child abduction and child

---

122 *U.S. v. Rodriguez-Pacheco*, 475 F3d 434; (First Cir. 2007) U.S. App. LEXIS 2497.

123 Ibid.

124 See generally, Kreston, S.S., 'Defeating the Virtual Defense in Child Pornography Prosecutions' (2004), *J. High Tech. L.* 4(49), 60–61.

125 See further, *U.S. v. Harms*, 371 F3d 1208, 1213 (10th Cir. 2004). Note further the more recent case of *U.S. v. Porter*, 184 Fed. Appx. 112 (2d Cir. 2006).

126 See further, *U.S. v. Riccardi*, 405 F3d 852, 870–71 (10th Cir. 2005); and *U.S. v. Cervini*, 379 F3d 987, 993 n.4 (10th Cir. 2004).

127 See for example the case of *U.S. v. Marchand*, 308 F. Supp. 2d 498, 504 (D.N.J. 2004). In this case, law enforcement agents from the United States, England and Brazil provided expert testimony and positively identified by name the children in eight of the pictures under consideration as children whom they had met in person at a time not distant from the age that the child was when he or she was photographed.

128 Note *U.S. v. Nolan*, 818 F.2d 1015 (1st Cir. 1987); and *U.S. v. Rodriguez-Pacheco*, 475 F3d 434; (First Cir. 2007) U.S. App. LEXIS 2497.

129 Note Child Obscenity and Pornography Prevention Act of 2003 (COPPA), H.R. 1161, 108th Cong. (2003); Prosecutorial Remedies and Other Tools to End the Exploitation of Children Today Act of 2003 (PROTECT), Pub. L. No. 108-21, 117 Stat. 650, 678 (current version at 18 U.S.C. § 2252 A(c)) (2000 and Supp. III 2003); Child Obscenity and Pornography

sexual offences within the United States.[130] Almost immediately the former US Attorney General, John Ashcroft, warned that child pornographers and others who exploit children would find little refuge in the Supreme Court decision stating that the government would 'continue to use every available resource to identify, investigate and prosecute child pornography cases to the fullest extent of the law'.[131] Echoing Ashcroft's words, Representative Jeff Miller from Florida attacked the high court for apparently placing 'a higher premium on the expression of paedophiles than on ensuring the psychological, emotional, and mental health of our country's children and society as a whole'.[132] Representative Miller accused the Supreme Court of turning 'its back on its long-standing recognition of the government's compelling interest in protecting American children'. He declared, 'despite the Supreme Court's decision, Congress is not required to, nor will it wait, on harm to our children before legislating against it.'[133]

New legislation to protect children from abuse and exploitation was announced by the Attorney General in May 2002. A press release from the Attorney General's Office stated:

> The protection of virtual child pornography by the Supreme Court threatens the de facto protection of all child pornography. In a world in which virtual images are increasingly indistinguishable from reality, prosecutors are now forced to prove that sexually explicit images involving children were in fact produced through the abuse of children, an extremely difficult task in today's worldwide Internet child pornography market.[134]

The Child Obscenity and Pornography Prevention Bill of 2002[135] proposed several changes to the existing law. First, the legislation proposed to tighten the definition

---

Prevention Act of 2002, H.R. 4623, 107th Cong. (2002); Prosecutorial Remedies and Tools against the Exploitation of Children Today Act of 2002, S. 2520, 107th Cong. (2002).

130 Note the Hearing Before the Subcommittee on Crime, Terrorism, and Homeland Security of the Committee on the Judiciary House of Representatives on *Enhancing Child Protection Laws after the April 16, 2002 Supreme Court Decision, Ashcroft v. Free Speech Coalition*, One Hundred Seventh Congress Second Session May 1, 2002 Serial No. 75, at <http://commdocs.house.gov/committees/judiciary/hju79366.000/hju79366_0.HTM>. Note also Hearing: Stopping Child Pornography: Protecting our Children and the Constitution. 2 October 2002. S.Hrg. 107-974. Serial No. J-107-108. GPO Stock No. 552-070-30170-4.

131 See Attorney General Transcript, Response to Supreme Court Decision in *Free Speech Coalition v. Ashcroft*, Tuesday, 16 April 2002, at <http://www.usdoj.gov/archive/ag/speeches/2002/041602newsconferenceresponse.htm>.

132 Mr Jeff Miller, Supreme Court ruling threatens our children, House of Representatives – 17 April 2002, Page: H1384.

133 Ibid.

134 Attorney General Transcript, News Conference with Attorney General John Ashcroft, Topic: Supreme Court decision on child pornography, Justice Department, Washington, DC, 1 May 2002, at <http://www.usdoj.gov/archive/ag/speeches/2002/050102ag-transcriptschildpornography.htm>.

135 Note, Child Abduction Prevention Act and the Child Obscenity and Pornography Prevention Act of 2003, Hearing before the Subcommittee on Crime, Terrorism, and Homeland Security of the Committee on the Judiciary of the House of Representatives, One Hundred

of 'child pornography', and ensure that child pornography prosecutions would not be barred merely because of the theoretical possibility that the material was created through computer imaging. At the same time, prosecutions that the Supreme Court had held to violate the First Amendment would be prevented. Secondly, the proposed legislation would generally prohibit the production, distribution and possession of any visual depictions, real or virtual, of prepubescent children engaged in sexually explicit conduct. Thirdly, the legislation would create more comprehensive offences prohibiting 'offers to sell or provide', and efforts to obtain child pornography, regardless of whether such depictions were actually provided or received. Finally, the legislation would establish a secure FBI database for identifying child pornography produced with actual children.

The proposed legislation included an affirmative defence that would permit defendants to prove that the images were produced without using real children. The creation of the FBI database of images already known to be of real children would facilitate the prosecution of others found to have those images in possession. The proposed legislation also aimed to encourage greater voluntary reporting of suspected child pornography found by Internet Service Providers on their systems.[136] Representative Mark Foley from Florida, supporting the proposed legislation, stated that the Supreme Court in siding with paedophiles over children, forced them into action. He said:

> Today, united, we begin reversing the damage of that decision. This legislation is a paedophile's worst nightmare. It virtually guarantees we are helping to protect America's children. It doesn't make a difference if the child engaged in sex is real or virtual. In other words, an old simple saying: If it walks like a duck, talks like a duck, it is a duck. The courts obviously didn't have a chance … to see the kind of virtual reality that is on computer terminals today. It's as close to reality as possible.[137]

Representative Foley's comments were echoed by Representative Hon. Lamar Smith who stated:

> Whether we agree or disagree with the Supreme Court, we now have to deal with the consequences of that decision. Based upon the Court's majority opinion, Congress needs to enact legislation that will prohibit all child pornography without limiting works of art and literature that are protected by the First Amendment and have a redeeming social value … Without amending the current law, this country faces a proliferation of child pornography.[138]

Eighth Congress, First Session on H.R. 1104 and H.R. 1161, 11 March 2003, at <http://commdocs.house.gov/committees/judiciary/hju85642.000/hju85642_0.htm>.

136 See US Department of Justice Fact Sheet: Preventing Child Pornography, A New Legislative Proposal, 1 May 2002.

137 Attorney General Transcript, News Conference with Attorney General John Ashcroft and Majority Whip Delay, Senators Sessions and Hutchinson, and House Representatives Foley, Smith and Pomeroy – Topic: Supreme Court decision on child pornography, Justice Department, Washington, DC, 1 May 2002.

138 [Chairman of the Subcommittee], Enhancing Child Protection Laws after the 16 April 2002 Supreme Court Decision, *Ashcroft v. Free Speech Coalition*. Hearing Before

President Bush also supported this legislative initiative, calling upon the US Congress to pass the Child Obscenity and Pornography Prevention Bill in October 2002.[139] This bill was passed by the House during the 107th Congress as HR 4623, but the Senate did not approve it. Representative Smith later introduced a similar bill during the 108th Congress as HR 1161: the Child Obscenity and Pornography Prevention Bill of 2003. Representative Smith later offered the language of this bill as an amendment to HR 1104, as the Prosecutorial Remedies and Other Tools to End the Exploitation of Children Today ('Protect') Bill 2003.

THE PROTECT ACT 2003

> The Supreme Court's 1982 *Ferber v. New York* decision holding that child pornography was not protected drove child pornography off the shelves of adult bookstores. Congressional action is necessary now to ensure that open and notorious trafficking in such materials does not reappear, and even increase, on the Internet.[140]

The Protect Act was enacted in April 2003[141] partly in response to the Supreme Court decision in *Ashcroft v. Free Speech Coalition*.[142] It was introduced in the US Senate in January 2003,[143] and passed the Senate by a vote of 84 to zero in February 2003.[144] The House of Representatives later moved to introduce a related bill entitled the Child Obscenity and Pornography Prevention Bill of 2003 in March 2003.[145] The Bill passed by a vote of 410 to 14.[146] A compromised version of the 2003 Protect Bill, with its amended sentencing provisions,[147] was introduced, and

---

the Subcommittee on Crime, Terrorism, and Homeland Security of the Committee on the Judiciary House of Representatives, One Hundred Seventh Congress Second Session, 1 May 2002 Serial No. 75, at <http://commdocs.house.gov/committees/judiciary/hju79366.000/hju79366_0.HTM>.

139 Office of the Press Secretary, President Increases Federal Efforts to Promote Online Safety, Remarks by the President on Children's Online Safety, 23 October 2002.

140 Title V – Obscenity and Pornography, Subtitle A–Child Obscenity and Pornography Prevention of the Protect Act 2003, section 501, para. 15.

141 S. 151, 108th Cong., 1st Sess. (2003). For a good summary of the legislative history see Dugan, K., 'Regulating What's Not Real: Federal Regulation in the Aftermath of *Ashcroft v. Free Speech Coalition*' (2004), 48 *Saint Louis University Law Journal* 1063 (Spring).

142 535 U.S. 234, 152 L. Ed. 2d 403, 122 S. Ct. 1389 (2002).

143 Cong. Rec. S230 (daily ed. Jan. 13, 2003).

144 149 CONG. REC. S2587–90 (daily ed. Feb. 24, 2003).

145 Cong. Rec. H1641 (daily ed. March 5, 2003).

146 149 CONG. REC. S5115 (daily ed. Apr.10, 2003).

147 See United States Sentencing Commission, Report to the Congress: Downward Departures from the Federal Sentencing Guidelines (in response to section 401(m) of Public Law 108–21), October 2003. See section G of the report in relation to the Protect Act, and Williams, E., 'Construction and Application of United States Sentencing Guideline § 2G2.1 et seq., Pertaining to Child Pornography', 145 *A.L.R. Fed.* 481. Note the following cases which involve constitutional challenges to sentencing guidelines involving child pornography cases: *U.S. v. Morell*, 429 F3d 1161 C.A.8 (Ark.), 2005; *U.S. v. Detwiler*, 338 F.Supp.2d 1166 D. Or., 2004.

passed the House on 10 April 2003 by a vote of 400–25 and the Senate by 98–0. The President signed the bill into law on 30 April 2003, declaring:

> The new law confronts an evil that is too often a cause of child abuse and abduction in America – the evil of child pornography. In the past, prosecutors have been hindered by not having all the tools needed to prosecute criminals who create child pornography. Under the Protect Act, we've seen images of children, even those created with computer technology, will now be illegal, giving prosecutors an important new tool. Obscene images of children, no matter how they are made, incite abuse, raise the dangers to children and will not be tolerated in America.[148]

According to Congressman Orrin Hatch, the Chairman of the Judiciary Committee, the Act strikes a necessary balance between the First Amendment and the Nation's critically important interest in protecting children.[149] Congressman Hatch claimed that technology had advanced so far that even experts often cannot say with absolute certainty that an image is real or virtual and computer-generated. For this reason the Act permits a prosecution to proceed when images include persons who appear virtually indistinguishable from actual minors, and even when this occurs, the accused is afforded a complete affirmative defence by showing that the images in question did not involve a minor.

The Congressional findings of the Protect Act[150] state that technology had advanced since the Supreme Court decided *Ferber* in 1982, and that at that time it was not possible to generate depictions of children that were indistinguishable from depictions of real children by using computer technology, nor was it possible to create composite images (pseudo-photographs) by using parts of images of real children. According to the Congressional findings, 'technological advances since *Ferber* have led many criminal defendants to suggest that the images of child pornography they possess are not those of real children, insisting that the government prove beyond a reasonable doubt that the images are not computer-generated. Such challenges increased significantly after the decision of the Supreme Court in *Ashcroft v. Free Speech Coalition*.'[151] It was further stated that the impact of the Supreme Court decision on the US Government's ability to prosecute child pornography offenders was already evident:[152]

> The Ninth Circuit has seen a significant adverse effect on prosecutions since the 1999 Ninth Circuit Court of Appeals decision in *Free Speech Coalition*. After that decision, prosecutions generally have been brought in the Ninth Circuit only in the most clear-cut cases in which the government can specifically identify the child in the depiction

148 President Signs PROTECT Act: President's Remarks Upon Signing of S. 151, the Protect Act, Office of the Press Secretary, 30 April 2003, at <http://www.whitehouse.gov/news/releases/2003/04/20030430-6.html>.

149 Mr Hatch, 1/13/2003, CR S236-237 at <http://thomas.loc.gov/cgi-bin/query/R?r108:FLD001:S00237>.

150 Title V – Obscenity and Pornography, Subtitle A – Child Obscenity and Pornography Prevention of the Protect Act 2003, section 501, para. 4.

151 Ibid., para. 7.

152 Ibid., para. 9.

> or otherwise identify the origin of the image. This is a fraction of meritorious child pornography cases. The National Center for Missing and Exploited Children testified that, in light of the Supreme Court's affirmation of the Ninth Circuit decision, prosecutors in various parts of the country have expressed concern about the continued viability of previously indicted cases as well as declined potentially meritorious prosecutions.[153]

It was further claimed that since the Supreme Court's decision in *Free Speech Coalition*,

> defendants in child pornography cases have almost universally raised the contention that the images in question could be virtual, thereby requiring the government, in nearly every child pornography prosecution, to find proof that the child is real. Some of these defence efforts have already been successful. In addition, the number of prosecutions being brought has been significantly and adversely affected as the resources required to be dedicated to each child pornography case now are significantly higher than ever before.[154]

An analysis of post-*Free Speech Coalition* cases indicates that this speculative observation is not borne out by the evidence, as previously discussed. The appeal courts have demonstrated their willingness and capacity to address defence contentions that images are virtual.[155] There was, moreover, no significant visible decrease in the number of child pornography convictions following the decision. In fact, as Slocum observed, the

> government has been quite successful since the *Free Speech* decision in meeting its burden of establishing that images depict actual children … Even more significantly, although the First Circuit has held that such evidence by itself is insufficient to meet the government's burden of proof, every other circuit that has considered the issue has held that the government can meet its burden of proof by merely introducing the images into evidence and allowing the factfinder to conclude that the images depict actual children.[156]

Regardless of these appeal decisions, the Congressional findings predicted that in the absence of congressional action, the difficulties in enforcing the child pornography laws would continue to grow increasingly worse.

> The mere prospect that the technology exists to create composite or computer-generated depictions that are indistinguishable from depictions of real children will allow defendants who possess images of real children to escape prosecution; for it threatens to create a reasonable doubt in every case of computer images even when a real child

---

153 Ibid., para. 9.

154 Ibid., para. 10.

155 *U.S. v. Kimler*, 335 F3d 1132, 1142 (10th Cir.), cert. denied, 157 L. Ed. 2d 759, 124 S. Ct. 945, 2003 U.S. LEXIS 9142, 72 U.S.L.W. 3392 (U.S. Dec. 8, 2003) (No. 03-7285); *U.S. v. Deaton*, 328 F3d 454, 2003 U.S. App. LEXIS 8751 (8th Cir. 2003) (*per curiam*); *U.S. v. Hall*, 312 F3d 1250, 1260 (11th Cir. 2002), cert. denied, 155 L. Ed. 2d 502, 123 S. Ct. 1646 (2003).

156 Slocum, B.G., 'Virtual Child Pornography: Does It Mean the End of the Child Pornography Exception to the First Amendment?' (2004), 14 *Alb. L.J. Sci. and Tech.* 637.

> was abused. This threatens to render child pornography laws that protect real children unenforceable. Moreover, imposing an additional requirement that the Government prove beyond a reasonable doubt that the defendant knew that the image was in fact a real child – as some courts have done – threatens to result in the de facto legalization of the possession, receipt, and distribution of child pornography for all except the original producers of the material.[157]

The following section outlines US federal child pornography laws as amended by the Protect Act 2003.

US FEDERAL CHILD PORNOGRAPHY LAWS AS AMENDED BY THE PROTECT ACT 2003

The Protect Act 2003 made several amendments to the child pornography provisions of Chapter 10 of the US Federal Code entitled *Sexual exploitation and other abuse of children*[158] which includes child pornography related offences. In its original incarnation the 1978 Protection of Children against Sexual Exploitation Act did not use the term 'child pornography' and instead criminalized visual depictions of minors engaging in sexually explicit conduct. In the original version, the use of the word 'minors' was a reference to 'real children'. However, as explained below, the current provisions of Chapter 10 provide a wider definition for 'child pornography'.

Defining Child Pornography

Section 2256(1) defines a child (minor) as any person under the age of 18 years. The definition of 'sexually explicit conduct' provided within section 2256(2) of title 18, United States Code, is amended to read as follows:

> (2) (A) Except as provided in subparagraph (B), 'sexually explicit conduct' means actual or simulated –
> (i) sexual intercourse, including genital-genital, oral-genital, anal-genital, or oral-anal, whether between persons of the same or opposite sex;
> (ii) bestiality;
> (iii) masturbation;
> (iv) sadistic or masochistic abuse; or
> (v) lascivious exhibition of the genitals or pubic area of any person.

157 Title V – Obscenity and Pornography, Subtitle A – Child Obscenity and Pornography Prevention of the Protect Act 2003, section 501, para. 13.

158 For a detailed history of this chapter of the US Federal Code see Buckman, D.F., 'Validity, Construction, and Application of 18 U.S.C.A. § 2252A(a), Proscribing Certain Activities Relating to Material Constituting or Containing Child Pornography', 2 *A.L.R. Fed.* 2d 533.

Subparagraph (B) of section 2256(2) provides a different definition of 'sexually explicit conduct' within the context of computer-generated images as referred to in 2256(8)(B):

> (B) For purposes of subsection 8(B) of this section, 'sexually explicit conduct' means –
> (i) graphic sexual intercourse, including genital-genital, oral-genital, anal-genital, or oral-anal, whether between persons of the same or opposite sex, or lascivious simulated sexual intercourse where the genitals, breast, or pubic area of any person is exhibited;
> (ii) graphic or lascivious simulated;
> (I) bestiality;
> (II) masturbation; or
> (III) sadistic or masochistic abuse; or
> (iii) graphic or simulated lascivious exhibition of the genitals or pubic area of any person.

The meaning of producing of child pornography includes producing, directing, manufacturing, issuing, publishing or advertising under section 2256(3). 'Visual depiction' includes undeveloped film and videotape, and data stored on computer disk or by electronic means which is capable of conversion into a visual image under section 2256(5).

Section 502 of the Protect Act 2003, entitled *Improvements to prohibition on virtual child pornography*, amended section 2256(8) of title 18 of the United States Code which provides a definition for child pornography, so that the current version reads as follows:

> 2256(8) 'child pornography' means any visual depiction, including any photograph, film, video, picture, or computer or computer-generated image or picture, whether made or produced by electronic, mechanical, or other means, of sexually explicit conduct, where –
>
> (A) the production of such visual depiction involves the use of a minor engaging in sexually explicit conduct;
> (B) *such visual depiction is a digital image, computer image, or computer-generated image that is, or is indistinguishable from, that of a minor engaging in sexually explicit conduct*;[159] or
> (C) such visual depiction has been created, adapted, or modified to appear that an identifiable minor is engaging in sexually explicit conduct.[160]

159 Emphasis added; this part has been added by section 502 of the Protect Act 2003. Note that this subsection used to include the following wording: '*such visual depiction is, or appears to be, of a minor engaging in sexually explicit conduct*'. However, a ban on sexually explicit images that appeared to depict minors, but were not produced using minors, as child pornography under 18 USCS §2256(8)(B) is unconstitutionally overbroad since it proscribes speech which is neither actual child pornography nor obscene and thus abridges the freedom to engage in substantial amount of lawful speech. See *Ashcroft v. Free Speech Coalition*, 122 S Ct 1389 (2002, US) 152 L Ed 2d.

160 Note for example *U.S. v. Fox*, 248 F3d 394 (5th Cir. 2001).

The definition provided within section 2256(8)(B) is intended to be narrower than the definition contained in the CPPA which was ultimately struck down by the Supreme Court. The Protect Act version relies on the new word 'indistinguishable' to 'cure the constitutional defects found by the Supreme Court, and to try, once again, to extend the ban to virtual child pornography'.[161]

Furthermore, an identifiable minor under section 2256(9) means a person:

> (A)(i)(I) who was a minor at the time the visual depiction was created, adapted, or modified; or
> (II) whose image as a minor was used in creating, adapting, or modifying the visual depiction; and
> (ii) who is recognizable as an actual person by the person's face, likeness, or other distinguishing characteristic, such as a unique birthmark or other recognizable feature; and
> (B) shall not be construed to require proof of the actual identity of the identifiable minor.

Section 2256 is also amended by the addition of two new paragraphs to provide explanations on the meaning of 'graphic' and 'indistinguishable':

> Section 2256(10) – 'graphic', when used with respect to a depiction of sexually explicit conduct, means that a viewer can observe any part of the genitals or pubic area of any depicted person or animal during any part of the time that the sexually explicit conduct is being depicted; and
>
> Section 2256(11) – the term 'indistinguishable' used with respect to a depiction, means virtually indistinguishable, in that the depiction is such that an ordinary person viewing the depiction would conclude that the depiction is of an actual minor engaged in sexually explicit conduct. This definition does not apply to depictions that are drawings, cartoons, sculptures, or paintings depicting minors or adults.

Child Pornography Offences under Section 2252A

Offences involving child pornography are included in 18 USCS § 2252A.[162] This section, entitled *Certain activities relating to material constituting or containing child pornography*, includes various possession, distribution and making offences which are similar to those provided under the Protection of Children Act 1978 in England and Wales.

---

161 Buckman, D.F., 'Validity, Construction, and Application of 18 U.S.C.A. § 2252A(a), Proscribing Certain Activities Relating to Material Constituting or Containing Child Pornography', 2 *A.L.R. Fed.* 2d 533.

162 For a detailed assessment see Buckman, D.F., 'Validity, Construction, and Application of 18 U.S.C.A. § 2252A(a), Proscribing Certain Activities Relating to Material Constituting or Containing Child Pornography', 2 *A.L.R. Fed.* 2d 533; and Parker, LJ, 'Validity, Construction, and Application of Federal Enactments Proscribing Obscenity and Child Pornography or Access Thereto on the Internet' (2005), 7 *A.L.R. Fed.* 2d 1.

If a person knowingly mails, or transports or ships in interstate or foreign commerce by any means, including by computer, any child pornography (§ 2252A(a)(1)); or knowingly[163] receives or distributes (§ 2252A(a)(2)) any child pornography (or any material that contains child pornography)[164] that has been mailed, or shipped or transported in interstate or foreign commerce by any means, including by computer (§ 2252A(a)(2)(A)); or knowingly reproduces any child pornography for distribution through the mail, or in interstate or foreign commerce by any means, including by computer (§ 2252A(a)(3)(A)) any material or purported material in a manner that reflects the belief, or that is intended to cause another to believe, that the material or purported material is, or contains …

(i) an obscene visual depiction of a minor engaging in sexually explicit conduct; or
(ii) a visual depiction of an actual minor engaging in sexually explicit conduct …

will be guilty of an offence under the above sections.

Pandering Offence

Similarly, section 2252A(a)(3)(B) includes the pandering provisions[165] and criminalizes knowingly advertising, promoting, presenting, distributing or soliciting through the mail the above-mentioned content.

The pandering provisions have been subject to constitutional review and in *U.S. v. Williams*[166] the Eleventh Circuit decided that these provisions are substantially overbroad and vague and therefore facially unconstitutional in violation of the First Amendment. In *Williams*, the defendant advertised pictures of himself with his daughter for swapping through an Internet chatroom. During appeal, the Eleventh Circuit was concerned about the regulation of advertised speech related to the illegal content, and argued that 'the First Amendment plainly protects speech

---

163 See for example *U.S. v. Matthews*, 209 F3d 338, 28 Media L. Rep. (BNA) 1673 (4th Cir. 2000) which established that the prosecution need to prove that the defendant was aware of both the images' sexually explicit nature and their depiction of minors.

164 § 2252A(a)(2)(B). Note for example *U.S. v. Bach*, 400 F3d 622 (8th Cir. 2005), cert. denied, 126 S. Ct. 243 (U.S. 2005).

165 The term pandering is explained in a footnote in *U.S. v. Williams*, 444 F3d 1286; 2006 U.S. App. LEXIS 8384; 19 Fla. L. Weekly Fed. C 418, and it is stated that 'as a legal concept, pandering is most commonly associated with prostitution. In that context, pandering provisions are statutes penalizing various acts by intermediaries who engage in the commercial exploitation of prostitution and are aimed at those who, as agents, promote prostitution rather than against the prostitutes themselves.' The Court noted that in some instances, the term is applied by 'Congress and the courts to the promotion of obscenity'. See, for example, 39 U.S.C. § 3008 (prohibiting pandering advertisements of sexually provocative materials by mail), *Ginzburg v. United States*, 383 U.S. 463, 86 S. Ct. 942, 16 L. Ed. 2d 31 (1966) (considering obscene nature of erotically advertised publications). Congress has characterized both the child pornography regulation at issue in this case (18 U.S.C. 2252A(a)(3)(B)) and its unconstitutional predecessor (18 U.S.C. § 2256(8)(D) (1996)) as 'pandering' provisions'.

166 *U.S. v. Williams*, 444 F3d 1286; 2006 U.S. App. LEXIS 8384; 19 Fla. L. Weekly Fed. C 418.

advocating or encouraging or approving of otherwise illegal activity, so long as it does not rise to "fighting word" status.[167] Thus, the non-commercial, non-inciteful promotion of illegal child pornography, even if repugnant, is protected speech under the First Amendment.'[168] The Court found

> particularly objectionable the criminalization of speech that 'reflects the belief' that materials constitute obscene synthetic or 'real' child pornography. Because no regard is given to the actual nature or even the existence of the underlying material, liability can be established based purely on promotional speech reflecting the deluded belief that real children are depicted in legal child erotica, or on promotional or solicitous speech reflecting that an individual finds certain depictions of children lascivious.[169]

Further, the Court stated that 'under the Protect Act pandering provision, mere talk is all that is required for liability and that does not square with Supreme Court First Amendment jurisprudence.'[170]

The Court accepted that the government had a compelling interest to protect children and was therefore justified in introducing legislation such as the Protect Act 2003, but held that the pandering provisions went further than necessary and abridged 'the freedom to engage in a substantial amount of lawful speech'.[171] The Court explained that the government's reasoning for such criminalization had 'no justification in the Supreme Court's First Amendment precedents'.[172] The Court further acknowledged that the decision of the Supreme Court in *Free Speech Coalition* gave the Congress 'ample authority to enact legislation that allows the Government to accomplish its legitimate goal of curbing child abuse without placing an unacceptably heavy burden on protected speech',[173] but the pandering provision reflected 'a persistent disregard of time-honoured and constitutionally-mandated principles relating to the Government's regulation of free speech and its obligation to provide criminal defendants due process'.[174] The Court reversed Williams' conviction for the pandering offence but affirmed his sentence of 60 months' imprisonment for possession of child pornography.

A petition for certiorari was filed by the Department of Justice with the Supreme Court in November 2006[175] arguing that the Eleventh Circuit's decision

---

167 See *Free Speech Coalition*, 535 U.S. at 253, 122 S. Ct. at 1403 (citing *Brandenburg v. Ohio*, 395 U.S. 444, 447, 89 S. Ct. 1827, 23 L. Ed. 2d 430 (1969) (holding advocacy of racist violence protected speech)). See also *Kingsley Int'l Pictures Corp. v. Regents of the Univ of State of N.Y.*, 360 U.S. 684, 79 S. Ct. 1362, 3 L. Ed. 2d 1512 (1959) (holding advocacy of immoral activities was protected speech).

168 *U.S. v. Williams*, 444 F3d 1286; 2006 U.S. App. LEXIS 8384; 19 Fla. L. Weekly Fed. C 418.

169 Ibid. Note 18 U.S.C. § § 2252A(a)(3)(B)(ii), 2256(2)(A)(v).

170 Ibid.

171 Ibid.

172 Ibid.

173 Ibid.

174 Ibid.

175 Rehearing, *en banc*, denied by *U.S. v. Williams*, 186 Fed. Appx. 983, 2006 U.S. App. LEXIS 25218 (11th Cir. Fla., 2006). Petition for certiorari filed at, 11/17/2006. See further, <http://

was incorrect. The Department of Justice argued in its petition that the Court of Appeals' 'misguided invalidation of the law undermines Congress's effort to protect children by eliminating the widespread market in child pornography'. The Supreme Court agreed to review the case and the petition for certiorari was granted in March 2007.[176]

Selling, Distribution and Possession Offences

Returning to the provisions of the Protect Act 2003, under section 2252A(a)(4)(A), whoever knowingly[177] sells or possesses with the intent to sell any child pornography;[178] or knowingly sells or possesses with the intent to sell any child pornography (2252A(a)(4)(B))[179] would commit an offence. Under section 2252A(a)(6), whoever knowingly distributes, offers, sends or provides to a minor any visual depiction, including any photograph, film, video, picture or computer-generated image or picture, whether made or produced by electronic, mechanical or other means, where such visual depiction is, or appears to be,[180] of a minor engaging in sexually explicit conduct …

(A) that has been mailed, shipped, or transported in interstate or foreign commerce by any means, including by computer;
(B) that was produced using materials that have been mailed, shipped, or transported in interstate or foreign commerce by any means, including by computer; or

---

www.usdoj.gov/osg/briefs/2006/2pet/7pet/2006-0694.pet.aa.html> for the text of the petition.

176 *U.S. v. Williams* (Supreme Court Docket No. 06-694) at <http://www.supremecourtus.gov/docket/06-694.htm>. The question presented to the Supreme Court is whether section 2252A(a)(3)(B) is overly broad and impermissibly vague, and thus facially unconstitutional.

177 The Court in *U.S. v. Grimes*, 244 F3d 375, 56 Fed. R. Evid. Serv 1048 (5th Cir. 2001) required the prosecution to establish knowledge both in relation to the sexually explicit nature of the conduct and age of persons depicted in the materials.

178 '… in the special maritime and territorial jurisdiction of the United States, or on any land or building owned by, leased to, or otherwise used by or under the control of the United States Government, or in the Indian country' (as defined in section 1151).

179 '… that has been mailed, or shipped or transported in interstate or foreign commerce by any means, including by computer, or that was produced using materials that have been mailed, or shipped or transported in interstate or foreign commerce by any means, including by computer.' Note *U.S. v. Grimes*, 244 F3d 375, 56 Fed. R. Evid. Serv 1048 (5th Cir. 2001) which held that 'postproduction computer alterations of visual depictions of unclothed girls that placed pixel blocks over their genital areas did not take depictions outside reach of child pornography statute prohibiting knowing possession of visual depictions whose production involved use of a minor engaging in sexually explicit conduct and which depict such conduct; depictions remained a lascivious exhibition.' Menninger, L.A., II, 'Cyberporn: Transmission of Images by Computer as Obscene, Harmful to Minors or Child Pornography' (2007), 61 *AMJUR POF 3d* 51 (updated in January 2007).

180 '18 USCS § 2252A's extension of prohibition on child pornography to visual depictions that "appear to be" or "convey the impression of" minors engaging in sexually explicit conduct is fully consistent with First Amendment; § 2252A is neither unconstitutionally vague nor overbroad.' See *U.S. v. Fox*, 248 F3d 394 (5th Cir. 2001).

(C) which distribution, offer, sending, or provision is accomplished using the mails or by transmitting or causing to be transmitted any wire communication in interstate or foreign commerce, including by computer,for purposes of inducing or persuading a minor to participate in any activity that is illegal …

would also be committing an offence.

According to section 2252A(b)(1), whoever violates, or attempts or conspires to violate, paragraph (1), (2), (3), (4) or (6) of subsection (a) shall be fined under this title and imprisoned for not less than five years and not more than 20 years. However, if such a person has a prior conviction under this chapter,[181] or under the laws of any State relating to aggravated sexual abuse, sexual abuse, or abusive sexual conduct involving a minor or ward, or the production, possession, receipt, mailing, sale, distribution, shipment or transportation of child pornography, such a person shall be imprisoned for not less than 15 years and not more than 40 years.

Under section 2252A(a)(5)(A), whoever knowingly possesses any book, magazine, periodical, film, videotape, computer disk or any other material that contains an image of child pornography;[182] or knowingly possesses such content[183] that was produced using materials that have been mailed, or shipped or transported in interstate or foreign commerce by any means, including by computer (2252A(a)(5)(B))[184] commits an offence. According to section 2252A(b)(2), whoever violates, or attempts or conspires to violate section 2252A(a)(5) shall be fined or imprisoned for not more than ten years, or both. However, if such a person has a prior conviction under this chapter,[185] or under the laws of any State relating to aggravated sexual abuse, sexual abuse, or abusive sexual conduct involving a minor or ward, or the production, possession, receipt, mailing, sale, distribution, shipment or transportation of child pornography, such a person could be imprisoned for not less than ten years and not more than 20 years.

Despite these provisions providing for long imprisonment terms, lighter sentences are also possible, and the conduct of the defendants may have an impact upon how these provisions are applied in practice by sentencing courts. In the case of *U.S. v. Stevens*,[186] the defendant was sentenced to only 12 months plus one day

---

181 Or under chapter 71, chapter 109A, or chapter 117 [18 USCS §§ 2251 et seq., §§ 1460 et seq., 2241 et seq., or 2421 et seq.], or under section 920 of title 10 (article 120 of the Uniform Code of Military Justice).

182 '… in the special maritime and territorial jurisdiction of the United States, or on any land or building owned by, leased to, or otherwise used by or under the control of the United States Government, or in the Indian country' (as defined in section 1151).

183 See for example *U.S. v. Tucker* (2002, CA10 Utah) 305 F3d 1193.

184 Note *U.S. v. Marcus* (2001, ED NY) 193 F Supp 2d 552: The defendant's constitutional attack on 18 USCS § 2252A(a)(5)(B) on First Amendment grounds was without merit given that the distinctions between adult and child pornography justified the prohibition of child pornography both *per se* and incidental to the government's right to prohibit the receipt and distribution of child pornography.

185 Or under chapter 71, chapter 109A, or chapter 117 [18 USCS §§ 2251 et seq., §§ 1460 et seq., 2241 et seq., or 2421 et seq.], or under section 920 of title 10 (article 120 of the Uniform Code of Military Justice).

186 *U.S. v. Stevens* (1998, DC Alaska) 29 F Supp 2d 592.

imprisonment for the possession of child pornography. Stevens had 400 images in his computer and these were downloaded through chat rooms. There was no evidence to suggest that he personally participated in any activities depicted, attempted to contact any person depicted, or had anything to do with producing child pornography or abusing children. According to the Court, the defendant had contributed only slightly to harms that Congress sought to prevent in 18 USCS § 2252A, and in such cases the sentencing courts could opt for less lenient penalties.[187]

Distribution of Child Pornography to Minors

A new subsection, 2252A(a)(6), was added by the Protect Act 2003 to the effect that any person who knowingly distributes, offers, sends or provides to a minor any visual depiction, including any photograph, film, video, picture or computer-generated image or picture, whether made or produced by electronic, mechanical or other means, where such visual depiction is, or appears to be, of a minor engaging in sexually explicit conduct …

> (A) that has been mailed, shipped, or transported in interstate or foreign commerce by any means, including by computer;
> (B) that was produced using materials that have been mailed, shipped, or transported in interstate or foreign commerce by any means, including by computer; or
> (C) which distribution, offer, sending, or provision is accomplished using the mails or by transmitting or causing to be transmitted any wire communication in interstate or foreign commerce, including by computer, for purposes of inducing or persuading a minor to participate in any activity that is illegal …[188]

shall be punished as provided in section 2252A(b) above.

Affirmative Defence

Section 2252A(c) provides limited defences to the above-mentioned charges; under this section it shall be an affirmative defence to a charge of violating paragraph (1),[189] (2),[190] (3)(A),[191] (4) or (5) of subsection (a) that …

> (1)(A) the alleged child pornography was produced using an actual person or persons engaging in sexually explicit conduct; and
> (1)(B) each such person was an adult at the time the material was produced; or
> (2) the alleged child pornography was not produced using any actual minor or minors.

187 For a detailed assessment of complicated US sentencing guidelines and their application see Williams, E., 'Construction and Application of United States Sentencing Guideline § 2G2.1 et seq., Pertaining to Child Pornography', 145 *A.L.R. Fed.* 481.

188 Added by section 503 of the Protect Act 2003.

189 '… knowingly mails, or transports or ships in interstate or foreign commerce by any means, including by computer, any child pornography …'.

190 '… knowingly receives or distributes' child pornography …

191 '… knowingly reproduces any child pornography for distribution …'.

However, the limited defences offered in this section shift the burden of proof to the defendants in child pornography cases 'to prove that the person depicted was not a minor and relieves the government of its burden of proof on an essential element of the offence'.[192]

No affirmative defence under subsection (c)(2) shall be available in any prosecution that involves child pornography depicting an identifiable minor engaging in sexually explicit conduct as described in section 2256(8)(C). Further affirmative defences are provided for the 2252A(a)(5) possession offences, and under section 2252A(d) it shall be an affirmative defence to a charge of violating subsection (a)(5) that the defendant …

(1) possessed less than three images of child pornography; and
(2) promptly and in good faith, and without retaining or allowing any person, other than a law enforcement agency, to access any image or copy thereof –
 (A) took reasonable steps to destroy each such image; or
 (B) reported the matter to a law enforcement agency and afforded that agency access to each such image.

It should be noted that this affirmative defence was not available to defendants charged with possession offences or offences involving virtual child pornography under the CPPA 1996 version of the defence. To this extent, this expansion of the affirmative defence is a welcome move.

Obscene Visual Representations of the Sexual Abuse of Children

A new section, 18 USCS § 1466A, entitled *Obscene visual representations of the sexual abuse of children*, was also added by the Protect Act 2003.[193] According to this section, any person who knowingly produces, distributes, receives or possesses with intent to distribute a visual depiction[194] of any kind, including a drawing, cartoon, sculpture or painting which depicts a minor engaging in sexually explicit conduct[195] (1466A(a)(1)(A)); and is obscene (1466A(a)(1)(B)); or depicts an image that is, or appears to be, of a minor engaging in graphic[196] bestiality, sadistic or

192 Feldmeier, J.P., 'Close Enough for Government Work: An Examination of Congressional Efforts to Reduce the Government's Burden of Proof in Child Pornography Cases' (2003), 30 *N. Ky. L. Rev* 205, 220–23. See further, Slocum, B.G., 'Virtual Child Pornography: Does It Mean the End of the Child Pornography Exception to the First Amendment?' (2004), 14 *Alb. L.J. Sci. and Tech.* 637.

193 Added 30 April 2003, P.L. 108-21, Title V, Subtitle A, § 504(a), 117 Stat. 681.

194 According to 1466A(f)(1), the term 'visual depiction' includes undeveloped film and videotape, and data stored on a computer disk or by electronic means which is capable of conversion into a visual image, and also includes any photograph, film, video, picture, digital image or picture, computer image or picture, or computer-generated image or picture, whether made or produced by electronic, mechanical or other means.

195 According to 1466A(f)(2) the term 'sexually explicit conduct' has the meaning given the term in section 2256(2)(A) or 2256(2)(B).

196 According to 1466A(f)(3), the term 'graphic', when used with respect to a depiction of sexually explicit conduct, means that a viewer can observe any part of the genitals or pubic

masochistic abuse, or sexual intercourse, including genital-genital, oral-genital, anal-genital or oral-anal, whether between persons of the same or opposite sex (1466A(a)(2)(A)); and lacks serious literary, artistic, political or scientific value; or attempts or conspires to do so, shall be subject to the penalties provided in section 2252A(b)(1), including the penalties provided for cases involving a prior conviction (1466A(a)(2)(B)). This newly introduced 'obscenity' section also includes the possession version of the above-mentioned offences in section 1466A(b), and those who committed possession offences shall be subject to the penalties provided in section 2252A(b)(2), including the penalties provided for cases involving a prior conviction. It is stated in section 1466A(c) that it is not a required element of any offence under this section that the minor depicted actually exists.

The circumstances referred to in subsections 1466A(a) and 1466A(b) are explained in 1466A(d):

(1) any communication involved in or made in furtherance of the offence is communicated or transported by the mail, or in interstate or foreign commerce by any means, including by computer, or any means or instrumentality of interstate or foreign commerce is otherwise used in committing or in furtherance of the commission of the offence;
(2) any communication involved in or made in furtherance of the offence contemplates the transmission or transportation of a visual depiction by the mail, or in interstate or foreign commerce by any means, including by computer;
(3) any person travels or is transported in interstate or foreign commerce in the course of the commission or in furtherance of the commission of the offence;
(4) any visual depiction involved in the offence has been mailed, or has been shipped or transported in interstate or foreign commerce by any means, including by computer, or was produced using materials that have been mailed, or that have been shipped or transported in interstate or foreign commerce by any means, including by computer; or
(5) the offence is committed in the special maritime and territorial jurisdiction of the United States or in any territory or possession of the United States.

According to 1466A(e), it shall be an affirmative defence to a charge of violating the possession offences provided in subsection 1466A(b) that the defendant ...

(1) possessed less than 3 such visual depictions; and
(2) promptly and in good faith, and without retaining or allowing any person, other than a law enforcement agency, to access any such visual depiction –
  (A) took reasonable steps to destroy each such visual depiction; or
  (B) reported the matter to a law enforcement agency and afforded that agency access to each such visual depiction.

The following section provides an overview of the prosecution and conviction statistics for child pornography offences.

---

area of any depicted person or animal during any part of the time that the sexually explicit conduct is being depicted.

US CHILD PORNOGRAPHY PROSECUTIONS

A considerable number of prosecutions have taken place in relation to Chapter 10 of the US Federal Code entitled *Sexual exploitation and other abuse of children*. The statistics provided under this heading include all the offences provided under Chapter 10. It was not possible to obtain the statistics for individual sections of the US Federal Code, or specifically in relation to the various child pornography offences described above. The statistics obtained through the *Transactional Records Access Clearinghouse*[197] cover the period 1995–2006.[198] An examination of Table 3.1 reveals that a total of 13,218 cases were referred to US prosecutors by the FBI. This resulted in a total of 9,026 prosecutions being filed with 6,567 convictions between 1995 and 2006. A total of 865 cases resulted in no conviction after prosecution within the same period. Out of the 6,567 convictions, 5,986 resulted in imprisonment.

Graph 3.1 and Table 3.1 also reveal that there has been a decrease in the case referrals made by the FBI since 2002. This could be said to be true with almost all referrals involving offences other than those related to terrorism since September 11. However, although priorities have changed, the FBI has continued to investigate offences related to child pornography under Chapter 10 of the US Federal Code with a considerable degree of success since 2002. The 2004–2006 statistics specifically indicate a recent up-turn in the number of referrals and prosecutions.

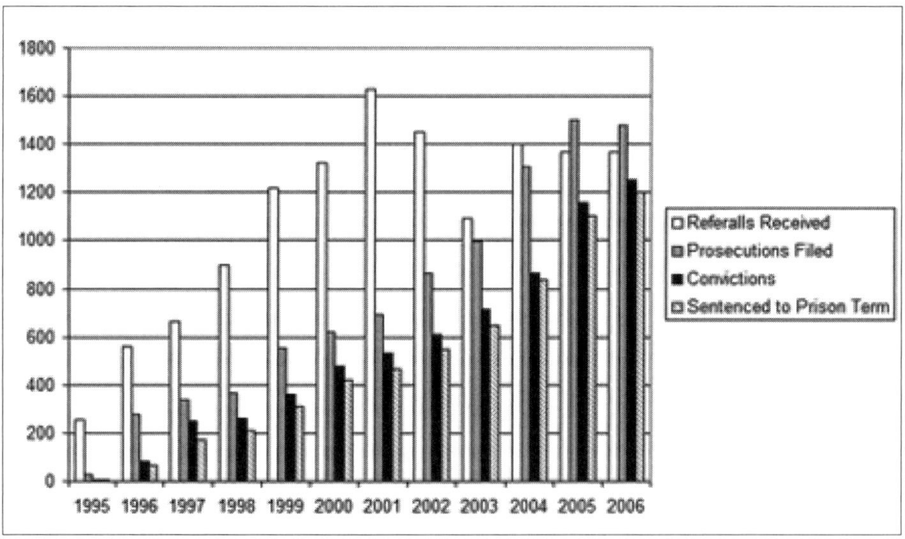

Graph 3.1 US sexual exploitation of children prosecutions (1995–2006)

197 The Transactional Records Access Clearinghouse (TRAC) is a data gathering, data research and data distribution organization associated with Syracuse University. See <http://trac.syr.edu/>.

198 More or less the statistics coincide with the launch of FBI's Innocent Images Operation in 1995. See generally, <http://www.fbi.gov/pressrel/candyman/iini.htm>.

Table 3.1 US child pornography prosecution and conviction statistics (1995–2006)

Fiscal Year	Referrals Received	Prosecutions Filed	Not Prosecuted	Convictions	Not Convicted after Prosecution	Prosecutions Completed	Sentenced to Prison Term
1995	254	30	34	5	4	9	5
1996	558	275	185	83	32	115	64
1997	664	338	235	249	43	292	174
1998	898	366	333	263	41	304	209
1999	1,221	553	424	360	58	418	311
2000	1,325	621	499	475	64	539	421
2001	1,626	695	680	532	60	592	466
2002	1,449	866	851	611	94	705	550
2003	1,092	995	929	716	98	814	649
2004	1,399	1,309	1,129	866	92	958	836
2005	1,366	1,499	1,373	1,156	123	1,279	1,101
2006	1,366	1,479	1,135	1,251	126	1,377	1,200
-All-	**13,218**	**9,026**	**7,807**	**6,567**	**865**	**7,402**	**5,986**

Table 3.2 reveals that 53 per cent of total referrals result in prosecution, with an 87 per cent conviction rate during the period 1995–2003.[199] 86 per cent of those prosecuted have been imprisoned with, in the period 1995–2006, an average prison term of 50 months. In 2006 the average imprisonment term for such offences reached 98 months among the 1,251 convictions for that year, the highest since 1995 as can be seen from Graph 3.2.

199 Data for 2004–2006 was not available at the time of writing.

Table 3.2 US child pornography prosecution and conviction statistics (averages)

Fiscal Year	Per cent Prosecuted	Per cent Not Prosecuted	Per cent Convicted (of prosecuted)	Per cent Prison Term (of convicted)	Median Prison Term (months)	Average Prison Term (months)	Median Days Referral to Court Disposal
1995	47	53	56	100	18	29	88
1996	60	40	72	77	15	34	167
1997	59	41	85	70	15	26	272
1998	52	48	87	79	24	38	329
1999	57	43	86	86	27	39	324
2000	55	45	88	89	27	44	328
2001	51	49	90	88	30	48	315
2002	50	50	87	90	30	50	335
2003	52	48	88	91	33	53	352
2004	N/A	N/A	N/A	N/A	41	64	N/A
2005	N/A	N/A	N/A	N/A	60	82	N/A
2006	N/A	N/A	N/A	N/A	60	98	N/A
-All-	**53**	**47**	**87**	**86**	**37**	**50**	**323**

A Department of Justice study based on the statistics received from the Executive Office for United States Attorneys (EOUSA) was published in July 2001.[200] The statistics and data provided within this study covers the period 1992–2000 (see Tables 3.3 and 3.4),[201] while the author's own research detailed above covers the period 1995–2006.

---

200 Dept. of Justice, Executive Office for US ATT'y, *Review of Child Pornography and Obscenity Crimes*, Rep. No. I-2001-07, t.3 (2001), 19 July 2001, at <http://www.usdoj.gov/oig/reports/plus/e0107/index.htm>. Note further the statistics provided for Fedaral prosecutions in child pornography and child abuse cases for the period of 1995–2005 in US Department of Justice, Office of the Attorney General, *Project Safe Childhood: Protecting Children from Online Exploitation and Abuse*, May 2006, at <http://www.projectsafechildhood.gov/guide.htm>. See in particular Part II: The Need for a National Initiative to Protect Children, at <http://www.projectsafechildhood.gov/part2.pdf>.

201 The data provided by EOUSA was obtained from its automated case management system, Legal Information Office Network System (LIONS). The LIONS database comprises caseload data entered by each of the 94 United States Attorneys' offices (USAOs). See Dept. of Justice, Executive Office for US ATT'y, Review of Child Pornography and Obscenity

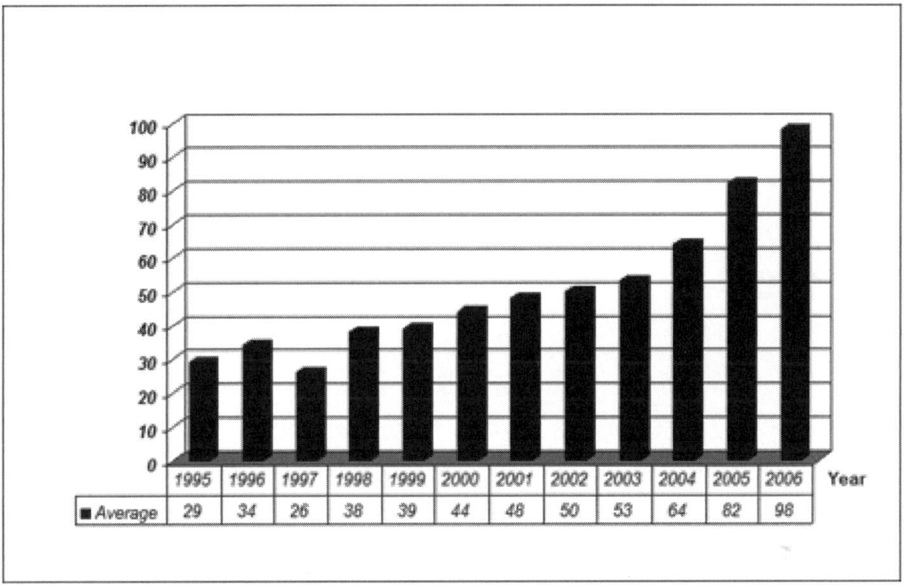

Graph 3.2 US average prison terms in sexual exploitation of children prosecutions (1995–2006)

Table 3.3 Federal prosecutions of child pornography cases (1992–2000)

Fiscal Year	Cases Referred	Cases Prosecuted	Cases Declined
1992	253	104	147
1993	221	79	162
1994	190	72	148
1995	**500**	**121**	**148**
1996	593	279	297
1997	716	320	283
1998	873	382	361
1999	1,131	510	422
2000	1,161	563	468
Total	**5,638**	**2,430**	**2,436**

Crimes, Rep. No. I-2001-07, t.3 (2001), 19 July 2001, at <http://www.usdoj.gov/oig/reports/plus/e0107/index.htm>.

Table 3.4 US child pornography conviction statistics (1992–2000)

Fiscal Year	Guilty Plea	Guilty Verdict	Acquitted	Dismissed	Other	Total
1992	85	9	0	9	2	105
1993	72	15	2	13	2	104
1994	61	4	0	9	4	78
1995	**79**	**3**	**2**	**6**	**4**	**94**
1996	135	9	0	10	8	162
1997	261	19	0	15	14	309
1998	265	19	3	28	9	324
1999	360	28	2	30	7	417
2000	422	23	1	45	7	498
Total	**1,740**	**119**	**10**	**165**	**57**	**2,091**

The two sets of data, one obtained from the Transactional Records Access Clearinghouse by the author, and the other from the 2001 Department of Justice study, do not match, but the only major discrepancies appear in the 1995 figures (see Tables 3.5 and 3.6).

Table 3.5 US child pornography prosecution statistics for 1995

Fiscal Year	Referrals Received	Prosecutions Filed	Not Prosecuted
1995	254	30	34

Source: Data obtained from the Transactional Records Access Clearinghouse.

Table 3.6 US child pornography prosecution statistics for 1995

Fiscal Year	Cases Referred	Cases Prosecuted	Cases Declined
1995	500	121	148

Source: Data obtained from the July 2001 Department of Justice study.

Interestingly, the Department of Justice study sets out to explain why a total of 2,436 referred cases[202] did not end up in prosecution. According to the study, there are several reasons, including suspects being prosecuted by other authorities as well as on other charges, lack of evidence or weak evidence, and jurisdictional problems. A detailed breakdown of the reasons for not prosecuting child pornography cases within the 1992–2000 period is provided in Table 3.7, taken from the Department of Justice study:

202 A total of 4,170 for the period 1995–2003 based upon the Transactional Records Access Clearinghouse data.

Table 3.7 Reasons for not prosecuting child pornography cases – US (1992–2000)

Basis for Declination	Total	Per cent
No crime		
No federal offence evident	280	11.5
Referred or handled in other prosecution		
Suspect prosecuted by other authority	510	20.9
Suspect prosecuted on other charges	54	2.2
Alternative resolution		
Civil, administrative, or other disciplinary	26	1.1
Pre-trial diversion complete	118	4.8
Suspect-related reasons		
Suspect a fugitive	3	0.1
No known suspect	38	1.6
Suspect deceased	43	1.8
Suspect deported	1	0.0
Suspect serving sentence	12	0.5
Case-related reasons		
Jurisdiction or venue problems	52	2.1
Lack of evidence	285	11.7
Stale case	23	0.9
Statute of limitations exceeded	10	0.4
Weak evidence	558	22.9
Witness problems	9	0.4
All other reasons		
Agency request	99	4.1
Court policy	1	0.0
Department instructions	5	0.2
Department policy	10	0.4
Juvenile suspect	23	0.9
Lack of resources	48	2.0
Minimal federal interest	77	3.2
Offender's health, age, prior record, or other personal circumstances	27	1.1
US Attorney policy	58	2.4
Petite policy	16	0.7
Suspect's co-operation	6	0.2
Other reasons	44	1.8
Total declinations	**2,436**	**99.9**

To these detailed statistical data we can add the FBI's Innocent Images National Initiative ('IINI') statistics. The IINI is a component of FBI's Cyber Crimes Program, and is an intelligence driven, proactive, multi-agency investigative operation to combat the proliferation of child pornography/child sexual exploitation facilitated by the Internet.[203] Between the fiscal years 1996 and 2006, the IINI resulted in 17,691 cases being investigated and 5,840 convictions.[204]

The statistical data shows that US prosecutors have enjoyed a remarkable degree of success in terms of conviction rates and that US courts take these offences very seriously. Evidence of this is the high percentage of imprisonments, averaging 98 months in 2006.

CONCLUSION

In terms of law and policy, many issues seem to have been resolved in the United States following the enactment of the Protect Act 2003. However, it is too soon to say whether the 2003 Act provisions will achieve the desired effect. This chapter has closely examined post-Free Speech cases, as well as the available statistical data. Prosecution statistics for 2002–2004 (see Table 3.8) suggest that the Supreme Court decision did not have a visible detrimental impact upon prosecutions and conviction rates as the government predicted.

Table 3.8 US child pornography prosecution statistics (2002–2004)

Fiscal Year	Referrals Received	Prosecutions Filed	Not Prosecuted	Convictions	Not Convicted after Prosecution	Prosecutions Completed	Sentenced to Prison Term
2002	1,449	866	851	611	94	705	550
2003	1,092	995	929	716	98	814	649
2004	1,399	1,309	1,129	866	92	958	836

The courts demonstrated their readiness to deal appropriately with defence claims that contested images were computer-generated images rather than depictions of real children. A conviction rate of 70 per cent was purportedly achieved in 2002, 71 per cent in 2003, and 66 per cent in 2004, down from 76 per cent in both 2000 and 2001. Contrary to the forecast of former US Attorney General, Mr Ashcroft, the above statistics do not suggest that the US Supreme Court decision rendered 'the ability to prosecute those who produce and possess child pornography immeasurably more difficult'.[205] Commentators who argued at the time that

203 See <http://www.fbi.gov/publications/innocent.htm> for further information.

204 Ibid.

205 See Attorney General Transcript, Response to Supreme Court Decision *in Free Speech Coalition v. Ashcroft*, Tuesday, 16 April 2002, at <http://www.usdoj.gov/archive/ag/speeches/2002/041602newsconferenceresponse.htm>.

such claims were 'grossly exaggerated'[206] have arguably been proved correct in their analysis. Only a handful of cases were cited by a US Senate Report[207] as evidence of this trend of defence hampering prosecutions. Cases in which the 'virtual pornography defence' was successful were cited as *U.S. v. Sims*,[208] *U.S. v. Bunnell*[209] and *U.S. v. Reilly*.[210] 'Left unchecked, this problem threatens to cripple a large number of child pornography prosecutions',[211] declared a 2003 US Senate report. Available evidence suggests that the information provided by the US Senate report provides a misleading impression.

In *Sims*,[212] an acquittal was granted with respect to one set of images (one count) out of four counts following the Supreme Court decision. The trial court in *Sims* noted, 'the government could have taken a more cautionary approach and presented evidence to prove the use of actual children, but it made the strategic decision not to do so.'[213] The prosecutors in *Sims* knew that the Child Pornography Prevention Act 1996 provisions were being considered at the Supreme Court level at the time of the prosecution, and were aware of the possibility that those provisions may be found unconstitutional. It was a strategic decision that ultimately led to Sims acquittal[214] rather than the 'virtual pornography defence' presenting a unique problem. As Feldmeier rightly observes, 'the acquittal in *Sims* was the product of the government's ill-conceived and neglectful strategy, not the defendant's skilful use of the "virtual child" defence.'[215] Feldmeier also notes that the defendant in the case of *Bunnell*[216] 'never went to trial, and thus, the "virtual child" defence was never presented, successfully or otherwise, to a jury.'[217] In *Reilly*,[218] the defendant

206 Feldmeier, J.P., 'Close Enough for Government Work: An Examination of Congressional Efforts to Reduce the Government's Burden of Proof in Child Pornography Cases' (2003), 30 *N. Ky. L. Rev* 205, 220–23.

207 US Senate Report, The PROTECT Act of 2003, No. 19-010, 108-2, 1st Session, 11 February 2003 (Hatch Report).

208 220 F. Supp. 2d 1222 (D.N.M. 2002).

209 2002 WL 927765 (D. Me. 2002).

210 01 Cr. 1114 (RPP), 2002 WL 31307170 (S.D.N.Y. Oct. 15, 2002).

211 US Senate Report, The PROTECT Act of 2003, No. 19-010, 108-2, 1st Session, 11 February 2003 (Hatch Report).

212 *U.S. v. Sims*, 220 F. Supp. 2d 1222 (D.N.M. 2002); 428 F3d 945; (Tenth Cir. 2005) U.S. App. LEXIS 24143.

213 Ibid.

214 Note a further appeal on sentencing: *U.S. v. Sims*, 428 F3d 945; (Tenth Cir. 2005) U.S. App. LEXIS 24143.

215 Feldmeier, J.P., 'Close Enough for Government Work: An Examination of Congressional Efforts to Reduce the Government's Burden of Proof in Child Pornography Cases' (2003), 30 *N. Ky. L. Rev* 205, 220–23.

216 2002 WL 927765 (D. Me. 2002).

217 Feldmeier, J.P., 'Close Enough for Government Work: An Examination of Congressional Efforts to Reduce the Government's Burden of Proof in Child Pornography Cases' (2003), 30 *N. Ky. L. Rev* 205, 220–23.

218 01 Cr. 1114 (RPP), United States District Court for the Southern District of New York, 2002 U.S. Dist. Lexis 19564, 11 October 2002, Decided, 15 October 2002, Filed, Motion denied by *U.S. v. Reilly*, 2003 U.S. Dist. Lexis 6005 (S.D.N.Y., 11 April 2003).

moved to withdraw his plea of guilty based on the Supreme Court judgment. The Court stated that Reilly did not acknowledge in his defence that he knew that the images he received were of actual children. Simply put, during the plea hearing, the Court did not inquire whether or not Reilly knew that the images were real. There was also no submission during the plea hearing that the Government would prove during trial that the defendant knew that the visual depictions were of actual minors. Even in *Sims* the Tenth Circuit ruled that even though the Government had the burden of proving beyond a reasonable doubt that the images at issue in a child pornography prosecution depict actual minors, 'this does not necessarily require expert testimony or identification of the actual child victims.'[219] The Tenth Circuit stated, 'juries often will be able to distinguish between real and virtual images, and "where no evidence suggests that the images are anything other than real, the government need offer no supporting evidence beyond the images themselves."'[220]

Did the Supreme Court decision really put prosecutors in a difficult position? An assessment of appeal cases suggests that prosecutors witnessed minor rather than substantial problems in a small number of cases.[221]

The author's own conclusions are supported by a recent analysis of the post-Free Speech cases by Buckman who summarized that sufficient evidence was provided in a number of cases[222] supporting convictions, indictments and guilty pleas[223] involving a variety of child pornography related offences in which 'the images in question were clearly of actual children'.[224] In one particular case,[225] images were alone deemed sufficient to show that real children were involved in the production of images and that expert testimony[226] is not always necessary to prove otherwise. Therefore, the alleged prosecutorial case for shifting the burden

---

219 *U.S. v. Sims*, 428 F3d 945; 2005 U.S. App. LEXIS 24143. *U.S. v. Morgan*, 2002 WL 975154 (D. Me. 2002) is another case in which the First Circuit decided that the government does bear a greater burden of proof since *Free Speech*.

220 Ibid.

221 Within this context note the cases of *U.S. v. Hilton*, 363 F3d 58 (1st Cir.), vacated, 386 F3d 13 (1st Cir. 2004); *U.S. v. Ellyson*, 326 F3d 522 (4th Cir. 2003); *U.S. v. Pearl*, 324 F3d 1210 (10th Cir. 2003), cert. denied, 539 U.S. 934, 123 S. Ct. 2591, 156 L. Ed. 2d 616 (2003); *U.S. v. Barbieri*, 43 Fed. Appx. 367 (10th Cir. 2002).

222 Note for example *Heidemann v. U.S.*, 2004 WL 633241 (M.D. Ala. 2004); *Padgett v. U.S.*, 302 F. Supp. 2d 593 (D.S.C. 2004), appeal dismissed, 119 Fed. Appx. 440 (4th Cir. 2005); *U.S. v. Cendejas*, 2004 WL 388960 (A.F.C.C.A. 2004); *U.S. v. Honzik*, 2003 WL 22862648 (A.F.C.C.A. 2003); *U.S. v. Rejkowski*, 2003 WL 649089 (N.M.C.C.A. 2003); *U.S. v. Marchand*, 308 F. Supp. 2d 498 (D.N.J. 2004).

223 See, for example, *U.S. v. James*, 55 M.J. 297 (C.A.A.F. 2001).

224 Buckman, D.F., 'Validity, Construction, and Application of 18 U.S.C.A. § 2252A(a), Proscribing Certain Activities Relating to Material Constituting or Containing Child Pornography', 2 *A.L.R. Fed.* 2d 533.

225 See *U.S. v. Wolford*, 62 M.J. 418 (C.A.A.F. 2006).

226 As was previously mentioned in this case, the prosecution can rely on expert testimony if and when necessary: *U.S. v. Rearden*, 349 F3d 608, 62 Fed. R. Evid. Serv 1255, 2 *A.L.R. Fed.* 2d 765 (9th Cir. 2003), cert. denied, 125 S. Ct. 32, 160 L. Ed. 2d 32 (U.S. 2004). See further, *U.S. v. Fuller*, 77 Fed. Appx. 371 (6th Cir. 2003).

of proof to the defendants to tackle the problem of 'virtual pornography defence' remains unsubstantiated.

Within this context it is appropriate to quote Feldmeier who claimed:

> The PROTECT Act's 'close enough' definitions of child pornography not only run afoul of First Amendment and due process requirements under the Constitution, they also undermine and insult the men and women serving as federal prosecutors who are more than capable of securing child pornography convictions without the assistance of dumbed-down evidentiary standards.[227]

A panic-led policy debate on criminalizing virtual child pornography started in the United States with the enactment of the Child Pornography Prevention Act 1996. The subsequent challenge at the Supreme Court was followed by the enactment of the Protect Act 2003. It remains to be seen whether the Protect Act 2003 provisions will help to reduce the problem of Internet child pornography in the United States, or whether it will lead into further constitutional challenges.[228]

---

227 Feldmeier, J.P., 'Close Enough for Government Work: An Examination of Congressional Efforts to Reduce the Government's Burden of Proof in Child Pornography Cases' (2003), 30 *N. Ky. L. Rev* 205, 220–23.

228 Note *U.S. v. Williams*, 444 F3d 1286; 2006 U.S. App. LEXIS 8384; 19 Fla. L. Weekly Fed. C 418.

Chapter 4

Legal Approaches in Canada

In 2001 the constitutionality of the Canadian possession of child pornography offence was challenged at the Supreme Court level in *Sharpe*.[1] This decision has had a major impact on debate and the development of laws in Canada with particular concerns centring on the courts' approach to written material. This chapter provides a detailed overview of these developments and highlights problematic features of the Canadian response to Internet child pornography.

LEGISLATIVE BACKGROUND

Although there were a number of attempts at legislation, there was no specific law in Canada criminalizing child pornography until 1993.[2] In 1993 the Canadian Parliament created a number of offences related to child pornography by introducing section 163.1 of the Criminal Code. By enacting these new provisions, Parliament's intention was to prevent harm to children by banning the production, publication, importation, distribution, sale and possession of child pornography, and by sending a stern message to Canadians 'that children need to be protected from the harmful effects of child sexual abuse and exploitation and are not appropriate sexual partners.'[3] It should be noted that unlike the provisions of the Protection of Children Act 1978 in England and Wales, the Canadian Criminal Code uses the words 'child pornography' within section 163.1(1), meaning:

(a) a photographic, film, video or other visual representation, whether or not it was made by electronic or mechanical means,
  (i) that shows a person who is or is depicted as being under the age of eighteen years and is engaged in or is depicted as engaged in explicit sexual activity, or
  (ii) the dominant characteristic of which is the depiction, for a sexual purpose, of a sexual organ or the anal region of a person under the age of eighteen years; or
(b) any written material or visual representation that advocates or counsels sexual activity with a person under the age of eighteen years that would be an offence under this Act.

1 *R v. Sharpe* (2001) SCC 2. File No. 27376, 26 January 2001.

2 The discussions started in the late 1970s. Note Canada, House of Commons, Standing Committee on Justice and Legal Affairs, 'Report on Pornography', No. 18–3, 22, March 1978 at 18:8 (Chairman: M. MacGuigan).

3 House of Commons Debates, 3rd Sess., 34th Parl., vol. XVI, 3 June 1993, at p. 20328 (as cited in *R v. Sharpe*, 2001 SCC 2. File No. 27376, 26 January 2001).

As far as the child pornography provisions are concerned, a child is defined as under the age of 18 in line with the UN Optional Protocol to the Convention on the Rights of the Child on the sale of children, child prostitution and child pornography. It may be noted that the above definition provided by the Canadian legislators is wider than the definition used in the Protection of Children Act 1978 which deals with indecent photographs and indecent pseudo-photographs of children in England and Wales. The Canadian version includes written material in addition to visual representations. Therefore text-based content such as writings as well as drawings could be regarded as child pornography if the other conditions within section 163.1 of the Canadian Criminal Code are satisfied.

In terms of the offences, under section 163.1(2), every person who makes, prints, publishes or possesses for the purpose of publication any child pornography is guilty of an indictable offence and liable to imprisonment for a term not exceeding ten years; or an offence punishable on summary conviction. According to section 163.1(5), an accused will not be able to rely on a defence to a charge under section 163.1(2) if he believes that a person shown in a visual representation that is alleged to constitute child pornography was or was depicted as being 18 years of age or more, unless the accused took all reasonable steps to ascertain the age of that person and took all reasonable steps to ensure that, where the person was 18 years of age or more, the representation did not depict that person under the age of 18 years.

Under section 163.1(3), every person who imports, distributes, sells or possesses for the purpose of distribution or sale any child pornography is guilty of an indictable offence and liable for imprisonment for a term not exceeding ten years; or an offence punishable on summary conviction. Similarly, under section 163.1(4), every person who possesses any child pornography is guilty of an indictable offence and liable to imprisonment for a term not exceeding five years; or an offence punishable on summary conviction.

According to section 163.1(6), where the accused is charged with an offence under subsection (2), (3) or (4), the court shall find the accused not guilty if the representation or written material that is alleged to constitute child pornography has artistic merit or an educational, scientific or medical purpose.

The above-mentioned provisions of section 163.1 are analysed below in light of the decision of the Canadian Supreme Court in *R v. Sharpe*.[4] This important case illustrates potential challenges on privacy and free-speech grounds to offences involving the 'private possession' of child pornography.

R V. SHARPE

Sharpe was charged on a four-count indictment after two seizures of material. The first seizure consisted of computer discs containing a text entitled 'Sam Paloc's

---

4 *R v. Sharpe* (2001) SCC 2. File No. 27376, 26 January 2001. Note also Ross, J., 'R v. Sharpe and Private Possession of Child Pornography' (2000), *Constitutional Forum* (11)50; Martin, R., 'Case Comment: R v. Sharpe' (2001), 39 *Alberta L. Rev.* 585.

Boyabuse – Flogging, Fun and Fortitude: A Collection of Kiddiekink Classics'.[5] The second seizure involved a collection of books, manuscripts, stories and photographs allegedly containing child pornography.[6] Four charges, namely, two for illegal possession under section 163.1(4) of the Criminal Code, and two for possession for the purposes of distribution or sale under section 163.1(3) of the Criminal Code, were made.

The case was first heard by the British Columbia Supreme Court (initial trial court) in which Shaw J controversially ruled[7] that the possession of child pornography provisions (as in section 163.1(4)) of the Canadian Criminal Code were unconstitutional. Shaw J held that the objective of the Canadian law was to combat material that puts children at risk of harm. Having reviewed the evidence in relation to child pornography and its associated risks, Shaw J ruled that there was little scientific evidence linking the simple possession of material containing child pornography with the grooming or seduction of children, or the use of children in its manufacture; confirming or augmenting cognitive distortions of paedophiles; and inciting paedophiles to commit offences against children.[8] Shaw J opined that the detrimental effects of criminalizing the possession of child pornography substantially outweighed the salutary effects, stating, 'the intrusion into freedom of expression and the right of privacy is so profound that it is not outweighed by the limited beneficial effects of the prohibition against possession'[9] of child pornography in the absence of scientific evidence.

The judge also challenged the effectiveness of possession provisions, expressing the view that the limited effectiveness of the prohibition was insufficient to warrant its highly invasive effects, as the simple possession prohibition deals with a very intimate and private aspect of an individual's life. In his reasoned judgment, Shaw J stated that subsections 2 and 3 of section 163.1 of the Canadian Criminal Code include 'powerful measures to tackle the problem of harm to children arising from pornography'.[10] He acknowledged that the offences of making, printing, publishing, importing, distributing, selling or possessing of child pornography for the purpose of publication, distribution or sale are aimed not only at the sources but also at the means of dissemination of child pornography. Whilst these provisions which tackle the root of the problem are in line with the Canadian government's objective of

5 For a detailed background for the case see Persky, S. and J. Dixon, *On Kiddie Porn: Sexual Representation, Free Speech and the Robin Sharpe Case*, Vancouver: New Star Books, 2001.

6 Doyle, K. and D. Lacombe, 'Scapegoat in Risk Society: The Case of Pedophile/Child Pornographer Robin Sharpe' (2000), 20, *Studies in Law, Politics and Society*, 183.

7 *R v. Sharpe* (1999), 22 C.R. (5th) 129, British Columbia Supreme Court.

8 Note that in relation to this aspect of the judgment, a study was commissioned by Department of Justice Canada following the decision of the British Columbia Supreme Court: Department of Justice Canada, *The Relationship between Child Pornography and the Commission of Sexual Offences against Children: A Review of the Literature*. Report prepared by Rettinger, L.J., Ottawa: Research and Statistics Division, Department of Justice Canada, 2000, at <http://www.justice.gc.ca/en/ps/rs/rep/2000/rr00-5.html>.

9 *R v. Sharpe* (1999), 22 C.R. (5th) 129, British Columbia Supreme Court.

10 Ibid.

protecting children from the harmful effects of child sexual abuse and exploitation, the possession provisions did not meet that objective he opined. Accordingly, the trial court declared section 163.1(4) of the Criminal Code void as being in violation of section 2(b) of the Canadian Charter and not justified under section 1 of the Charter. The two charges which related to simple possession of child pornography were dismissed, whilst two other charges related to section 163.1(3) which forbid the possession of child pornography for the purpose of distribution or sale were confirmed, the court ruling that the criminalization of possession of child pornography for the purpose of distribution or sale was constitutional. Shaw J reasoned, 'possession for the purpose of sale or distribution is far less invasive of an individual's freedom of expression and right of privacy than a total ban on possession.'[11]

British Columbia Court of Appeal

On appeal, the British Columbia Court of Appeal, by a margin of two to one, upheld Shaw J's conclusion.[12] Southin JA, in agreement with Shaw J's approach, made the distinction between simple possession and possession for the purposes of distribution and sale of child pornography, stating that 'legislation which makes simple possession of expressive materials a crime can never be a reasonable limit in a free and democratic society. Such legislation bears the hallmark of tyranny.'[13] Rowles JA also held the law invalid on the ground that it was unjustifiably overbroad. Acknowledging that the Canadian Parliament had a reasonable basis for concluding that criminalizing possession of child pornography would reduce the risk of harm to children, Rowles JA nevertheless observed that the law failed as 'it caught much more material than necessary to achieve the objective, mainly relating to teenage sexuality, an intrusion on free expression aggravated by its impact on privacy.'[14]

In a dissenting judgment, McEachern CJBC considered Shaw J to have erred, arguing that he had failed to consider the suppression of the market for child pornography and the government's overall aim of preventing abuse of children in the course of producing child pornography. McEachern CJBC strongly argued that 'any balancing of the risk of harm to children against the risk of harm to "innocent" possessors of child pornography as defined must be resolved in favour of children.'[15]

The British Columbia Court of Appeal judgment was bound to be challenged at the Canadian Supreme Court level and, as Martin observes, the appeal to the Canadian Supreme Court 'was portrayed publicly as a contest between freedom of expression and the protection of children. The idea was promoted that unless the Supreme Court upheld the *Code* prohibitions against child pornography, all Canadian children would be at risk of serious harm.'[16]

---

11 Ibid.

12 *R v. Sharpe* (1999), 136 C.C.C. (3d) 97, British Columbia Court of Appeal.

13 Ibid.

14 Ibid.

15 Ibid.

16 Martin, R., 'Case Comment: R v. Sharpe' (2001), 39 *Alberta L. Rev.* 585.

Supreme Court Decision in *Sharpe*

The question before the Supreme Court of Canada was whether Canada's law banning the possession of child pornography was constitutional or, conversely, it unjustifiably intruded on the constitutional right of Canadians to free expression.[17] All nine Supreme Court Justices were present for the appeal and, in a 6–3 majority judgment, the Supreme Court of Canada concluded that the Canadian Criminal Code's provision on possession of child pornography was 'constitutional, except for two peripheral applications relating to expressive material privately created and kept by the accused, for which two exceptions can be read into the legislation'.[18]

The Supreme Court of Canada stated that the Parliament was not required to adduce scientific proof based on concrete evidence that the possession of child pornography causes harm to children;[19] a reasoned apprehension of harm would suffice. By applying this test, the Supreme Court concluded that the evidence established several connections between the possession of child pornography and harm to children, namely:

(1) child pornography promotes cognitive distortions;
(2) it fuels fantasies that incite offenders to offend;
(3) it is used for grooming and seducing victims; and
(4) children are abused in the production of child pornography involving real children.

At the same time, the Supreme Court noted that the Canadian law captured the possession of two categories of material that one would not normally think of as child pornography, namely:

(1) written materials or visual representations created and held by the accused alone, exclusively for personal use; and
(2) visual recordings created by or depicting the accused that do not depict unlawful sexual activity and are held by the accused exclusively for private use.

In relation to these two categories the Supreme Court ruled that these would raise little or no risk of harm to children, arguing:

> ... the bulk of the material falling within these two classes engages important values underlying the s. 2(b) [of the Canadian Charter of Rights and Freedoms] guarantee while posing no reasoned risk of harm to children. In its main impact, s. 163.1(4) is proportionate and constitutional. Nonetheless, the law's application to materials in the two problematic classes, while peripheral to its objective, poses significant problems at the final stage of the proportionality analysis. In these applications the restriction imposed by

---

17 Ibid. Note that Sharpe did not challenge the constitutionality of the offence of possession for the purposes of distribution and sale.

18 Ibid.

19 Note Department of Justice Canada, *The Relationship between Child Pornography and the Commission of Sexual Offences against Children: A Review of the Literature*. Report prepared by Rettinger, L.J., Ottawa: Research and Statistics Division, Department of Justice Canada, 2000, at <http://www.justice.gc.ca/en/ps/rs/rep/2000/rr00-5.html>.

> s. 163.1(4) regulates expression where it borders on thought. The cost of prohibiting such materials to the right of free expression outweighs any tenuous benefit it might confer in preventing harm to children. To this extent, the law cannot be considered proportionate in its effects, and the infringement of s. 2(b) [of the Canadian Charter of Rights and Freedoms] contemplated by the legislation is not demonstrably justifiable under s. 1.[20]

Although McLachlin CJ disagreed with the general 'contention that prohibiting possession of expressive material does not raise free expression concerns',[21] he upheld the law as constitutional with two exceptions: 'where the prohibition's intrusion into free expression and privacy is most pronounced and its benefits most attenuated.'[22]

The first exception protects 'the possession of expressive material created through the efforts of a single person and held by that person alone, exclusively for his or her own personal use. This exception applies to deeply private expression, such as personal journals and drawings, intended solely for the eyes of their creator.'[23] The second exception protects 'a person's possession of visual recordings created by or depicting that person, but only where these recordings do not depict unlawful sexual activity, are held only for private use, and were created with the consent of those persons depicted.'[24] The Supreme Court ruled that 'while excluding the offending applications [would] not subvert Parliament's object, striking down the statute altogether would most assuredly do so.'[25] This explains why the law was upheld as constitutional. According to McLachlin CJ, these two exceptions apply equally to the offence of 'making' child pornography under section 163.1(2) of the Canadian Criminal Code. However, neither exception affords protection to a person 'harbouring any other intention than private possession; any intention to distribute, publish, print, share or in any other way disseminate these materials will subject a person to the full force of section 163.1.'[26] These exceptions should therefore be seen as very limited.[27]

In their dissenting judgment L'Heureux-Dube, Gonthier and Bastarache J stated:

> child pornography is harmful whether it involves real children in its production or whether it is a product of the imagination. Section 163.1 was enacted to protect children, one of the most vulnerable groups in society. It is based on the clear evidence of direct harm caused by child pornography, as well as Parliament's reasoned apprehension that child pornography also causes attitudinal harm. The lack of scientific precision in the social science evidence relating to attitudinal harm is not a valid reason for attenuating the Court's deference to Parliament's decision.[28]

---

20 *R v. Sharpe* (2001) SCC 2. File No. 27376, 26 January 2001.

21 Ibid.

22 Ibid.

23 Ibid.

24 Ibid.

25 Ibid.

26 Ibid.

27 Martin labels the first exception as the 'closet paedophile exception', and the second exception as the 'horny teenager exception': See Martin, R., 'Case Comment: R v. Sharpe' (2001), 39 *Alberta L. Rev.* 585.

28 *R v. Sharpe* (2001) SCC 2. File No. 27376, 26 January 2001.

The dissenting judgment appears unconcerned with whether the content in question involved real children in its production or not,[29] but argues that harm 'exists independently of dissemination or any risk of dissemination and flows directly from the existence of the pornographic representations, which on their own violate the dignity and equality rights of children'.[30]

Despite strong dissenting arguments, the appeal was allowed by a 6–3 majority judgment and a re-trial was ordered.[31]

Sharpe Retrial

In the retrial of *R v. Sharpe*,[32] the alleged child pornography consisted of both written materials (Counts 1, 2, 3 and 4) and photographs (Counts 2 and 4). The written material in question involved computer discs containing a collection of 17 short stories entitled 'Sam Paloc's *Boyabuse – Flogging, Fun and Fortitude: A Collection of Kiddiekink Classics*' ('Boyabuse'), which was 245 pages in length, and *Stand By America, 1953*, a short story of 32 pages in length authored by the defendant, Robin Sharpe. The retrial was conducted at the British Columbia Court of Appeal level in March 2002.

During the retrial, Sharpe raised two defences in relation to the written material. He first argued that the written material did not advocate or counsel the commission of sexual crimes against children. Second, Sharpe argued that these stories had artistic merit.

Three English professors and a psychiatrist gave evidence at the trial as expert witnesses to assess the nature of the written material on trial. Two professors, Miller of the University of Western Ontario, and Weir of the University of British Columbia, testified that 'Boyabuse' and *Stand By America, 1953* had literary or artistic merit. Delaney, a professor of English at Simon Fraser University, appeared as a witness for the Crown and expressed the opinion that 'Boyabuse' and *Stand By America, 1953* could not reasonably be viewed as art and therefore had no evidence of literary merit. Shaw J, delivering the British Columbia Court of Appeal judgment, rejected Professor Delaney's testimony, expressing the view that 'moral considerations played a significant role'[33] in the formulation of Delaney's opinion. Finally, Dr Lohrasbe, a forensic psychiatrist with considerable experience in the assessment and treatment

---

29 See generally, Benedet, J., 'Children in Pornography After Sharpe' (2002), 43 *C. de D.* 327 which argues that the majority of the Court erred in considering the value of freedom of expression in a detached and abstract manner.

30 *R v. Sharpe* (2001) SCC 2. File No. 27376, 26 January 2001.

31 An interesting observation in relation to media coverage and misreporting of the Supreme Court is provided in Sauvageau, F., D. Schneiderman and D. Taras, *The Last Word: Media Coverage of the Supreme Court of Canada*, Vancouver: University of British Columbia Press, 2006.

32 *R v. Sharpe* (2002) B.C.D. Crim. J. 2149; 2002 B.C.D. Crim. J. LEXIS 183; [2002] B.C.D. Crim. 250.90.60.00-01, decided on 26 March 2002.

33 Ibid., para. 94.

of sex offenders, admitted that he had no qualifications to express any view on the literary merit of Sharpe's writings and said that he did not purport to do so.[34]

The British Columbia Court of Appeal ruled that the Crown had failed to prove beyond reasonable doubt that 'Boyabuse' advocated or counselled the commission of sexual crimes against children. Section 163.1(1)(b) of the Criminal Code required that such written material 'advocates or counsels sexual activity with a person under the age of 18 years', and unless this was the case no possession offence would be committed. According to the presiding judge, Shaw J, whilst the written material in question arguably glorified the acts described therein, they did not go so far as to actively promote their commission. Quoting the Supreme Court decision in *R v. Sharpe*,[35] Sharpe J. drew comparisons with works of literature:

> While Nabokov's *Lolita*, Boccaccio's *Decameron*, and Plato's *Symposium* portray or discuss sexual activities with children, on an objective view they cannot be said to advocate or counsel such conduct in the sense of actively inducing or encouraging it.[36]

The descriptions within 'Boyabuse' and *Stand By America, 1953*, in his words,

> … may well be designed to titillate or excite the reader (if the reader is so inclined) but these descriptions do not actively advocate or counsel the reader to engage in the acts described … Where written material is simply a thinly disguised exhortation to seduce children or to otherwise make them prey to sexual crimes, such writing may well advocate or counsel such crimes. But that is not the case with *Boyabuse* and *Stand By America, 1953*. These writings simply describe morally repugnant acts.[37]

In terms of Sharpe's second defence,[38] McLachlin CJ had stated at the Supreme Court:

> 'artistic merit' should be interpreted as including any expression that may reasonably be viewed as art. Any objectively established artistic value, however small, suffices to support the defence. Simply put, artists, so long as they are producing art, should not fear prosecution under s. 163.1(4).[39]

With relevance to this statement Shaw J added:

> Sharpe's portrayal of people, events, scenes and ideas are reasonably well written. He uses parody and allegory, not expertly, but he does use them. His characterization is thin, but it does exist and at times is expressed with a reasonable degree of skill. His plots show some imagination and are sometimes fairly complex. In my view, *Boyabuse* and *Stand By America, 1953* are properly termed transgressive literature. Mr. Sharpe shows skill in the

---

34 Ibid., paras 97–100.

35 *R v. Sharpe* (2001) SCC 2. File No. 27376, 26 January 2001.

36 Ibid.

37 *R v. Sharpe* (2002) B.C.D. Crim. J. 2149; 2002 B.C.D. Crim. J. LEXIS 183; [2002] B.C.D. Crim. 250.90.60.00-01, decided on 26 March 2002.

38 See further, Ryder, B., 'The Harms of Child Pornography Law' (2003), 36 *U.B.C. L. Rev.* 101 (Winter).

39 *R v. Sharpe* (2001) SCC 2. File No. 27376, 26 January 2001.

> literary quality of his work and the literary devices that he uses, although not to the level of most established writers.[40]

Based on this assessment, Shaw J ruled that there was some objectively established artistic value to 'Boyabuse'. Therefore Sharpe's second defence succeeded and Sharpe was found not guilty on count one. Similarly, count three, involving the possession of *Stand By America, 1953* for the purpose of distribution or sale, was dismissed by Shaw J on the grounds that it had some artistic merit.

With regards to the possession charges involving various photographs of boys in sexual poses in counts two and four (400 photographs), Sharpe, in his defence, argued that he came within an exception to the child pornography provisions of the Canadian Criminal Code enunciated by the Supreme Court of Canada in *R v. Sharpe*.[41] This argument was rejected by Shaw J, and Sharpe was found guilty with respect to photographs constituting child pornography. There was no evidence to suggest that Sharpe kept the photographs in strict privacy as was required by the Supreme Court decision. There was also no evidence to suggest that the photographs in question were intended for the private use of the two boys who appeared in those photographs. According to the British Columbia Court of Appeal, the second exception would only protect auto-depictions, such as photographs taken by a child or adolescent of him- or herself alone, kept in strict privacy, and intended for personal use only. This would also extend to protect the recording of lawful sexual activity, provided certain conditions were met. Shaw J identified the following conditions as necessary:

- The person possessing the recording must have personally recorded or participated in the sexual activity in question.
- That activity must not be unlawful, thus ensuring the consent of all parties, and precluding the exploitation or abuse of children.
- All parties must also have consented to the creation of the record.
- The recording must be kept in strict privacy by the person in possession, and intended exclusively for private use by the creator and the persons depicted therein.[42]

For example, it was stated that 'a teenage couple would not fall within the law's purview for creating and keeping sexually explicit pictures featuring each other alone, or together engaged in lawful sexual activity, provided these pictures were created together and shared only with one another.'[43]

While the *Sharpe* judgments triggered the Canadian government to review child pornography legislation,[44] Sharpe was subsequently charged with one count of gross indecency contrary to section 157 of the Canadian Criminal Code, and one count of indecent assault against an 11-year-old boy contrary to section 156 of the

40 *R v. Sharpe* (2002) B.C.D. Crim. J. 2149; 2002 B.C.D. Crim. J. LEXIS 183; [2002] B.C.D. Crim. 250.90.60.00-01, decided on 26 March 2002.

41 *R v. Sharpe* (2001) SCC 2. File No. 27376, 26 January 2001.

42 *R v. Sharpe* (2002) B.C.D. Crim. J. 2149; 2002 B.C.D. Crim. J. LEXIS 183; 2002 B.C.D. Crim. 250.90.60.00-01, decided on 26 March 2002.

43 Ibid.

44 Note Gotell, L., 'Inverting Image and Reality: *R v. Sharpe* and the Moral Panic Around Child Pornography' (2001/2002), 12 *Const. Forum Const.* 9.

Canadian Criminal Code in February 2004. It was claimed that these offences were committed by Sharpe in the late 1970s and early 1980s. Sharpe was found guilty of these crimes.[45] These offences carried a maximum sentence of ten years, and Sharpe was sentenced to two years less a day imprisonment in July 2004.[46]

CANADIAN CHILD PORNOGRAPHY LAWS FOLLOWING *SHARPE*

An immediate reaction to the Supreme Court decision in *Sharpe* came from the Canadian Parliament with the introduction of Bill C-15A to amend the child pornography provisions of the Canadian Criminal Code.[47] The Minister of Justice and Attorney General of Canada, the Honourable Martin Cauchon, stated:

> While the Internet allows us many positive opportunities, we know that criminals use the Internet to target vulnerable children. These laws better equip us to effectively protect Canadian youth from those who use technology to victimize them … Law enforcement agencies will have more appropriate tools to bring offenders to justice and prevent future offences from occurring.[48]

Bill C-15A received Royal Assent in June 2002.[49] Apart from amending the existing provisions on child pornography, the new Bill also introduced new offences of accessing child pornography, and communicating with children via a computer system for the purpose of facilitating or committing certain sexual offences, such as child luring or abduction.[50]

The definition of child pornography provided within section 163.1(1) of the Canadian Criminal Code has not been modified by the provisions of Bill C-15A.[51] The definition of the making offence provided in section 163.1(2) of the Canadian Criminal Code also remained unchanged.

Section 163 of the Canadian Criminal Code included various offences relating to child pornography; namely, the making, distribution, possession and accessing of child pornography offences. In each of the child pornography related offences, child pornography is an indictable offence, for which any offender is liable to imprisonment for a term of up to five or ten years, depending on the offence; or

---

45 *R v. Sharpe* [2004] B.C.J. No. 1565; 2004 BCSC 240; 2004 BC.C. LEXIS 1676, Judgment: 20 February 2004.

46 See 'Kid porn figure guilty of assault', *Calgary Sun*, 20 July 2004; 'Jail for champion of kid porn', *The Toronto Sun*, 20 July 2004.

47 See generally, Criminal Code of Canada: Child Pornography and Luring of Children on the Internet – Summary, at <http://www.media-awareness.ca/english/resources/legislation/canadian_law/federal/criminal_code/criminal_code_child.cfm>.

48 Department of Justice Press Release, 10 June 2002, at <http://www.justice.gc.ca/en/news/nr/2002/doc_30529.html>.

49 Bill C-15A: An Act To Amend The Criminal Code And To Amend Other Acts: Prepared by: David Goetz, Gérald Lafrenière, Law and Government Division, 12 October 2001: Revised 30 September 2002. Royal Assent 4 June 2002. Statutes of Canada 2002, c.13.

50 For this final offence see section 172.1.

51 R.S.C. 1985, c. C-46, s. 163.1.

an offence punishable on summary conviction. Section 163.1(3) of the Canadian Criminal Code has been amended by Bill C-15A and the amended version defined the distribution of child pornography as:

> Every person who *transmits*, *makes available*, distributes, sells, imports, *exports* or possesses for the purpose of *transmission*, *making available*, distribution, sale or *exportation* any child pornography is guilty of
>
> (a) an indictable offence and liable to imprisonment for a term not exceeding ten years; or
> (b) an offence punishable on summary conviction.

Bill C-15A amendments added the words 'transmits', 'makes available', 'exports', 'transmission', and 'making available' in relation to the definition of 'distribution of child pornography' within this section.[52] These amendments were made in order to ensure that the distribution offence extends to the distribution of child pornography in electronic format on the Internet.

The possession offence provided in section 163.1(4) of the Canadian Criminal Code has not been modified by Bill C-15A. However, clause 5(3) of Bill C-15A introduced a new offence of 'accessing child pornography' and introduced section 163.(4.1), which states:

> Every person who accesses any child pornography is guilty of
>
> (a) an indictable offence and liable to imprisonment for a term not exceeding five years; or
> (b) an offence punishable on summary conviction.[53]

Subsection 4.2 states, for the purposes of subsection (4.1), that a person accesses child pornography who knowingly causes child pornography to be viewed by, or transmitted to, himself or herself. It is not clear why this section was deemed necessary in addition to the possession offence provided in section 163.1(4). It appears that the new access offence would cover those who merely view the material through an Internet browser without downloading or making further copies of such material. This would, for example, cover cached images in an Internet browser's cache directory. Subsection 4.2 requires an intentional access. If there is any evidence (for example, cached images) to suggest that an accused knowingly viewed child pornography on the Internet, then the appropriate charge would be 'accessing child pornography' rather than 'possession of child pornography' under the new provisions. It is worth noting that this type of distinction does not exist under the Protection of Children Act 1978 in England and Wales. In England and Wales an accused could be charged with a 'making offence' or a 'possession offence' under the 1978 Act[54] if there is any evidence to suggest that an accused viewed or accessed child pornography.

---

52 See Clause 5(2) of Bill C-15A.

53 Maximum penalty: fine of up to $2,000 and/or imprisonment for up to six months.

54 *R v. Smith and Jayson*, CA, [2002] EWCA Crim 683, and note Akdeniz, Y., Case Report: Court of Appeal Clarifies the Law on Downloading Child Pornography from the Web (2002), *Computer Law and Security Report*, 18(6), 433–5. See further, Ormerod, D.C., 'Case Comment on *R v. Smith (Graham Westgarth)*' (2002), *Crim. L.R.*, August, 659–63.

In terms of the above-mentioned offences, section 163.1(6) provided some limited defences and these remain unchanged but now cover the newly introduced subsection 4.1:

> Where the accused is charged with an offence under subsection (2), (3), (4) or (4.1), the court shall find the accused not guilty if the representation or written material that is alleged to constitute child pornography has artistic merit or an educational, scientific or medical purpose.

The content of the defence was not changed and the 'artistic merit' defence as well as the *Sharpe* retrial interpretation remain under the new provisions.

FURTHER AMENDMENTS TO THE CANADIAN LAW

After the Bill C-15A amendments were made, Bill C-2[55] – an Act to amend the Criminal Code (protection of children and other vulnerable persons) – and the Canada Evidence Act were introduced in the House of Commons of Canada on 8 October 2004.[56] Bill C-2[57] was designed to amend further the child pornography provisions of the Canadian Criminal Code.

The amendments were triggered by unhappiness regarding the nature of child pornography laws following the *R v. Sharpe* judgment of the Supreme Court and its application by the courts in Canada, as well as being due to the obligations arising following the ratification of the United Nations' Optional Protocol to the Convention on the Rights of the Child on the Sale of Children, Child Prostitution and Child Pornography by the Canadian government. Bill C-2 was enacted on 20 July 2005[58] and it amended the child pornography provisions with respect to the type of written and audio material that constitutes child pornography, and with respect to the child pornography offences, defences and penalties. Following the enactment of Bill C-2, Canada ratified the United Nations Optional Protocol in September 2005.[59]

Bill C-2 increased the penalties from six months to a maximum of 18 months for making of child pornography under section 163.1(2)(b); distribution of child pornography under 163.1(3)(b); possession of child pornography under section 163.1(4)(b); and for accessing child pornography under section 163.1(4.1)(b).

---

55 See generally, Legislative History of BILL C-2 at <http://www.parl.gc.ca/common/Bills_ls.asp?Parl=38&Ses=1&ls=C2>.

56 See generally, MacKay, R., Bill C-2: An Act to Amend the Criminal Code (Protection of Children and Other Vulnerable Persons) and the Canada Evidence Act, Parliamentary Information and Research Centre, Library of Canadian Parliament, 13 October 2004, at <http://www.parl.gc.ca/38/1/parlbus/chambus/house/bills/summaries/c2-e.pdf>.

57 Formerly known as Bill C-12 and Bill C-20.

58 See <http://www.parl.gc.ca/38/1/parlbus/chambus/house/bills/government/C-2/C-2_4/C-2_cover-E.html>.

59 See Department of Justice, Canada, Press Release: Ratification of the United Nations Optional Protocol to the Convention on the Rights of the Child on the Sale of Children, Child Prostitution and Child Pornography, 14 September 2005, at <http://www.justice.gc.ca/en/news/fs/2005/doc_31622.html>.

However, many members of the House of Commons of Canada argued that 'increasing maximum sentences is meaningless if the courts do not impose these increased sentences.'[60] It has been argued that there was no corresponding pattern in the actual sentencing practices when maximum sentences were raised. Many called for mandatory minimum sentences, elimination of statutory release and no conditional sentences for child predators.[61] There is no statistical data available on child pornography prosecutions and convictions in Canada, but news reports, parliamentary debates and reported court cases suggest that many prosecutions result in conditional sentences, mainly house arrests in prosecutions involving not only the possession of child pornography but also the distribution of child pornography.

The final version of Bill C-2 included mandatory minimum sentences for a term of one year for making and distribution offences on indictment, and for a term of forty-five days for possession and access offences on indictment. For the summary offences the amended legislation provides a mandatory minimum sentence term of ninety days for making and distribution offences, and a term of 14 days for the possession and access offences.

The amendments also created a new prohibition against advertising child pornography and the words 'advertises' and 'advertisement' were added to section 163.1(3) in relation to the distribution of child pornography offence with the enactment of Bill C-2 in July 2005.

More substantially, the words 'audio recording' became part of the definition of child pornography in section 163.1(1) following the enactment of Bill C-2. Paragraph 7 of the Bill proposed that the following extended definition is adopted:

(a) a photographic, film, video or other visual representation, whether or not it was made by electronic or mechanical means,
   (i) that shows a person who is or is depicted as being under the age of eighteen years and is engaged in or is depicted as engaged in explicit sexual activity, or
   (ii) the dominant characteristic of which is the depiction, for a sexual purpose, of a sexual organ or the anal region of a person under the age of eighteen years;
(b) any written material, visual representation *or audio recording* that advocates or counsels sexual activity with a person under the age of eighteen years that would be an offence under this Act;
(c) any written material whose dominant characteristic is the description, for a sexual purpose, of sexual activity with a person under the age of eighteen years that would be an offence under this Act; or
(d) any audio recording that has as its dominant characteristic the description, presentation or representation, for a sexual purpose, of sexual activity with a person under the age of eighteen years that would be an offence under this Act.

With these amendments, the definition of 'child pornography' within the Canadian Criminal Code became broader to include data in audio format[62] as well as written material whose dominant characteristic is the description of sexual activity with a

60 See speech of Mr Rob Moore (Fundy Royal, CPC), First Reading of Bill C-2, Hansard, 38th Parliament, 1st Session, No. 007, House of Commons of Canada, 8 October 2004, at <http://www.parl.gc.ca/38/1/parlbus/chambus/house/debates/007_2004-10-13/toc007-E.htm>.

61 Ibid.

62 There are, however, no known cases involving audio recordings as of June 2007.

person under the age of 18 years as long as the description is done for a sexual purpose. A similar wording is also used for audio recordings (see above) within the Bill C-2 amendments.[63]

Bill C-2 also introduced a new provision (subsection 4.3), and the commission of a child pornography offence with intent to profit became an aggravating factor for sentencing purposes.[64]

Robin Sharpe Amendments

The wording used in subsections 163.1(6) and (7) of the Act in relation to the defences was also amended by Bill C-2 and the following amended version was introduced:

> Defence
>
> (6) No person shall be convicted of an offence under this section if the act that is alleged to constitute the offence
>
> (*a*) has a legitimate purpose related to the administration of justice or to science, medicine, education or art; and
>
> (*b*) does not pose an undue risk of harm to persons under the age of eighteen years.
>
> Question of law
>
> (7) For greater certainty, for the purposes of this section, it is a question of law whether any written material, visual representation or audio recording advocates or counsels sexual activity with a person under the age of eighteen years that would be an offence under this Act.

Previously, the Canadian legislators used the words ‘public good’ instead of ‘legitimate purpose’ in Bill C-12 and Bill C-20. This wording generated discomfort and anxiety during the Parliamentary debate. Many argued that the ‘legitimate purpose’ defence, as in the case of the ‘artistic merit’ and the previously proposed ‘public good’ defences, would continue to create a dangerous loophole. The opposition accused the Liberal Government of failing to protect Canadian children adequately and failing to address the controversial ‘artistic merit’ defence created by the Supreme Court. Many argued that there was ‘nothing artistic about child pornography’.[65] One member of Parliament, Mr James Moore, stated:

---

63 See generally, Department of Justice Canada, Backgrounder: Key Highlights of Proposed Amendments to Protect Children and Other Vulnerable Persons, October 2004, at <http://www.justice.gc.ca/en/news/nr/2004/doc_31248.html>.

64 Subsection 4.3 states, ‘if a person is convicted of an offence under this section, the court that imposes the sentence shall consider as an aggravating factor the fact that the person committed the offence with intent to make a profit.’

65 See speech of Mrs Nina Grewal (Fleetwood—Port Kells, CPC), First Reading of Bill C-2, Hansard, 38th Parliament, 1st Session, No. 007, House of Commons of Canada, 8 October 2004, at <http://www.parl.gc.ca/38/1/parlbus/chambus/house/debates/007_2004-10-13/toc007-E.htm>.

> To successfully prosecute, the police and prosecutors now have to prove that the child pornography in question lacks John Robin Sharpian artistic merit. In other words, the best efforts of our law enforcement community to stop child pornography will be like cobwebs trying to lasso a locomotive; simply impossible.[66]

With the Bill C-2 amendments, literally known as the 'Robin Sharpe amendments', the Canadian legislators abolished and removed the defence of 'artistic merit' from section 163.1(6). The new version of the defence introduced by Bill C-2 still provides a limited 'legitimate purpose related to art' defence under the new subsection 163.1(6)(a). This limited defence is part of a two-pronged defence which can only be raised if the content in question has a legitimate purpose related to the administration of justice or to science, medicine, education or art and does not pose an undue risk of harm to persons under the age of 18 years.[67] According to Department of Justice Canada, the amendments narrow and clarify the test for the child pornography defence. The Department of Justice Canada argued, 'this single legitimate purpose defence incorporates the harm-based standard used by the Supreme Court of Canada in upholding the existing child pornography provisions in 2001.'[68]

The fate of these provisions remains to be seen. It is possible that they will face renewed challenge on constitutional grounds.[69] It is also unclear how the new test will ultimately be interpreted by the courts.[70] The wording used by the Canadian legislators remains extremely vague and arguably lacks sufficient clarity. It is now speculated that 'the amended law could conceivably also capture Plato's *Symposium*, Nabokov's *Lolita*, and such films as Franco Zeffirelli's version of Shakespeare's *Romeo and Juliet*, notwithstanding the Supreme Court's explicit exemption of such works from the charge of advocating illegal sexual acts.'[71]

---

66 See speech of Mr James Moore (Port Moody–Westwood–Port Coquitlam, CPC), First Reading of Bill C-2, Hansard, 38th Parliament, 1st Session, No. 007, House of Commons of Canada, 8 October 2004, at <http://www.parl.gc.ca/38/1/parlbus/chambus/house/debates/007_2004-10-13/toc007-E.htm>.

67 Note the Debates of the Senate (Hansard), 1st Session, 38th Parliament, Volume 142, Issue 14, Tuesday, November 16, 2004, Child Pornography Legislation–Definition Applied to Art Works. (Response to question raised by Hon. A. Raynell Andreychuk on 21 October, 2004.)

68 Department of Justice Canada, Backgrounder: Key Highlights of Proposed Amendments to Protect Children and Other Vulnerable Persons, October 2004, at <http://www.justice.gc.ca/en/news/nr/2004/doc_31248.html>.

69 Note the criticisms of the British Columbia Civil Liberties Association, 'Brief of the British Columbia Civil Liberties Association re Bill C-2', at <http://www.bccla.org/othercontent/05billc2.htm>.

70 There are no known cases as of June 2007 involving section 163.1(6).

71 British Columbia Civil Liberties Association, 'Brief of the British Columbia Civil Liberties Association re Bill C-2', at <http://www.bccla.org/othercontent/05billc2.htm>.

CONCLUSION

The period 2001–2005 has been a lively one in terms of the Canadian government's response to Internet child pornography prompted by the decision of the Supreme Court in *Sharpe*. As mentioned above, there have been two major legislative initiatives to amend Canadian law on child pornography. During this period Canada also ratified the UN Optional Protocol to the Convention on the Rights of the Child on the Sale of Children, Child Prostitution and Child Pornography. Despite extensive policy initiatives and legislative attempts at reform, the Canadian law remains problematic for a number of reasons, explored below.

Images vs. Written Material

Firstly, a distinction needs to be made between 'real images of child abuse' and 'written material describing such abuse'. As it stands, the definition of 'child pornography' provided within the Canadian Criminal Code includes both visual representations (as well as audio recordings) and written material, as well as depictions of real children under the age of 18, or persons depicted as under the age of 18 (virtual content). The definition provided in section 163.1(1)(i) also includes persons engaged (real content) or depicted as engaged (virtual content) in explicit sexual activity.

The current version of section 163.1(1)(b) of the Canadian Criminal Code states that any written material that advocates or counsels sexual activity with a person under the age of 18 years will be prosecuted. Bill C-2 added a subsection (c) to clarify further what type of written material is covered. Following the amendments any written material the dominant characteristic of which is the description of sexual activity with a person under the age of 18 years for a sexual purpose can be the subject matter of a criminal investigation. Why is this so?

It is submitted that the Canadian legislation would have been no less effective and significantly clearer if the definition of child pornography under section 163.1 did not include 'written material' at all. Laws such as the Protection of Children Act 1978 in England and Wales and the US child pornography laws as described in the previous chapter, concentrate on visual representations rather than the criminalization and prosecution of written material. When indecent photographs and sexually explicit images involve real children, the children used in such images are abused and sexually exploited in the process, and the need to protect them from such abuse and sexual exploitation is clear. However, it is much more difficult to argue that there is such a direct link and harm to children when pen and paper are used to describe the sexual abuse of children. There is no doubt that such written material may be used for grooming purposes, but if that is the case, the grooming activity should be criminalized rather than the writings themselves. In fact, luring a child by means of a computer system has been considered a criminal activity under section 172.1 of the Canadian Criminal Code since 2002.[72]

72 Note for example *R v. Deck* (2006) W.C.B.J. LEXIS 479; 2006 W.C.B.J. 62; 69 W.C.B. (2d) 88; 2006 ABCA 92; and *R v. Brown* (2006) W.C.B.J. LEXIS 1013; 2006 W.C.B.J. 23; 69 W.C.B. (2d) 780.

The Canadian Supreme Court in *Sharpe*[73] did not go as far as to say that any written material involving sexual activity with a person under the age of 18 years is protected speech. It created a limited exception in which the possession of expressive material created through the efforts of a single person and held by that person alone, exclusively for his or her own personal use is protected. The Supreme Court described such written material as 'deeply private expression, such as personal journals and drawings, intended solely for the eyes of their creator'.[74] It would have been better to leave the application of this exception to the courts rather than trying to clarify it within the Canadian Parliament and trying to define such words as 'legitimate purpose', 'artistic merit' or 'public good' by legislation. Many were displeased by the fact that Robin Sharpe had been found not guilty in relation to his writings which according to Shaw J had some artistic merit.[75] However, it should be recalled that Robin Sharpe was found guilty by the same judge in relation to two counts of possession of child pornography involving various photographs.

It appears that the debate on whether written materials should or should not be regarded as child pornography will continue for some time. Within this context it is worth noting the case of *R v. Beattie*,[76] in which the defendant was charged with the possession of child pornography involving 33 stories which described, in graphic language, sexual activities between adults and children contrary to section 163.1(4) of the Criminal Code. The trial judge found that the stories 'viewed objectively' did not actively induce or encourage sexual activity with children by sending the message 'sex with children can and should be pursued'. The trial judge therefore dismissed the charge. On appeal, the Court of Appeal for Ontario ruled that the stories in question did not explicitly advocate or counsel having sex with children. However, the Court considered that these stories sent two explicit and clear messages to the objective reader of them:

> First, they send the message that children want and enjoy sex with adults. Children encourage sex with adults – even their fathers – by becoming precocious, flirtatious, even manipulative. They are sexually insatiable and ready for repeated sexual encounters. And they enjoy sexual activity even when it is painful and violent.[77]
>
> Second, these stories send the message that although society seemingly disapproves of sex between adults and children, those adults who love children the most and understand them the best (their parents) and those adults who are responsible for their well-being (their parents and doctors) routinely have sex with children. According to the stories, adults do so because they appreciate that children not only enjoy but benefit from sexual activity.[78]

Laskin JA, delivering the appeal court's judgment, stated, 'the trial judge's approach does not recognize that active inducement or encouragement may come from a message that is implicit in the stories themselves. Material that describes sex with

73 *R v. Sharpe* (2001) SCC 2. File No. 27376, 26 January 2001.

74 Ibid.

75 *R v. Sharpe* (2002) B.C.D. Crim. J. 2149; 2002 B.C.D. Crim. J. LEXIS 183; [2002] B.C.D. Crim. 250.90.60.00-01, decided on 26 March 2002.

76 *R v. Beattie* (2005) 75 O.R. (3d) 117; Ont. Rep. LEXIS 69.

77 Ibid., para. 14.

78 Ibid., para. 15.

children as enjoyable, normal and beneficial, and the children as willing may send the message that sex with children can and should be pursued.'[79]

The appeal was allowed and a retrial was ordered. An appeal to the Supreme Court of Canada was denied in November 2005.[80] However, regardless of Laskin JA's clear reasoning, the question remains whether such written materials simply 'describe morally repugnant acts', as was stated by Shaw J in the *Sharpe* retrial, and therefore should constitute deeply private expression in the absence of any further distribution or showing to or sharing of the stories with children, or any other use as part of a luring activity involving children. If there was any evidence to suggest that the stories were used for any such purpose, then alternative charges including a luring charge under section 172.1 of the Canadian Criminal Code[81] could have been brought. Laskin JA did not address the Supreme Court's exceptions while reaching the appeal court's judgment and it remains to be seen whether the same decision will be supported by other courts.[82]

Most child pornography related prosecutions in the UK, the United States Canada and elsewhere involve offences related to images and films. In rare instances written materials are involved and in any event most defendants charged with offences related to child pornography are found to possess or distribute images involving child pornography rather than written material. Cases like *Sharpe* and *Beattie* remain exceptional.

If Canadian politicians, law enforcement bodies and prosecutors are committed to better protecting the children of Canada, efforts should centre on the prosecution of offenders who create, distribute and possess abusive images of real children. Obviously, there may be instances in which a suspect may have in his possession writings and drawings rather than photographs or images in data format. It is the view of the author that these cases should not be brought to trial.

Introduction of Mandatory Minimum Sentences

As mentioned above, Bill C-2 increased the summary convictions from six months to a maximum of 18 months in relation to child pornography offences. The commission of such an offence with an intent to profit is also seen as an aggravating factor for sentencing purposes following the Bill C-2 amendments.

Prior to this, most possession and distribution prosecutions resulted in conditional sentences and house arrests. These types of sentences were seen as unsatisfactory and mandatory minimum sentences for child pornography offences were introduced as a response to public criticism.

79 Ibid., para. 23.

80 *R v. Beattie* (2005) CanLII 41352 (S.C.C.), 10 November 2005 Docket no 30999.

81 Note for example *R v. Deck* (2006) W.C.B.J. LEXIS 479; 2006 W.C.B.J. 62; 69 W.C.B. (2d) 88; 2006 ABCA 92; and *R v. Brown* (2006) W.C.B.J. LEXIS 1013; 2006 W.C.B.J. 23; 69 W.C.B. (2d) 780.

82 Note further *R v. Missions*, 196 C.C.C. (3d) 253; 2005 C.C.C. LEXIS 111, a decision of the Nova Scotia Court of Appeal which endorsed the view adopted in *R v. Beattie*.

It should be recalled that there are no minimum mandatory sentences for child pornography related offences under the Protection of Children Act 1978 in England and Wales. However, as was explained in Chapter 2, the Court of Appeal in *R v. Oliver*[83] laid down the sentencing guidelines in terms of child pornography prosecutions. These vary from a simple fine to a maximum imprisonment of ten years. Detailed sentencing guidelines similar to the Oliver guidelines would have been preferable to mandatory minimum sentences of one year for making and distribution offences on indictment, and for a term of 45 days for possession and access offences on indictment.

Under the Oliver guidelines there needs to be an element of distribution or possession of large amounts of images involving sexual activity between children, or solo masturbation by a child, or a small amount of material involving non-penetrative sexual activity between adults and children to be able to pass the custody threshold in a prosecution. The Oliver guidelines also make a distinction between less and more serious crimes and first time offenders and repeat offenders. A wide range of penalties were additionally made available to the sentencing courts including fines, conditional discharges, community sentences, and community rehabilitation orders with a sex offender programme in addition to custodial sentences.

Development of Sentencing Guidelines by the Canadian Courts

When sentencing offenders in relation to child pornography related offences 'the objectives of greatest concern are denunciation, deterrence of other offenders and acknowledgement of the harm done to victims',[84] according to the Court in *R v. R.A.B.*[85] To assist the sentencing courts, a categorization of the varying levels of child pornography, ranging from erotica, non-criminal images (Level 1) to sadistic sexual images (Level 5) was submitted by the Crown and adopted by the Provincial Court of British Columbia in *R v. G.H.K.*:[86]

> Level 1 – Non erotic, non sexualized material including nudity (not subject to criminal sanctions).
>
> Level 2 – Material where the dominant characteristic demonstrates a sexual purpose. (Emphasis on the genital area, a sex organ or anal region.)

83 (CA Criminal Division), [2002] EWCA Crim 2766; [2003] 2 Cr App R (S) 64; [2003] 1 Cr App R 28; [2003] 2 Cr App R (S.) 15, *The Times*, 6 December 2002; 2002 WL 31599711. See further, Gillespie, A.A., 'Sentences for Offences Involving Child Pornography' (2003), *Crim. L.R.*, 81–92 (February); and Thomas, D.A., 'Sentencing: Making Indecent Photographs or Pseudo Photographs of Children – Sentencing Guidelines' (2003), *Crim. L.R.*, 127–33 (February).

84 *R v. R.A.B.* [2006] B.C.J. No. 1808; 2006 BCPC 367; 2006 BC.C. LEXIS 1858 (British Columbia Provincial Court); *R v. M.H.* [2002] B.C.J. No. 771; *R v. E.O.* [2003] O.J. No. 563.

85 Ibid.

86 *R v. G.H.K.* [2005] B.C.J. No. 2874; (2005) BCPC 618. The Provincial Court of Alberta also referred to the Provincial Court of British Columbia categorization: *R v. Peterson* [2006] A.J. No. 827; 2006 ABPC 177; 2006 AB.C. LEXIS 817 (Alberta Provincial Court).

Level 3 – Explicit sexual activity and assaults, involving adults and children and sexual acts between young children.
Level 4 – Gross assaults, penetrative assaults involving adults.
Level 5 – Sadistic sexual images involving children.

This resembles the image description scale set up by the Court of Appeal in *Oliver*[87] in England and Wales based upon the COPINE[88] typology. Although there is no reference either to the work of COPINE or to the Court of Appeal's decision in *Oliver*, the striking similarities suggest that the Provincial Court of British Columbia relied upon the Oliver image description scale while formulating its own categorization. This type of categorization is not yet widely used by the Canadian courts and it remains to be seen whether it will be adopted by the Federal Courts.

Prosecution Statistics

Detailed statistics are not available for Canadian child pornography prosecutions. However, in a study conducted by Statistics Canada in 2003 on 'Sexual Offences in Canada' it was stated that between 1997 and 2002, the Canadian police brought charges against 226 men and 11 women for the production or distribution of child pornography.[89] In a later study conducted in 2005 on 'Children and Youth as Victims of Violent Crime', Statistics Canada revealed that there were 166 persons charged with the production and distribution of child pornography in 2003 based upon the Uniform Crime Reporting Survey conducted within 122 police services in Canada.[90] According to the 2005 study, almost 'all offenders were male (99 per cent) and the majority were aged 25 to 54 years (53 per cent)'.[91] The study also revealed that 'there has been an eight-fold increase in the number of charges laid by police for child pornography'[92] since 1998 'from a low of 20 charges in 1998 to a high of 159 charges in 2003.'[93] In terms of conviction rates, these 'have increased from 41 per cent of cases in 1999 to 58 per cent in 2001, at which point the rate has remained relatively stable.'[94] Finally, in terms of punishment, the study based upon the Adult Criminal Court Survey revealed that 'offenders charged and found guilty of distributing child pornography were mostly sentenced to probation (52 per cent), followed by prison

87 (CA Criminal Division), [2002] EWCA Crim 2766; [2003] 2 Cr App R (S) 64.

88 For further information see <http://www.copine.ie/>.

89 Kong, R., H. Johnson, S. Beattie and A. Cardillo, *Sexual Offences in Canada*, 2003, Statistics Canada, Catalogue no. 85-002-XIE, vol. 23, no. 6, at <http://www.statcan.ca/english/freepub/85-<002-XIE/0060385-002-XIE.pdf>.

90 AuCoin, K., *Children and Youth as Victims of Violent Crime*, Statistics Canada, Catalogue no. 85-002-XIE, vol. 25, no. 1 (April, 2005) at <http://www.statcan.ca:8096/bsolc/english/bsolc?catno=85-002-XIE2005001>.

91 Ibid.

92 Ibid.

93 Ibid.

94 Ibid.

(33 per cent)'[95] between 1996 and 2003.[96] Obviously, compared to England and Wales and the United States these statistics are low, but they do not seem to take into consideration the possession charges or any other related charges. It is therefore difficult to comment further in terms of success, and effectiveness of the working practices based upon the current child pornography laws in Canada.

Overall, Canada treats online sexual exploitation of children as a growing problem and has therefore developed a strategy that has entailed amendment of the Canadian Criminal Code as well as support for self-regulatory initiatives such as Cybertip.ca[97] in co-ordination and in co-operation with the private sector. Only time will tell whether the new provisions and amended defences within the Criminal Code will withstand constitutional scrutiny.

---

95 Ibid.

96 Note also a discussion of these statistics in Proceedings of the Canadian Standing Senate Committee on Legal and Constitutional Affairs, Issue 18 – Evidence for July 7 2005.

97 See <http://www.cybertip.ca> for further information.

Part Two

Supranational and International Approaches

> There is no doubt that the future development of the international legal system will not only rest on the activities of states, but also increasingly on the international organizations they have created themselves to overcome the limits of the capacity of national governments to deal effectively with transnational problems.[1]

The rights of children and their protection from sexual exploitation and child pornography has generally been recognized as an international problem,[2] and there have been significant policy initiatives at the supranational, regional international and international levels to address this. Following on from the assessment of national approaches in three different jurisdictions, namely, England and Wales, the United States of America, and Canada, Part Two of this book assesses harmonization efforts to combat child pornography at the European Union, Council of Europe and United Nations levels.

Although many would assume that strict child pornography laws are in place in most countries, in reality, this is not necessarily the case. Part of the ongoing problem is that there are variations between the criminal laws of different countries and at the same time there are still many countries around the world with no specific legislation dealing with child pornography.[3] What constitutes child pornography in one country may well not be considered child pornography in another. Equally, certain states may decide not to criminalize certain activities such as possession of child pornography, or similar crimes may not result in similar penalties in different countries.

---

1 See Malanczuk, P., *Akehurst's Modern Introduction to International Law*, 7th edn, London: Routledge, 1997, at 96.

2 Note also the following instruments in relation to the need to extend particular care to children: Geneva Declaration of the Rights of the Child of 1924 and in the Declaration of the Rights of the Child adopted by the General Assembly on 20 November 1959; the Universal Declaration of Human Rights, in the International Covenant on Civil and Political Rights (in particular in articles 23 and 24), in the International Covenant on Economic, Social and Cultural Rights (in particular in article 10). See further the Convention on the Rights of the Child Adopted and opened for signature, ratification and accession by General Assembly resolution 44/25 of 20 November 1989 entry into force 2 September 1990, in accordance with article 49, <http://www.unhchr.ch/html/menu3/b/k2crc.htm>.

3 See generally Report of the Special Rapporteur on the sale of children, child prostitution and child pornography (Mr Juan Miguel Petit), E/CN.4/2005/78, 23 December 2004, Commission on Human Rights, at <http://daccessdds.un.org/doc/UNDOC/GEN/G05/100/19/PDF/G0510019.pdf>.

Such disparities, in turn, result in complications with regards to combating child pornography on a borderless and global environment like the Internet. For example, cross-border law enforcement operations could be hampered if both the countries involved in such operations do not criminalize the same conduct or content. Furthermore, problems of extradition may be witnessed, especially if similar crimes do not exist in certain countries and requirements for dual-criminality can not be satisfied. Traditional forms of national criminal investigation and evidence-gathering may also be undermined if the suspects are outside the jurisdiction, and cross-border co-operation is not possible due to disparities between the criminal laws or due to the non-existence of mutual assistance agreements. Definitional problems and differences therefore add to the problems associated with the detection and successful prosecution of such crimes at a national level.

Furthermore, in some cases the non-existence of laws dealing with child pornography may lead to the creation of a commercial market for child pornography with organized crime involvement. There is already evidence to suggest that commercial websites based in Eastern Europe supply child pornography to those interested in such content around the globe.[4]

Undoubtedly, the harmonization of common legal standards would be a significant step in the global fight against child pornography. However, harmonization efforts to combat child pornography have been protracted and are ongoing. As will be seen in Part Two, various agreements and conventions developed by the European Union, the Council of Europe and the United Nations provide reservations for member states and the right not to apply certain provisions at state level. Harmonization rests upon how each member state implements these provisions. Chapters 5 (European Union), 6 (Council of Europe) and 7 (United Nations) will provide an assessment of how these provisions have been implemented to date.

4 Ibid., para. 25.

Chapter 5

European Union Policy

At European Union (EU) Member State level there is a strong commitment, based on global economic competition, but equally political populism, to embrace in principle 'the age of the Information Society'.[1] At the same time it is recognized that because of cultural, historical and socio-political diversity there will inevitably be divergent approaches to the growth and governance of the Internet in different European societies. The European Parliament is convinced that

> … such divergences weaken Member States' ability to fight cybercrime and that Member States and the European institutions must define a coherent legal framework for criminal investigations and sanctions for high-tech crime and computer-related offences (as proposed by the Commission in its communication) in order to protect European citizens, the internal market and the internal security of the Union itself and of its Member States.[2]

As far as the problem of child pornography is concerned, the European Union has been working towards a common approach to tackle this problem within Member States and within the candidate countries. The EU also co-operates with regional organizations such as the Council of Europe and international organizations such as the United Nations and G8 to fight cybercrime more generally and child pornography specifically. The development of an EU-wide policy on how to combat Internet child pornography is explored in this chapter.

THE EUROPEAN UNION AND THE INTERNET

As well as being concerned with telecommunications liberalization, the creation of a European Information Society,[3] the development of electronic commerce, data protection and privacy, the EU is also committed to steer co-operation for

---

1 See House of Lords Select Committee on Science and Technology, *Information Society* (1995–96 HL 77, HMSO, London) paras 1.1, 1.6 (the *Government Response* is at Cm.3450, 1996); European Commission Communication, *The Information Society and Development: the Role of the European Union* (COM(97) 351, Brussels–Luxembourg, 1997).

2 *Strategy for Creating a Safer Information Society* (A5-0284/2001), text adopted by the European parliament on 6 September 2001: Recommendation of the European Parliament on the *Strategy for Creating a Safer Information Society by Improving the Security of Information Infrastructures and Combating Computer-related Crime* (2001/2070(COS)), C 72 E/323-329 *Official Journal of the European Communities*, 21.3.2002, paragraph G.

3 European Commission, *eEurope – An Information Society for All –* Progress report for the Special European Council on Employment, Economic reforms and social cohesion towards

fighting crime within Member States in relation to exploitation of women, sexual exploitation of children, and high-tech crime amongst other things.[4] In 1997 the European Parliament recognized that national solutions do not address the problems of a global communication system and emphasized the importance of co-operation between Member States in the sphere of justice and home affairs.[5] The European Parliament stressed, in a Resolution in October 1997, that measures to protect minors and human dignity can be effective only if they are co-ordinated at a global level, and called on the European Commission and the Member States to seek to bring such international co-ordination with the United Nations, the G8 and the OECD and to engage in bilateral talks with the United States and Japan.[6]

Initiatives at the EU level with respect to combating Internet child pornography are of crucial significance for Member States and may also have an impact upon candidate countries during the EU integration and enlargement period for full membership to the EU.

---

a Europe based on innovation and knowledge Lisbon, 23–24 March 2000, COM/2000/0130 final, March 8, 2000. European Commission, *eEurope 2002 – An Information Society for All – Draft Action Plan* prepared by the European Commission for the European Council in Feira, 19–20 June 2000, COM/2000/0330 final. European Commission, Communication from the Commission to the Council and European Parliament, *The eEurope 2002 update* prepared by the European Commission for the European Council in Nice, 7 and 8 December 2000, COM/2000/0783 final. Communication from the Commission to the Council and the European Parliament, *eEurope 2002: Impact and Priorities: A Communication to the Spring European Council in Stockholm*, 23–24 March 2001, COM/2001/0140 final. Opinion of the Economic and Social Committee on *eEurope 2002 An information society for all: Draft Action Plan*, OJ C 123, 25 April 2001 pp. 36–46, 25 April 2001.

4 Conclusions of the Tampere European Council: Bull. 10-1999, point I.14: The Council of the European Union at its Tampere meeting in October 1999 stated that the fight against cybercrime is a priority in developing the Union as an area of freedom, security and justice (Article 2 of the EU Treaty). See furthermore Joint Action 97/154/JHA *concerning action to combat trafficking in human beings and sexual exploitation of children*: OJ L 63, 4 March 1997. But note that this joint action has been repealed by article 11 of the Council Framework Decision 2004/68/JHA of 22 December 2003 on *combating the sexual exploitation of children and child pornography* (see OJ L 013 20 January 2004, pp. 44–8), at <http://register.consilium.europa.eu/pdf/en/03/st10/st10748en03.pdf>.

5 See European Parliament Resolution on the Commission communication *on illegal and harmful content on the Internet*, 24 April 1997 and European Parliament Resolution of 24 October 1997 on the Commission Green Paper *on the protection of minors and human dignity in audiovisual and information services* (COM(96) 483).

6 Ibid. See further, *Strategy for Creating a Safer Information Society* (A5-0284/2001), text adopted by the European parliament on 6 September 2001: Recommendation of the European Parliament on the *Strategy for Creating a Safer Information Society by Improving the Security of Information Infrastructures and Combating Computer-related Crime* (2001/2070(COS)), C 72 E/323-329 *Official Journal of the European Communities*, 21 March 2002, paragraph F.

EUROPEAN UNION POLICY DEVELOPMENTS

In April 1996 Irish Minister of State for European Affairs, Gay Mitchell, called on the EU to investigate controls on the transmission of child pornography on the Internet at a joint meeting organized by UNICEF and the Council of Europe.[7] This was followed by the informal meeting of the EU culture and telecommunications ministers in Bologna, Italy to discuss Internet regulation. The ministers agreed at that time to ask the European Commission to draw up a report on the issue. Subsequently, a resolution was adopted by the Telecommunications Council of Ministers in September 1996 on preventing the dissemination of illegal content on the Internet, especially child pornography. As a response to these calls, a Communication Paper on illegal and harmful content was published by the European Commission in which the Commission stated:

> … the answer to the challenge will be a combination of self-control of the service providers, new technical solutions such as rating systems and filtering software, awareness actions for parents and teachers, information on risks and possibilities to limit these risks and of international co-operation.[8]

The Communication Paper was launched together with a Green Paper on the Protection of Minors and Human Dignity in Audio-visual and Information Services in October 1996.[9] While the Communication Paper provided policy options for immediate action to fight against harmful and illegal content on the Internet, the Green Paper set out to examine the broader challenges that society faces in ensuring that these issues of overriding public interest are adequately taken into account in the rapidly evolving world of audio-visual and information services. It suggested:

> If such mechanisms of international governance and re-regulation are to be initiated then the role of nation states is pivotal. Nation states are now simply one class of powers and political agencies in a complex system of power from world to local levels but they have a centrality because of their relationship to territory and population.[10]

The UK Government welcomed the European Commission's approach, with its emphasis on self-regulation by the Internet industry, as entirely consistent with the

---

7 Smyth, P., 'Mitchell argues for world wide register of paedophiles', *Irish Times* (Dublin), 26 April 1996. See also Human Rights Watch 'Silencing The Net: The Threat to Freedom of Expression On-line' (1996), *Monitors: A Journal of Human Rights and Technology* 1, Special Release available at <http://www.epic.org/free_speech/intl/hrw_report_5_96.html>.

8 See European Commission Communication to the European Parliament, The Council, The Economic and Social Committee and the Committee of the Regions, *Illegal and Harmful Content on the Internet* (COM(96) 487, Brussels–Luxembourg, 16 October 1996.

9 See European Commission, *Green Paper on the Protection of Minors and Human Dignity in Audovisual and Information Services* (COM (96) 483 final, Brussels–Luxembourg, 16 October 1996.

10 Hirst, P. and G. Thompson, 'Globalization and the Future of the Nation State' (1995), *Economy and Society* 24(3), 408–42, at 430.

UK's own approach. A House of Commons Select Committee Report on European legislation acknowledged this in November 1996 by stating:

> The UK strongly agrees with the Commission that since a legal framework for regulation of the Internet already exists in Member States, new laws or regulations are unnecessary.[11]

Chris Smith, the then Secretary of State for National Heritage, stated in July 1997:

> It is vital, however, in considering how best to address [the problem of illegal and harmful content on the Internet], that we bear in mind that only a small fraction of the material available to the public poses a threat to the protection of minors or human dignity. It will be important, therefore, not to impose hasty regulation upon these new services and thereby constrain their development and the educational, commercial and social opportunities and other benefits they can engender.[12]

The Communication Paper and the Green Paper were followed by the European Commission Working Party Report[13] in November 1996. According to the Working Party Report, a self-regulatory system, including representatives of industry and users, should be developed to advise on whether or not a breach of the code of conduct has occurred. The next stage in the discussion was the adoption of a resolution on the Commission Communication Paper by the European Parliament in April 1997.[14] The European Commissioner for industrial affairs and information and telecommunications technologies, Martin Bangemann, recognized that it was difficult to pass legislation at international level on 'harmful' content on the Internet, but stated there was less scope for cultural difference in defining what was 'illegal', and the response had to be global.[15] He also emphasized the need for co-ordination between initiatives relating to the subjects, both in the EU framework and in other international fora.

These issues were further discussed at the 'Global Information Networks, Ministerial Conference' in Bonn in July 1997.[16] The resultant 'Bonn Declaration'[17] underlined the importance of clearly defining the relevant legal rules on responsibility for content of the various actors in the chain between creation and use. The ministers

---

11 Select Committee on European Legislation (1996) Fourth Report, London: HMSO, November 1996, para. 14.8.

12 See House of Commons, Select Committee on European Legislation, Second Report: Session 1997–98, London: HMSO, 22 July 1997, HC 155-ii. See particularly 'The Information Society and Protection of Human Dignity' section at para. 60. An online copy is available at <http://www.parliament.the-stationery-office.co.uk/pa/cm199798/cmselect/cmeuleg/155ii/el0262.htm>.

13 European Commission Working Party Report, *Illegal and Harmful Content on the Internet* (1996).

14 See European Commission, *Communication on illegal and harmful content on the Internet* (COM(96)0487 – C4-0592/96) Committee on Civil Liberties and Internal Affairs, 20 March 1997.

15 Ibid.

16 See 'Global Information Networks, Ministerial Conference', Bonn, 6–8 July 1997.

17 Ibid.

recognized the need to make a clear distinction between the responsibility of those who produce and place content in circulation and that of intermediaries such as Internet service providers (ISPs), thus beginning to accept that it is producers and users who must exercise normative choice and discernment and that carriers are not in a position to act as content guardians in this medium. However, historically, one should also note that despite these calls and initiatives, CompuServe Germany was successfully prosecuted in May 1998 for the dissemination of child pornography to its customers in Germany[18] (discussed in Chapter 8).

EU ministers also declared at the Bonn Conference 'their intention to co-operate fully with the Council of Europe, the OECD, and other appropriate international fora, in order to identify and dismantle existing obstacles to the use of new services on global information networks, to prevent the establishment of new barriers, and to establish a clear and predictable legal framework at national and, where appropriate, European and global levels.'[19] This statement serves to emphasize that Internet-related problems deserve not only national and supranational attention but also global levels of governance and co-operation as the Internet remains beyond the control of any single nation state or even the EU Member States combined.

The Bonn Declaration was followed in September 1997 by Martin Bangemann's call for an Internet charter, which would focus on issues to do with technical standards, illegal content, licenses, encryption and data privacy:

> The current situation may lead to the adoption of isolated global rules with different countries signing up to different rules agreed under the auspices of different international organizations. An international charter would provide a suitable answer.[20]

The idea was given further substance when Martin Bangemann and fellow-Commissioner, Sir Leon Brittan, launched a proposed framework for international policy co-operation and sought to start a process which could lead to the adoption of an International Communications Charter for the Internet in February 1998.[21] However this initiative was never followed up.

In July 1998 the Austrian government, during its presidency of the European Union, called for action against child pornography following the discovery of a paedophilia ring using the Internet in Netherlands.[22] This was immediately followed by calls by the former German Chancellor, Helmut Kohl, for stronger international

18 See the *Criminal case of Somm, Felix Bruno*, File No: 8340 Ds 465 JS 173158/95, Local Court (Amtsgericht) Munich. See also Associated Press, 'Ex-CompuServe Executive Convicted', Berlin, 28 May 1998.

19 'Global Information Networks, Ministerial Conference', Bonn, 6–8 July 1997.

20 See 'A New World Order for Global Communications', a speech by Martin Bangemann to Telecom Inter@ctive '97, ITU Geneva, 8 September 1997.

21 See the European Commission, *Communication on International Charter: The need for strengthened international co-ordination – Communication from the Commission to the European Parliament, the Council, the Economic and Social Committee and the Committee of the Regions* (COM (98) 50, Brussels–Luxembourg. See also Tucker, E., 'Internet: EU tries to forge system of rules', *Financial Times*, 5 February 1998.

22 Reuters, 'Austria urges European action against Net porn', Vienna, 17 July 1998.

co-operation in the struggle against child pornography.[23] Kohl said at the time, 'the Dutch case showed that the international community needed to intensify its efforts to protect children from such abuses.'[24]

The outcome of all these political developments was the production of a number of important policy documents by the EU. These are:

- the EU Action Plan on promoting safer use of the Internet,[25] and its follow-up decision;[26]
- the Council Recommendation of 24 September 1998 on the development of the competitiveness of the European audiovisual and information services industry by promoting national frameworks aimed at achieving a comparable and effective level of protection of minors and human dignity;[27]
- the Council Decision of 29 May 2000 to combat child pornography on the Internet;[28]
- the Directive 2000/31/EC of the European Parliament and of the Council of 8 June 2000 on certain legal aspects of information society services, in particular electronic commerce, in the Internal Market (Directive on Electronic Commerce);[29]
- the communication to the Council and the European Parliament on combating trafficking in human beings and combating the sexual exploitation of children and child pornography;[30]
- the communication to the Council and the European Parliament on Creating a Safer Information Society by Improving the Security of Information Infrastructures and Combating Computer-related Crime;[31] and
- the Council Framework Decision on combating the sexual exploitation of children and child pornography.[32]

---

23 Reuters, ' Kohl urges fight against online child pornography', Bonn, 19 July 1998.

24 BBC News, 'Call for action on Net porn', 18 July 1998.

25 Decision no 276/1999/EC of the European Parliament and of the Council of 25 January 1999 adopting a *Multiannual Community Action Plan on promoting safer use of the Internet by combating illegal and harmful content on global networks*.

26 European Commission Communication, *Follow-up to the Multiannual Community Action Plan on Promoting Safer Use of the Internet by combating illegal and harmful content on global networks*: Proposal for a decision of the European Parliament and of the Council amending Decision No. 276/1999/EC adopting a Multiannual Community Action Plan on promoting safer use of the Internet by combating illegal and harmful content on global networks, COM 2002 152, Brussels, 22 March 2002, INFSO/D/5.

27 OJ L 270 of 7 October 1998, p. 48.

28 Council Decision of 29 May 2000 *to combat child pornography on the Internet* (2000/375/JHA) OJ L 138, 9 July 2000 p. 1.

29 *Official Journal of the European Communities*, L 178/1, 17 July 2000.

30 Communication to the Council and the European Parliament *on combating trafficking in human beings and combating the sexual exploitation of children and child pornography*, COM(2000)854 final /2, Brussels, 22 January 2001.

31 Communication from the Commission to the Council, the European Parliament, the Economic and Social Committee and the Committee of the Regions on *Creating a Safer Information Society by Improving the Security of Information Infrastructures and Combating Computer-related Crime*, COM(2000) 890 final, Brussels, 26 January 2001. See generally, <http://europa.eu.int/ISPO/eif/InternetPoliciesSite/Crime/crime1.html>.

32 *Council Framework Decision on combating the sexual exploitation of children and child pornography*, Communication to the Council and the European Parliament COM(2000)

The following sections analyse these significant developments towards the establishment of a common EU-wide policy in the fight against child pornography.

EU ACTION PLAN ON PROMOTING SAFER USE OF THE INTERNET

In November 1997 the European Commission adopted a proposal for an action plan promoting the safe use of the Internet which would cover a three year period between 1999 and 2002.[33] The Action Plan recognized that the Internet does not exist in a 'legal vacuum'. However, because of the global nature of the Internet, the EU preferred self-regulatory solutions for the regulation of illegal and harmful content. The Action Plan therefore encouraged one, the creation of a European network of hotlines (such as the UK's Internet Watch Foundation which was mentioned in Chapter 2) to report illegal content such as child pornography by online users, and two, the development of self regulatory and content-monitoring schemes by access providers and content providers for combating illegal content.

The Commission's Action Plan was supported by the UK Government. According to Barbara Roche, the former Parliamentary Under-Secretary of State for Small Firms, Trade and Industry at the Department of Trade and Industry:

> The Government support the actions to be promoted by the action plan [EU Action plan on the safe use of the Internet, COM (97) 582], whose approach builds on the UK's successful experience with the Internet Watch Foundation. The Government consider that international co-operation between national hotlines, and in the development of filtering systems, is crucial to the control of illegal and harmful content on the Internet.[34]

Following over a year of discussions within the institutions of the European Union, in December 1998 the Council of the European Union approved the Action Plan on promoting safer use of the Internet by combating illegal and harmful content on global networks.[35] The name of the Action Plan was changed slightly from 'safe use of the

---

854 final 2, Brussels, 22 January 2001. *Combating trafficking in human beings and combating the sexual exploitation of children and child pornography*: Proposal for a Council Framework Decision on combating trafficking in human beings. Proposal for a Council Framework Decision on combating the sexual exploitation of children and child pornography. (See <http://europa.eu.int/eur-lex/en/com/pdf/2000/en_500PC0854_01.pdf>). See OJ C E/2001/62/E/25 327, pp. 327–30, 27 February 2001. Note also the Anna Karamanou report of the Committee on Citizens' Freedoms and Rights, Justice and Home Affairs in relation to this Communication, A5-0206/2001.

33 See Communication from the Commission to the European Parliament, the Council, the Economic and Social Committee and the Committee of the Regions for an *Action Plan on promoting safe use of the Internet*, November 1997.

34 According to Mrs Barbara Roche, the Department of Trade and Industry, Internet, Commons Written Answers, 25 February 1998. See further, the Select Committee on European Legislation Sixteenth Report, HC 155-xvi, 27 February 1998 for the comments on the Safe use of the Internet COM(97)582.

35 Decision No. /98/EC of the European Parliament and of the Council of adopting a Multiannual Community Action Plan *on promoting safer use of the Internet by combating illegal and harmful content on global networks*, December 1998.

Internet' to 'safer use of the Internet'. Members of the European Parliament (MEPs) thought the words 'safer use' would be more appropriate since the EU legislation did not cover criminal law, and it would not be an easy task to promote 'safe' Internet use.[36] Furthermore, according to the MEPs, it was illusory to believe that this action plan alone could stop illegal and harmful content on the Internet. However, during the discussions of the adoption of the Action Plan, the MEPs thought that the Action Plan was a step in the right direction.

Critique of the EU Action Plan on Illegal Content

While all the EU Action Plan initiatives appear attractive to concerned users, there are certain matters which should be carefully addressed. Although the new EU Action Plan suggests that 'harmful content needs to be treated differently from illegal content', what is illegal or harmful is not clearly defined within the context of the Action Plan. The Action plan states that illegal content is related to a wide variety of issues such as instructions on bomb-making (national security), pornography (protection of minors), incitement to racial hatred (protection of human dignity) and libel (protection of reputation), but none of these are necessarily 'illegal content', or even considered as 'harmful content' (probably undefinable in a global context) by many European countries.[37]

In July 1998 the Economic and Social Committee of the European Commission published its opinion on the EU Action Plan.[38] Although favourably disposed in general, the Committee noted that very little attention has been given to illegal content in relation to protection of intellectual property, human dignity, and privacy or to offences relating to national and economic security.[39]

In the view of the Committee, the scope of the Action Plan should have been restricted to combating illegal content such as child pornography, and a lower priority should have been assigned to the development of means of combating harmful content. It may be noted that the Civil Liberties Committee of the European Parliament has also adopted a report on the EU Action Plan which concluded that combating Internet content that is liable to prosecution is a matter for the Member

36 Economic and Social Committee of the European Commission, *Opinion on the Proposal for a Council Decision adopting a Multiannual Community Action Plan on promoting safe use of the Internet* (*Official Journal of the European Communities*, 98/C 214/08, Brussels–Luxembourg, 10 July 1998) pp. 29–32.

37 See further, the Interim report on Initiatives in EU Member States with respect to Combating Illegal and harmful content on the Internet, Version 7, European Commission, 4 June 1997.

38 Economic and Social Committee of the European Commission, 'Opinion on the Proposal for a Council Decision adopting a Multiannual Community Action Plan on promoting safe use of the Internet', *Official Journal of the European Communities*, 98/C 214/08, July 10, 1998, pp. 29–32.

39 Ibid., para. 3.1.1.1.

States.[40] The Commission policy in relation to harmful Internet content also received criticism, but this issue is beyond the scope of this book.[41]

Safer Internet Plus

Although originally planned as a three year Action Plan, in 2002[42] the European Commission prolonged the work in this field for another two years expanding the Action Plan related work and projects to cover the EU candidate countries.[43] One of the main reasons for expanding the Action Plan programme was the fact that illegal and harmful content on the Internet remained a continuing concern for lawmakers, the private sector and parents. The coverage of the Action Plan was also extended to new online technologies:

> … including mobile and broadband content, online games, peer-to-peer file transfer, and all forms of real-time communications such as chat rooms and instant messages. Action will be taken to ensure that a broader range of areas of illegal and harmful content and conduct of concern are covered, including racism and violence.[44]

The European Commission had a budget of EUR 13.3 million over two years for the follow-up programme. Overall, the Safer Internet Action Plan ran between 1999 and 2004 with a total budget of EUR 38.3 million. As a result, approximately 89 projects were financially sponsored under the Safer Internet Action Plan across Europe.[45]

---

40 European Parliament, News report, 'Promote use of Internet but crack down on illegal content', 8 June 1998.

41 See Walker, C. and Y. Akdeniz, 'The Governance of the Internet in Europe with Special Reference to Illegal and Harmful Content' (1998), *Crim. L.R.*, December Special Edition: Crime, Criminal Justice and the Internet, 5–19; Akdeniz, Y., 'The Regulation of Internet Content in Europe: Governmental Control vs. Self-Responsibility' (1999), *Swiss Political Science Review*, 5(2), 123–31; Akdeniz, Y., 'The European Union and Illegal and Harmful Content on the Internet' (1998), *Journal of Civil Liberties* 3(1), March, 31–6; and Akdeniz, Y. and N. Strossen, 'Sexually Oriented Expression', in Y. Akdeniz, C. Walker and D. Wall (eds), *The Internet, Law and Society*, Harlow: Addison Wesley Longman, 2000, 207–31.

42 European Commission Communication, Follow-up to the Multiannual Community *action plan on promoting safer use of the Internet by combating illegal and harmful content on global networks*: Proposal for a decision of the European Parliament and of the Council amending Decision No. 276/1999/EC adopting a Multiannual Community Action Plan on promoting safer use of the Internet by combating illegal and harmful content on global networks, COM 2002 152, Brussels, 22 March 2002, INFSO/D/5.

43 Decision No. 1151/2003/EC of the European Parliament and of the Council of 16 June 2003, amending Decision No. 276/1999/EC *adopting a Multiannual Community Action Plan on promoting safer use of the Internet by combating illegal and harmful content on global networks*, at <http://europa.eu.int/information_society/activities/sip/docs/pdf/programmes/extenstion/extenstion_decision_en.pdf>.

44 Ibid.

45 Note the first evaluation of the Safer Internet Action Plan covered 1999–2000. The Commission adopted a communication COM(2001) 690 on this evaluation which is available at <http://europa.eu.int/eur-lex/en/com/cnc/2001/com2001_0690en01.pdf>. The Commission has also adopted a communication COM(2003) 653 on the evaluation of the

In May 2005 the EU extended the Action Plan on 'Safer Internet Plus'[46] for the period 2005–2008 to continue to promote safer use of the Internet and new online technologies, particularly to fight against illegal content such as child pornography and racist material and content which are potentially harmful to children or content unwanted by the end-user. It is suggested by the Safer Internet Plus document that 'practical measures are still needed to encourage reporting of illegal content to those in a position to deal with it, to encourage assessment of the performance of filter technologies and the benchmarking of those technologies, to spread best practice for codes of conduct embodying generally agreed canons of behaviour, and to inform and educate parents and children on the best way to benefit from the potential of new online technologies in a safe way.'[47] The four-year programme will have a budget of EUR 45 million and it will focus more closely on end-users, especially parents, educators and children. The Safer Internet Plus Plan will continue to be extended to EU candidate countries. The indicative breakdown of the budget suggests that almost half will be spent on awareness raising (47–51 per cent). Fighting against illegal content will receive 25–30 per cent, tackling unwanted and harmful content, 10–17 per cent, and promoting a safer environment, 8–12 per cent of the budget.

The EU Action Plan programme initiatives sit well with self-regulatory initiatives to be discussed in Part Three. For example, the formation of a number of European hotlines has been supported by EU Action Plan funding.

THE COUNCIL RECOMMENDATION OF 24 SEPTEMBER 1998

The Council Recommendation of 24 September 1998 on the development of the competitiveness of the European audiovisual and information services industry by promoting national frameworks aimed at achieving a comparable and effective level of protection of minors and human dignity.[48] The development of the September 1998 Recommendation followed from adoption of the European Commission Green

Safer Internet programme 1999–2002 which is available at <http://europa.eu.int/information_society/activities/sip/docs/pdf/communication/acte_en.pdf>. The full evaluation reports can be obtained through <http://europa.eu.int/information_society/activities/sip/programme/evaluations/index_en.htm>.

46 See the fact sheet for the Safer Internet Plus Programme at <http://europa.eu.int/information_society/doc/factsheets/018-saferinternetplus.pdf>. Note also the Commission Staff Working paper, Ex Ante Evaluation: Safer Internet Plus, SEC(2004) 148, 12 March 2004, at <http://europa.eu.int/information_society/activities/sip/docs/pdf/si_plus/exante.pdf>.

47 See para. 7 of Decision No. 854/2005/EC of the European Parliament and of the Council establishing a Multiannual Community Programme on promoting safer use of the Internet and new online technologies, PE-CONS 3688/1/04 REV1, Strasbourg, 11 May 2005, at <http://europa.eu.int/information_society/activities/sip/docs/prog_decision_2005/sip_decision_2005_en.pdf>.

48 (98/560/EC), L 270/48, *Official Journal of the European Communities*, 7 October 1998.

Paper on the protection of minors and human dignity in audiovisual and information services of October 1996[49] by the European Parliament.[50]

The Council Recommendation addressed, in particular, 'issues of protection of minors and of human dignity'[51] and encouraged the industry to 'develop a national self-regulatory framework'.[52] Like other initiatives, the Recommendation recognized that the 'global nature of communications networks necessitates an international approach to the question of the protection of minors and human dignity in audiovisual and information services.'[53]

The Council urged Member States to foster 'a climate of confidence which would promote the development of the audiovisual and information services industry'[54] by promoting self-regulatory and voluntary solutions by industry and encouraging the participation of all relevant parties (such as users, consumers, businesses and public authorities) 'in the definition, implementation and evaluation of national measures in the fields covered by this recommendation'.[55] The use of hotlines in relation to illegal Internet content was also recommended by the Council[56] which encouraged the transnational co-operation of similar hotlines to 'strengthen the effectiveness of national measures'.[57]

As far as industry co-operation is concerned, the Council recommended industry to 'co-operate in the drawing up of codes of conduct for the protection of minors and human dignity applying to the provision of on-line services, *inter alia* to create an environment favourable to the development of new services.'[58] The European Commission was invited by the Council to facilitate the 'networking' of the bodies responsible for self-regulation within the Member States.[59] The Council also provided indicative guidelines for the implementation of a self-regulatory framework at national level.[60] According to the Council, its guidelines related to four key components of a national self-regulation framework:

- consultation and representation of the parties concerned,
- code(s) of conduct,
- national bodies facilitating co-operation at Community level,
- national evaluation of self-regulation frameworks.

---

49 COM (96) 483 final.

50 OJ C 339, 10 November 1997, p. 420.

51 Paragraph 5 of the Council Recommendation, L 270/48, *Official Journal of the European Communities*, 7 October 98.

52 Paragraph 13, L 270/49.

53 Paragraph 16, L 270/49.

54 Ibid.

55 Recommendation I (1), L 270/50.

56 Recommendation I (3), L 270/50.

57 Ibid.

58 Recommendation II (2), L 270/51.

59 Recommendation III, L 270/51.

60 See the Annex of the Council recommendation, L 270/52.

An evaluation report from the Commission was also requested within two years after the adoption of this Council Recommendation,[61] and this was provided by the Commission in February 2001.[62] The Commission Evaluation Report stated, 'the development of the Internet had further complicated the situation for protecting minors',[63] and noted the difficulties encountered with digital broadcasters or content providers where it was either difficult or sometimes impossible to identify the source of content on the Internet. The Commission explained that in most of the Member States associations of Internet-operators[64] have already been founded,[65] and ISPs from 11 Member States[66] are members of the European Internet Service Providers Association organization (EuroISPA).[67] As far as hotlines are concerned, these were established in nearly all Member States or were under construction[68] with the financial support provided by the above-mentioned EU Action Plan on safer use of the Internet.

The 2001 evaluation report pointed out that 'in five Member States, especially in the context of child pornography, it was the law enforcement agencies who operated such hotlines.[69] However, this is not the case within the United Kingdom (as will be explained in Chapter 9). The report stated that 'the efficiency of hotlines may be increased, if their existence is well known to the Internet users.'[70] Furthermore, the report stated:

> Overall, the Member States consider the existence of hotlines as an important issue but there is divergence with respect to the appreciation of their efficiency. Probably it is still too early to draw a definite conclusion to this respect.[71]

---

61 Recommendation III (4), L 270/51.

62 European Commission, Evaluation Report from the Commission to the Council and the European Parliament on the application of Council Recommendation of 24 September 1998 concerning the protection of minors and human dignity, COM(2001) 106 final, Brussels, 27 February 2001. Note also the EU Council conclusions of 21 June 2001 in relation the protection of minors from harmful media content and human dignity as a follow-up to the Commission's Evaluation Report on the implementation of the Council Recommendation of 24 September 1998, 2361st Council meeting (Culture), 9755/01 (Presse 233), at <http://europa.eu.int/comm/avpolicy/c2361.htm>. The Council conclusions welcomed the Commission's Evaluation Report of 27 February 2001. Council Conclusions of 23 July 2001 on the Commission's Evaluation Report on the application of the recommendation concerning the protection of minors and human dignity (2001/C 213/03), 2001 OJ C 213, 31 July 2001.

63 Ibid.

64 Austria, Belgium, Denmark, Germany, Spain, France, Ireland, Italy, Netherlands, Sweden, Finland, United Kingdom.

65 See 3.1.1. Self-regulation and codes of conduct, the Commission Evaluation Report.

66 Austria, Belgium, Germany, Denmark, France, Ireland, Italy, Netherlands, Finland, United Kingdom.

67 See 3.1.1. Self-regulation and codes of conduct, the Commission Evaluation Report.

68 Ibid.

69 Austria, Belgium, Germany, Denmark, Finland.

70 See 3.1.1. Self-regulation and codes of conduct, the Commission Evaluation Report.

71 Ibid.

Another important fact as noted by the report was that nearly all Member States who replied to the European Commission confirmed that the vast majority of those websites carrying illegal content were 'located outside of the European Union',[72] mainly in the United States (for example, politically extremist and sexually explicit content) and in Russia and in Asia (for example, paedophilia). In its conclusion, the 2001 evaluation report stated that 'the results of the application of the Recommendation were encouraging, although interested parties and in particular consumers should have been more involved in the establishment of codes of conduct.'[73] Furthermore, the report pointed out:

> ... approaches like the establishment of the Dutch NICAM-Institute and the British Communications White Paper demonstrate that much can be achieved under co-regulation or self-regulation and may constitute an orientation for further implementation of the Recommendation.[74]

Overall this Recommendation emphasized further support for co-regulation and/or self-regulation at the national level, but the evaluation report's conclusions in relation to the diverse nature of hotlines within the Member States should be noted. Openness, transparency and accountability of such hotlines may be better established within those countries in which the hotlines are operated by public bodies or by the police[75] rather than in the hands of industry based organizations such as in the UK.

A second evaluation report by the Commission was adopted in December 2003.[76] The second report noted some differences in terms of application by the Member States, but these were generally regarded as positive. The report was, however, once again critical of the limited involvement of consumer associations and other interested parties in the establishment of codes of conduct and other self-regulatory initiatives.

An additional recommendation was proposed by the Commission in April 2004 and was adopted by the European Parliament in September 2005. An amended proposal for a recommendation was adopted by the Commission in January 2006.[77] A political agreement was reached on this recommendation in late 2006.[78] There is nothing specific within the proposed recommendation in relation to combating

---

72 Ibid.

73 Ibid.

74 Ibid.

75 Austria, Belgium, Germany, Denmark, Finland.

76 The second evaluation report from the Commission to the Council and the European Parliament on the application of Council Recommendation of 24 September 1998 concerning the protection of minors and human dignity, COM(2003)776 final, adopted on 12 December 2003, <at http://eur-lex.europa.eu/LexUriServ/site/en/com/2003/com2003_0776en01.pdf>.

77 An amended proposal for a Recommendation of the European Parliament and of the Council *on the Protection of Minors and Human Dignity and the Right of Reply in relation to the Competitiveness of the European Audiovisual and Information Services Industry*, 20 January 2006, COM(2006)31 final, at <http://eur-lex.europa.eu/LexUriServ/site/en/com/2006/com2006_0031en01.pdf>.

78 Recommendation of the European Parliament and of the Council *on the protection of minors and human dignity and on the right of reply in relation to the competitiveness of the*

child pornography but the most recent recommendation includes the strengthening of self-regulatory initiatives including improvement of reporting illegal content to appropriate authorities within the EU as well as developing and improving codes of conduct to fight illegal content on the Internet.

COUNCIL DECISION OF MAY 2000 TO COMBAT CHILD PORNOGRAPHY ON THE INTERNET[79]

In April 1997 Recommendation 5 of the EU Action Plan to combat organized crime[80] called for a cross-pillar study on high-tech crime. The Austrian Presidency produced the strategic guidelines in the area of high tech crime in late 1998.[81] The purpose of the document was to progress towards an agreement for an EU strategy on these issues. This initiative by the Austrian presidency of the European Union was broadly endorsed and supported by the UK government.[82] The Guidelines called Member States 'to take account of work being done in other fora, and to adopt joint positions where possible',[83] with special reference to the work of the Council of Europe on the Cybercrime Convention. Guideline 4 emphasized the need for a balance between self-discipline and regulation for ISPs and suggested the development of international codes of conduct. As far as the UK government was concerned, this was welcome with a special reference to the joint work of the Association of Chief Police Officers (ACPO) and ISPs (see further in Chapter 8).[84]

The European Union, under the presidency of the Austrian government, started to develop a draft joint action[85] to combat child pornography on the Internet.[86] The

---

European audiovisual and online information services industry, 2004/0117 (COD), LEX 775, PE-CONS 3683/06, Brussels, 20 December 2006.

79 OJ L 138, 9 June 2000 pp. 1–4.

80 The European Council in Dublin, in December 1996, underlined its absolute determination to fight organized crime and stressed the need for a coherent and co-ordinated approach by the European Union. Turning this resolve into concrete action, the European Council in Amsterdam, in June 1997, endorsed an Action Plan to Combat Organized Crime, in which, among other things, it called on the Council and the Commission to examine and address, by the end of 1998, the issue of fraud and counterfeiting relating to all non-cash payment instruments, including electronic payment instruments. See Action Plan to Combat Organized Crime, adopted by the Council on 28 April 1997, OJ C 251, 97/C 251/01, 15 August 1997.

81 See European Scrutiny Committee Reports, First Report, 7 December 1998, HC 34-I, Session 1998–99 – High Tech Crime (elements of the Union's strategy against high 'tech' crime).

82 See ibid., para. 7.2.

83 Guideline 1.

84 See ibid. The comments are of The Parliamentary Under-Secretary of State for the Home Department, Kate Hoey.

85 Initiative of the Republic of Austria with a view to adopting a Council Decision to combat child pornography on the Internet, OJ C 362, 16 December 1999 pp. 8–10.

86 See European Scrutiny Committee Reports, Second Report, 15 December 1998, HC 34-ii, Session 1998–99 – Child Pornography on the Internet. This is a contribution to the

joint action has been supported by the UK government, and former Parliamentary Under-Secretary of State for the Home Department, Kate Hoey, commented:

> The Government endorses the need for effective action by Member States to deal with child pornography and broadly supports the provisions of the draft joint Action. The UK has been a leader within the EU in developing measures of the kind envisaged in Articles 1 and 3.[87]

The Minister's comments directly referred to the setting up of the Internet Watch Foundation, and she added:

> In general, Internet service providers in the UK are not required to vet the material which their customers store and transmit. They do however acquire responsibilities once they become aware of material which is illegal. Should they not remove child pornography from their servers once they are made aware of it, they could be prosecuted under the Protection of Children Act 1978 for the dissemination of such material. In general, UK Internet service providers are diligent in removing illegal material once they are made aware of it and in co-operating with law enforcement when investigations into crime are under way.[88]

The Minister finally reinforced the fact that 'in respect of child pornography, the law has adequately accommodated technical developments and should enable law enforcement authorities to take necessary measures to combat this activity on computer networks.'[89] Therefore, no changes to UK legislation were deemed necessary to meet the provisions of the joint action.[90] The EU Justice and Home Affairs Council gave its agreement to the draft joint action on combating child pornography on the Internet in December 1998, while noting that the text could not be formally adopted until the European Parliament had given its opinion.[91] According to the Austrian Presidency Conclusions,

> The European Council welcomes the initiatives on the protection of children. In particular child pornography on the Internet was recognized as a global problem requiring a coordinated approach also at international level, especially at the United Nations. The Council is called upon to ensure an effective follow-up to these initiatives at European and international level.[92]

---

implementation of Recommendation 5 of the EU Action Plan to Combat Organized Crime which was endorsed by the Amsterdam European Council in June 1997.

87 Ibid., para. 12.3.

88 See further, Leong, G., 'Computer Child Pornography: The Liability of Distributors?' (1998), *Crim. L.R.*, Special Edition: Crime, Criminal Justice and the Internet, December 1998, 19–29.

89 European Scrutiny Committee Reports, Second Report, 15 December 1998, HC 34-ii, Session 1998–99 – Child Pornography on the Internet, para. 12.3.

90 Ibid., para. 12.4.

91 See Lords Written Answers, 'Home Affairs Council, 3–4 December', 14 December 1998, columns WA126 and WA127.

92 See para. 92 of the Presidency Conclusions, Vienna European Council, 11 and 12 December 1998, at <http://europa.eu.int/council/off/conclu/dec98.htm>.

It took almost two years for the Council of the European Union to adopt a *Decision to combat child pornography on the Internet.*[93] The decision which was adopted on 29 May 2000 took into account the above-mentioned European Commission *Communication on illegal and harmful content on the Internet,*[94] various resolutions adopted by the European Parliament,[95] the *Resolution of the Council and of the Representatives of the Governments of the Member States on illegal and harmful content on the Internet,*[96] and the *Joint Action adopted by the Council concerning action to combat trafficking in human beings and sexual exploitation of children.*[97] The decision also took into consideration the *Recommendation adopted by the Council on 24 September 1998 on the development of the competitiveness of the European audiovisual and information services industry by promoting national frameworks aimed at achieving a comparable and effective level of protection of minors and human dignity.*[98]

The Council Decision also referred to the Recommendation of the European Council in Vienna on 11–12 December 1998 to ensure an effective follow-up to the initiatives for the protection of children at European and international level, especially in the area of child pornography in the Internet; and to the Council common position on negotiations relating to the Council of Europe's Draft Convention on Cybercrime.[99]

The Council stated that it was aware of the fact that 'the sexual abuse of children and the production, processing, possession and distribution of child pornography material may constitute an important form of international organized crime, the extent of which within the European Union gives cause for ever-increasing concern',[100] and expressed the view that further measures were needed within the Union 'to promote the safer use of the Internet'.

The Council therefore required Member States 'to take the necessary measures to encourage Internet users to inform law enforcement authorities, either directly or indirectly, on suspected distribution of child pornography material on the Internet,

93 2000/375/JHA. Note also the Report (Rapporteur: Timothy Kirkhope) of the Committee on Citizens' Freedoms and Rights, Justice and Home Affairs on the initiative of the Republic of Austria with a view to adopting a Council Decision to combat child pornography on the Internet (10317/1999 – C5-0318/1999 – 1999/0822(CNS)), A5-0090/2000, 28 March 2000.

94 OJ C 150, 19 May 1997, p. 38.

95 19 September 1996 on minors who are victims of violence, OJ C 320, 28 October 1996, p. 190; 12 December 1996 on measures to protect minors in the European Union(3), OJ C 20, 20 January 1997, p. 170.

96 Meeting within the Council, of 17 February 1997, OJ C 70, 6 March.1997, p. 1.

97 Joint Action 97/154/JHA of 24 February 1997, (8) OJ L 63, 4 March 1997, p. 2. Note that this has been repealed by article 11 of the 2003 EU Framework Decision.

98 OJ L 270, 7 October 1998, p. 48.

99 1999/364/JHA of 27 May 1999, OJ L 142, 5 June 1999, p. 1.

100 2000/375/JHA. Note also the Report (Rapporteur: Timothy Kirkhope) of the Committee on Citizens' Freedoms and Rights, Justice and Home Affairs on the initiative of the Republic of Austria with a view to adopting a Council Decision to combat child pornography on the Internet (10317/1999 – C5-0318/1999 – 1999/0822(CNS)), A5-0090/2000, 28 March 2000.

if they come across such material'[101] under article 1(1) of the decision in order 'to intensify measures to prevent and combat the production, processing, possession and distribution of child pornography material and to promote the effective investigation and prosecution of offences in this area'.[102] Article 1(2) stated that further measures may include the setting-up of specialized units within law enforcement authorities with the necessary expertise and resources to be able to deal swiftly with child pornography related offences. Co-operation between Member States to facilitate an effective investigation and prosecution of offences concerning child pornography was encouraged by article 2(1) and for that purpose 'existing channels for communication, such as Europol and Interpol shall be used'.[103]

Apart from the encouragement of co-operation in the field of law enforcement, the Council decision also emphasized the importance of co-operation and constructive dialogue with the Internet industry and specifically with ISPs.[104] This would involve industry co-operation with law enforcement agencies or relevant authorities (for example, the IWF, or ISP organizations such as ISPA at the UK level) in the search for appropriate measures, of a voluntary or a legally binding nature, to eliminate child pornography from the Internet. ISPs were also required to retain traffic-related data,[105] 'where applicable and technically feasible' according to the Council decision 'for such time as may be specified under the applicable national law, to allow the data to be made available for inspection by the criminal prosecution authorities in accordance with the applicable rules of procedure.'[106] The requirement for retaining traffic data and setting up ISP control systems for individual ISPs may be burdensome. It may also be said that such a requirement goes further than necessary in a democratic society, turning ISPs into private policing organizations and also undermining the privacy of communications of Internet users.[107] There was no agreement at the EU level on the limits of retention of traffic data for law enforcement purposes or how long such data should be retained at the time the Council Decision was finalized.

Following the terrorist attacks of 11 September 2001, governments started to adopt more surveillance powers, including measures related to data retention by communication service providers. A European Union Directive 2002/58/ concerning the processing of personal data and the protection of privacy in the electronic communications sector (Directive on privacy and electronic communications)[108]

---

101 Ibid.

102 Ibid.

103 See article 2(2) of the Council Decision.

104 See article 3 of the Council Decision.

105 In accordance with the Council resolution of 17 January 1995 on the lawful interception of telecommunications, OJ C 329, 4 November 1996, p. 1.

106 See article 3(c) of the Council Decision.

107 See further, Akdeniz, Y. and N. Bohm, 'Internet Privacy: New Concerns about Cyber-Crime and the Rule of Law' (1999), *Information Technology and Communications Law Journal* (5) 20–24.

108 EU Directive 2002/58/ concerning the processing of personal data and the protection of privacy in the electronic communications sector (Directive on privacy and electronic communications) of 12 July 2002, *Official Journal of the European Communities*, 31 July 2002, L 201 pp. 37–47.

allowed for (but without requiring) the retention of data for a limited period to safeguard national security, defence, public security or the prevention, investigation, detection and prosecution of criminal offences or of unauthorized use of the electronic communications system, as referred to in Article 13(1) of Directive 95/46/EC.

The inclusion of such a provision within the Directive was primarily prompted by a request of the Council of the European Union on 20 September 2001 from the European Commission to submit proposals 'for ensuring that law enforcement authorities[109] are able to investigate criminal acts involving the use of electronic communications systems and to take legal measures against their perpetrators'.[110] It was also no secret that the UK government strongly lobbied for the explicit reference to the scope for data retention provisions during negotiations in Council.[111] Despite strong criticism from civil liberties organizations,[112] the communications industry[113] and Radical Party MEPs,[114] and this being a third pillar issue under Title VI of the EU Treaty, data retention provision was included within article 15 of the new first pillar EU Directive on privacy and electronic communications. Even before the new Directive on privacy and electronic communications was adopted in May 2002, the UK government introduced voluntary data retention provisions for the communication service providers through the provisions of Part XI of the Anti-terrorism, Crime and Security Act 2001, enacted in December 2001.[115]

---

109 Note also Enfopol 55: Council Resolution on law enforcement operational needs with respect to public telecommunication networks and services, 9194/1, Brussels, 20 June 2001.

110 Extraordinary Council meeting, Justice, Home Affairs and Civil Protection, Brussels, 20 September 2001, 12019/01 (Presse 327), para. 4.

111 See, for example, House of Commons European Scrutiny Committee Thirty-Second Report, HC 152-xxxii, Session 2001–02, July 2002 (19. DTI (23528) Personal data and privacy in telecommunications).

112 Global Internet Liberty Campaign (representing around 60 public interest organizations) letter dated 22 May 2002, at <http://gilc.org/cox_en.html>.

113 EuroISPA, ETNO and ECPA, Joint Industry Memo in view of the 2nd Reading of the Cappato Report: The Implications of 'Data Retention' in Article 15.1 of the Common Position on the Electronic Communications Data Protection Directive addressed to the Members of the Committee on Citizens' Freedoms and Rights, Justice and Home Affairs. 16 April 2002, at <http://www.euroispa.org/docs/160402_dataretent.doc>.

114 Open letter of Marco Cappato, Radical MEP and EP draftsman on privacy in electronic communications, to the President of the EU Council and to the President of the EU Telecoms Council: the fight against terrorism shall not hinder fundamental freedoms and rights such as the right to privacy, 5 December 2001, at <http://www.radicalparty.org/privacy/lett_cap_e.htm>. See further, Committee on Citizens' Freedoms and Rights, Justice and Home Affairs (Rapporteur: Marco Cappato), Recommendation for Second Reading on the Council common position for adopting a European Parliament and Council directive concerning the processing of personal data and the protection of privacy in the electronic communications sector (15396/2/2001 – C5-0035/2002 – 2000/0189(COD)), A5-0130/2002, 22 April 2002.

115 See generally, Walker, C. and Y. Akdeniz, 'Anti-Terrorism Laws and Data Retention: War is Over?' (2003), *Northern Ireland Legal Quarterly*, 54(2), Summer, 159–82, at <http://www.cyber-rights.org/documents/data_retention_article.pdf>.

After years of debate, and following the July 2005 London bombings,[116] a Data Retention Directive was adopted at the European Union level in January 2006[117] to harmonize Member States' provisions concerning the obligations of providers of publicly available electronic communications services with respect to the retention of traffic data. Member States will have to implement the provisions of the Data Retention Directive into national law by 15 September 2007.[118] Member States shall ensure that the categories of data specified in Article 5 are retained for periods of not less than six months and not more than two years from the date of the communication.

Finally, it is worth noting that article 8 of the 2000 Council Decision required measures contained in the 2000 Decision to be implemented by the Member States by 31 December 2000. At the time of writing there has not been a follow up document or study associated with the Council Decision.

THE EU DIRECTIVE ON ELECTRONIC COMMERCE

The European Union Directive on certain legal aspects of information society services, in particular electronic commerce, in the Internal Market ('Directive on electronic commerce')[119] was finalized during the summer of 2000. The Directive on electronic commerce is related to the issue of ISP liability and will be discussed in Chapter 8.

116 On 13 July 2005, the Council of the European Union reaffirmed in its declaration condemning the terrorist attacks on London the need to adopt common measures on the retention of telecommunications data as soon as possible.

117 See Directive 2006/24/EC of the European Parliament and of the Council of 15 March 2006 on the retention of data generated or processed in connection with the provision of publicly available electronic communications services or of public communications networks and amending Directive 2002/58/EC, L 105 13.04.2006, pp. 54–63, at <http://eur-lex.europa.eu/LexUriServ/site/en/oj/2006/l_105/l_10520060413en00540063.pdf>.

118 See generally, the European Parliament Legislative Observatory pages on data retention through <http://www.europarl.eu.int/oeil/file.jsp?id=5275032>.

119 Directive 2000/31/EC of the European Parliament and of the Council of 8 June 2000 on certain legal aspects of information society services, in particular electronic commerce, in the Internal Market, *Official Journal of the European Communities*, vol 43, OJ L 178, 17 July 2000 p. 1. Note also Common Position (EC) No. 22/2000 of 28 February 2000 adopted by the Council, acting in accordance with the procedure referred to in Article 251 of the Treaty establishing the European Community, with a view to adopting a Directive on electronic commerce, OJ C 128, 8 May 2000, pp. 32–50.

COMMISSION COMMUNICATION ON CREATING A SAFER INFORMATION SOCIETY BY IMPROVING THE SECURITY OF INFORMATION INFRASTRUCTURES AND COMBATING COMPUTER-RELATED CRIME

The Commission Communication on creating a safer information society by improving the security of information infrastructures and combating computer related crime[120] was launched in January 2001. This Communication had a wider context and 'discussed the need for and possible forms of a comprehensive policy initiative in the context of the broader Information Society and Freedom, Security and Justice objectives for improving the security of information infrastructures and combating cybercrime, in accordance with the commitment of the European Union to respect fundamental human rights.'[121]

As far as child pornography is concerned, the Commission believed there was a clear need for an EU instrument to 'ensure that Members States have effective sanctions in place to combat child pornography on the Internet', and this was a short-term objective set up by the Commission. The paper emphasized the fact that it 'attaches great importance to ensuring that the European Union is able to take effective action in particular against child pornography on the Internet'.[122] Although the Commission welcomed the above-mentioned Council decision on combating child pornography on the Internet, it shared the view of the European Parliament that further action was required to approximate national laws.[123] The Communication stated that for this purpose, a Council Framework Decision would be necessary.

PROPOSAL FOR A COUNCIL FRAMEWORK DECISION ON COMBATING THE SEXUAL EXPLOITATION OF CHILDREN AND CHILD PORNOGRAPHY

A more substantial European Communication paper which dealt with combating trafficking in human beings and combating the sexual exploitation of children and child pornography with a view to harmonize EU Member States laws was published in January 2001. This included a proposal for a Council Framework Decision in this field.[124] This paper once again emphasized that 'trafficking in human beings and

120 The Communication to the Council and the European Parliament on *Creating a Safer Information Society by Improving the Security of Information Infrastructures and Combating Computer-related Crime*, COM(2000) 890 final, Brussels, 26 January 2001, at <http://europa.eu.int/ISPO/eif/InternetPoliciesSite/Crime/CrimeCommEN.html>.

121 Ibid.

122 Ibid.

123 Ibid.

124 Communication to the Council and the European Parliament COM(2000) 854 final 2, Brussels, 22 January 2001. *Combating trafficking in human beings and combating the sexual exploitation of children and child pornography*: Proposal for a Council Framework Decision on combating trafficking in human beings. Proposal for a Council Framework Decision on combating the sexual exploitation of children and child pornography. (See <http://europa.eu.int/eur-lex/en/com/pdf/2000/en_500PC0854_01.pdf>). See OJ C E/2001/62/E/25 327, pp. 327–30,

the sexual exploitation of children, including child pornography are abhorrent and increasingly worrying phenomena.'[125] The Commission's intention was to establish 'common rules relating to the constituent elements of criminal law linked with trafficking in human beings and the sexual exploitation of children, with particular reference to child pornography on the Internet'.[126]

The objective of the Commission was to illustrate the European Union's determination 'to implement common penal provisions in this field [the worrying issue of child pornography on the Internet] and to provide Internet users with a safe and crimeless environment'[127] as a matter of urgency. The Commission acknowledged the work of the Council of Europe in relation to the Cybercrime Convention, and the United Nations Optional Protocol to the Convention of the Rights of the Child on the sale of children and stated that its work has taken into account and reflected these other international developments. The CoE Convention provisions and UN Optional Protocol provisions are discussed in subsequent chapters.

The European Commission called upon the Council to 'demonstrate clearly its will to take on the fight against these unacceptable violations of human rights and human dignity by providing a common approach on criminal law and to develop law enforcement and judicial co-operation.'[128] The Commission took the view that 'a further response to the issue of sexual exploitation of children and child pornography is required at the level of the European Union',[129] and stated that the use of a Framework Decision[130] would 'reinforce a common approach of the European Union in these areas and fill gaps in existing legislation'.[131]

The Committee of the Regions was supportive of the proposal for a Council Framework Decision and believed that 'these problems should be addressed at the pan-European level, which should also involve co-operation at regional level and the participation of both the applicant states and other non-EU states.'[132] In September 2001 the Council of the European Union at a Justice, Home Affairs and Civil Protection meeting[133] examined certain key questions identified by the Presidency

---

27 February 2001. Note also the Anna Karamanou report of the Committee on Citizens' Freedoms and Rights, Justice and Home Affairs in relation to this Communication, A5-0206/2001.

125 Ibid., p. 2.

126 Ibid., p. 3.

127 Ibid., p. 4.

128 Ibid., p. 5.

129 Ibid., p. 21.

130 Framework decisions are used to align the laws and regulations of the Member States. Proposals are made on the initiative of the Commission or a Member State and they have to be adopted unanimously by the Member States. See further, the EU Glossary on Institutions, policies and enlargement of the European Union at <http://europa.eu.int/scadplus/leg/en/cig/g4000.htm>.

131 Commission Communication, p. 22.

132 Opinion of the Committee of the Regions on the 'Proposal for a Council Framework Decision on combating the sexual exploitation of children and child pornography', *Official Journal of the European Communities*, C 357/41–43, 14 December 2001, para. 3.

133 2370th Council meeting – Justice, Home Affairs and Civil Protection, Brussels, 27–28 September 2001, C/01/334: Combating the Sexual Exploitation of Children and Child Pornography.

on the draft Framework Decision on combating the sexual exploitation of children and child pornography, namely whether the draft Framework Decision definition of child pornography covered realistic images of children in particular,

- when the person represented appears to be a child but is actually over 18 years of age on the date of the image,
- when a real person is not represented (virtual pornography).

Ultimately, the Council adopted the general approach of providing for an exception where images of a person over the age of sexual consent are produced, acquired and possessed with the agreement of the persons concerned and solely for their own private use. The Council instructed its preparatory bodies to continue their work expeditiously on the basis of the guidelines agreed by the Council, with a view to reaching political agreement as soon as possible.

In its December 2001 meeting, the Council[134] noted that there was very broad consensus on a Presidency compromise proposal regarding the key elements of a Framework Decision on combating the sexual exploitation of children and child pornography. In its April 2002 meeting, the Council[135] re-examined the draft Framework Decision and asked the Article 36 Committee to continue discussions with a view to resolving the very limited number of outstanding questions which related to the definition of offences concerning child pornography and the penalties to be applied for these offences. It was the intention of the Council to reach an agreement on the draft Framework Decision by mid June 2002. However, there were further delays[136] and the draft Framework Decision was not finalized and adopted until December 2003.[137]

The Council Framework Decision finally entered into force on 20 January 2004, the day it was published in the *Official Journal of the European Union*. Member States were required to take the necessary measures to comply with the Framework Decision by 20 January 2006.[138]

---

134 2396th Council meeting – Justice, Home Affairs and Civil Protection, Brussels, 6–7 December 2001, C/01/444: Combating the Sexual Exploitation of Children and Child Pornography.

135 2423rd Council meeting – Justice, Home Affairs, and Civil Protection, Luxembourg, 25/26 April 2002, 7991/02 (Presse 104): Sexual Exploitation of Children and Child Pornography.

136 See the written question (E-0964/02) put by Anna Karamanou (PSE) on 17 April 2002 to the Council.

137 Council Framework Decision 2004/68/JHA of 22 December 2003 *on combating the sexual exploitation of children and child pornography* (see OJ L 013 20 January 2004, pp. 44–8), at <http://register.consilium.europa.eu/pdf/en/03/st10/st10748en03.pdf>.

138 Article 12(1). Note European Parliament legislative resolution on the proposal for a Council Framework Decision on combating the sexual exploitation of children and child pornography (COM(2000) 854-C5-0043/2001–2000/0025(CNS)), 12 June 2001.

The Provisions of the Council Framework Decision

The Council Framework Decision on combating the sexual exploitation of children and child pornography[139] defined a child as any person 'below the age of 18 years',[140] and child pornography in article 1(b) as pornographic material that visually depicts or represents:

(i) a real child involved or engaged in sexually explicit conduct, including lascivious exhibition of the genitals or the pubic area of a child; or
(ii) a real person appearing to be a child involved or engaged in the conduct mentioned in (i); or
(iii) realistic images of a non-existent child involved or engaged in the conduct mentioned in (i).

Visual depiction and representation was the agreed format for defining child pornography under the Framework Decision while some of the earlier drafts included references to 'textual or written material of whatever type' in addition to audiovisual material.[141] There was ultimately no support for the inclusion of textual or written material for defining child pornography. In the original draft proposal for a Framework Decision child pornography was defined as 'pornographic material that visually depicts a child engaged in sexually explicit content'. The final version, as referred above, is close to this original definition. As may be noted from the definition provided in article 1(b)(iii), the EU approach includes pseudo-photographs of non existing children within its definition of child pornography.

Article 2 requires Member States to introduce offences concerning sexual exploitation of children including coercing and/or recruiting a child into prostitution or into participating in pornographic performances, and engaging in sexual activities with a child. These offences aim to combat the sexual exploitation of children and are included within the broader aims of the Framework Decision. Obviously, the commission of such crimes could lead into the production and dissemination of child pornography and their inclusion and introduction within the Framework Decision is welcome.

Article 3 deals with offences concerning child pornography and each Member State is required to 'take the necessary measures to ensure that the following intentional conduct, whether undertaken by means of a computer system or not, when committed without right is punishable':[142]

---

139 Council Framework Decision 2004/68/JHA of 22 December 2003 *on combating the sexual exploitation of children and child pornography* (see OJ L 013 20 January 2004, pp. 44–8), at <http://register.consilium.europa.eu/pdf/en/03/st10/st10748en03.pdf>. For a summary of the Framework Decision see <http://europa.eu/scadplus/leg/en/lvb/l33138.htm>.

140 Article 1(a) of the Council Framework Decision.

141 See the European Parliament report *on Sexual exploitation of Children* (A5-0206/2001), European Parliament legislative resolution *on the proposal for a Council Framework Decision on combating the sexual exploitation of children and child pornography* (COM(2000) 854-C5-0043/2001–2001/0025(CNS)), 2002/C 53 E/108-113, vol. 45, 28 February 2002.

142 Ibid., article 3(1).

(a) production of child pornography;
(b) distribution, dissemination or transmission of child pornography;
(c) supplying or making available child pornography;
(d) acquisition or possession of child pornography.

Offences of procuring, importing, exporting, purchasing, selling and offering of child pornography were removed from the final version of the article 3 offences as well as the inducement or the facilitation of the offences provided in article 3. However, under article 3(2) a Member State may exclude from criminal liability conduct relating to child pornography:

(a) referred to in Article 1(b)(ii) where a real person appearing to be a child was in fact 18 years of age or older at the time of the depiction;
(b) referred to in Article 1(b)(i) and (ii) where, in the case of production and possession, images of children having reached the age of sexual consent are produced and possessed with their consent and solely for their own private use. Even where the existence of consent has been established, it shall not be considered valid, if for example superior age, maturity, position, status, experience or the victim's dependency on the perpetrator has been abused in achieving the consent;
(c) referred to in Article 1(b)(iii), where it is established that the pornographic material is produced and possessed by the producer solely for his or her own private use, as far as no pornographic material as referred to in Article 1(b)(i) and (ii) has been used for the purpose of its production, and provided that the act involves no risk for the dissemination of the material.

These exceptions were agreed after long discussions within various EU institutions between the Member States and in the absence of such exceptions an agreement may not have been reached at all. The offences and the wording within article 3 are consistent with the Council of Europe's Cybercrime Convention (article 9) which is discussed in the following chapter. Under article 4, the instigation, aiding, abetting and attempting to commit the offences provided in articles 2 and 3 are required to be criminalized. The offences provided in the above section are not medium specific and the Commission's intention was to provide a general legal mechanism for combating child pornography.

In terms of penalties, article 5 requires Member States to provide criminal penalties of at least between one and three years of imprisonment for the offences provided in articles 2, 3 and 4 of the Framework Decision. However, Member States may provide other sanctions including non-criminal sanctions or measures, concerning conduct relating to child pornography referred to in article 1(b)(iii) according to article 5(4).

As far as aggravated offences are concerned, Member States are required to ensure under article (5)(2) that they are punishable with criminal penalties of at least between five and ten years of imprisonment subject to article 5(4) which provides:

(a) the offences referred to in Article 2(a), consisting in 'coercing a child into prostitution or into participating in pornographic performances', and the offences referred to in Article 2(c)(i);

(b) the offences referred to in Article 2(a), consisting in 'profiting from or otherwise exploiting a child for such purposes', and the offences referred to in Article 2(b), in both cases as far as they refer to prostitution, where at least one of the following circumstances may apply:
— the victim is a child below the age of sexual consent under national law,
— the offender has deliberately or by recklessness endangered the life of the child,
— the offences involve serious violence or caused serious harm to the child,
— the offences are committed within the framework of a criminal organization within the meaning of Joint Action 98/733/JHA, irrespective of the level of the penalty referred to in that Joint Action;

(c) the offences referred to in Article 2(a), consisting in 'profiting from or otherwise exploiting a child for such purposes', and the offences referred to in Article 2(b), in both cases as far as they refer to pornographic performances, Article 2(c)(ii) and (iii), Article 3(1)(a), (b) and (c), where the victim is a child below the age of sexual consent under national law and at least one of the circumstances referred to under the second, third and fourth indent under point (b) of this paragraph may apply.

In terms of child pornography offences provided in article 3(1)(a) (production of child pornography), article 3(1)(b) (distribution, dissemination or transmission of child pornography), article 3(1)(c) (supplying or making available child pornography), these will be punishable with criminal penalties of at least between five and ten years of imprisonment where the victim is a child below the age of sexual consent under national law and at least one of the circumstances referred to under the second, third and fourth indent under article 5(2)(b) is present. Possession of child pornography would receive a penalty of between one and three years of imprisonment under article 5(1).

The issue of Internet Service Providers' liability is addressed in article 6 (liability of legal persons) which requires Member States to 'take the necessary measures to ensure that legal persons can be held liable for offences referred to in Articles 2, 3 and 4 committed for their benefit by any person, acting either individually or as part of an organ of the legal person.'[143] However, it may be argued that provided the offences are not committed for the 'benefit' of an ISP, then this section does not apply to ISPs. It should also be noted that article 6 does not affect the provisions of the above-mentioned Electronic Commerce Directive,[144] which deal with the liability of ISPs in more detailed and clear terms.

With regards to the issue of jurisdiction, article 8 suggests that Member States will take the necessary measures to establish their jurisdiction over the offences referred to in articles 2, 3 and 4 where,

(a) the offence is committed in whole or in part within its territory;
(b) the offender is one of its nationals; or
(c) the offence is committed for the benefit of a legal person established in the territory of that Member State.

143 See further, article 7 of the Framework Decision in terms of the sanctions provided for legal persons.

144 OJ L 178, 17 July 2000, p. 1.

In relation to Internet child pornography, under article 8(5) Member States are required to ensure that their jurisdiction includes situations where an offence under article 3 and, insofar as it is relevant, under article 4, is committed by means of a computer system accessed from its territory, whether or not the computer system is on its territory.

Another parallel development in terms of EU efforts to combat the sexual exploitation of children and child pornography is an initiative to recognize and enforce prohibitions (which, for example, involve exercising professional activities related to the supervision of children) arising from convictions for sexual offences committed against children.[145] This was an initiative of the Belgium government which in late 2004 proposed a draft Framework Decision that would apply to the offences covered in articles 2, 3 and 4 of the Council Framework Decision on combating the sexual exploitation of children and child pornography.[146] The European Parliament adopted a resolution on the draft Framework Decision in June 2006,[147] but this has yet to be finalized.

CONCLUSION

As this chapter has demonstrated, there have been a considerable number of initiatives to address the problem of Internet child pornography at the European Union level over the last decade. Generally, the EU prefers to play an advisory role for its Member States and favours common measures to be adopted at the national level in relation to criminal matters. However, in the fight against child pornography the EU approach has been directive rather than advisory with the development of two binding policies, namely the Electronic Commerce Directive which is related to the issue of ISP liability within the context of illegal Internet content, including child pornography (which will be detailed in Chapter 8), and the Council Framework Decision on combating the sexual exploitation of children and child pornography.

It is clear that there has been some duplication of effort at EU level with documents and initiatives covering similar ground which could have been usefully avoided. After ten years of discussions and several attempts the EU Member States have finally moved towards achieving EU-wide harmonization to fight child pornography under the provisions of the Council Framework Decision. This is an EU-wide binding document which was to be implemented by each EU Member State by January 2006 subject to various reservations by Member States. A full assessment of the implementation of the Framework Decision will be made by the European Commission by February 2008.

Delay in finalizing the EU policies may be attributed, in part, to the development of a Cybercrime Convention by the Council of Europe which will be detailed in the

145 Combating the sexual exploitation of children and child pornography: recognition and enforcement of prohibitions arising from convictions for sexual offences. Framework decision, CNS/2004/0818. See generally, <http://www2.europarl.eu.int/oeil/file.jsp?id=5219892>.

146 2004/68/JHA of 22 December 2003.

147 CNS/2004/0818: 01/06/2006 – EP: legislative opinion, 1st reading or single reading. See <http://www.europarl.europa.eu/oeil/file.jsp?id=5219892>.

next chapter. The EU remains supportive of the CoE Convention and participated in the policy making process that led to its development.[148] However, it is still unsatisfactory that the Council Framework Decision took so long in the planning.

A wider programme for child protection on the Internet was drafted by the Economic and Social Committee in February 2001.[149] The main purpose of this programme was to complement and strengthen the EU Safer Internet Action Plan.[150] The Committee noted that 'bringing child pornographers to justice is taking too long', and the Committee remains concerned 'that police remain unable to trace the majority of children abused for child pornography on-line.'[151] However, no further progress has been made to date.

The development of a common policy in relation to the problem of Internet child pornography at the European Union level is significant. Whilst it may not have a strong impact on UK policy which already parallels EU policies described in this chapter, it will certainly have an impact upon the policies of more recent EU Member States and the policies of the candidate countries under the EU enlargement plan. Harmonization can also be expected to improve police and judicial co-operation between the EU Member States.

---

148 European Union, Common Position on the CoE Convention, 27 May 1999. (OJ L 142, 5 June 1999 pp. 1–2) adopted by the Council on the basis of Article 34 of the Treaty on European Union, on negotiations relating to the Draft Convention on Cyber Crime held in the Council of Europe.

149 See Opinion of the Economic and Social Committee on *A programme for child protection on the Internet* (2002/C 48/06), C 48/27-32 *Official Journal of the European Communities*, 21 February 2002.

150 Ibid., para. 1.2.

151 Opinion of the Economic and Social Committee on *A programme for child protection on the Internet* (2002/C 48/06), C 48/27-32 *Official Journal of the European Communities*, 21 February 2002, para. 5.2.

Chapter 6

Council of Europe Policy

This chapter describes and analyses the work and policies of the Council of Europe in the fight against child pornography.

The Council of Europe (CoE)[1] was the first international organization to be founded in Europe after the Second World War and its main role is to strengthen democracy, human rights and the rule of law throughout its member states. The defence and promotion of these fundamental values is no longer simply an internal matter for governments but has become a shared and collective responsibility of all the countries concerned. Furthermore, the CoE's work involves close co-operation with other regional European organizations such as the European Union and the Organization for Security and Co-operation in Europe (OSCE).

The CoE's fight against the sexual exploitation of children started in 1991[2] when the Committee of Ministers of the CoE adopted *Recommendation R (91)11 concerning sexual exploitation, pornography and prostitution of, and trafficking in, children and young adults*.[3] The Committee of Ministers noted, 'the well-being and interests of children and young adults are fundamental issues for any society',[4] and 'sexual exploitation of children and young adults for profit-making purposes in the form of pornography, prostitution and traffic of human beings has assumed new and alarming dimensions at national and international level.'[5] According to the Committee of Ministers it was

> … in the interests of member States of the Council of Europe to harmonize their national legislation on sexual exploitation of children and young adults in order to improve the co-ordination and effectiveness of action taken at national and international level with a view to tackling this problem.[6]

The Committee of Ministers recommended that governments of member states review their legislation and practice with a view to introducing, and implementing

---

1 See <http://www.coe.int>.

2 But note the earlier work of the Council of Europe in this field: Recommendation 1065 (1987) of the Parliamentary Assembly of the Council of Europe *on the traffic in children and other forms of child exploitation*; Resolution No. 3 *on sexual exploitation, pornography and prostitution of, and trafficking in, children and young adults*, 16th Conference of European Ministers of Justice (Lisbon, 1988).

3 Adopted by the Committee of Ministers on 9 September 1991 at the 461st meeting of the Ministers' Deputies.

4 Ibid.

5 Ibid.

6 Ibid.

measures relating to pornography involving children.[7] The Committee of Ministers specifically recommended that governments should:

- Provide for appropriate sanctions taking into account the gravity of the offence committed by those involved in the production and distribution of any pornographic material involving children;
- Examine the advisability of introducing penal sanctions for mere possession of pornographic material involving children;
- Ensure, particularly through international co-operation, the detection of firms, associations or individuals often linked with two or more countries, using children for the production of pornographic material;
- Envisage informing the public, in order to raise awareness, of the implementation of penal policy, the number of prosecutions and convictions in cases involving child pornography, while ensuring the anonymity of the children concerned and of the alleged offenders.

Taking high priority action for the protection of children with a view to preventing all forms of exploitation of children, including the production, sale, marketing and possession of pornographic material involving children was also one of the aims of the Action Plan adopted at the Second Council of Europe Summit in October 1997. A more direct approach was adopted by including a provision on criminalizing child pornography and by introducing a variety of child pornography offences within the Cybercrime Convention which was finalized and opened to signature in November 2001.

CYBERCRIME CONVENTION

The CoE's Cybercrime Convention 2001[8] is the first international treaty to address criminal law and procedural aspects of various types of offensive behaviour directed against computer systems, networks or data in addition to content related crimes such as child pornography. In general, the Convention aims to harmonize national legislation in this field, facilitate investigations, and allow efficient levels of co-operation between the authorities of different member states of the CoE and other third party states who would be party to the Convention following a ratification process at the national level.

---

7 Ibid.

8 The text of the Cybercrime Convention can be found at <http://conventions.coe.int/treaty/en/projects/cybercrime.htm>. See further, Akdeniz, Y., *An Advocacy Handbook for the Non Governmental Organizations: The Council of Europe's Cybercrime Convention 2001 and the Additional Protocol on the Criminalisation of Acts of a Racist or Xenophobic Nature Committed through Computer Systems*, Cyber-Rights and Cyber-Liberties, 2003 (revised February 2007), at <http://www.cyber-rights.org/cybercrime/coe_handbook_crcl.pdf>.

A Committee of Experts on crime in cyber-space ('PC-CY') was set up in 1997 to develop the Cybercrime Convention. The CoE Committee of Ministers decided to establish this committee in recognition that:[9]

> the fast developments in the field of information technology have a direct bearing on all sections of modern society. The integration of telecommunication and information systems, enabling the storage and transmission, regardless of distance, of all kinds of communication opens a whole range of new possibilities ... By connecting to communication and information services users create a kind of common space, called cyberspace, which is used for legitimate purposes but may also be the subject of misuse. These cyberspace offences are either committed against the integrity, availability and confidentiality of computer systems and telecommunication networks or they consist of the use of such networks of their services to commit traditional offences. The transborder character of such offences, e.g. when committed through the Internet, it is in direct conflict with the territoriality of national law enforcement authorities.[10]

Within this context, the PC-CY Committee also considered child pornography related offences. Prior to the inclusion of child pornography offences within the Cybercrime Convention, the Committee conducted a questionnaire based enquiry about CoE member states' legislation.[11] Nineteen member states of the CoE, including the UK, 'considered a provision on child pornography distributed in electronic networks as necessary to be included in the draft Convention'.[12] The arguments put forward for inclusion were 'the increasing danger posed by such behaviour at global level, the need for harmonising the relevant legal provisions in national laws (for example, for the purposes of international co-operation) and for enhancing deterrence.'[13] On the basis of the replies to the questionnaire, the PC-CY Committee decided to opt for drafting a *sui generis* provision criminalizing child pornography distributed through computer networks.[14]

Title 3 of the Convention, entitled 'content-related offences', includes provisions related to child pornography and this is the only content related provision that has been included within the Cybercrime Convention. The PC-CY Committee discussed including other content related offences such as the distribution of racist propaganda

9 See further, Csonka, P. (Secretary to Committee PC-CY, Council of Europe), Contribution to the Conference on combating child pornography on the Internet, Vienna, 29 September – 1 October 1999, through <http://www.stop-childpornog.at/>.

10 Terms of reference of the Committee – document PC-CY (97) 1.

11 See Csonka, P. Contribution to the Conference on combating child pornography on the Internet.

12 Ibid.

13 Ibid.

14 Ibid.

through computer systems,[15] but provisions on racist propaganda were ultimately not included.[16]

As far as child pornography related offences are concerned, these are contained within article 9 of the Cybercrime Convention. Several offences related to child pornography are included within this provision. The intention of the CoE was 'to strengthen protective measures for children, including their protection against sexual exploitation, by modernising criminal law provisions to more effectively circumscribe the use of computer systems in the commission of sexual offences against children'.[17]

> This provision responds to the preoccupation of Heads of State and Government of the Council of Europe, expressed at their 2nd summit (Strasbourg, 10–11 October 1997) in their Action Plan (item III.4) and corresponds to an international trend that seeks to ban child pornography, as evidenced by the recent adoption of the Optional Protocol to the UN Convention on the rights of the child, on the sale of children, child prostitution and child pornography and the recent European Commission initiative on combating sexual exploitation of children and child pornography (COM2000/854).[18]

---

15 See further, Council of Europe, Parliamentary Assembly, Report of debates of the Second Part of the 2001 Ordinary Session: *Draft convention against cyber crime*, Assembly Spring Session – 23–27 April 2001, 24 April 2001, at <http://www.cyber-rights.org/documents/coe_assembly.htm>; European Committee on Crime Problems, Explanatory Memorandum related to the Cybercrime Convention, CDPC (2001) 17, Strasbourg, 29 June 2001, at <http://www.privacyinternational.org/issues/cybercrime/coe/cybercrimememo-final.html>, paragraph 35.

16 The Parliamentary Assembly of the Council of Europe voted against such inclusion only by one vote of difference and the racist propaganda issue will be included within an additional protocol to the Cybercrime Convention. See the Report of debates of the Second Part of the 2001 Ordinary Session on the Draft Cybercrime Convention, Council of Europe, Parliamentary Assembly (Assembly Spring Session, 23–27 April 2001), 24 April 2001. See further, PC-RX(2002)15E Draft of the First Additional Protocol to the Convention on Cybercrime concerning the criminalisation of acts of a racist and xenophobic nature committed through computer systems and its Explanatory Report, Strasbourg, 14 May 2002. Note also the Additional Protocol concerning the Criminalisation of Acts of a Racist and Xenophobic Nature Committed Through Computer Systems which came into force on 1 March 2006. See generally, Akdeniz, Y., *Stocktaking on Efforts to Combat Racism on the Internet*, background report for the High Level Seminar on Racism and the Internet, Intergovernmental Working Group on the Effective Implementation of the Durban Declaration and Programme of Action, Fourth session, Geneva, 16–27 January 2006, E/CN.4/2006/WG.21/BP.1, published by the United Nations High Commissioner for Human Rights (UNHCHR) Office: Geneva, January 2006, at <http://www.ohchr.org/english/issues/racism/groups/docs/e_cn4_2006_wg21_bp1.doc> and <http://www.cyber-rights.org/reports/ya_un_paper_int_06.pdf>.

17 European Committee On Crime Problems (CDPC), Explanatory Memorandum to the Convention on Cybercrime, document prepared by the Secretariat and former experts of the PC-CY Committee, Strasbourg, 14 February 2001, EXPC-CY (2001) 1, adopted on 8 November 2001, at para. 91.

18 Ibid., at para. 92.

Under article 9(2) of the Cybercrime Convention, for the purposes of article 9(1), child pornography should include pornographic material that visually depicts:

(a) a minor engaged in sexually explicit conduct;
(b) a person appearing to be a minor engaged in sexually explicit conduct;
(c) realistic images representing a minor engaged in sexually explicit conduct.

As can be seen from the above definition, realistic images or pseudo-photographs are also covered by the Convention as 'it is widely believed that such material and on-line practices, such as the exchange of ideas, fantasies and advice among paedophiles, play a role in supporting, encouraging or facilitating sexual offences against children.'[19] This was the reason behind the inclusion of paragraphs 2(b) and 2(c) which 'aim at providing protection against behaviour' rather than abusive conduct as in paragraph 2(a).[20] According to the Explanatory Memorandum of the Cybercrime Convention, 'sexually explicit conduct' covers real or simulated:

> a) sexual intercourse, including genital-genital, oral-genital, anal-genital or oral-anal, between minors, or between an adult and a minor, of the same or opposite sex; b) bestiality; c) masturbation; d) sadistic or masochistic abuse in a sexual context; or e) lascivious exhibition of the genitals or the pubic area of a minor. It is not relevant whether the conduct depicted is real or simulated.[21]

The term 'minor' shall include all persons under 18 years of age according to article 9(3), though a member state may 'require a lower age-limit, which shall be not less than 16 years'. This is in accordance with the definition of a 'child' in the United Nation's Convention on the Rights of the Child (article 1), as it was considered 'an important policy matter to set a uniform international standard regarding age'.[22]

Article 9(1) requires each member state of the CoE to adopt such legislative and other measures as may be necessary to establish as criminal offences under their domestic laws when committed intentionally and without right the following conduct:

(a) producing child pornography for the purpose of its distribution through a computer system;
(b) offering or making available child pornography through a computer system;
(c) distributing or transmitting child pornography through a computer system;
(d) procuring child pornography through a computer system for oneself or for another;
(e) possessing child pornography in a computer system or on a computer-data storage medium.

These offences are similar to those provided under the European Union's Framework Decision on combating the sexual exploitation of children and child pornography[23]

---

19 Ibid., at para. 93.

20 Ibid., para. 102.

21 Ibid., at para. 100.

22 Ibid., at para. 104.

23 Council Framework Decision 2004/68/JHA of 22 December 2003 on combating the sexual exploitation of children and child pornography (see OJ L 013 20 January 2004, pp. 44–8),

discussed in the previous chapter. There are also similarities with the United Nations' Optional Protocol to the Convention on the Rights of the Child on the Sale of Children, Child Prostitution and Child Pornography[24] which will be discussed in Chapter 7.

The term 'without right' within article 9(1) does not exclude legal defences, excuses or similar relevant principles that relieve a person of responsibility under specific circumstances. According to the Explanatory Memorandum,

> … the term 'without right' allows a Party to take into account fundamental rights, such as freedom of thought, expression and privacy. In addition, a Party may provide a defence in respect of conduct related to 'pornographic material' having an artistic, medical, scientific or similar merit.[25]

Intention is also a crucial element of the various child pornography offences provided in article 9. Liability will not be imposed if there is no intention to commit such offences.[26] It is also acknowledged that member states and other signing states may adopt more specific standards such as those provided for Internet Service Providers in relation to the availability of illegal content in their servers under the EU E-Commerce Directive.[27] Moreover, 'liability may be imposed if there is "knowledge and control" over the information which is transmitted or stored.'[28] Therefore, as far as Internet Service Providers' liability is concerned '[i]t is not sufficient, for example, that a service provider served as a conduit for, or hosted a website or newsroom containing such material, without the required intent under domestic law in the particular case.'[29]

However, a service provider is not required to monitor conduct to avoid criminal liability, and this is consistent with the provisions of article 15 of the European Union E-Commerce Directive.

Ratification and Harmonization

The Parliamentary Assembly of the CoE approved the Cybercrime Convention in its April 2001 session, and the Council of Europe's Committee on Crime Problems approved the final draft of Cybercrime Convention in June 2001.[30] Finally, the

---

at <http://register.consilium.europa.eu/pdf/en/03/st10/st10748en03.pdf>. For a summary of the Framework Decision see <http://europa.eu/scadplus/leg/en/lvb/l33138.htm>.

24 Optional Protocol to the Convention on the Rights of the Child on the Sale of Children, Child Prostitution and Child Pornography, New York, 25 May 2000, Fifty-fourth session (97th plenary meeting), Agenda item 116 (a), Distr. General A/RES/54/263, 26 June 2000.

25 Ibid., para. 103.

26 Ibid., para. 105.

27 Ibid. See further, Chapter 6 in relation to this issue.

28 Ibid.

29 Ibid.

30 Council of Europe's Committee on Crime Problems approved the final draft of Cybercrime Convention, Strasbourg, 22 June 2001. See further, Report of debates of the Second Part of the 2001 Ordinary Session on the Draft Cybercrime Convention, Council of Europe, Parliamentary Assembly (Assembly Spring Session, 23–27 April 2001), 24 April 2001. Note also First international treaty to combat crime in cyberspace approved by Ministers' Deputies – 646a(2001), Strasbourg, 19 September 2001, at <http://press.coe.int/cp/2001/646a(2001).htm>.

Cybercrime Convention[31] was opened to signature by the member states and the non-member states which have participated in its elaboration and for accession by other non-member states in November 2001. The UK, the United States and Canada immediately signed the Convention in November 2001.

The provision and harmonization of these common legal standards by the CoE member states in relation to the child pornography offences could constitute a significant step towards fighting this problem within the wider European region. However, there have been two major hurdles.

To begin with, the signing, ratification and implementation of the Convention by member states has been extremely slow. Following the first five ratifications, the Cybercrime Convention came into force on 1 July 2004. As of June 2007, 38 member states (plus the external supporters United States, Canada, South Africa, Japan and Montenegro) have signed and 21 countries (Albania, Armenia, Bosnia and Herzegovina, Bulgaria, Croatia, Cyprus, Denmark, Estonia, Finland, France, Hungary, Iceland, Latvia, Lithuania, Netherlands, Norway, Romania, Slovenia, the former Yugoslav Republic of Macedonia, Ukraine and the United States[32]) have ratified the main convention out of the potential 50 countries (45 CoE member states plus the above mentioned external supporters). The UK and Canada are notably yet to ratify the Cybercrime Convention, and it could take many more years before a substantial number of member states do so.

Research by the author reveals (see Table 6.1) only four CoE member states (Albania, Azerbaijan, Moldova and Monaco) do not have specific child pornography legislation already in place at the time of writing. While the production and dissemination of child pornography is generally already criminalized in the majority of the CoE member states, 15 member states (Albania, Armenia, Azerbaijan, Czech Republic, Georgia, Latvia, Macedonia, Moldova, Monaco, Portugal, Russia, San Marino, Serbia, Slovenia and Ukraine) do not have specific laws criminalizing the *possession* of child pornography.

Out of these 15 member states Albania, Latvia, Macedonia, Slovenia and Ukraine are the only member states to have signed and ratified the Cybercrime Convention. Therefore, it can be expected that specific child pornography related criminal provisions, including possession, will be provided in these states in the very near future. The Czech Republic, Portugal and Slovenia have signed but have yet to ratify the Cybercrime Convention. As members of the European Union these states are required to take the necessary measures to comply with the Council Framework Decision on combating the sexual exploitation of children and child pornography by 20 January 2006.[33] As mentioned in the previous chapter, the Council Framework

31 Convention on Cybercrime, ETS No. 185. See generally, <http://conventions.coe.int/Treaty/EN/WhatYouWant.asp?NT=185&CM=8&DF=10/04/02>.

32 The US Senate approved the ratification of the Cybercrime Convention on 3 August 2006. See CNet News, 5 August 2006, at <http://news.com.com/Senate+ratifies+controversial+cybercrime+treaty/2100-7348_3-6102354.html>.

33 For details see the previous chapter: Council Framework Decision 2004/68/JHA of 22 December 2003 on combating the sexual exploitation of children and child pornography (see OJ L 013 20 January 2004, pp. 44–8).

Table 6.1 Child pornography laws in the Council of Europe region

Member States	CP Law	Possession	CoE Signature	CoE Ratification	EU Framework	UN Optional Prot.
Albania	X	X	✓	✓		X
Andorra	✓	✓	X	X		✓
Armenia	✓	X	✓	✓		✓
Austria	✓	✓	✓	X	✓	✓
Azerbaijan	X	X	X	X		✓
Belgium	✓	✓	✓	X	✓	✓
Bosnia and Herzegovina	✓	✓	✓	✓		✓
Bulgaria	✓	✓	✓	✓	✓	✓
Croatia	✓	✓	✓	✓		✓
Cyprus	✓	✓	✓	✓	✓	✓
Czech Republic	✓	X	✓	X	✓	X
Denmark	✓	✓	✓	✓	✓	✓
Estonia	✓	✓	✓	✓	✓	✓
Finland	✓	✓	✓	✓	✓	X
France	✓	✓	✓	✓	✓	✓
Georgia	✓	X	X	X		✓
Germany	✓	✓	✓	X	✓	X
Greece	✓	✓	✓	X	✓	X
Hungary	✓	✓	✓	✓	✓	X
Iceland	✓	✓	✓	✓		✓
Ireland	✓	✓	✓	X	✓	X
Italy	✓	✓	✓	X	✓	✓
Latvia	✓	X	✓	✓	✓	✓
Liechtenstein	✓	✓	X	X		X
Lithuania	✓	✓	✓	✓	✓	✓
Luxembourg	✓	✓	✓	X	✓	X
Macedonia	✓	X	✓	✓		✓

Table 6.1 Continued Child Pornography Laws in the Council of Europe Region*

Member States	CP Law	Possession	CoE Signature	CoE Ratification	EU Framework	UN Optional Prot.
Malta	✓	✓	✓	X	✓	X
Moldova	X	X	✓	X		✓
Monaco	X	X	X	X		X
Netherlands	✓	✓	✓	✓	✓	✓
Norway	✓	✓	✓	✓		✓
Poland	✓	✓	✓	X	✓	✓
Portugal	✓	X	✓	X	✓	✓
Romania	✓	✓	✓	✓	✓	✓
Russian Federation	✓	X	X	X		X
San Marino	✓	X	X	X		X
Serbia	✓	X	✓	X		✓
Slovakia	✓	✓	✓	X	✓	✓
Slovenia	✓	X	✓	✓	✓	✓
Spain	✓	✓	✓	X	✓	✓
Sweden	✓	✓	✓	X	✓	✓
Switzerland	✓	✓	✓	X		✓
Turkey	✓	✓	X	X		✓
Ukraine	✓	X	✓	✓		✓
United Kingdom	✓	✓	✓	X	✓	X
The following countries are external supporter states.						
Canada	✓	✓	✓	X		✓
Costa Rica	✓	X	X	X		✓
Japan	✓	X	✓	X		✓
Mexico	✓	X	X	X		✓
Montenegro	✓	X	✓	X		✓
South Africa	✓	✓	✓	X		✓
United States	✓	✓	✓	✓		✓

* Information for this table is gathered from CoE Cybercrime Convention related documents, Europol, Child Pornography Legislation within the European Union report, Europol, 2005, International Centre for Missing and Exploited Children, Child Pornography: *Model Legislation and Global Review 2006 Report*, second edition.

Decision includes similar child pornography related measures to those provided in article 9 of the Cybercrime Convention. A full assessment of the implementation of the Framework Decision will be made by the European Commission by February 2008, but it is safe to say that the Czech Republic,[34] Latvia,[35] Portugal and Slovenia will have specific child pornography legislation including criminal measures for possession sometime soon. Additionally, Armenia, Azerbaijan, Georgia, Latvia, Macedonia, Moldova, Portugal, Serbia, Slovenia and Ukraine signed and ratified the UN Optional Protocol on the Sale of Children, Child Prostitution and Child Pornography[36] and therefore have obligations to the UN in terms of introducing child pornography related offences.

Following this assessment, it may be said that child pornography related criminal provisions are either non-existent or below supranational and international standards in only six CoE member states; namely Albania,[37] the Czech Republic, Moldova, Monaco, Russia[38] and in San Marino. This, in turn, means that only a minority of CoE member states do not have strong child pornography legislation.

In terms of the Cybercrime Convention, it should be noted that member states 'may reserve the right not to apply, in whole or in part, paragraph 1(d)[39] and 1(e),[40] and 2(b)[41] and 2(c)'[42] under article 9(4). Only the offences of producing (for the purpose of distribution through a computer system), offering (soliciting others to obtain child pornography) and distribution of child pornography under article

34 The *Prague Post* reports that the Czech Parliament is considering outlawing the possession of child pornography later in 2007: see 'Law sought to ban child porn', *Prague Post*, 14 February 2007, at <http://www.praguepost.com/articles/2007/02/14/law-sought-to-ban-child-porn.php>. Note further Information for the UN Special Rapporteur on the sale of children, child prostitution and child pornography for the study of child pornography on the Internet – situation in the Czech Republic, Enclosure No. 2745/2004, at <http://www.ohchr.org/english/issues/children/rapporteur/ Czech Republic Gov.doc>.

35 Latvia currently criminalizes first time possession offenders with a fine (150–400 USD) with confiscation. Repeated offenders could be imprisoned for up to one year. See Latvian letter to Interpol, 2006, at <http://www.interpol.int/Public/Children/SexualAbuse/NationalLaws/csaLatvia.pdf>.

36 Optional Protocol to the Convention on the Rights of the Child on the Sale of Children, Child Prostitution and Child Pornography, New York, 25 May 2000, Fifty-fourth session (97th plenary meeting), Agenda item 116 (a), Distr. General A/RES/54/263, 26 June 2000.

37 Note UN Special Rapporteur of the Commission on Human Rights on the sale of children, child prostitution and child pornography, Mission to Albania (October 2005), E/CN.4/2006/67/Add.2, at <http://daccess-ods.un.org/access.nsf/Get?Open&DS=E/CN.4/2006/67/Add.2&Lang=E>.

38 Note UN Special Rapporteur of the Commission on Human Rights on the sale of children, child prostitution and child pornography, Mission to the Russian Federation (October 2000), E/CN.4/2001/78/Add.2, at <http://daccess-ods.un.org/access.nsf/Get?Open&DS=E/CN.4/2001/78/Add.2&Lang=E>.

39 Procuring child pornography through a computer system for oneself or for another.

40 Possessing child pornography in a computer system or on a computer-data storage medium.

41 A person appearing to be a minor engaged in sexually explicit conduct.

42 Realistic images representing a minor engaged in sexually explicit conduct.

9(1)(a), (b) and (c) will be harmonized by the member states of the CoE and by the other signing states, while the procuring (actively obtaining child pornography, for example, by downloading it), and possession offences will be discretionary under article 9(4). This is despite the fact that possession is recognized by the CoE to stimulate demand for such material, and an effective way 'to curtail the production of child pornography is to attach criminal consequences to the conduct of each participant in the chain from production to possession'.[43]

In accordance with Article 9(4), Denmark, one of the ratifying states, reserved the right not to adopt the offence of possession of obscene pictures of a person who has attained the age of 15, if the person concerned had given his or her consent to the possession in regards to article 9(1)(e). Ukraine also reserved the right not to apply to the full extent article 9(1)(d) and (e) of the Convention.

The same approach was adopted for establishing what may or may not constitute child pornography under article 9(2). The decision concerning persons appearing to be a minor engaged in sexually explicit conduct (for example, a 24-year-old posing as a 17-year-old teenager), and realistic images representing a minor engaged in sexually explicit conduct (for example, pseudo-photographs created by computers) is left to the discretion of the member states of the Council of Europe and the other signing states under article 9(4). In accordance with Article 9(4), Denmark and Iceland reserved the right not to introduce a criminal offence relating to visual representations of a person appearing to be a minor engaged in sexually explicit conduct in regards to article 9(2)(b).[44] Hungary reserved the right not to apply Article 9(2)(b) while ratifying the Cybercrime Convention. The United States reserved the right to apply article 9(2)(b) and article 9(2)(c) only to the extent consistent with the Constitution of the US and as provided for under its federal law. France, on the other hand, decided, in accordance with article 9(2)(b) of the Convention, that it would apply article 9(1) to any pornographic material that visually depicts a person appearing to be a minor engaged in sexually explicit conduct, in so far as it is not proved that the said person was 18 years old on the day of the fixing or the registering of his or her image.

The member states' right not to apply certain parts of article 9 offences could lead to disparities between criminal provisions related to child pornography within the ratifying states. Such legal differences could then hinder cross-border law enforcement operations if the countries involved in such an operation do not both criminalize the same conduct or content. The crucial issue in relation to cross-border policing and mutual assistance[45] is 'dual criminality' as a safeguard – that the legal systems of the parties to a mutual assistance request (both the country requesting information and the requested party) have equivalent offences within their national legal systems in relation to the alleged offences that are part of the investigation.

43 CoE Cybercrime Explanatory Memorandum, para. 98.

44 Iceland also reserved the right not to introduce a criminal offence relating to visual representations involving realistic images representing a minor engaged in sexually explicit conduct in regards to article 9(2)(c).

45 See further, article 25 of the Cybercrime Convention in relation to provisions on mutual assistance.

The Cybercrime Convention includes provisions in relation to mutual assistance and aims to overcome these difficulties, but these problems will only be surmounted if the Convention is ratified by all member states.

CoE RECOMMENDATION REC(2001)16 ON THE PROTECTION OF CHILDREN AGAINST SEXUAL EXPLOITATION

A parallel policy development to the Cybercrime Convention is the formulation of the CoE *Recommendation on the protection of children against sexual exploitation* in 2001.[46] The intention of the CoE was to contribute effectively to the common goal of affording children adequate protection against sexual exploitation.[47] To this end, the CoE recommended that the member states' governments

> ... ensure that effective measures are taken to protect children against sexual exploitation, review their legislation and practice in the light of the principles contained in the present recommendation and ensure that their implementation is followed closely, assessed on a permanent basis and accompanied by adequate technical assistance.[48]

As far as the problem of child pornography is concerned, the CoE recommendation has the aim of:

> ... eliminating child pornography, child prostitution and trafficking in children, committed by natural or legal persons on an individual or organized basis, within the country or outside of it, by nationals or residents, with or without the child's consent.

In paragraph (c) the recommendation adopts the same definition and offences provided by article 9 of the Cybercrime Convention but without restricting these to computer systems. Instead, the CoE recommended that criminal sanctions take into account 'the gravity of the offence committed by those involved in the production and distribution of any pornographic material, by whatever means, involving children or simulating the images of children'.[49] Moreover, member states are urged to 'introduce criminal sanctions for mere possession, in whatever form, of pornographic material involving children or simulating the images of a child'.[50]

Additionally, the CoE recommended the adoption of general measures to protect children from sexual exploitation including in relation to public awareness, education and information in this field, collection and exchange of information, prevention, identification and assistance, the media and the Internet.[51] As far as Internet related measures are concerned, the recommendation states that member states should:

---

46 Adopted by the Committee of Ministers on 31 October 2001at the 771st meeting of the Ministers' Deputies.

47 Note also the CoE Recommendation No. R (91) 11 concerning sexual exploitation, pornography and prostitution of, and trafficking in, children and young adults.

48 Recommendation Rec(2001)16 on the protection of children against sexual exploitation.

49 Ibid., para. 44.

50 Ibid., para. 45.

51 Ibid., II. General measures.

Involve ISPs in raising awareness about sexual exploitation and its risks, especially on the Internet and through the use of modern communication technologies.[52]

Ensure that ISPs work alongside the authorities to identify and to combat the various means through which the Internet can be used for the purpose of sexual exploitation of children.[53]

Encourage ISPs to develop a code of conduct appropriate to the modern information and communications technologies to prevent the sexual exploitation of children, identify abuses of such a code and to take measures to inhibit and suppress such abuses.[54]

Recognize that it is necessary for law-enforcement agencies to be able to use connection data to trace suspicious content and subsequently locate, identify and question those who edit or disseminate child pornography or encourage or incite child prostitution.[55]

Provide information to parents, carers, all others responsible for children and children themselves on the risks of sexual exploitation on the Internet, the forms it may take and on how to limit access to it.[56]

Create hotlines and encourage citizens to report cases of child pornography or of incitement to child prostitution on the website, thus enabling the appropriate law enforcement authorities to take specific action.[57]

CoE RECOMMENDATION (2001) 8 ON SELF-REGULATION CONCERNING CYBER-CONTENT

A further politically important CoE *Recommendation on self-regulation concerning both illegal and harmful content* was adopted on 5 September 2001.[58] The intention of this Recommendation was to highlight the importance of self-regulatory organizations within a co-regulatory framework in relation to the regulation of illegal and harmful Internet content. The CoE recommended that the governments of member states implement in their domestic law and/or practice the principles appended to this Recommendation.

It was specifically recommended that the member states should encourage the establishment of content complaints systems, such as hotlines (for example, similar to the Internet Watch Foundation hotline in the UK), which are provided by Internet service providers, content providers, user associations or other institutions. According to the CoE Recommendation, such content complaints systems should,

52 Ibid., para. 22.
53 Ibid., para. 23.
54 Ibid., para. 24.
55 Ibid., para. 25.
56 Ibid., para. 26.
57 Ibid., para. 27.
58 Recommendation Rec(2001)8 was adopted by the Committee of Ministers on 5 September 2001 at the 762nd meeting of the Ministers' Deputies. See further, the Explanatory Memorandum to Recommendation (2001) 8 of the Committee of Ministers to member States on self-regulation concerning cyber content: self-regulation and user protection against illegal or harmful content on new communications and information services.

where necessary for ensuring an adequate response against presumed illegal content, be complemented by hotlines provided by public authorities.[59] This should be supplemented at the domestic level, by the setting up of an

> ... adequate framework for co-operation between content complaints bodies and public authorities with regard to presumed illegal content. For this purpose, member states should define the legal responsibilities and privileges of bodies offering content complaints systems when accessing, copying, collecting and forwarding presumed illegal content to law enforcement authorities.[60]

Member states were also encouraged to foster Europe-wide and international co-operation between content complaints bodies,[61] and co-operation between law enforcement authorities with regard to complaints and investigations concerning presumed illegal content from abroad.[62]

When assessing the likely impact of the above-mentioned recommendations it has to be borne in mind that any recommendation of the Committee of Ministers of the CoE is an instrument of political commitment and not a legally enforceable instrument. Although valuable, the advisory nature of these recommendations may not necessarily result in state-level implementation.

CONCLUSION

The Council of Europe has taken the protection of children against sexual exploitation issue very seriously and as a result the above-discussed provisions of the Cybercrime Convention and two related recommendations have been adopted in recent years. In a related development, the Parliamentary Assembly of the CoE adopted a Resolution in September 2002 calling member states to take a zero tolerance approach to crimes committed against children, and acknowledged that 'child pornography in itself represents sexual abuse of children and encourages further such abuse.'[63] Furthermore, the protection of children against sexual exploitation and abuse has recently become part of a CoE programme called 'Building a Europe for and with

59 Ibid., para. 12.

60 Ibid., para. 14.

61 Ibid., para. 15.

62 Ibid., para. 16.

63 Parliamentary Assembly of the CoE, *Sexual exploitation of children: zero tolerance*, Resolution 1307 (2002). Text adopted by the Assembly on 27 September 2002 (32nd Sitting). See <http://assembly.coe.int/Main.asp?link=/Documents/AdoptedText/ta02/ERES1307.htm>. See further, Report of the Social, Health and Family Affairs Committee, Rapporteur: Mr Provera; at <http://assembly.coe.int//Main.asp?link=http://assembly.coe.int/Documents/WorkingDocs/doc02/EDOC9535.htm>; the opinion of the Committee on Legal Affairs and Human Rights, Rapporteur: Mr Piscitello, at <http://assembly.coe.int//Main.asp?link=http://assembly.coe.int/Documents/WorkingDocs/doc02/EDOC9573.htm>; and the opinion of the Committee on Culture, Science and Education, Rapporteur: Baroness Hooper, at <http://assembly.coe.int//Main.asp?link=http://assembly.coe.int/Documents/WorkingDocs/doc02/EDOC9575.htm>.

Children'.[64] This programme was launched in early 2006 and will run for three years from 2006 to 2008. The programme has two main objectives: the promotion of children's rights within the CoE member States and the protection of children against all forms of violence, including sexual violence.

In a further development, a Group of Specialists on the protection of children against sexual exploitation (PC-S-ES)[65] within the CoE was charged with the task of developing measures designed to ensure the protection of children against sexual exploitation in 2002. This group will carry out its work in the light of the Recommendation (2001) 16 *on the protection of children against sexual exploitation*, and the Commitment and Plan of Action, adopted at the preparatory Conference for the Second World Congress in Yokohama,[66] which formally requested the CoE to provide follow-up and support for the practical application of Recommendation (2001) 16.[67] Currently the group is working on a draft Convention on the protection of children against sexual exploitation and sexual abuse.[68] When finalized, this will constitute a broader Convention with the aim of addressing the root of the problem, which continues to be the sexual exploitation and sexual abuse of children.

In February 2007 Terry Davis, Secretary General of the CoE, criticized governments for not doing enough to hunt down child predators in cyberspace by reference to the low number of ratifications to the Cybercrime Convention. Davis stated, 'governments must either improve international co-operation, or accept that they will always be one step behind criminals.'[69] The Cybercrime Convention is not directly binding on any member states, and, as mentioned previously, the ratification process is a very long one. This does not necessarily mean that CoE member states do not have legal provisions criminalizing child pornography, however. Within the Council of Europe region, only Albania, the Czech Republic, Moldova, Monaco, Russia and San Marino fall within this category. Nevertheless, the signing and ratification of the Cybercrime Convention has the potential to improve and harmonize procedural provisions within state laws in the fight against cybercrimes and facilitate cross-border police operations. Criticism of some governments for their slow response is therefore not unwarranted.

64 See <http://www.coe.int/T/TransversalProjects/Children/>.

65 See <http://www.coe.int/childprotection>.

66 Budapest, November 2001.

67 The work of the Group will also take into account the Yokohama Global Commitment 2001, and the United Nations Convention on the Rights of the Child.

68 Proposals of provisions of the draft Convention on the protection of children against sexual exploitation and sexual abuse – PC-ES (2006) 6 E REV 3. See <http://www.coe.int/t/e/legal_affairs/legal_co-operation/Fight_against sexual_exploitation_of_children/>. Note further Committee of Experts on the protection of children against sexual exploitation and sexual abuse (PC-ES), Draft Convention on the protection of children against sexual exploitation and sexual abuse: Invitation to the Parliamentary Assembly to give an opinion, CM(2007)24, 14 February 2007, 989 Meeting, 14 March 2007.

69 Council of Europe press release, 'We are not doing enough to hunt down child predators in cyberspace', 086(2007), Strasbourg, 7 February 2007.

Chapter 7

United Nations Policy

As the largest existing international organization, with 192 states as its members, the United Nations could politically and strategically provide an ideal platform for addressing the problem of Internet child pornography and the sexual exploitation of children. Following on from discussion of supranational and regional international approaches to combat Internet child pornography at the European Union and Council of Europe levels, this chapter will provide an assessment of important policy developments at the United Nations level.

UN CONVENTION ON THE RIGHTS OF THE CHILD

Following the establishment of the 1989 United Nations Convention on the Rights of the Child, the United Nations has been conducting research and studying the issues of child sexual exploitation and child pornography since the early 1990s.[1] Specifically, in July 1996 the German government called upon the United Nations to help create and develop international standards for acceptable content on the Internet to protect women and children from violence and sexual exploitation online.[2]

According to the 1989 United Nations' Convention on the Rights of the Child, the need to extend particular care to the child has been provided in a number of international instruments including

> … in the Geneva Declaration of the Rights of the Child of 1924 and in the Declaration of the Rights of the Child adopted by the General Assembly on 20 November 1959 and recognized in the Universal Declaration of Human Rights, in the International Covenant on Civil and Political Rights (in particular in articles 23 and 24), in the International Covenant on Economic, Social and Cultural Rights (in particular in article 10) and in the statutes and relevant instruments of specialized agencies and international organizations concerned with the welfare of children.[3]

Article 1 of the 1989 Convention defines a child as a 'human being below the age of 18 years unless under the law applicable to the child, majority is attained earlier'.

---

1 See generally, United Nations, Commission on Human Rights, 'Rights of the Child: Report of the Special Rapporteur (Mrs Ofelia Calcetas-Santos) on the sale of children, child prostitution and child pornography', E/CN.4/1996/100, 17 January 1996.

2 'Germany asks U.N. for Web guidance', *Wired News*, 17 July 1996.

3 See the Convention on the Rights of the Child Adopted and opened for signature, ratification and accession by General Assembly resolution 44/25 of 20 November 1989 entry into force 2 September 1990, in accordance with article 49, <http://www.unhchr.ch/html/menu3/b/k2crc.htm>.

Definitional differences are still witnessed within different jurisdictions. After years of disagreement on the age of a child, a number of policy documents, including the previously discussed Council of Europe Cybercrime Convention and the EU Council Framework Decision on the sexual exploitation of children and child pornography, are finally in line with the definition provided by the UN Convention. In the absence of a harmonized definition of persons to be considered children, definitional variations will be witnessed in terms of what sort of content could be regarded as child pornography within different jurisdictions. As established in the previous chapter, this could, for example, hinder cross-border law enforcement operations if similar definitions are not used.

Article 34 of the 1989 Convention states that state parties undertake to protect children from all forms of sexual exploitation and sexual abuse including:

(a) The inducement or coercion of a child to engage in any unlawful sexual activity;
(b) The exploitative use of children in prostitution or other unlawful sexual practices;
(c) The exploitative use of children in pornographic performances and materials.[4]

Following the 1989 Convention, the UN Commission on Human Rights, at its forty-sixth session, by its resolution 1990/68 of 7 March 1990, decided to appoint a Special Rapporteur to consider matters relating to the sale of children, child prostitution and child pornography, including the problem of the adoption of children for commercial purposes. According to the 1994 report of the Special Rapporteur,

> child pornography has become increasingly transnational, and is interwoven with child prostitution. The advent of new technology raises many questions regarding the efficacy of existing laws on the subject.[5]

4 See also the Declaration of the Rights of the Child Proclaimed by General Assembly resolution 1386(XIV) of 20 November 1959, <http://www.unhchr.ch/html/menu3/b/25.htm>. United Nations High Commissioner for Human Rights – Reports submitted by the Special Rapporteur on the sale of children, child prostitution and child pornography to the General Assembly <http://ap.ohchr.org/documents/dpage_e.aspx?m=102>. *Sale of children, child prostitution and child pornography*, Note by the Secretary-General, 16 October 1997; *Sale of children, child prostitution and child pornography*, A51-456.EN, A/51/456, 7 October 1996; *Sale of children, child prostitution and child pornography*, A/50/456, 20 September 1995; *Sale of children, child prostitution and child pornography*, A/49/478, 5 October 1994. See further, *The Rights of the Child, General Assembly Resolution* 51/77 of 12 December 1996; *The Rights of the Child, General Assembly Resolution* 50/153 of 21 December 1995; Report of the Special Rapporteur on the sale of children, child prostitution and child pornography (Ms Ofelia Calcetas-Santos), Report on the mission of the Special Rapporteur to the United States of America on the issue of commercial sexual exploitation of children (9–20 December 1996), 7 February 1997; Commission on Human Rights Resolution 1995/78, *Question of a draft optional protocol to the Convention on the Rights of the Child on the sale of children, child prostitution and child pornography, as well as the basic measures needed for their prevention and eradication.*

5 Special Rapporteur (Mr Vitit Muntarbhorn) Report of the Commission on Human Rights *on the sale of children, child prostitution and child pornography*, E/CN.4/1994/84, 14 January 1994, presented at the fiftieth session of the General Assembly of the United Nations, para. 173.

States who did not criminalize the production, distribution, or possession of child pornography were urged to enact legislation in this field.[6] Following on from the 1994 report, the 1995 report of the Special Rapporteur[7] noted the 'complications brought about by the advent of modern technology'[8] in the field of child pornography, and its impact upon the law and successful prosecution of offenders:

> Even where legislation already includes measures against the proliferation of pornographic materials, actual detection and monitoring may pose serious barriers to effective prosecution of offenders.[9]

The Rapporteur also noted that due to globalization and the advancement of new technologies, some specific problems could arise in relation to the treatment of pseudo images, in which images may be created 'without the use of actual children',[10] and that this sort of activity was not necessarily criminalized by many nation states. According to the report, jurisdiction and the degree of culpability of 'those who merely use or possess the materials vis-à-vis those who distribute and manufacture them'[11] would be additional problems to be addressed in the near future. A year later, the 1996 Report noted:

> ... challenges to a study on child pornography include the lack and/or obsolescence of any uniform definition of what child pornography entails, lack of data regarding the production and distribution of child pornography in many parts of the world and shifting global patterns of production and consumption of child pornography. Furthermore, the development of home video equipment and computer technology has revolutionized the international production and distribution of child pornography. Expanding international access to increasingly inexpensive technology has transformed child pornography into a sophisticated industry. Computer alteration of images and the potential for creating computer generated pornography pose formidable challenges for courts and law enforcement officials worldwide.[12]

Difficulties in relation to international co-operation within this field were also noted in the 1996 report. Additionally, the 1997 report noted the 'spread of child pornography material, especially through the new media',[13] and argued that 'the

6 Ibid., para. 174.

7 Special Rapporteur (Ms Ofelia Calcetas-Santos) Report of the Commission on Human Rights *on the sale of children, child prostitution and child pornography*, A/50/456, 20 September 1995, presented at the fiftieth session of the General Assembly of the United Nations, para. 22.

8 Ibid.

9 Ibid., para. 59.

10 Ibid., para. 61.

11 Ibid.

12 Special Rapporteur (Ms Ofelia Calcetas-Santos) Report of the Commission on Human Rights *on the sale of children, child prostitution and child pornography*, A/51/456, 7 October 1996, presented at the fifty-first session of the General Assembly of the United Nations, para. 30.

13 Special Rapporteur (Ms Ofelia Calcetas-Santos) Report of the Commission on Human Rights *on the sale of children, child prostitution and child pornography*, A/52/482, 16 October

Internet renders the traditional legal definition of child pornography, namely the visual depiction or use of a child for pornographic purposes outdated.'[14] The Special Rapporteur encouraged the Committee on the Rights of the Child to

> ... reaffirm that the scope of article 34 of the Convention on the Rights of the Child should be interpreted to include an absolute prohibition on 'pseudo-child pornography', including the 'morphing' of child and adult bodies to create virtual child pornographic images.[15]

The 1997 report emphasized the importance of self-regulation in this field alongside the legal measures[16] stating, 'one of the main problems in Western Europe and other States region appears to be the spread of child pornography material, especially through the new media, as well as rings of paedophiles co-operating in the abuse of children.'[17] The Special Rapporteur welcomed the continuing process of adopting extraterritorial legislation by countries of origin of tourists who engage in child sex abuse.[18]

OPTIONAL PROTOCOL TO THE CONVENTION ON THE RIGHTS OF THE CHILD ON THE SALE OF CHILDREN, CHILD PROSTITUTION AND CHILD PORNOGRAPHY

Concerns regarding child pornography and its availability and distribution through the Internet at the UN level led to the drafting of an Optional Protocol on the Sale of Children, Child Prostitution and Child Pornography[19] to the 1989 Convention on the Rights of the Child in the late 1990s by the Commission on Human Rights. This Optional Protocol was introduced by a Resolution of the Economic and Social Council of the United Nations[20] in May 2000. All states who have signed, ratified or acceded to the Convention on the Rights of the Child were invited to sign, ratify or accede to the Optional Protocol.

1997, presented at the fifty-second session of the General Assembly of the United Nations, para. 34.

14 Ibid., para. 53.

15 Ibid.

16 Ibid., para. 103. See further, the *Promotion and Protection of the Rights of Children: Sale of children, child prostitution and child pornography*, Note by the Secretary-General, A/52/482, 16 October 1997. See further, Alexander, S., S. Meuwese and A. Wolthuis, 'Policies and developments relating to the sexual exploitation of children: The legacy of the Stockholm Conference' (2000), *European Journal on Criminal Policy and Research* (8) 479–501.

17 Ibid., para. 34.

18 Ibid. Within this context note the UK's Sexual Offences (Conspiracy and Incitement) Act 1996 which deals with British sex offenders abroad, and section 2 of the 1996 Act made it an offence to incite another person to commit certain sexual acts against children abroad. The scope of incitement for the purposes of section 2 extends to the use of the Internet, and any incitement will be deemed to take place in the UK if the message is received in the UK. See <http://www.uk-legislation.hmso.gov.uk/acts/acts1996/1996029.htm>.

19 Optional Protocol to the Convention on the Rights of the Child on the Sale of Children, Child Prostitution and Child Pornography, New York, 25 May 2000, Fifty-fourth session (97th plenary meeting), Agenda item 116 (a), Distr. General A/RES/54/263, 26 June 2000.

20 A/54/L.84 of 16 May 2000.

The Optional Protocol to the Convention on the Rights of the Child on the Sale of Children, Child Prostitution and Child Pornography declares that state parties to the Optional Protocol are 'gravely concerned at the significant and increasing international traffic in children for the purpose of the sale of children, child prostitution and child pornography'.[21] Concern was also raised 'about the growing availability of child pornography on the Internet and other evolving technologies',[22] and the Optional Protocol noted the conclusions of the International Conference on combating child pornography on the Internet, held in Vienna in 1999, 'in particular its conclusion calling for the world wide criminalisation of the production, distribution, exportation, transmission, importation, intentional possession and advertising of child pornography, and stressing the importance of closer co-operation and partnership between Governments and the Internet industry'.[23]

With this Optional Protocol, state parties agreed under article 1 to 'prohibit the sale of children, child prostitution and child pornography'.[24] Child pornography is defined as 'any representation, by whatever means, of a child engaged in real or simulated explicit sexual activities or any representation of the sexual parts of a child for primarily sexual purposes' under article 2(c). Article 3(1) requires the state parties to ensure that, as a minimum, the 'producing, distributing, disseminating, importing, exporting, offering, selling or possessing'[25] of child pornography (as defined in article 2) offences are fully covered by criminal law whether such offences are committed domestically or trans-nationally or on an individual or organized basis.

Article 3(4) requires state parties to take measures to establish the liability of legal persons for offences established in paragraph 1 'where appropriate'. This is an emphasis on Internet Service Providers (ISPs) liability within the context of illegal Internet content which will be further detailed in Chapter 8. However, the 2001 Special Rapporteur report[26] acknowledged, with respect to the dissemination of child pornography through the servers of ISPs, that 'given the decentralized nature of the Internet over which no one entity has control, traditional legislation penalizing the dissemination of child pornography cannot be applied to those ISPs which may unwittingly facilitate such crimes.'[27] Therefore, although liability (whether criminal, civil or administrative to be decided at the nation-state level) could occur, the nature of the Internet and the technical capabilities of ISPs were factors to be taken into account when policies were developed during the implementation of the Optional Protocol by ratifying states.

---

21 See the Optional Protocol to the Convention on the Rights of the Child on the Sale of Children, Child Prostitution and Child Pornography at <http://www.unhchr.ch/html/menu2/dopchild.htm>.

22 Ibid.

23 See <http://www.stop-childpornog.at/>.

24 Optional Protocol.

25 Article 3(1)(c) of the Optional Protocol.

26 Special Rapporteur (Ms Ofelia Calcetas-Santos) Report of the Commission on Human Rights *on the sale of children, child prostitution and child pornography*, E/CN.4/2001/78, 25 January 2001, presented at the fifty-seventh session of the General Assembly of the United Nations.

27 Ibid., para. 76.

A further requirement under the Optional Protocol is to make child pornography offences extraditable offences under article 5(1), to be included in any extradition treaty existing between state parties to facilitate the prosecution and conviction of those who commit such offences. Furthermore, mutual legal assistance is encouraged in article 6, including assistance in obtaining evidence at their disposal necessary for the proceedings. The UN Optional Protocol in article 10(1) required state parties to

> … take all necessary steps to strengthen international co-operation by multilateral, regional and bilateral arrangements for the prevention, detection, investigation, prosecution and punishment of those responsible for acts involving the sale of children, child prostitution, child pornography and child sex tourism.[28]

More important, article 10(3) requires states parties to

> … promote the strengthening of international co-operation in order to address the root causes, such as poverty and underdevelopment, contributing to the vulnerability of children to the sale of children, child prostitution, child pornography and child sex tourism.[29]

Status of the Optional Protocol

According to article 14, the Optional Protocol was expected to 'enter into force three months after the deposit of the tenth instrument of ratification or accession'.[30] Following the required number of ratifications, the Optional Protocol entered into force on 18 January 2002. As of June 2007, 115 countries[31] have signed the Optional Protocol including the United Kingdom,[32] the United States and Canada, and 119 member states have ratified or acceded to the Optional Protocol.[33]

Status of the signatures, ratification and accession to the Optional Protocol as of June 2007 (115 Signatories, 119 Parties) is given in Table 7.1.[34]

---

28 Optional Protocol.

29 Ibid.

30 Article 14(1).

31 See <http://www.unicef.org/crc/opsx-tableweb.htm>. See further, Special Rapporteur (Mr Juan Miguel Petit) Report of the Commission on Human Rights *on the sale of children, child prostitution and child pornography*, E/CN.4/2002/88, 4 February 2002, presented at the fifty-eighth session of the General Assembly of the United Nations, para. 57.

32 The UK government signed the optional protocol at the Millennium Summit of the United Nations, which was convened from 6 to 8 September 2000 in New York. Agence France-Presse, 'UN summit produces flood of treaty signatures', 9 September 2000.

33 See generally, Office of the UN High Commissioner for Human Rights, Status of ratifications of the principal international human rights treaties, at <http://www.unhchr.ch/pdf/report.pdf>.

34 Taken from <http://www.ohchr.org/english/countries/ratification/11_c.htm>.

Table 7.1 UN optional protocol signatures and ratifications

Participant States	Signature	Ratification, Accession (a)
Afghanistan	–	19 Sept 2002 (a)
Algeria	–	27 Dec 2006 (a)
Andorra	7 Sept 2000	30 Apr 2001
Angola	–	24 Mar 2005 (a)
Antigua and Barbuda	18 Dec 2001	30 Apr 2002
Argentina	1 Apr 2002	25 Sept 2003
Armenia	24 Sept 2003	30 Jun 2005
Australia	18 Dec 2001	8 Jan 2007
Austria	6 Sept 2000	6 May 2004
Azerbaijan	8 Sept 2000	3 Jul 2002
Bahrain	–	21 Sep 2004 (a)
Bangladesh	6 Sept 2000	6 Sept 2000
Belarus	–	23 Jan 2002 (a)
Belgium	6 Sept 2000	17 Mar 2006
Belize	6 Sept 2000	1 Dec 2003
Benin	22 Feb 2001	31 Jan 2005
Bhutan	15 Sept 2005	–
Bolivia	10 Nov 2001	3 Jun 2003
Bosnia and Herzegovina	7 Sept 2000	4 Sept 2002
Botswana	–	24 Sept 2003 (a)
Brazil	6 Sept 2000	27 Jan 2004
Brunei Darussalam	–	21 Nov 2006 (a)
Bulgaria	8 Jun 2001	12 Feb 2002
Burkina Faso	16 Nov 2001	31 Mar 2006
Cambodia	27 Jun 2000	30 May 2002
Cameroon	5 Oct 2001	–
Canada	10 Nov 2001	14 Sept 2005
Cape Verde	–	10 May 2002 (a)
Chad	8 May 2002	28 Aug 2002
Chile	28 Jun 2000	6 Feb 2003
China	6 Sept 2000	3 Dec 2002
Colombia	6 Sept 2000	11 Nov 2003

Table 7.1 Continued UN optional protocol signatures and ratifications

Participant States	Signature	Ratification, Accession (a)
Comoros	–	23 Feb 2007 (a)
Costa Rica	7 Sept 2000	9 Apr 2002
Croatia	8 May 2002	13 May 2002
Cuba	13 Oct 2000	25 Sept 2001
Cyprus	8 Feb 2001	6 Apr 2006
Czech Republic	26 Jan 2005	–
Democratic Republic of the Congo	–	11 Nov 2001 (a)
Denmark	7 Sept 2000	24 Jul 2003
Djibouti	14 Jun 2006	–
Dominica	–	20 Sept 2002 (a)
Dominican Republic	–	6 Dec 2006 (a)
Ecuador	6 Sept 2000	30 Jan 2004
Egypt	–	12 Jul 2002 (a)
El Salvador	13 Sept 2002	17 May 2004
Equatorial Guinea	–	7 Feb 2003 (a)
Eritrea	–	16 Feb 2005 (a)
Estonia	24 Sept 2003	3 Aug 2004
Fiji	16 Sept 2005	–
Finland	7 Sept 2000	–
France	6 Sept 2000	5 Feb 2003
Gabon	8 Sept 2000	–
Gambia	21 Dec 2000	–
Georgia	–	28 Jun 2005 (a)
Germany	6 Sept 2000	–
Ghana	24 Sept 2003	–
Greece	7 Sept 2000	–
Guatemala	7 Sept 2000	9 May 2002
Guinea-Bissau	8 Sept 2000	–
Haiti	15 Aug 2002	–
Holy See	10 Oct 2000	24 Oct 2001
Honduras	–	8 May 2002 (a)

Table 7.1 Continued UN optional protocol signatures and ratifications

Participant States	Signature	Ratification, Accession (a)
Hungary	11 Mar 2002	–
Iceland	7 Sept 2000	9 Jul 2001
India	15 Nov 2004	16 Aug 2005
Indonesia	24 Sept 2001	–
Ireland	7 Sept 2000	–
Israel	14 Nov 2001	–
Italy	6 Sept 2000	9 May 2002
Jamaica	8 Sept 2000	–
Japan	10 May 2002	24 Jan 2005
Jordan	6 Sept 2000	4 Dec 2006
Kazakhstan	6 Sept 2000	24 Aug 2001
Kenya	8 Sept 2000	–
Kuwait	–	26 Aug 2004 (a)
Kyrgyzstan	–	12 Feb 2003 (a)
Lao People's Democratic Republic	–	20 Sept 2006 (a)
Latvia	1 Feb 2002	22 Feb 2006
Lebanon	10 Oct 2001	8 Nov 2004
Lesotho	6 Sept 2000	24 Sept 2003
Liberia	22 Sept 2004	–
Libyan Arab Jamahiriya	–	18 Jun 2004 (a)
Liechtenstein	8 Sept 2000	–
Lithuania	–	5 Aug 2004 (a)
Luxembourg	8 Sept 2000	–
Madagascar	7 Sept 2000	22 Sept 2004
Malawi	7 Sept 2000	–
Maldives	10 May 2002	10 May 2002
Mali	–	16 May 2002 (a)
Malta	7 Sept 2000	–
Mauritius	11 Nov 2001	–
Mexico	7 Sept 2000	15 Mar 2002
Micronesia (Federated States of)	8 May 2002	–

Table 7.1 Continued UN optional protocol signatures and ratifications

Participant States	Signature	Ratification, Accession (a)
Moldova	8 Feb 2002	12 Apr 2007
Monaco	26 Jun 2000	–
Mongolia	12 Nov 2001	27 Jun 2003
Montenegro	–	23 Oct 2006 (a)
Morocco	8 Sept 2000	2 Oct 2001
Mozambique	–	6 Mar 2003 (a)
Namibia	8 Sept 2000	16 Apr 2002
Nauru	8 Sept 2000	–
Nepal	8 Sept 2000	20 Jan 2006
Netherlands	7 Sept 2000	23 Aug 2005
New Zealand	7 Sept 2000	–
Nicaragua	–	2 Dec 2004 (a)
Niger	27 Mar 2002	26 Oct 2004
Nigeria	8 Sept 2000	–
Norway	13 Jun 2000	2 Oct 2001
Oman	–	17 Sept 2004 (a)
Pakistan	26 Sept 2001	–
Panama	31 Oct 2000	9 Feb 2001
Paraguay	13 Sept 2000	18 Aug 2003
Peru	1 Nov 2000	8 May 2002
Philippines	8 Sept 2000	28 May 2002
Poland	13 Feb 2002	4 Feb 2005
Portugal	6 Sept 2000	16 May 2003
Qatar	–	14 Dec 2001 (a)
Republic of Korea	6 Sept 2000	24 Sept 2004
Romania	6 Sept 2000	18 Oct 2001
Rwanda	–	14 Mar 2002 (a)
Saint Vincent and the Grenadines	–	15 Sept 2005 (a)
San Marino	5 Jun 2000	–
Senegal	8 Sept 2000	5 Nov 2003
Serbia	8 Oct 2001	10 Oct 2002

Table 7.1 Continued UN optional protocol signatures and ratifications

Participant States	Signature	Ratification, Accession (a)
Seychelles	23 Jan 2001	–
Sierra Leone	8 Sept 2000	17 Sept 2001
Slovakia	30 Nov 2001	25 Jun 2004
Slovenia	8 Sept 2000	23 Sept 2004
South Africa	–	30 Jun 2003 (a)
Spain	6 Sept 2000	18 Dec 2001
Sri Lanka	8 May 2002	22 Sept 2006
Sudan	–	2 Nov 2004 (a)
Suriname	10 May 2002	–
Sweden	8 Sept 2000	19 Jan 2007
Switzerland	7 Sept 2000	19 Sept 2006
Syrian Arab Republic	–	15 May 2003 (a)
Tajikistan	–	5 Aug 2002 (a)
Thailand	–	11 Jan 2006 (a)
The Former Yugoslav Republic of Macedonia	17 Jul 2001	17 Oct 2003
Togo	15 Nov 2001	2 Jul 2004
Tunisia	22 Apr 2002	13 Sept 2002
Turkey	8 Sept 2000	19 Aug 2002
Turkmenistan	–	28 Mar 2005 (a)
Uganda	–	30 Nov 2001 (a)
Ukraine	7 Sept 2000	3 Jul 2003
United Kingdom of Great Britain and Northern Ireland	7 Sept 2000	–
United Republic of Tanzania	–	24 Apr 2003 (a)
United States of America	5 Jul 2000	23 Dec 2002
Uruguay	7 Sept 2000	3 Jul 2003
Vanuatu	16 Sept 2005	–
Venezuela	7 Sept 2000	8 May 2002
Viet Nam	8 Sept 2000	20 Dec 2001
Yemen	–	15 Dec 2004 (a)

According to article 12(1) of the Optional Protocol, each State Party shall, 'within two years following the entry into force of the present Protocol for that State Party, submit a report to the Committee on the Rights of the Child providing comprehensive information on the measures it has taken to implement the provisions of the Protocol'; guidelines for this purpose were published by the Committee on the Rights of the Child in February 2002.[35] As the ratification process is slow, only 13 states[36] had provided initial reports as of July 2006. As of June 2007, the examination process of the Committee on the Rights of the Child was yet to commence, but this will eventually 'contribute to developing a common understanding of definitions and their implications'[37] within the ratifying member states.

In December 2004 the Special Rapporteur on the sale of children, child prostitution and child pornography published a thematic report on child pornography on the Internet.[38] The report was based on the information received from governments, international organizations and non-governmental organizations (NGOs) in reply to a questionnaire sent by the Special Rapporteur. Information was received from 51 countries and, according to the report, many countries still do not have legislation on child pornography. As of June 2007, 73 out of 192 UN member states are not party to the Optional Protocol, and despite the fact that more than half (119 as of June 2007) of the UN member states became party to the Optional Protocol, it has been observed that 'this legal vacuum leaves a dangerous gap that exposes children to the risk of abuse, further increased by the impunity factor.'[39]

In his report, the Special Rapporteur called for the ratification of the Optional Protocol and the adoption of its definition of child pornography by the UN member states, and recommended that further legislation creating the offence of 'Internet grooming or luring' should be introduced to combat the sexual exploitation of children on the Internet. He called for the introduction of legislation on ISPs, establishing a minimum monitoring obligation to prevent online child pornography, and an obligation to remove or prevent accessibility to illegal material of which they have knowledge. There was also a call for criminalizing child erotica, and a call to ensure that 'legislation on child pornography protects all children under the age

35 Committee on the Rights of the Child, Guidelines regarding initial reports to be submitted by States Parties under article 12 (1) of the Optional Protocol to the Convention on the Rights of the Child on the Sale of Children, Child Prostitution and Child Pornography (unedited version), CRC/OP/SA/1, adopted by the Committee at its 777th meeting (Twenty-ninth session), 1 February 2002.

36 These are Turkey, Syrian Arab Republic, Bangladesh, Costa Rica, Viet Nam, Denmark, Qatar, China, Iceland, Morocco, Andorra, Kazakhstan and Norway.

37 Special Rapporteur on the sale of children, child prostitution and child pornography, *Thematic Report on child pornography on the Internet*, E/CN.4/2005/78, Economic and Social Council, Commission on Human Rights, 23 December 2004, at <http://daccessdds.un.org/doc/UNDOC/GEN/G05/100/19/PDF/G0510019.pdf>, p. 22, para. 119.

38 Ibid. Note also Addendum: Communications sent to Governments and replies received, E/CN.4/2005/78/Add.3, 8 March 2005, at <http://daccessdds.un.org/doc/UNDOC/GEN/G05/127/92/PDF/G0512792.pdf>. See also <http://www.ohchr.org/english/issues/children/rapporteur/annual05.htm> for the individual state responses.

39 See E/CN.4/2005/78, p. 2.

of 18, regardless of the age of consent to sexual activity, which can be under 18.'[40] According to the Special Rapporteur, 'a child under 18 should not be considered as able to consent to engagement in pornography, prostitution or trafficking.'[41]

The Special Rapporteur was concerned with the limited action taken so far to protect the victims of child pornography and called for more efforts to identify the victims of abuse and provide them with assistance and compensation. The report identified the private sector as an 'indispensable ally' in the fight against Internet child pornography and emphasized the importance of self-regulatory initiatives. The Special Rapporteur urged credit-card companies to make all possible efforts to avoid accepting payment for child pornography web sites.

OTHER UN-LEVEL DEVELOPMENTS

Another politically important development took place at the United Nations Educational, Scientific, and Cultural Organization (UNESCO) level with an expert meeting on 'sexual abuse of children, child pornography and paedophilia on the Internet: an international challenge', in January 1999.[42] The expert meeting resulted in a declaration and an action plan which proposed certain measures primarily for UNESCO and for governments, international agencies, NGOs, industry, educators, parents, law enforcement agencies and the media. The meeting declared, *inter alia*, that 'action against illegal content on the Internet needs industry co-operation in restricting circulation and a fully functioning system of self-regulation and that protection must go hand-in-hand with effective law enforcement.'[43]

Following the conference, UNESCO set up 'Innocence in Danger', an international Internet education and safety programme.[44] The programme has been designed to gather information and create networks among all industries and community action groups to avoid duplication of efforts regarding Internet education for children and for adults.[45] This was followed by an international conference on combating child pornography on the Internet organized by Austria in October 1999.[46] During this conference, the participants

40 Ibid.

41 Ibid.

42 See generally, <http://www.innocenceindanger.org>. See further, Special Rapporteur (Ms Ofelia Calcetas-Santos) Report of the Commission on Human Rights *on the sale of children, child prostitution and child pornography*, A/54/411, 29 September 1999, presented at the fifty-fourth session of the General Assembly of the United Nations.

43 Special Rapporteur (Ms Ofelia Calcetas-Santos) Report of the Commission on Human Rights *on the sale of children, child prostitution and child pornography*, E/CN.4/2001/78, 25 January 2001, presented at the fifty-seventh session of the General Assembly of the United Nations, para. 79.

44 See <http://www.innocenceindanger.org/>. See further, Arnaldo, C.A. (ed.), *Child Abuse on the Internet: Ending the Silence*, New York: Berghahn Books, Paris: UNESCO, 2001.

45 The 1999 Special Rapporteur Report, para. 7.

46 Ibid., para. 31.

> … agreed that a policy of zero tolerance with regard to child pornography must be pursued in all jurisdictions, which will require effective legislation and law enforcement. Participants also committed themselves to the strengthening of partnerships at national and international levels among governments, the Internet industry, hotlines and NGOs.[47]

More important, the Second World Congress[48] against the Commercial Sexual Exploitation of Children took place in Yokohama, Japan in December 2001.[49] The Congress brought together over 3,000 participants, including representatives of 132 Governments and of NGOs, United Nations agencies and the private sector.[50] Child pornography was one of the main topics discussed during the conference. The outcome of the conference was the Yokohama Global Commitment 2001 document, which stated:

> We have come together to … take adequate measures to address negative aspects of new technologies, in particular child pornography on the Internet, while recognizing the potential of new technologies for the protection of children from commercial sexual exploitation, through dissemination and exchange of information and networking among partners.[51]

However, according to the UN Special Rapporteur report of 2002, the conference

> … demonstrated the lack of progress made by Governments since the first World Congress. There was little evidence of concrete steps having been taken by Governments to implement the Stockholm Agenda for Action, which they committed themselves to do five years ago. It was reported that less than half have adopted national plans of action against the commercial sexual exploitation of children, and of those which have adopted such plans, none have committed adequate financial resources for their implementation.[52]

---

47 Ibid., para. 32.

48 The first Congress was held in Stockholm, Sweden, in August 1996.

49 See <http://www.unicef.org/events/yokohama/outcome.html>. Prior to the Congress, six regional preparatory meetings had been held – in Bangkok for the East Asia and Pacific region (16–18 October 2001), in Rabat for Africa and the Middle East (24–26 October 2001), in Dhaka for South Asia (5–6 November 2001), in Montevideo for Latin America and the Caribbean (7–9 November 2001), in Budapest for Eastern and Western Europe (20–21 November 2001) and in Philadelphia for the United States, Canada and Mexico (2–3 December 2001).

50 Special Rapporteur (Mr Juan Miguel Petit) Report of the Commission on Human Rights *on the sale of children, child prostitution and child pornography*, E/CN.4/2002/88, 4 February 2002, presented at the fifty-eighth session of the General Assembly of the United Nations, para. 47.

51 See <http://www.unicef.org/events/yokohama/outcome.html>.

52 Special Rapporteur (Mr Juan Miguel Petit) Report of the Commission on Human Rights *on the sale of children, child prostitution and child pornography*, E/CN.4/2002/88, 4 February 2002, presented at the fifty-eighth session of the General Assembly of the United Nations, para. 56.

The Special Rapporteur, in his 2002 report, encouraged all states to review their commitments in this respect and to make the adoption and implementation of such plans of action a matter of the utmost priority.[53]

CONCLUSION

Child pornography has been recognized as a global problem by a number of international organizations including not only the United Nations but also the European Union and the Council of Europe. Although most of the policy related developments described in this chapter are important, the most significant development remains the UN Optional Protocol to the Convention on the Rights of the Child on the Sale of Children, Child Prostitution and Child Pornography, which entered into force in January 2002. This now provides the basis for individual governments to show their commitment to the fight against child pornography and the sexual exploitation of children. Progress is evidently[54] slow in this field, even though there seems to be much agreement[55] on how to deal with the problem of child pornography at the UN level. Although a considerable number of UN member states have signed and ratified the Optional Protocol, others need to follow suit to ensure that safe havens for the provision and dissemination of child pornography are not created in those countries which do not criminalize child pornography. Many member states, it must be said, are still 'at the stage of equipping themselves with the normative, institutional and policy instruments to tackle the issue'.[56]

---

53 Ibid.

54 Special Rapporteur (Mr Juan Miguel Petit) Report of the Commission on Human Rights *on the sale of children, child prostitution and child pornography*, E/CN.4/2002/88, 4 February 2002, presented at the fifty-eighth session of the General Assembly of the United Nations, para. 56.

55 See for example the Yokohama Global Commitment 2001.

56 Special Rapporteur on the sale of children, child prostitution and child pornography, *Thematic Report on child pornography on the Internet*, E/CN.4/2005/78, Economic and Social Council, Commission on Human Rights, 23 December 2004, at <http://daccessdds.un.org/doc/UNDOC/GEN/G05/100/19/PDF/G0510019.pdf>. Note also Addendum: Communications sent to Governments and replies received, E/CN.4/2005/78/Add.3, 8 March 2005, at <http://daccessdds.un.org/doc/UNDOC/GEN/G05/127/92/PDF/G0512792.pdf>, p. 22, para. 117.

Part Three

Internet Service Providers' Liability and Self-Regulatory Approaches

> Close cooperation and interaction with the industry, and in particular, Internet service providers is absolutely necessary in order to find solutions that are not only juridically sound but also technically achievable.[1]

Although a degree of harmonization has been established at the supranational (European Union), regional international (Council of Europe), as well as at the international (United Nations) level, there still exist different legal approaches between states. As states continue to amend their legal frameworks to achieve a greater degree of harmonization, states and international organizations can be expected to look to the Internet industry for assistance in the fight against child pornography. An examination of policy initiatives within the three jurisdictions included within this book, as well as at the European level, reveals that a strong partnership between governments and the Internet industry emerged in the mid-1990s with an emphasis on self and co-regulation. The private sector, most notably Internet Service Providers (ISPs), have been encouraged to develop voluntary ethical codes of conduct, self-regulatory measures, policies and practices aimed at combating illegal and harmful content on the Internet to avoid prosecution for carrying illegal content such as child pornography on their servers.

Part Three examines child pornography specific initiatives and policies developed by the Internet industry aimed at reducing the circulation of illegal content through properly functioning systems of self-regulation (such as codes of conduct and the establishment of hotlines to report illegal Internet activity) in compliance with and supported by the legal system. These levels of intervention may be said to reflect late modernity in that there is a dispersal of regulatory power in shifting the boundaries between public and private organizations, with the latter taking a strong role in policing.[2] The issues surrounding Internet ISP liability are a key part of this debate and are detailed in Chapter 8. This is followed by an analysis of self-regulatory and co-regulatory initiatives viewed from UK, North American and European perspectives in Chapter 9.

---

1 Council of the European Union, *Conclusions of the First High Level Political Dialogue on Counter-Terrorism between the Council, the Commission, and the European Parliament*, JAI 240, 9246/06, Brussels, 18 May 2006.

2 See generally, Walker, C. and Y. Akdeniz, 'The Governance of the Internet in Europe with Special Reference to Illegal and Harmful Content' (1998), *Crim. L.R.*, December Special Edition: Crime, Criminal Justice and the Internet, 5–19. See further, Rose, N. and P. Miller, P., 'Political Power beyond the State' (1992), 43 *British Journal of Sociology* 173; Jones, T. and T. Newburn, *Private Security and Public Policing*, Oxford: Clarendon, 1998.

Chapter 8

Internet Service Providers' Liability

Internet Service Providers (ISPs) differ in nature in different countries but the main function remains the commercial provision of Internet access services such as dial-up and broadband to the online users. It is not possible (especially for home users) to access the Internet without the services of an ISP, and therefore the role of an ISP is crucial. Although no ISP controls third-party content or all of the backbones of the Internet, the role they play in providing access has made them visible targets for the control of content on the Internet, and their responsibility as gateways to communication for the mass public has been brought into question, especially in relation to the availability of such illegal content as child pornography. While ISPs are not directly part of the chain of liability in terms of offending behaviour, they are considered by many states, as well as international agreements and conventions, to be part of the chain which contributes to the distribution of child pornography on the Internet. In most instances, liability will only be imposed if there is 'knowledge and control' over the information which is transmitted or stored by an ISP. Nevertheless, difficult issues surround ISP liability.

THE ROLE OF THE ISPS

The role of ISPs can vary from pure conduit (for example, dial-up service and broadband) to pure publisher and accordingly the term ISP should be seen as an umbrella term covering different characteristics. ISPs may be content providers themselves, offering content to customers. Some offer content on a small scale (for example, no more than the provision of a web page with information relevant to their customers), while others such as AOL create and provide content for their customers such as news, sport and entertainment.

By performing diverse roles as described above, the duties and responsibilities of the ISPs may considerably vary. While the provision and transmission of private communications such as electronic mail is not different from the role of a traditional post office or telephone company, the role and duties of an ISP as a content creator may be different. However, this content-related responsibility does not necessarily or feasibly extend to third-party content that is available over the Internet.

While ISPs have been the target of defamation lawsuits in both the United States (CompuServe and AOL[1]) and the UK (Demon Internet[2]), and copyright suits[3] in the United States, they have also been charged with criminal offences of providing child pornography within the European Union member states, specifically Germany,[4] France[5] and Austria.[6] The availability of hate speech on the Internet remains another concern for the German government and for French courts,[7] and ISPs have become the 'usual suspects' for the provision of such material on the Internet in these cases.[8]

1 See *Cubby, Inc. v. CompuServe Inc.* 776 F. Supp. 135 (1991), *Stratton Oakmont, Inc. v. Prodigy Servs. Co.* 23 Media L. Rep. (BNA) 1794 (1995), and *Kenneth M. Zeran v. America Online, Inc.* U.S. District Court, E.D. Virginia, 958 F.Supp (1997); U.S Court of Appeals, 4th Circuit, CA-96-1564-A, 129 F.2d 327 (1997); U.S. Supreme Court, Certiorari denied, Pet. 97-1488.

2 *Godfrey v. Demon Internet Ltd*, QBD, [1999] 4 All ER 342; [2000] 3 WLR 1020; [2001] QB 201. See further, Akdeniz, Y., 'Case Analysis: Laurence Godfrey v. Demon Internet Limited' (1999), *Journal of Civil Liberties*, 4(2), 260–67.

3 See *Religious Technology Center v. F.A.C.T.Net, Inc.*, 901 F. Supp. 1519 (D. Colo. 1995), *Religious Technology Center v. Netcom On-line Communication Services, Inc.*, 907 F. Supp. 1361 (N.D. Cal. 1995).

4 Macavinta, C., 'CompuServe manager convicted', *Cnet News.Com*, 28 May 1998.

5 The managers of two Internet providers, WorldNet and FranceNet, have been charged with distribution of child pornography on 'alt.binaries' newsgroups. They faced the possibility of three years in jail and £65,000 fines. See Rooney, B., 'Net porn crackdown', *Daily Telegraph*, 15 May 1996.

6 There has been a cyber-protest of two hours organized by the Austrian ISPs following the Austrian government's decision that ISPs must remain liable for illegal content fed through their access points. This followed a police raid on a Vienna based ISP, VIPnet, whose computers have allegedly been used to feed child pornography into the Internet. See 'Austria persists in Net smut war', Reuters, 27 March 1997.

7 *League Against Racism and Antisemitism (LICRA), French Union of Jewish Students v. Yahoo! Inc. (USA), Yahoo France*, Tribunal de Grande Instance de Paris (The County Court of Paris), Interim Court Order, 20 November 2000. Note also *Yahoo!, Inc. v. La Ligue Contre Le Racisme Et L'Antisemitisme*, Case Number C-00-21275 JF [Docket No. 17], United States District Court for the Northern District of California, San Jose Division, 169 F. Supp. 2d 1181; 2001 U.S. Dist. LEXIS 18378, November 7 2001, Decided; *Yahoo! Inc. v. La Ligue Contre Le Racisme et L'Antisemitisme*, 379 F3d 1120 (9th Cir. 2004); *Yahoo! Inc. v. La Ligue Contre Le Racisme et L'Antisemitisme*, 399 F3d 1010 (9th Cir. 2005); *Yahoo! Inc. v. La Ligue Contre Le Racisme et L'Antisemitisme*, 433 F3d 1199 (9th Cir. 2006). See further, Akdeniz, Y., 'Case Review: League Against Racism and Antisemitism' (LICRA), *French Union of Jewish Students v. Yahoo! Inc. (USA),* Yahoo France (2001), *Electronic Business Law Reports* 1(3) 110–20; Akdeniz, Y., 'Governing Racist Content on the Internet: National and International Responses' (2007), *University of New Brunswick Law Journal* (Canada) 56, Spring, 103–61.

8 See for example 'German Government Pushes Blockage of Netherlands Web Sites', *Global Alert*, 1996, September 18, <http://www.hartford-hwp.com/archives/61/250.html>, AP News, 'Effective blockade on the Internet impossible', 22 April 1997. For further information about the Radikal incident, see Akdeniz, Y., 'To Link or Not to Link: Problems with World Wide Web Links on the Internet' (1997), *International Review of Law, Computers and Technology* 11(2), 281–98. In another similar incident in January 1996, Deutsche Telekom (DT) blocked users of its T-Online computer network from accessing Internet sites used to

There are technical factors which prevent an ISP from blocking the free flow of information on the Internet. First, an Internet service provider cannot easily stop the incoming flow of material through newsgroups. No one can hope to monitor the enormous quantity of network traffic, which may consist of hundreds of thousands of emails, newsgroup messages, files, Web pages and peer-to-peer (P2P) activity that travels in dozens of text and binary formats, some of them readable only by particular proprietary tools, through the servers of an ISP. ISPs do have a limited technical ability to detect and control content, but in most cases it would be impossible for a single ISP to control, monitor or judge whether this enormous amount of Internet content and activity contains illegal content according to the laws of the country of service. It should also be noted that in technical terms, ISPs cannot remove content from the Internet which is not physically residing on their servers. ISPs can only take action in terms of their own servers, though it is also possible for an ISP to block access to content which is available through other sources.

In this way, ISPs differ from newspaper editors or broadcast companies for example, as they do not have control over most Internet content. Rather, as an EU communication paper stated, 'ISPs play a key role in facilitating user access to Internet content.'[9]

IMPLICATIONS FOR CRIMINAL LIABILITY

Although it should be realized that the initial responsibility for content generation and dissemination lies with authors and not content providers, CompuServe has been successfully prosecuted in Germany.[10] This section analyses the *CompuServe* case as it is relevant to policy developments in Europe, leading to an assessment of European-wide proposals to address issues surrounding legal liability of ISPs.

COMPUSERVE GERMANY CASE

Felix Somm was the General Manager of CompuServe in Germany until he resigned in April 1997. Before that date Somm was indicted by the Bavarian prosecutors following allegations that he was responsible for the distribution of illegal content over the Internet. Somm was found guilty of having assisted in the dissemination of child pornography and other Internet content deemed illegal in Germany, including

---

spread anti-Semitic propaganda, which is a crime in Germany. The company was responding to demands by Mannheim prosecutors who were investigating Ernst Zundel, a German-born neo-Nazi living in Toronto who denies the existence of the Holocaust. See 'German Service Cuts Net Access', *San Jose Mercury News*, 27 January 1996.

9 See European Commission Communication to the European Parliament, The Council, The Economic and Social Committee and the Committee of the Regions: Illegal and Harmful Content on the Internet, Com (96) 487, Brussels, 16 October 1996.

10 Note also the Yahoo! case in France, *League Against Racism and Antisemitism (LICRA), French Union of Jewish Students v. Yahoo! Inc. (USA), Yahoo France*, The County Court of Paris, Interim Court Order, 20 November 2000.

popular computer games such as Doom, Heretic and Wolfenstein 3D[11] in violation of the German Dissemination of Publications Morally Harmful to Youth Act. Somm received a two-year suspended sentence and a fine of DM100,000 from the Munich district court in May 1998.[12]

The decision was the first of its kind, with an ISP being found liable under criminal law, and involved the availability and distribution of child pornography through Usenet discussion groups and the above-mentioned computer games through the services of CompuServe. The content in question (both child pornography and the computer games) involved third-party content over which CompuServe had no control whatsoever. The content in question was available not only to German customers but also to other CompuServe customers through their global system, with a large number of customers based in the United States.

At the time the German prosecution took place, ISPs could only be held accountable under the German Teleservices Act 1997 (known also as the 'Multimedia Act') for the dissemination of illegal material through their services if they knew about the content and blocking or removing the content in question was technically possible. However, according to the *CompuServe* judgement, 'the conditions for an exemption from liability pursuant to section 5(3) of the Teleservices Act were not met, since CompuServe Germany was not an access provider.'[13] According to the defence, the court made a methodical error in applying the 1997 Act to the *CompuServe* case.[14] The defence argued:

> The judgment suggestively attempts at winning the reader over to the harsh punishment of disseminators of child pornography. This aim may not be objected to as such if the judgment is given against the true offenders, namely those who sexually abuse children and store for retrieval child-pornographic content in the network.[15]

---

11 The German Federal Review Board decided to put the games on the index for publications morally harmful to youth. This was effected with regard to their social-ethical disorientation (including, but not limited to deliberate, realistically reproduced killings) or elements glorifying National Socialism. The decisions of the Federal Review Board for Publications Morally Harmful to Youth were published in the Federal Gazette No. 100 of 31 May 1994 ('Doom'), in the Federal Gazette No. 141 of 29 July 1995 ('Heretic') and in the Federal Gazette No. 20 of 29 January 1994 ('Wolfenstein 3D'). See the Criminal case of Somm, Felix Bruno, File No. 8340 Ds 465 JS 173158/95, Local Court (Amtsgericht) Munich. An English version of the decision is available at <http://www.cyber-rights.org/isps/somm-dec.htm>.

12 See Macavinta, C., 'CompuServe manager convicted', *Cnet News.Com*, 28 May 1998.

13 See the Criminal case of Somm, Felix Bruno, File No. 8340 Ds 465 JS 173158/95, Local Court (Amtsgericht) Munich. An English version of the decision is available at <http://www.cyber-rights.org/isps/somm-dec.htm>.

14 See Bender, G., 'Bavaria v. Felix Somm: The Pornography Conviction of the Former CompuServe manager', *International Journal of Communications Laws and Policy* (1), Summer 1998, at <http://www.digital-law.net/IJCLP/1_1998/ijclp_webdoc_14_1_1998.html>.

15 Ibid.

The decision was taken despite the efforts of the state prosecutors who agreed with the defence that 'it was technically impossible to filter out all such material'[16] over the Internet. Judge Wilhelm Hubbert disagreed with the assertions and described ISPs as accomplices to crimes carried out over their networks, stating:

> Even on the Internet, there can be no law-free zones … The accused is not a victim. He abused the medium.[17]

Following the *Somm* decision, in an unusual move, the prosecutors in the case filed an appeal against the conviction of Felix Somm in May 1998,[18] and Landgericht München (Regional Court of Munich I, 20th Criminal Division) quashed the *Somm* decision in November 1999, resulting in Somm's acquittal.[19]

Undoubtedly, the availability and distribution of child pornography should be regulated, whether on the Internet or elsewhere. However, prosecuting ISPs would achieve little in the fight against child pornography and will not necessarily contribute to the reduction of the real-life problem of child abuse and sexual exploitation of children. It may conversely have a chilling effect on the development of the Internet.[20]

LIABILITY FOR ACTUAL KNOWLEDGE

Following on from the *CompuServe* prosecution in Germany, it was suggested that ISPs should only be held liable if they had actual knowledge of the illegal content that they carried on their own servers (for example on news servers). A similarity can be found in civil law within section 1 of the Defamation Act 1996 in England and Wales which provides that:

> In defamation proceedings a person has a defence if he shows that –
>
> (a) he was not the author, editor or publisher of the statement complained of,
> (b) he took reasonable care in relation to its publication, and
> (c) he did not know, and had no reason to believe, that what he did caused or contributed to the publication of a defamatory statement.

Section 1 of the 1996 Act directly refers to Internet Service Providers, but there is no such provision provided for criminal liability for ISPs within the English legal system. Although pressured to self-regulate, ISPs have not been prosecuted within the

---

16 See *Associated Press*, Ex-CompuServe Executive Convicted, Berlin, 28 May 1998.

17 See the Criminal case of Somm, Felix Bruno, File No. 8340 Ds 465 JS 173158/95, Local Court (Amtsgericht) Munich. An English version of the decision is available at <http://www.cyber-rights.org/isps/somm-dec.htm>.

18 Reuters, 'Prosecutors appeal Somm's case', *Wired News*, 3 June 1998.

19 'Germany clears Net chief of child porn charges', *Independent*, 18 November 1999; 'CompuServe ex-official's porn-case conviction reversed', *Associated Press*, 17 November 1999.

20 Compare the *CompuServe* Germany case with the US case of *Doe v. America Online, Inc.*, 25 Media L. Rep. (BNA) 2112; 1997 WL 374223 (Fla. Cir. Ct. 26 June 1997); Case No. 97-2587 (Fourth District Court of Appeal, Fla., 14 October 1998).

UK even though they may well be considered liable under section 3 of the Protection of Children Act 1978 if they carry illegal content such as child pornography on their servers.[21] However, *Net Benefit: the electronic commerce agenda for the UK*,[22] a long forgotten policy document launched by the Department of Trade and Industry in October 1998, stated:

> Primary responsibility for illegal material on the Internet would clearly lie with the individual or entity posting it. Under UK law, however, an Internet Service Provider which has been made aware of the illegal material (or activity) and has failed to take reasonable steps to remove the material could also be liable to prosecution as an accessory to a crime.[23]

The statement could be interpreted to mean that 'knowingly' carrying illegal content would bring liability for the UK ISPs even though actual knowledge is not a requirement under the 1978 Act. Furthermore, *Net Benefit* claimed that 'clarification of the liability of ISPs has been addressed by collaboration among UK industry, Government and the police',[24] referring to the establishment of the Internet Watch Foundation (discussed in the next chapter), and the development of an industry code of conduct by the Internet Service Providers Association (ISPA). On this issue *Net Benefit* stated:

> Compliance with this code of practice (essentially the removal of material from their UK servers following IWF notification) would likely be taken in court as evidence of the ISP having made reasonable efforts to comply with the law.[25]

This would mean that despite the existence of a criminal provision within the 1978 Act, a UK-based ISP will avoid prosecution in a court of law if the ISP in question complies with the ISPA code of conduct and is subject to the Internet Watch Foundation hotline notification and notice and takedown procedure. However, reliance on the ISPA code of practice and the IWF scheme does not settle the ISP liability issue, and the current legal situation in England and Wales may be criticized for a lack of clarity and certainty.

Leaving aside uncertainty in terms of the 1978 Act, the UK ISP liability regime ought to be interpreted in the light of European developments, as the European

---

21 Section 3 of the 1978 Act states, 'where a body corporate is guilty of an offence under this Act and it is proved that the offence occurred with the consent or connivance of, or was attributable to any neglect on the part of, any director, manager, … he, as well as the body corporate, shall be deemed to be guilty of that offence and shall be liable to be proceeded against and punished accordingly.' See, for an interpretation, Leong, G., 'Computer Child Pornography: The Liability of Distributors?' (1998), *Crim. L.R.*, Special Edition: Crime, Criminal Justice, and the Internet, December, 19–29.

22 DTI, Net Benefit: the electronic commerce agenda for the UK, DTI/Pub 3619, October 1998. See also Speech by Mrs Barbara Roche MP at the OECD Electronic Commerce Ministerial Meeting, Ottawa: 9 October 1998.

23 Ibid., at p. 20.

24 Ibid.

25 Ibid.

Union had the final word on ISP liability. Although complete immunity from prosecution was desired for European ISPs, the EU Directive on certain legal aspects of electronic commerce in the Internal Market[26] offered limited protection to ISPs with the introduction of an 'actual knowledge' test for removal of third-party content from ISP servers.[27] The practice known as 'notice and takedown'[28] became common practice for the removal of Internet content through ISP servers following the implementation of the EU Directive. Such notices can be given either by hotlines, like the Internet Watch Foundation in England and Wales, for the removal of allegedly illegal content, or by private companies or individuals for the removal of other forms of content including content deemed to be defamatory[29] or that infringed copyright and trademark laws.[30] A more thorough analysis of the Directive is required at this point.

THE EU DIRECTIVE ON ELECTRONIC COMMERCE

The European Union Directive on certain legal aspects of information society services, in particular electronic commerce, in the Internal Market ('Directive on electronic commerce')[31] was finalized during the summer of 2000. The issue of

---

26 European Commission, 'Proposal for a European Parliament and Council Directive on certain legal aspects of electronic commerce in the internal market', COM(1998) 586 final, 98/0325 (COD), Brussels, 18 November 1998; European Commission, Amended proposal for a European Parliament and Council Directive on certain legal aspects of electronic commerce in the Internal Market (presented by the Commission pursuant to Article 250 (2) of the EC-Treaty), COM(1999) 427 final, 98/0325 (COD). Directive 2000/31/EC of the European Parliament and of the Council of 8 June 2000 on certain legal aspects of information society services, in particular electronic commerce, in the Internal Market ('Directive on electronic commerce') v 43, OJ L 178, 17 July 2000, p. 1.

27 See articles 13 and 14 of the Directive.

28 For a critique of notice and takedown provisions in relation to defamation, see Cyber-Rights and Cyber-Liberties (UK) Press Release, 'UK ISP found liable for defamation', 26 March 1999, at <http://www.cyber-rights.org/press>. See also; Uhlig, R., 'Libel setback for Demon', *Daily Telegraph*, 'Connected' Section, 1 April 1999; and Akdeniz, Y., 'The case for free speech', *Guardian* (Online Section), 27 April 2000.

29 This is already possible under section 1 of the Defamation Act, and 'notice and takedown' is common practice for the removal of content alleged to be defamatory. See for example Akdeniz, Y., 'Case Analysis: Laurence Godfrey v. Demon Internet Limited' (1999), *Journal of Civil Liberties*, 4(2), 260–67; 'Cyber-Rights and Cyber-Liberties' (UK), *Hulbert's Case, the Lord Chancellor and Censorship of the Internet*, 11 November 1999; and Akdeniz, Y. and W.R.H. Rogers, 'Defamation on the Internet', in Y. Akdeniz, C. Walker and D. Wall (eds), *The Internet, Law and Society*, Harlow: Addison Wesley Longman, 2000, 294–317.

30 This is the case in the United States with the Digital Millennium Copyright Act 1998.

31 Directive 2000/31/EC of the European Parliament and of the Council of 8 June 2000 on certain legal aspects of information society services, in particular electronic commerce, in the Internal Market, *Official Journal of the European Communities*, v 43, OJ L 178, 17 July 2000, p. 1. Note also Common Position (EC) No. 22/2000 of 28 February 2000 adopted by the Council, acting in accordance with the procedure referred to in Article 251 of the Treaty

ISP liability was taken on board in this Directive due to the fact that 'existing and emerging disparities in Member States' legislation and case-law concerning liability of service providers acting as intermediaries prevent the smooth functioning of the internal market',[32] a reference to the *CompuServe* prosecution in Germany. The Directive suggested, 'it is in the interest of all parties involved in the provision of information society services to adopt and implement procedures',[33] to remove and disable access to illegal information. The Directive provides some limited exemptions from liability,[34] and these are explained in paragraph 42 as covering:

> ... only cases where the activity of the information society service provider is limited to the technical process of operating and giving access to a communication network over which information made available by third parties is transmitted or temporarily stored, for the sole purpose of making the transmission more efficient; this activity is of a mere technical, automatic and passive nature, which implies that the information society service provider has neither knowledge of nor control over the information which is transmitted or stored.[35]

However, this does not affect the possibility of court injunctions of different kinds 'requiring the termination or prevention of any infringement, including the removal of illegal information or the disabling of access to it'.[36] These issues are dealt with in section four of the Directive entitled 'Liability of intermediary service providers'. Article 12 therefore deals with the issue of 'mere conduit' and under article 12(1) 'Member States shall ensure that the service provider is not liable for the information transmitted, on condition that the provider:

> (a) does not initiate the transmission;
> (b) does not select the receiver of the transmission; and
> (c) does not select or modify the information contained in the transmission.

This would cover 'automatic, intermediate and transient storage of the information transmitted' which is not stored for any period longer than is reasonably necessary for the transmission under article 12(2). It is also provided that the provisions of this article shall not affect the possibility for a court or administrative authority, in accordance with Member States' legal systems, of requiring the service provider to terminate or prevent an infringement.[37]

Issues related to the transmission or carrying of information (such as caching) by ISPs to their users is covered under article 13(1), which requires Member States

---

establishing the European Community, with a view to adopting a Directive on electronic commerce, OJ C 128, 8 May 2000 pp. 32–50.

32 Ibid., para. 40.

33 Ibid.

34 See generally, section 4 of the Directive: Liability of intermediary service providers: Articles 12 (Mere Conduit), 13 (Caching), 14 (Hosting), 15 (No General Obligation to Monitor).

35 Ibid.

36 Ibid., para. 45.

37 Article 12(3).

to ensure that the service provider is not liable for the automatic, intermediate and temporary storage of that information, performed for the sole purpose of making more efficient the information's onward transmission to other recipients of the service upon their request, on condition that:

> (a) the provider does not modify the information;
> (b) the provider complies with conditions on access to the information;
> (c) the provider complies with rules regarding the updating of the information, specified in a manner widely recognized and used by industry;
> (d) the provider does not interfere with the lawful use of technology widely recognized and used by industry, to obtain data on the use of the information; and
> (e) the provider acts expeditiously to remove or to disable access to the information it has stored upon obtaining actual knowledge of the fact that the information at the initial source of the transmission has been removed from the network, or access to it has been disabled, or that a court or an administrative authority has ordered such removal or disablement.

Termination or prevention of an infringement is also possible by a court or administrative authority order as in article 12.

As far as hosting issues by ISPs or information society service providers are concerned, article 14(1) requires Member States to

> … ensure that the service provider is not liable for the information stored at the request of a recipient of the service, on condition that:
>
> (a) the provider does not have actual knowledge of illegal activity or information and, as regards claims for damages, is not aware of facts or circumstances from which the illegal activity or information is apparent; or
> (b) the provider, upon obtaining such knowledge or awareness, acts expeditiously to remove or to disable access to the information.

Therefore, there is no absolute protection provided within the Directive for ISPs, who are required to act expeditiously 'upon obtaining actual knowledge' of illegal activity or content 'to remove or to disable access to the information concerned'.[38] Such removal or disabling of access 'has to be undertaken in the observance of the principle of freedom of expression and of procedures established for this purpose at national level',[39] according to the Directive. Termination or prevention of an infringement is also possible by a court or administrative authority order as in articles 12 and 13. Article 14(3) also states that the provisions of article 14 do not 'affect the possibility for Member States of establishing procedures governing the removal or disabling of access to information'. It was decided that notice and take down procedures should not be regulated in the Directive itself.[40] Rather the

38 Ibid., para. 46.

39 Ibid.

40 See Report from the Commission to the European Parliament, the Council and the European Economic and Social Committee – First report on the application of Directive 2000/31/EC on electronic commerce, COM(2003) 702 final, Brussels, 21 November 2003, at <http://europa.eu.int/eur-lex/en/com/rpt/2003/com2003_0702en01.pdf>, section 4.7.

Directive, through Recital 40 and article 16, encourages self-regulatory solutions and procedures to be developed by the Internet industry to implement and bring into action notice and takedown procedures.[41]

In addition to the notice based limited liability exceptions, the Directive prevents member states from imposing a monitoring obligation on service providers only with respect to obligations of a general nature, but 'this does not concern monitoring obligations in a specific case and, in particular, does not affect orders by national authorities in accordance with national legislation.'[42] Under article 15, the Directive specifically requires Member States not to 'impose a general obligation on providers, when providing the services covered by Articles 12, 13 and 14, to monitor the information which they transmit or store, nor a general obligation actively to seek facts or circumstances indicating illegal activity.' However, Member States 'may establish obligations for information society service providers promptly to inform the competent public authorities of alleged illegal activities undertaken or information provided by recipients of their service or obligations to communicate to the competent authorities, at their request.'[43]

While a general monitoring obligation cannot be imposed upon ISPs, this does not stop states issuing 'blocking orders'. During 2002 North Rhine Westphalia, Germany's most populous state, issued a blocking order to prevent German-based ISPs from providing access to websites based outside Germany (mainly in the United States) if those sites host racist and neo-Nazi content.[44] The blocking order affected approximately 76 ISPs within that region.[45] Although there have been legal cases and appeals surrounding the blocking orders, a number of Administrative courts have ruled that German authorities can continue to ask ISPs to block such pages. Prior to the issuing of the blocking order, the Dusseldorf District Authority President, Jurgen Bussow, wrote to four US ISPs in August 2000 requesting that they prevent access to four websites containing racist, neo-Nazi material. As this action was unsuccessful, Bussow issued the blocking order to German ISPs within the North Rhine Westphalia region.[46] Similarly, an attempt in France to block access to

41 Out of those Member States which have transposed the Directive, only Finland has included a legal provision setting out a notice and take down procedure concerning copyright infringements only: This information has been taken from the above-mentioned Commission Report: COM(2003) 702 final.

42 Ibid., para. 47.

43 Article 14(2).

44 'Ban on neo-Nazi web content in German state; upheld', *National Journal's Technology Daily*, 22 December 2004.

45 Between 2002 and 2004 the Dusseldorf District Administration issued 90 ordinances against Internet providers in North Rhine-Westphalia, forcing them to block access to certain websites with rightwing extremist content. See US Bureau of Democracy, Human Rights, and Labor, *Report on Global Anti-Semitism*, January 2005, at <http://www.state.gov/g/drl/rls/40258.htm>. Note also Combating racism, racial discrimination, xenophobia and related intolerance and comprehensive implementation of and follow-up to the Durban Declaration and Programme of Action Note by the UN Secretary-General, A/59/330, 4 October 2004.

46 See generally, Eberwine, E.T., 'Note and Comment: Sound and Fury Signifying Nothing?: Jurgen Bussow's Battle against Hate-speech on the Internet' (2004), 49 *N.Y.L. Sch.*

the Front14.org portal[47] and the racist sites that it hosted for free was unsuccessful in 2001. *J'accuse!*, an association aimed at eradicating racism on the Internet, sued 14 major French ISPs,[48] and although the Court agreed that the racist portal violated the French law, the Court did not require ISPs to block access to the portal.[49] However, in June 2005 a Paris court ordered French ISPs to block the website of the French revisionist organization, Association of Former Connoisseurs of War and Holocaust Stories (AAARGH), to French viewers.[50] Two US-based ISPs have also agreed to stop hosting AAARGH's website. The utility and effectiveness of such a 'blocking regime' remains to be seen, but ISPs may be asked to block access to certain websites and content in the future within EU Member States.

Overall, the Directive provides limited and notice-based liability with takedown procedures for illegal content and requires Member States and the Commission to encourage the development of codes of conduct.[51]

UK Implementation of the Directive on Electronic Commerce

Within the UK, the Department of Trade and Industry conducted a consultation in relation to the implementation of the EU E-Commerce Directive and this was

---

L. Rev 353; and Van Blarcum, C.D., 'Internet Hate Speech: The European Framework and the Emerging American Haven' (2005), 62 *Wash and Lee L. Rev* 781.

47 The Front14.org website had the following disclaimer: 'Only front 14 offers free web hosting and e mail exclusively to racialists. Join today. Many White people don't have the time and energy to put into hosting their own domain, so they join Geocities, Angelfire, etc., in an attempt to get their voices heard. But these "free" services (who bombard you with ads) have adopted an aggressive anti-White policy. We decided to provide an alternative to proud White men and women, one that would be for our White interests only.'

48 In the course of 1996, the four principal network providers in France (Imaginet, Calvacon, Internetway and Internet France) blocked access to 14 discussion forums of French antisemitic and Holocaust-denying propaganda, advertisements for Nazi memorabilia and banned literature. In March 1997 the UEJF took out a court injunction against nine network providers guilty of transmitting Holocaust-denial material. It was the country's first Internet trial. No penalty has been announced, but the network providers have been ordered to revise contracts to ensure that racist and Holocaust-denial propaganda is removed from the sites on which they appear. See Institute for Jewish Policy Research and American Jewish Committee, *Antisemitism World Report 1997*.

49 Référé 30 October 2001 TGI Paris: j'Accuse, et autres/14 fournisseurs d'accès Internet, Ordonnance de référé du Tribunal de grande instance de Paris, 30 October 2001 <http://www.chez.com/aipj/ordonnance30oct2001>. See generally, Frydman, B. and I. Rorive, 'Regulating Internet Content through Intermediaries in Europe and the USA' (2002), *Zeitschrift für Rechtssoziologie* 23(1), S. 41–59, Max Planck Institute, at <http://www.isys.ucl.ac.be/etudes/cours/linf2202/Frydman_&_Rorive_2002.pdf>.

50 US Bureau of Democracy, Human Rights, and Labor, *International Religious Freedom Report 2005*, section on France, 8 November 2005, at <http://www.state.gov/g/drl/rls/irf/2005/51552.htm>.

51 Ibid., para. 49.

concluded in November 2001.[52] Member States had until 16 January 2002 to implement the Directive into national law. The UK was slightly delayed and the Directive was finally implemented in the form of the Electronic Commerce (EC Directive) Regulations 2002 No. 2013. The main body of the regulations came into force on 21 August 2002.

Mere conduit, caching and hosting related provisions of the EU Directive in relation to ISP liability are provided by regulations 17, 18 and 19 of the 2002 UK Regulations.[53] The notice and takedown provisions are incorporated in regulation 19 on hosting as far as third-party content is concerned. A service provider under regulation 19(a) shall not be liable for any criminal sanction as a result of third-party content storage as long as the service provider –

(i) does not have actual knowledge of unlawful activity or information and, where a claim for damages is made, is not aware of facts or circumstances from which it would have been apparent to the service provider that the activity or information was unlawful; or
(ii) upon obtaining such knowledge or awareness, acts expeditiously to remove or to disable access to the information.

Regulation 19 defines the burden of proof issue in relation to the above provisions, and under subsection 2 the service provider will have an evidential burden in relation to the defence in regulation 19(a)(i), and the court or jury 'shall assume that the defence is satisfied unless the prosecution proves beyond reasonable doubt that it is not'.

A definition of 'notice' for the purposes of 'actual knowledge' in terms of regulations 18(b)(v) and 19(a)(i) has been provided by regulation 22. This is a welcome addition as the EU Directive failed to provide any such definition. In determining whether a service provider has actual knowledge, a court shall take into account all matters which appear to it in the particular circumstances to be relevant and, among other things, shall have regard to

(a) whether a service provider has received a notice through a means of contact made available in accordance with regulation 6(1)(c), and
(b) the extent to which any notice includes –
  (i) the full name and address of the sender of the notice;
  (ii) details of the location of the information in question; and
  (iii) details of the unlawful nature of the activity or information in question.

The Regulations do not include any 'statutory notice and takedown procedures' as far as illegal Internet content is concerned. The government continues to support industry self-regulation and industry-wide codes of conduct which 'would be more

52 See The E-Commerce Directive (00/31/EC): UK Government Consultation Paper. See further, questions for consultees 6.1 of the above consultation document. See further, DTI Consultation on Implementation of the Directive on Electronic Commerce (2000/31/Ec): <http://www.dti.govuk/sectors/ictpolicy/ecommsdirective/page10133.html>. Note also the Government's Response to the Public Consultation, 31 July 2002.

53 Note the case of *Bunt v. Tilley and others* [2006] EWHC 407 (QB); [2006] 3 All ER 336 which clarifies these provisions in relation to liability for defamation.

appropriate to the different circumstances that will be relevant in each case than the horizontal provisions that would have to be set out in the Regulations'.[54] With an emphasis on co-regulation, the government has preferred to act as a facilitator and actively encourages the development of such codes of conduct and industry self-regulation as detailed in the following chapter.

The concept of notice-based liability is emerging in relation to other types of content, including terrorism related materials, over the Internet.[55] The British government's proposed criminalization of the encouragement of terrorism and the dissemination of terrorist material through the Internet following the July 2005 terrorist attacks in London is one example.[56] The Terrorism Act 2006, which came into force in March 2006, contains provisions criminalizing the encouragement of terrorism[57] and the dissemination of terrorist publications.[58] The 2006 Act also includes notice and takedown provisions if the encouragement or dissemination takes place over the Internet.[59] Hazel Blears, the Minister of State for the Home Office, explained that the intention behind section 3 is 'to provide a method by which webmasters could be made aware of content on their websites, thus ensuring that they could not claim not to have known about it if they were subsequently prosecuted'.[60]

Article 15 of the EU Directive, including a 'no general obligation to monitor' provision, was not included within the UK Electronic Commerce Regulations 2002. The government was concerned that such an inclusion 'would not only confer no additional legal certainty on intermediaries but could even introduce uncertainty if the prohibition were interpreted differently from its meaning in the Directive. The Regulations do not, therefore, transpose this provision.'[61]

Technically, the UK ISPs could be asked to monitor their systems for illegal activity and content in the future. Overall, ISP liability remains a hotly debated topic

---

54 Government's Response to the Public Consultation, 31 July 2002.

55 See for example Brynjar Lia, 'Al-Qaeda Online: Understanding Jihadist Internet Infrastructure', *Jane's Intelligence Review*, 1 January 2006, at <http://www.mil.no/multimedia/archive/00075/Al-Qaeda_online__und_75416a.pdf>.

56 But note the human rights considerations, especially in relation to freedom of expression: ODIHR, *Background Paper on Human Rights Considerations in Combating Incitement to Terrorism and Related Offences*, 2006, at <http://www.osce.org/documents/odihr/2006/10/21814_en.pdf>.

57 Terrorism Act 2006, c. 11, section 1: 'This section applies to a statement that is likely to be understood by some or all of the members of the public to whom it is published as a direct or indirect encouragement or other inducement to them to the commission, preparation or instigation of acts of terrorism …'.

58 Ibid., section 2(2): dissemination of terrorist publications includes: 'distributing or circulating a terrorist publication; giving, selling, or lending such a publication; offering such a publication for sale or loan; providing a service to others that enables them to obtain, read, listen to or look at such a publication, or to acquire it by means of a gift, sale or loan; transmitting the contents of such a publication electronically.'

59 Ibid., ss. 3, 4.

60 U.K., H.C., *Parliamentary Debates*, vol. 442, col. 1471, 15 February 2006.

61 Government's Response to the Public Consultation, 31 July 2002.

which is often questioned in the UK in relation to not only illegal content but also other types of Internet content deemed violent,[62] harmful, defamatory or offensive.

An assessment of the transposition and application of the Directive on Electronic Commerce was provided by the European Commission in November 2003.[63] According to the Commission report, the preliminary analysis indicated that one or two adopted laws within the EU Member States contain problems related, in particular, to the transposition of the provisions concerning the liability of Internet intermediaries.[64] It appears from the Commission report that the Member States have, in general, transposed articles 12–14 correctly. The Commission report notes that some Member States have decided to provide limitations on the liability of providers of hyperlinks and search engines in addition to ISPs.[65] However, at the time the first report was published, there was little information about how the ISP liability provisions of the E-Commerce Directive were being applied in practice by the Member States.

62 Note the Home Office Paper entitled '*Consultation: On the Possession of Extreme Pornographic Material*' (London: Home Office), August 2005; Home Office, *Consultation on the Possession of Extreme Pornographic Material: Summary of responses and next steps*, August 2006, at <http://www.homeoffice.govuk/documents/cons-extreme-porn-3008051/Gvt-response-extreme-porn.pdf>. Note also the responses received by the Scottish Executive at <http://www.scotland.govuk/Topics/Justice/criminal/17543/ExtremePornograhicMateria/Response> and the analysis of the Scottish Responses to the joint Scottish Executive and Home Office consultation on the possession of extreme pornographic material at <http://www.scotland.govuk/Topics/Justice/criminal/17543/ExtremePornograhicMateria/AnalysisReport>. Note further the Cyber-Rights.Org Response to the initial consultation paper, December 2005, at <http://www.cyber-rights.org/cyber-rights.org_response.pdf>; Petley, J., 'Press furore fuels knee-jerk response to "extreme" pornography' (2006), *Index on Censorship*, October, at <www.indexonline.org/en/news/articles/2006/3/britain-violent-porn-bill-addresses-public-a.shtml>; Rowbottom, J., 'Obscenity Laws and the Internet: Targeting the Supply and Demand' (2006), *Crim. L.R.*, February, 97–109.

63 Report from the Commission to the European Parliament, the Council and the European Economic and Social Committee – First report on the application of Directive 2000/31/EC on electronic commerce), COM(2003) 702 final, Brussels, 21 November 2003, at <http://europa.eu.int/eur-lex/en/com/rpt/2003/com2003_0702en01.pdf>.

64 Ibid., section 3.3.

65 Spain and Portugal have opted for the model of Article 14 both for search engines and hyperlinks, whereas Austria and Liechtenstein have opted for the model of Article 12 for search engines and of Article 14 for hyperlinks. This information has been taken from footnote 69 of the above-mentioned Commission Report: COM(2003) 702 final. The Department for Trade and Industry (DTI) issued a consultation paper *on the Liability of Hyperlinkers, Location Tool and Content Aggregators* in June 2005. The consultation paper considered whether the provisions of the Electronic Commerce (EC Directive) Regulations 2002 should extend to providers of hyperlinks, location tool and content aggregation services or not. See <http://www.dti.govuk/files/file13986.pdf>. Note also the Government Response and the summary of responses, December 2006, at <http://www.dti.govuk/files/file35905.pdf>.

US POLICY ON ISP LIABILITY

In the United States a very different approach to ISP liability has been adopted. While a 'notice' based liability policy appears to be preferred in Europe, ISPs have more protection in the United States for third-party content that travels through their servers regardless of any 'knowledge' on their part.

Section 230(c)(1) of the Communications Decency Act 1996 provides that 'no provider or user of an interactive computer service shall be treated as the publisher or speaker of any information provided by another information content provider.'[66] However, section 230(c)(1) would not immunize US ISPs with respect to any information the ISPs develop or create entirely by themselves; it only applies to 'third-party content' that travels through their servers.

Section 230 became law in February 1996. The US Congress chose to 'promote the continued development of the Internet and other interactive computer services and other interactive media'[67] and 'to preserve the vibrant and competitive free market' for such services, largely 'unfettered by Federal or State regulation'.[68] In recognition of the speed with which information may be disseminated and the near impossibility of regulating information content, the US Congress decided not to treat providers of interactive computer services like other information providers such as newspapers, magazines or television and radio stations, all of which may be held liable for publishing or distributing obscene or defamatory material written or prepared by others.[69]

Section 230 was considered and tested by the Fourth Circuit Court of Appeals in *Zeran v. America Online Inc*,[70] a defamation case which held, 'by its plain language, section 230 created a federal immunity to any cause of action that would make service

66 Section 230 defines 'interactive computer service' as 'any information service, system, or access software provider that provides or enables computer access by multiple users to a computer server, including specifically a service or system that provides access to the Internet and such systems operated or services offered by libraries or educational institutions.' 47 U.S.C. § 230(e)(2). The term 'information content provider' is defined as 'any person or entity that is responsible, in whole or in part, for the creation or development of information provided through the Internet or any other interactive computer service.' Ibid., § 230(e)(3). The statute goes on to define the term 'Information content provider' as 'any person or entity that is responsible, in whole or in part, for the creation or development of information provided through the Internet or any other interactive computer service.' 47 U.S.C. § 230(e)(3). However, for copyright infringement a different policy has been established with the passage of the Digital Millennium Copyright Act (H. R. 2281) 1998.

67 Ibid.

68 47 USC § 230(b)(1) and (2).

69 However, for copyright infringement a notice and actual knowledge-based liability policy has been established with the enactment of the Digital Millennium Copyright Act (H. R. 2281) 1998.

70 129 F 3d 327 (1997). Cert. den. 48 S Ct 2341 (1998). The plaintiff's claim, which arose out of a false bulletin board posting that the plaintiff was selling t-shirts with offensive messages about the Oklahoma City bombing, was framed as one for negligence in failing to remove the posting, but the court stated that the allegations were in substance indistinguishable from a 'garden variety defamation action': 129 F 3d at 332.

providers liable for information originating with a third-party user of the service.'[71] Nor did the fact that the provider had notice of the transmission of wrongful material prevent the operation of this immunity.

Section 230 precludes courts from entertaining claims that would place an Internet service provider in a publisher's role. Thus, lawsuits seeking to hold a service provider liable for its exercise of a publisher's traditional editorial functions – such as deciding whether to publish, withdraw, postpone or alter content, are barred. As Chief Judge Wilkinson wrote for the Fourth Circuit in *Zeran v. America Online*,[72] 'section 230 was enacted, in part, to maintain the robust nature of Internet communication and, accordingly, to keep government interference in the medium to a minimum.'[73]

Doe v. America Online

Within this context, it is important to note the case of *Doe v. America Online*,[74] which considered the issue of transmission of child pornography by US ISPs and whether any liability should arise.

In this case America Online (AOL) faced criminal prosecution following allegations by the mother of an 11-year-old that AOL had created 'a home shopping network for paedophiles'.[75] According to the lawsuit[76] brought by the mother named as Jane Doe, 'AOL was responsible for the content of the material available on its services but had failed to enforce its rules and monitor its subscribers.'[77] One subscriber, a former school teacher, Ron Russell, who was named in the suit, was convicted of an array of sexual charges. Russell allegedly used the service to sell

---

71 Ibid., at 330.

72 *Zeran v. America Online* [1997] 129 F3d 327. Note that Zeran was adopted by other state and federal appeal courts: *Blumenthal v. Drudge* (D.D.C. 1998) 992 F.Supp. 44, 51; *Ben Ezra, Weinstein, and Co. v. AOL, Inc.*, 206 F3d 980, 986 (10th Cir. 2000); *Doe One v. Oliver* (Conn.Super.Ct. 2000) 755 A.2d 1000, 1003–4; *Morrison v. America Online, Inc.* (N.D.Ind. 2001) 153 F.Supp.2d 930, 933–4; *Schneider v. Amazon.com, Inc.* (Wn.App. 2001) 31 P.3d 37, 40–42; *PatentWizard, Inc. v. Kinko's, Inc.* (D.S.D. 2001) 163 F.Supp.2d 1069, 1071; *Green v. AOL*, 318 F3d 465, 471 (3d Cir. 2003); *Batzel v. Smith*, 333 F3d 1018, 1027 n.10 (9th Cir. 2003); *Carafano v. Metrosplash.com, Inc.* (9th Cir. 2003) 339 F3d 1119, 1123–4; *Barrett v. Fonorow* (Ill.App.Ct. 2003) 799 N.E.2d 916, 923–5; *Donato v. Moldow* (N.J. Super.Ct.App. Div 2005) 865 A.2d 711, 720–27; *Austin v. CrystalTech Web Hosting* (Ariz.App. 2005) 125 P.3d 389, 392–4. See further, Dowling, J., 'Noah v. AOL Time Warner: Are There Legitimate Barriers to Civil Rights Protection on the Internet?' (2004), 14 *Alb. L.J. Sci. and Tech.* 775.

73 Ibid.

74 *Doe v. America Online, Inc.*, 25 Media L. Rep. (BNA) 2112; 1997 WL 374223 (Fla. Cir. Ct. 26 June 1997); Case No. 97-2587 (Fourth District Court of Appeal, Fla., 14 October 1998).

75 'AOL faces child porn suit', Reuters, 24 January 1997.

76 See *Jane Doe v. America Online, Inc.*, Case No. CL 97-631 AE; Decision: 1997 WL 374223 (Fla. Cir. Ct. 26 June 1997).

77 Ibid.

images of sexual acts involving himself, Jane Doe's 11-year-old son and two other boys he had befriended in 1994.[78]

Count IV of the complaint claimed that AOL was negligent, contending that AOL breached an alleged duty to exercise reasonable care to ensure that its services should not be used for the 'purposes of the sale and or distribution of child pornography'.[79] In its defence, AOL argued that all Doe's claims were barred by section 230 of the Communications Decency Act (47 U.S.C 230). The Court ruled:

> Making AOL liable for Russell's chat room communications would treat AOL as the 'publisher or speaker' of those communications. Second, it would subject AOL to principles of liability that govern traditional publishers (such as newspapers and magazines) but that do not govern entities (such as telephone companies) that provide a service over which numerous third parties may communicate with one another.[80] Third, it would impose on AOL, as a matter of law, a standard of care that would require AOL to monitor, screen and censor the great volumes of information transmitted over its system by third parties, which are the quintessential activities in which traditional publishers must engage … Moreover, the federal court in *Zeran* rejected[81] the same argument now made by Doe, holding that suits for 'negligent distribution' of harmful third-party material are simply a species of the broader category of suits for 'publishing' such material.[82]

AOL or any other US ISP is therefore not liable for customers who misuse their services to distribute illegal content;[83] the courts having held that 'such publication of obscene literature or computer pornography is analogous to the defamatory publication at issue in the *Zeran* decision.'[84] However, it should be noted that the *Zeran* decision is often criticized.[85] In *Doe v. America Online, Inc.*, Lewis J. dissenting argued that 'the so-called "Decency Act" has, contrary to well-established legal

---

78 Russell is serving a 22-year sentence for attempted sexual battery and a 14-year sentence on child pornography charges following Operation Innocent Images conducted by the FBI in 1995 with the help of AOL.

79 See *Jane Doe v. America Online, Inc.*, Case No. CL 97-631 AE; Decision: 1997 WL 374223 (Fla. Cir. Ct. 26 June 1997). See also 'Judge: America Online not liable for porn peddlers', *Associated Press*, 14 June 1997.

80 See, for example, *Braun v. Soldier of Fortune Magazine, Inc.*, 968 F.2d 1110, 1118–19 (11th Cir. 1992).), cert. denied, 506 U.S. 1071 (1993).

81 See *Zeran*, 958 F.Supp. at 1133.

82 See *Jane Doe v. America Online, Inc.*, above.

83 *Doe v. America Online, Inc.*, 783 So. 2d 1010 (Fla. 2001), in approving the decision of *Doe v. America Online, Inc.*, 718 So. 2d 385, 27 Media L. Rep. (BNA) 1119 (Fla. Dist. Ct. App. 4th Dist. 1998), review granted, 729 So. 2d 390 (Fla. 1999) and decision approved, 2001 WL 228446 (Fla. 2001).

84 Zitter, J.M., 'Annotation: Liability of Internet Service Provider for Internet or E-Mail Defamation' (2000), *84 A.L.R. 5th 169*.

85 Note for example the Seventh Circuit decision in *Doe v. GTE Corp.* 347 F3d. 655 (7th Cir. 2003) which thought *Zeran* was flawed. Note also *Barrett v. Rosenthal*, 112 Cal. App. 4th 1379, 1395 (1st Dist., Div 2 2004) which was subsequently overruled by the California Supreme Court: *Barrett v. Rosenthal*, 40 Cal.4th 33, 146 P.3d 510, 51 Cal.Rptr.3d 55 (Cal. Sup. Ct., 20 November 2006). See further, Myers, D.A., 'Defamation and the Quiescent Anarchy of the Internet: A Case Study of Cyber Targeting' (2006), 110 *Penn St. L. Rev* 667 (Winter).

principles, been transformed from an appropriate shield into a sword of harm and extreme danger which places technology buzz words and economic considerations above the safety and general welfare of our people.'[86] He added:

> it is inconceivable that Congress intended the CDA to shield from potential liability an ISP alleged to have taken absolutely no actions to curtail illicit activities in furtherance of conduct defined as criminal, despite actual knowledge that a source of child pornography was being advertised and delivered through contact information provided on its service by an identified customer, while profiting from its customer's continued use of the service. Such an interpretation transforms a statute intended to further and support responsible ISP efforts to protect children and the public from even questionably harmful and illegal materials into a statute which both condones and exonerates a flagrant and reprehensible failure to act by an ISP in the face of allegedly specific, known dissemination of material unquestionably harmful to children.[87]

Notwithstanding such criticism, section 230 protection was extended to individuals for the republication of defamatory content on the Internet in *Barrett v. Rosenthal*.[88] The California Supreme Court held that section 230 prohibits distributor liability for Internet publications and that section 230(c)(1) immunizes individual users of interactive computer services in addition to the ISPs. At the same time, the California Supreme Court was critical of section 230's broad scope and stated that it had 'some troubling consequences'.[89] *Zeran* remains the authority on ISP liability, but whether or not this is a desirable state of affairs is a matter for debate. The present state of the law in the United States would seem to leave the victim of Internet attack in the position where he or she may be dependent for an effective remedy upon the grace of the ISP.[90]

Despite such protection being granted to ISPs, US regulators have introduced provisions for legal responsibility for the reporting *of child pornography by electronic communication service providers* in 2004 under 42 USC 13032. This provision includes a 'duty to report' when an electronic communication service provider 'obtains knowledge of facts or circumstances from which a violation of section 2251, 2251A, 2252, 2252A, 2252B or 2260 of title 18, United States Code, involving child pornography (as defined in section 2256 of that title), or a violation of section 1466A of that title is apparent'.[91]

The ISP in question is required, as soon as reasonably possible, to 'make a report of such facts or circumstances to the CyberTipLine,[92] a hotline to report cases of child sexual exploitation including child pornography, at the National Center for

86 Dissent by Lewis J in *Doe v. America Online, Inc.*, 783 So. 2d 1010 (Fla. 2001).

87 Ibid.

88 40 Cal.4th 33, 146 P.3d 510, 51 Cal.Rptr.3d 55 (Cal. Sup. Ct., 20 November 2006).

89 Ibid.

90 See generally, Akdeniz, Y. and W.R.H. Rogers, 'Defamation on the Internet', in Y. Akdeniz, C. Walker and D. Wall (eds), *The Internet, Law and Society*, Harlow: Addison Wesley Longman, 2000, 294–317.

91 42 USCS § 13032 (b)(1).

92 See generally, < http://www.cybertipline.com/>.

Missing and Exploited Children'.[93] The CyberTipLine will then forward the report involving a child pornography related incident to a law enforcement agency or agencies designated by the Attorney General. Under the above provisions, an initial failure to report by an ISP could result in a fine of up to $50,000, and any subsequent failures could result in a fine of up to $100,000.[94] In line with the EU E-Commerce Directive provisions, the US law does not require the service providers to actively 'engage in the monitoring of any user, subscriber, or customer of that provider, or the content of any communication of any such person'.[95]

Within this context, it is also worth noting that in Canada, Bill C-15A introduced provisions for courts to order a 'custodian of the computer system', for example, an ISP, to delete material containing child pornography from their servers. Canadian courts need to be satisfied on a balance of probabilities under section 164.1(5) of the Canadian Criminal Code that the material in question contains child pornography as described in section 163.1. Apart from the court-ordered removal of the illegal content, Canadian ISPs could be compelled to provide an electronic copy of the material to the court; and compelled to provide information on the identity and location of the person who posted the material on the system under section 164.1. For these purposes the Canadian courts would have to issue a 'warrant of seizure'. Under this section, the courts are required to give notice to the person who posted the material and provide that person with an opportunity to show cause why the content in question should not be deleted prior to issuing the removal order.

CONCLUSION

ISPs often find themselves within the chain of liability in terms of the provision and transmission of child pornography. While a notice-based liability approach has been adopted in Europe, ISPs are immune from prosecution within the United States even though they may be aware of the availability of such content on their servers. US ISPs are required to report to the relevant authorities if they become aware of the availability of child pornography on their servers, however. As the debate surrounding ISP liability continues ISPs will inevitably find themselves increasingly enmeshed in policy developments targeting the availability of illegal Internet content. Emerging self-regulatory initiatives are the subject of the following chapter.

93 'Under the Electronic Communications Privacy Act, an ISP could not turn information over to law enforcement officials without a warrant. However, this Act requires, without a warrant, ISPs to turn over whatever information they might acquire. (See 18 U.S.C. § 2702(b)(6)(B) amending ECPA to permit disclosure.)' See CyberTelecom: An Open Law Project, 'Reporting Child Pornography', at <http://www.cybertelecom.org/cda/cppa.htm>.

94 See 42 USCS § 13032 (b)(4).

95 See 42 USCS § 13032 (e).

Chapter 9

Self-Regulator
and Co-Regulatory Initia

This chapter provides an overview of self-regulatory initiatives in relation to the fight against Internet child pornography. Industry self-regulation, with the development of industry-wide codes of conduct and hotlines for reporting illegal content such as child pornography, has been seen as an additional tool to aid the objective of combating Internet child pornography and bolster state regulation.[1] Self-regulation[2] in this field can also lead into a co-regulatory framework in which there is a strong partnership between states, international organizations and the Internet industry either directly or through quasi-regulatory industry-based organizations such as the UK's Internet Watch Foundation. This chapter will explore these issues from a UK, North American and European perspective with the main focus on the development of industry-wide codes of conduct to combat illegal Internet content and the development of Internet hotlines to report child pornography.

INDUSTRY SELF-REGULATION

Self-regulation with respect to Internet content and other Internet related activities may have a number of advantages such as flexibility and cost-effectiveness. Self-regulation can address complex areas and may also be 'tailor-made for the needs and problems of that particular sector, and will (at both design and enforcement stages) reflect inside knowledge about the realities of that sector'.[3] Self-regulation can be a sensitive tool to avoid heavy-handed legislation, government control, and heavy burdens and legal liability for the Internet Service Providers (ISPs), given that the Internet is a global and fast changing medium. It may also be said that the Internet industry is more specialized and has more knowledge and experience than policy makers and is therefore adequately equipped to self-regulate. The involvement of ISPs in the self-regulatory process for Internet regulation has potential advantages for the Internet industry itself. ISPs can decide (or at least inform) their own means of regulation and this promises to be more flexible and speedy than government

---

1 See generally, Better Regulation Task Force report, *Alternatives to State Regulation*, July 2000, <http://www.cabinet-office.gov.uk/regulation/TaskForce/2000/StateRegulation.pdf>.

2 See generally, National Consumer Council report, *Models of Self-regulation: an overview of models in business and the professions*, November 2000 (reprinted with amendments from October 1999), and Better Regulation Task Force interim report on *Self-Regulation*, October 1999, at <http://www.ncc.org.uk/pubs/pdf/models_self_regulation.pdf>.

3 Ibid., p. 21.

tion. From an ISP’s perspective, self-regulation is inevitably preferable to le mandatory government regulation which includes ISPs within the chain of lity. Supporting this view Swire writes:

> Industry expertise might not be given its full effect in a government-controlled system. Individual ethics and community norms might be more effective when arising from the community itself than when mandated by government agencies.[4]

Within a self-regulatory system the role of the government is not excluded, though its traditional functions as a law making and enforcing body would be limited.

At the same time self-regulation may have certain disadvantages. For example, self-regulatory practices or schemes may not apply to those ISPs who are not members of an ISP trade organization. This could potentially lead to partial coverage and a lack of universal standards for the ISP sector, and to a distortion of the market with non-members not following the self-regulatory rules and codes of practice. It is also possible that standards in practice may vary amongst participating ISPs. A limited range of sanctions are available for breach of self-regulatory rules through ISP codes of conduct. It is possible that some codes of practice may not have any sanctions compared with the coercive and universal application of government laws and regulation. This could generate scepticism about the commitment of business interests to self-regulation and the enforcement of rules, and therefore public confidence may be lacking. As with government legislation and regulation, if there is no commitment and resources for monitoring and enforcement, effectiveness could be limited.[5]

INDUSTRY CODES OF CONDUCT

Within the context of self-regulation it is important to note the development of industry-wide codes of conduct in relation to tackling illegal Internet content. The UK Internet Service Providers Association (ISPA) has a code of practice which was adopted in January 1999, and amended in April 2002.[6] This code is intended to govern the conduct of ISPA members. The ISPA code includes references to the work of the Internet Watch Foundation (IWF), with whom the ISPA co-operates in its efforts to remove illegal material from websites and newsgroups and through the servers of its member ISPs.[7] ISPA members are required to adhere to the IWF procedure discussed later in this chapter.

---

4 Swire, P.P., ‘Markets, Self-Regulation, and Government Enforcement in the Protection of Personal Information’, <http://www.ntia.doc.gov/reports/privacy/selfreg1.htm> in US Department of Commerce, *Privacy and Self-regulation in the Information Age*, Washington, DC, June 1997, at <http://www.ntia.doc.gov/reports/privacy/privacy_rpt.htm>.

5 See generally, National Consumer Council, *Models of Self-regulation: an overview of models in business and the professions*, November 2000.

6 See <http://www.ispa.org.uk/about_us/page_16.html>.

7 See section 5 of the ISPA Code of Practice at <http://www.ispa.org.uk/html/code_of_practice.htm>.

The development of ISP codes of conduct are notably encouraged at the European Union level. A recommendation on the protection of minors and human dignity in audiovisual and information services was adopted by the Council in May 1998 (formal adoption in September 1998)[8] following a proposal through the European Commission.[9] This Recommendation aimed to provide guidelines for national legislation and urged European ISPs to develop codes of good conduct so as to better apply existing legislation. The recommendation also offered guidelines for the development of national self-regulatory policies regarding the protection of minors and human dignity.[10] According to the EU recommendation, self-regulation should be based on three key elements:

- firstly, the involvement of all the interested parties (Government, industry, service and access providers, user associations) in the production of codes of conduct;
- secondly, the implementation of codes of conduct by the industry;
- thirdly, the evaluation of measures taken.[11]

Different codes of conduct presently exist within different European states.[12] The above-mentioned recommendation of the European Commission suggests that there may be a need for greater harmonization of these codes at a European level. Europe's leading ISPs announced their intention to promote industry codes of conduct in July 1998. The declared aim was to create a pan-European code of conduct and principles on issues such as how to keep illegal material off the Internet and protect children from harmful online content.[13] According to David Phillips, the former Vice-President and legal counsel of AOL in Europe, there was a window of

8 Council Recommendation of 24 September 1998 on the development of the competitiveness of the European audiovisual and information services industry by promoting national frameworks aimed at achieving a comparable and effective level of protection of minors and human dignity as published in the OJ L 270 of 7 October 1998, p. 48 (98/560/EC). See also the Opinion of the Economic and Social Committee on the Proposal for a Council Recommendation concerning the protection of minors and human dignity in audiovisual and information services (98/C 214/07), 10 July 1998, EN C 214/25 *Official Journal of the European Communities*, C 214/25.

9 Commission Communication to the European Parliament, the Council and the Economic and Social Committee on the follow-up to the Green paper on the protection of minors and human dignity in audiovisual and information services including a Proposal for a Recommendation, COM (97) 570 final.

10 See the Annex to the above recommendation of 24 September 1998: Indicative Guidelines for the Implementation, at National Level, of a Self-Regulation Framework for the Protection of Minors and Human Dignity in on-line Audiovisual and Information Services.

11 The Recommendation is closely linked to the EU Action Plan of promoting Safer Use of the Internet: EU Decision No. 276/1999/EC of the European Parliament and of the Council of 25 January 1999 adopting a Multiannual Community Action Plan on promoting safer use of the Internet by combating illegal and harmful content on global networks, OJ L 33, 6 February 1999.

12 For example, there are ISP codes of conduct in Belgium, France, Germany, Italy, Netherlands and Austria apart from the UK. See <http://www.euroispa.org/coc.html>.

13 See Reuters, 'European ISPs plan code of conduct', Vienna, 14 July 1998.

opportunity to 'implement meaningful self-regulatory measures and prevent more burdensome and ill-fitted government and regulatory initiatives'.[14] However, this initiative has not been followed by European ISPs to date, and the European Internet Service Providers Association (EuroISPA), does not have its own Europe-wide code of conduct at present.[15]

The potential harmonization of codes of conduct is problematic for a number of reasons. For example, with respect to illegal content, a European Commission Communication Paper notes, 'each country may reach its own conclusion in defining the borderline between what is permissible and not permissible.'[16] This 'margin of appreciation' is of course very much in line with the approach fostered by the Council of Europe's European Court of Human Rights.[17] While ISPs may take all conceivable action against material which has been declared 'illegal' in a given state, it is not necessarily the case that the same activity will be regarded as illegal in a neighbouring European territory. In the context of child pornography, there have been some minimal EU-wide standards on child pornography offences under the EU Council Framework Decision on combating the sexual exploitation of children and child pornography (discussed in Chapter 5). This suggests that codes of conduct should not differ all that much from one another. The Council of Europe's Cybercrime Convention 2001 (discussed in Chapter 6) also aims to harmonize child pornography laws in its member states and these efforts could aid the future development of ISP codes of conduct. The task of developing a specific ISP code of conduct on combating Internet child pornography may be more feasible than trying to develop a much broader code of conduct on combating 'illegal and harmful Internet content'. With a narrow focus it is more likely that agreement could be reached at a European level.

CO-REGULATION

> Self-regulation and legal regulation are not black-and-white opposites. It is widely accepted that the right balance has to be found between the two. Self-regulation, at its best, can be seen as a co-operation between the regulator, regulated and those in whose interests regulation is made. But for self-regulation to work effectively, there may be a need for a concept of co-regulation which is underpinned by legal regulation.[18]

---

14 Ibid.

15 See <http://www.euroispa.org/32.htm>. EuroISPA has nine ISP associations as its members.

16 See European Commission Communication to the European Parliament, The Council, The Economic and Social Committee and the Committee of the Regions: Illegal and Harmful Content on the Internet, Com (96) 487, Brussels, 16 October 1996.

17 See *Handyside v. UK*, App. no. 5493/72, Ser A vol. 24 (1976). The European Court of Human Rights in *Handyside* stated that the steps necessary in a democratic society for the protection of morals will depend on the type of morality to which a country is committed – there was no single universal standard but states had a margin of appreciation to set their own standards.

18 National Consumer Council, Models of self-regulation: an overview of models in business and the professions, November 2000, p. 48.

The UK government White Paper, *A New Future for Communications*, described co-regulation as indicating 'situations in which the regulator would be actively involved in securing that an acceptable and effective solution is achieved'.[19] According to the White Paper, the regulator may, for example, 'set objectives which are to be achieved, or provide support for sanctions available, while still leaving space for self-regulatory initiatives by industry, taking due account of the interests and views of other stakeholders, to meet the objectives in the most efficient way'.[20]

Co-regulation could act as a 'bridge to self-regulation'[21] within the Internet industry. With a co-regulatory approach the government would take the leading role in shaping policy initiatives according to its objectives. Given that these may be expected to change over time, co-regulatory and self-regulatory solutions have the benefit of flexibility. If the objectives cannot be achieved through self or co-regulation, states can still opt to legislate. In these circumstances the ISP industry would be forced to adapt to the new policy and requirements of the government, as was witnessed following the enactment of the Regulation of Investigatory Powers Act 2000,[22] and Part XI of the Anti-terrorism, Crime and Security Act 2001[23] in the UK in terms of new surveillance measures and requirements.

The relationship between the UK government and the formation of the Internet Watch Foundation provides an example of a co-regulatory approach and is explored below.

THE INTERNET WATCH EXPERIENCE IN THE UK

Concerns over the availability of child pornography over the Internet and pressure to regulate on ISPs can be traced in the UK to 1996.[24] The initial warning to ISPs providing services within the UK came from the former Science and Technology Minister, Ian Taylor, in August 1996 following the Metropolitan Police attempt to ban approximately 130 Usenet discussion groups carried by UK ISPs.[25] At that

19 White Paper, *A New Future for Communications*, December 2000, Cm 5010, at <http://www.communicationswhitepaper.gov.uk/>, p. 83. See further, Culture, Media and Sport Committee (HC), *Second Report on the Communications White Paper*, Volume I HC 161-I, 15 March 2001.

20 Ibid.

21 OFTEL consultation document, *Encouraging self and co-regulation in telecoms to benefit consumers*, June 2000.

22 See generally, Akdeniz, Y., N. Taylor and C. Walker, 'Regulation of Investigatory Powers Act 2000 (1): Bigbrother.gov.uk: State Surveillance in the Age of Information and Rights' (2001), *Crim. L.R.*, February, 73–90.

23 See generally, Walker, C. and Y. Akdeniz, 'Anti-Terrorism Laws and Data Retention: War is Over?' (2003), *Northern Ireland Legal Quarterly*, 54(2), Summer, 159–82.

24 'Police get tough on Internet's hard-core porn', *Independent*, 16 August 1996; 'Yard move to close Internet porn lines', *Evening Standard*, 15 August 1996.

25 A copy of the Metropolitan Police letter is at <http://www.cyber-rights.org/documents/themet.htm>. See Uhlig, R., 'Minister's warning over Internet porn', *Daily Telegraph*, 18 August 1996, and 'The list and the hysteria; When the police moved to ban pornography on the Net, it set off a storm in the press and in the industry itself', *Independent*, 2 September 1996.

time both Taylor and the Metropolitan Police made it clear that the police would act against ISPs who provided users with pornographic and violent material. The main concern was the availability of child pornography on Usenet discussion groups.[26]

Historically, this was the first time the responsibility of ISPs for carrying illegal content was questioned within the UK, and it was prompted by the actions of Bavarian police against CompuServe for carrying child pornography and racist content in 1995 (discussed in the Chapter 8).[27] Following this warning by the Metropolitan Police, self-regulation of the Internet industry rather than government regulation was considered the best way forward. The former Science and Technology Minister stated:

> In the absence of self-regulation, the police will inevitably act against service providers as well as the originators of illegal materials …[28] UK ISP must devise a Code of Practice[29] to control access to illegal and unsuitable material or face increasing political pressure for curbing legislation.[30]

Taylor added that the UK Government was keen to see the Internet fully exploited for business, education and leisure, but warned that this would not happen if people were afraid of what they might find online. A self-regulatory system also suited the commercial interests of Internet Service Providers who wanted security and certainty.

These discussions led to the establishment of the Internet Watch Foundation in September 1996 (initially known as the Safety-Net)[31] and the publication by the Internet industry of *Rating, Reporting, Responsibility, for Child Pornography and Illegal Material on the Internet*.[32] The Home Office, the Department for Trade and Industry (DTI), the Metropolitan Police and ISPs all played a crucial role in the establishment of the Internet Watch Foundation. This co-operation between government and industry was the first step towards the establishment of a co-regulatory framework to fight illegal content in which the industry would develop the

---

See also the DTI Press Release P/96/636, 'Ian Taylor challenges Internet Service Providers: develop new software to come clean', 14 August 1996.

26 But it was noted that some of these groups identified by the Metropolitan Police did not carry or provide any images at all. See generally, Akdeniz, Y., 'The Regulation of Pornography and Child Pornography on the Internet' (1997), *The Journal of Information, Law and Technology* (1) at <http://elj.warwick.ac.uk/jilt/internet/97_1akdz/default.htm>.

27 Uhlig, R., 'Internet firms in talks to close porn access', *Daily Telegraph*, 1 January 1996, Langton, J., 'German court tries to block Internet porn', *Sunday Telegraph*, 20 April 1997, Uhlig, R., 'Internet provider is convicted in test case on pornography', *Daily Telegraph*, 29 May 1998.

28 Per Ian Taylor (see above).

29 See Internet Services Providers Association of the UK (ISPA-UK) web page at <www.ispa.org.uk> for a copy of its Code of Practice.

30 See Uhlig, R., 'Minister calls for Internet controls', *Daily Telegraph*, 22 March 1996.

31 See <http://www.internetwatch.org.uk>.

32 See DTI, 'Rating, Reporting, Responsibility, For Child Pornography and Illegal Material on the Internet', September 1996, at <http://www.mit.edu/activities/safe/labeling/r3.htm>.

self-regulatory mechanisms for reporting such content. Within this newly established system the government, industry and law enforcement agencies all pledged to work together. Welcoming the Industry's proposals, Ian Taylor stated:

> This is a ground-breaking proposal and an opportunity for the UK to take a world lead. It is a major industry-led initiative to clean up the net, to reassure the public and business that the Internet can be a safe and secure place to work, learn and play.[33]

The Safety-Net proposal required UK ISPs to implement reasonable, practicable and proportionate measures to hinder the use of the Internet for illegal purposes, and to provide a response mechanism in cases where illegal material or activity is identified.[34] This led to the formation of the IWF Hotline.

Hotlines for Reporting Illegal Activity

Several ISPs and/or their trade associations, especially in the Western world, have developed hotlines to report illegal Internet content. Most of the current Internet hotlines are run privately by industry-based organizations and in many countries they are funded by ISPs. In many cases they constitute centres of expertise providing guidance to ISPs as to what content might be illegal.

Internet hotlines usually allow members of the public to report illegal Internet content that often takes the form of child pornography but may include other forms of illegality including racist material. In most cases the hotline will assess the report and if the reported content is deemed illegal by the hotline operator, it is reported to the appropriate bodies, including the police, ISPs, and to a corresponding hotline (if one exists) when the content is hosted in a different jurisdiction. Upon receipt of the notice ISPs will generally remove the reported illegal content from their servers.

IWF Hotline

IWF launched its hotline for reporting illegal material on the Internet in December 1996, and the foundation received charitable status in 2005. It is fully funded and supported by UK Internet Service Providers who oversee its operation. The IWF has an email, telephone and fax hotline for users to report Internet content involving child pornography and other illegal content such as criminally obscene content, incitement to racial hatred content as well as content involving inappropriate chat or behaviour with or towards a child online.[35] The IWF undertook to inform all British ISPs once they had located allegedly illegal content such as child pornography. The ISPs concerned then have no excuse in law that they are unaware of the allegedly

33 See the DTI Press Release, 'Internet Safety-Net to Tackle Child Porn', 23 September 1996.

34 See Safety-Net proposal, 'Rating, Reporting, Responsibility, for Child Pornography and Illegal Material on the Internet' adopted and recommended by the Executive Committee of ISPA – Internet Services Providers Association, LINX – London Internet Exchange and The Safety-Net Foundation at <http://www.mit.edu/activities/safe/labeling/r3.htm>.

35 See <http://www.internetwatch.org.uk/hotline/>.

illegal content, and the UK police would[36] be entitled to take action against any ISP which does not remove the relevant content.[37] In addition, the Internet Service Providers Association (ISPA) member ISPs provide a 24-hour point of contact to the IWF, allowing all ISPA members to be on constant alert for notices of illegal material which they then, in most cases, immediately remove from their servers. The IWF will then report the material to the relevant police forces for further investigation and possible prosecution if the originator of the content is based in the UK. If the content in question is made available by a person outside the UK, the IWF will contact other hotlines (if one exists) as well as police forces in the country of origin.

To date the activities of the IWF have mainly concentrated on the availability of child pornography through Usenet discussion groups and to some extent through websites, even though illegal content is available and distributed through a variety of sources and systems, including through peer-to-peer (P2P) networks.[38]

An examination of the IWF annual statistics reveal that a considerable number of reports were made to the hotline by members of the public between 1997 and 2006. For obvious reasons reporting was low during the first few years of the hotline's activities, but the number of reports exceeded 10,000 in 2001, 20,000 in 2005 and 30,000 in 2006 (see Graph 9.1).

Out of a total of 138,603 reports made by the end of 2006, the IWF took action in relation to 34,630 (approximately 25 per cent). The majority of these reports involved child pornography found in newsgroups. However, in 2004 a considerable proportion of the actioned reports (3,195) involved websites rather than newsgroups (approximately 58). The 6,128 actioned reports in 2005 involved 21,017 child abuse images.

More interestingly, it was revealed in the 1999 annual report that only 4 per cent of items on which the IWF took an action originated in the UK.[39] The UK contribution remained significantly low in 2004 (1 per cent), while the United States led with 40 per cent, and Russia followed close behind with 31 per cent.[40] In 2005 only 0.4 per cent of potentially illegal child abuse content was hosted in the UK, while 40 per cent was traced to the United States; 28 per cent was traced to Russia; 17 per cent to Asian countries including Thailand, China, Japan and South Korea,

---

36 Reports of material considered illegal by the IWF are also passed on to the law enforcement body in the country where the material originated, via the National Criminal Intelligence Service.

37 See Safety-Net proposal, 'Rating, Reporting, Responsibility, for Child Pornography and Illegal Material on the Internet' adopted and recommended by the Executive Committee of ISPA – Internet Services Providers Association, LINX – London Internet Exchange (1996).

38 United States General Accounting Office, *File Sharing Programs: Users of Peer-to-Peer Networks can readily access child pornography*, Statement of Linda D. Koontz, Director, Information Management Issues, Testimony Before the Subcommittee on Commerce, Trade, and Consumer Protection, Committee on Energy and Commerce, House of Representatives, GAO-04-757T, May 2004.

39 For example, in 2004, out of about 17,000 reports, 82 per cent involved (14,185) child pornography.

40 See IWF, Annual Report 2004 (January 2005), at <http://www.iwf.org.uk/documents/20050204_annual_report_2004.pdf>.

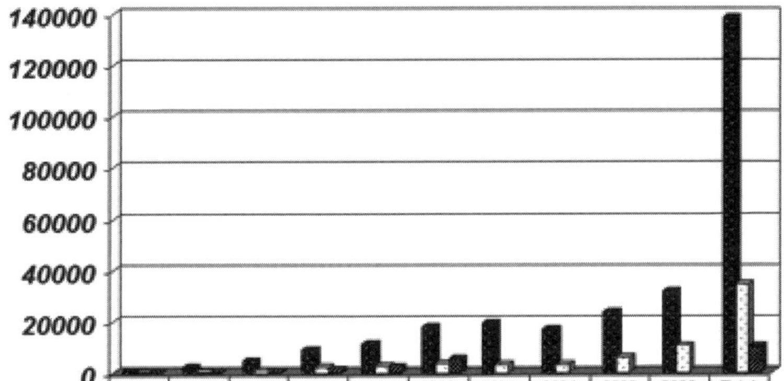

	1997	1998	1999	2000	2001	2002	2003	2004	2005	2006	Total
■ Reports	898	2407	4869	8942	11357	17868	19553	17255	23658	31776	138603
□ Action Taken	249	447	1196	2376	2930	3783	3427	3438	6126	10656	34630
■ Previously Actioned	63	124	504	1406	2377	5819					10293

Graph 9.1 Internet Watch Foundation statistics (1997–2006)

and 13 per cent to Europe.[41] 47 per cent of potentially illegal child abuse websites were deemed commercial pay-per-view websites, and 70 per cent of all commercial pay-per-view websites appeared to be hosted in either Russia or the United States. The 2006 annual report[42] indicates that less than 1 per cent of potentially illegal child abuse content continues to be hosted in the UK, while 82.5 per cent of all domains apparently featuring child abuse content were hosted in the United States, up from 40 per cent the previous year. The United States continues to head the league table for commercial pay-per-view websites with 62.8 per cent of the reported sites originating there, up from 36.4 per cent the previous year. The United States is followed by Russia with 28 per cent.

Though useful at one level, the IWF statistics reveal little about the actual amount of child pornography on the Internet.[43] Limited visible distribution within the UK for example, does not necessarily mean that illegal content such as child pornography has not been obtained (downloaded) within the UK jurisdiction. It is therefore

41 See generally, the IWF Annual Report 2005, at <http://www.iwf.org.uk/documents/20060306_iwf_annual_report_2005_-_high_res.pdf>.

42 See generally, the IWF Annual Report 2006 at <http://www.iwf.org.uk/documents/20070412_iwf_annual_report_2006_(web).pdf>.

43 COPINE project dealt with the availability of child pornography through the newsgroups. See the Proceedings of the First Copine Conference, 20–21 January 1998, Dublin, Ireland; and Proceedings of the Second Copine Conference, 1–2 April 1999, Brussels. Please note that these reports are not online. See further, a summary of the Cork Study in the Irish Department of Justice, Equality and Law Reform, *Illegal and Harmful Use of the Internet* (Pn.5231, Dublin, 1998) pp. 33–5.

difficult to judge how successful the UK hotline and the Internet Watch experience have been so far, despite its own and the UK government's claims to success.[44] It is true that the hotline has managed to raise awareness of the grave problem of Internet child pornography, and a considerable number of illegal items have been removed from the servers of UK ISPs. However, it is not known how many new images are posted to various newsgroups (replacing those removed images) and websites (replacing those blocked or removed websites) or circulated by any other means (such as through P2P networks), nor is it known how much child pornography is available on the world wide web or elsewhere on the Internet.

It should also be noted that the efforts of the IWF have concentrated on newsgroups carried by UK ISPs. Illegal material has been removed from UK ISP newsgroup servers as a result but the same material continues to be available on the Internet carried by foreign ISPs in their own newsgroup servers (as well as through commercial newsfeed providers) accessible to UK residents from computers and servers located abroad.[45]

Banning Newsgroups

Almost five years into its operation the IWF broadened its scope and decided to take action against certain newsgroups frequently containing child pornography. The IWF identified 28 such newsgroups in July 2000.[46] Initial research conducted by the IWF in August 1999 indicated that some 77 per cent of the illegal material reported to the organization had been found in just three newsgroups. A proposal to block these and other newsgroups was made in a discussion paper in late 2000.[47] Ironically, the IWF's suggestion that 'all UK ISPs should cease hosting those groups known to account for the most frequent instances of child pornography'[48] echoes the August

44 See House of Commons Hansard Written Answers for 2 February 2000 (pt 7); House of Commons Hansard Written Answers for 7 November 2000 (pt 4); Lords Hansard text for 27 October 2000 (201027-01) (E-Commerce in the EU: EUC Report); House of Commons Hansard Written Answers for 28 February 2000 (pt 32); (Internet Watch Foundation), House of Commons Hansard Written Answers for 11 May 2006; Child Abuse (Internet), House of Commons Hansard Debates for 30 April 2007.

45 Usenet discussion groups are different from World Wide Web pages and they are copied and carried by all Internet servers all around the world. A message sent to, for example, uk.legal will appear in any server carrying the uk.legal newsgroup. A message deleted from uk.legal in Britain does not necessarily mean that the same message is also deleted in, for example, Australia.

46 IWF Discussion Paper on Newsgroups, November 2000.

47 See generally, Cyber-Rights and Cyber-Liberties (UK) response to the Internet Watch Foundation on its discussion paper on the availability of child pornography through the Usenet discussion groups (newsgroups), 30 January 2001, at <http://www.cyber-rights.org/reports/crcl_iwf_newsgroups.htm>.

48 IWF Discussion Paper on Newsgroups, November 2000.

1996 Metropolitan Police request to ban 130 Usenet discussion groups allegedly carrying child pornography, which led to the formation of the IWF.[49]

Despite strong criticism from civil liberties organizations,[50] the IWF signalled a change in policy in November 2001 by urging 'all ISPs serving UK customers not to host newsgroups which the IWF identifies as regularly containing child pornography, the criteria for "regular" being determined by the IWF Board.'[51] In 2002 the IWF Board agreed that the criteria for 'regular' to be 'finding an average of at least 1 per cent of images viewed as illegal' during the close monitoring period of a specific newsgroup.[52] The Board also agreed that a further test would be used in the 'close monitoring' phase 'whereby in each of six consecutive monitoring rounds finding any illegal content would lead to immediate listing of the group, and six "clear" rounds would remove the group from monitoring.'[53]

The IWF argued that a newsgroup name could, in certain circumstances, be an illegal advertisement under the Protection of Children Act 1978, and an ISP which knowingly carries such a group with such a name would be committing an offence under section 1(1)(d) of the Act. Although highly likely, it does not always follow that a specific newsgroup with an allegedly illegal name would also contain illegal content. While the original list contained 28 newsgroups to be banned, following the expansion of this policy in July 2002 a list of around 162 newsgroups was compiled and UK ISPs were advised not to carry them. According to the IWF 2005 Annual Report, 211 newsgroups are currently listed as potentially illegal in the UK.[54]

Whilst it may be tempting to identify and block particular newsgroups, websites or other Internet forums that appear to be devoted to illegal material, such measures arguably set dangerous precedents. These are in effect acts of privatized censorship which could change the role and relationship of Internet service providers to their customers if applied too broadly.[55]

---

49 See the letter from the Metropolitan Police to the UK ISPs, August 1996, at <http://www.cyber-rights.org/documents/themet.htm>.

50 See, for example, Cyber-Rights and Cyber Liberties (UK) response to the Internet Watch Foundation on its discussion paper on the availability of child pornography through the Usenet discussion groups (newsgroups), 30 January 2001.

51 See the IWF Definition of 'Regular' (In the context of newsgroups receiving potentially illegal articles) document, February 2002. See further, <http://www.iwf.org.uk/corporate/page.49.231.htm>.

52 See <http://www.iwf.org.uk/corporate/page.49.231.htm>.

53 Ibid.

54 According to the 2005 report, 226 notices were issued to Internet service providers to take-down a further 12,777 images that were published in newsgroups not included in the 211 listed.

55 Akdeniz, Y., 'The case for free speech', *Guardian* (Online Section), 27 April 2000; Akdeniz, Y., 'Policing the Internet: Regulation and Censorship', in Gibson, R. and S. Ward (eds), *Reinvigorating Democracy? British Politics and the Internet*, Aldershot: Ashgate, 2000, 169–88; Akdeniz, Y., 'Case Analysis: Laurence Godfrey v. Demon Internet Limited' (1999), *Journal of Civil Liberties*, 4(2), July, 260–67.

Blocking Access to Websites

Until recently, content involving child pornography on the Internet has been predominantly available through newsgroups. However, in the last few years the work of the IWF suggests that websites (including commercial pay-per-view websites) rather than newsgroups are becoming the main source of dissemination of child pornography on the Internet. The above-mentioned annual reports of the IWF revealed that these websites are predominantly located outside the UK jurisdiction, and are traceable mainly to the United States, Russia and various Eastern European and Asian countries.[56] As discussed in the previous chapter, in some countries' courts and/or other legal authorities issue 'blocking orders' to ISPs to prevent access to websites carrying illegal content based outside their jurisdictions.

In the UK, British Telecom (BT), in partnership with the IWF, developed the CleanFeed Project[57] in late 2003. This follows the decision of the IWF to assist its subscribing members in filtering potentially illegal content from their client services through the use of the Child Abuse Images URL (CAI URL) service.[58] The CleanFeed Project is aimed towards blocking access to any images or websites that contain child pornography within the IWF database. Customers of BT are prevented from accessing the blocked content and websites. In July 2004 BT claimed that within the first three weeks of its launch the CleanFeed system had blocked 230,000 attempts to access child abuse websites. According to the Register, 'the announcement caused a flurry of media attention raising fears that thousands of people in the UK are trying to access illegal child abuse websites.'[59] In response, the ISPA stated that while it welcomed 'any developments in the fight against child abuse images appearing on the Internet, it is concerned that the statistics could be misleading'.[60] The ISPA specifically questioned the nature of the material CleanFeed was detecting.

---

56 See generally, the IWF Annual Report 2005, at <http://www.iwf.org.uk/documents/20060306_iwf_annual_report_2005_-_high_res.pdf>, and the IWF Annual Report 2006, at <http://www.iwf.org.uk/documents/20070412_iwf_annual_report_2006_(web).pdf>.

57 IWF/BT Project CleanFeed, at <http://www.iwf.org.uk/media/news.archive-2004.39.htm>.

58 See generally, Child Abuse Images URL database at <http://www.iwf.org.uk/public/page.148.htm>. See further, the IWF discussion paper, *Commercialising the CAI URL Database*, June 2004, at <http://www.iwf.org.uk/corporate/page.94.176.htm>, and Addendum to the discussion paper at <http://www.iwf.org.uk/corporate/page.94.177.htm>. Note further Recommendations from the Board and FC Working Group on Commercialising the CAI Database, February 2005, at <http://www.iwf.org.uk/corporate/page.128.277.htm>, as well as the revised recommendations of May 2005, at <http://www.iwf.org.uk/corporate/page.141.304.htm>.

59 Richardson, T., 'ISPA seeks analysis of BT's "Cleanfeed" stats', *Register*, 21 July 2004, at <http://www.theregister.co.uk/2004/07/21/ispa_bt_cleanfeed/>. See further, Richardson, T., 'BT blocks 230k attempts to access child porn', *Register*, 20 July 2004, at <http://www.theregister.co.uk/2004/07/20/bt_internet_block/>.

60 See ibid. for the ISPA statement in full.

> As with any technical solution, care must be taken to ensure blocking web sites offering illegal images does not cause unacceptable levels of collateral damage. Any such technical measures must be evaluated by ISPs over time to judge their success. The CleanFeed solution by BT will only prevent 'casual' browsing of known web sites. It will not hinder organized distribution of such images. It will not prevent access to new web sites offering illegal content, nor will it prevent children being abused. The very presence of images of child abuse on the Internet is a problem. Preventing access is not a solution to the presence of these websites.

BT responded by stating:

> BT has always said the technology is not a total solution to this challenging problem, but it is a start. BT agrees with ISPA that the IWF has made great progress with tackling the hosting of such sites in the UK and BT sees this technology as a step forward. It is different in that it tackles the problem from another angle by preventing people from deliberately or accidentally accessing sites including those located overseas. The fight against child abuse is a global one and so it is important that everyone works as closely as they can with the relevant law enforcement agencies and bodies such as the IWF. As a result, we have said we are willing to share the technology with other service providers on a non commercial basis and so we look forward to discussions with them.[61]

Research by Clayton[62] showed that BT's CleanFeed system can also be used to discover the contents of the secret blacklist that it uses to find out which sites are blocked.[63] BT subsequently agreed that it is possible to manipulate the system in this way but maintained that 'Clayton ha[d] overestimated the effectiveness of his back-door approach.'[64] The IWF also concluded that the benefits of CleanFeed outweigh its weaknesses:

> Individuals who would want to use this system as an 'oracle' to locate illegal child abuse websites and who also have the specialist knowledge to do so, are vastly outnumbered by Internet consumers who benefit from protection of exposure to this content online.[65]

In 2006 BT claimed that its CleanFeed system was blocking 35,000 attempts to access websites known to carry child pornography every day.[66] Currently, the government is trying to ensure that all British ISPs offering broadband Internet connectivity to the UK public use the CleanFeed system to restrict access to the sites identified by the IWF by the end of 2007.[67] At present the use of such a blocking system by British

---

61 ISP Review, 'BT Responds with Cleanfeed Clarity', 22 July 2004, at <http://www.ispreview.co.uk/cgi-bin/news/viewnews.cgi?id=EpApuAlVFkFFXOlkSX>.

62 Clayton, R., 'Failures in a Hybrid Content Blocking System', research paper presented at the Workshop on Privacy Enhancing Technologies, Dubrovnik, Croatia, 30 May 2005 – 1 June 2005, at <http://www.cl.cam.ac.uk/~rnc1/cleanfeed.pdf>.

63 See further, Mathieson, S.A., 'Back door to the black list', *Guardian*, 26 May 2005.

64 Ibid.

65 Ibid.

66 'Porn blocks', *Evening Chronicle*, 7 February 2006.

67 Child Abuse (Internet), House of Commons Hansard Debates for 30 April 2007. Note further Child Pornography, House of Commons Hansard Written Answers for 7 November

ISPs is voluntary and there is no legal requirement to implement such a system, but it is estimated that the 'biggest UK ISPs who between them provide over 90 per cent of domestic broadband connections are either currently blocking or had plans to implement blocking systems by the end of 2006.'[68] The government has hinted that it will review 'the options for stopping UK residents accessing websites on the IWF list'[69] if ISPs elect not to use blocking systems. With government pressure many ISPs may follow BT's approach, but others are concerned about the costs of implementing such a system (which government admits is a genuine issue),[70] as well as its possible benefits.[71] Many support the view that the small amount of child abuse content available through websites does not warrant a huge investment for blocking and that more often such content is distributed by other means, including through private forums, ftp servers and peer-to-peer networks.[72] In a similar vein, it is claimed that blocking systems have their limitations as circumvention is possible. The ISPA recently stated that it supported the government's action against child abuse sites, but cautioned it would 'only curtail casual browsing and will not hinder organized distribution of such images'.[73]

US CYBERTIPLINE EXPERIENCE

The UK co-regulatory framework can be usefully contrasted with the current situation in the United States, where ISPs have a legal responsibility to report when they encounter child pornography on their servers under the US Code, section 42 USC 13032 (2004) (mentioned in previous chapter). Unlike the UK, there is no 'banning policy' as far as newsgroups are concerned. It is a requirement under US law that the service provider in question 'make a report of such facts or circumstances to the CyberTipLine[74] at the National Center for Missing and Exploited Children'[75] as soon as reasonably possible. CyberTipLine will then forward the report to a law enforcement agency or agencies designated by the Attorney General, including to the

---

2006; Internet Service Providers, House of Commons Hansard Written Answers for 25 October 2006.

68 Child Abuse (Internet), House of Commons Hansard Written Answers for 15 May 2006.

69 Ibid.

70 Internet Service Providers, House of Commons, Hansard Written Answers for 25 October 2006.

71 'Surfing with a safety net: The government is leaning on ISPs to install web filters for home broadband, at huge cost', *Guardian*, 29 June 2006.

72 Ibid.

73 Ibid.

74 See generally, <http://www.cybertipline.com/>. See further, <http://www.cybertip.org/en_US/documents/CyberTiplineFactSheet.pdf>.

75 'Under the Electronic Communications Privacy Act, an ISP could not turn information over to law enforcement officials without a warrant. However, this Act requires, without a warrant, ISPs to turn over whatever information they might acquire. (See 18 U.S.C. § 2702(b)(6)(B) amending ECPA to permit disclosure.)' See CyberTelecom: An Open Law Project, 'Reporting Child Pornography', at <http://www.cybertelecom.org/cda/cppa.htm>.

members of the Internet Crimes Against Children (ICAC) task force programme.[76] According to the Department of Justice report *Project Safe Childhood: Protecting Children from Online Exploitation and Abuse*, 'the ICAC task forces have been the leading recipient of the CyberTipline referrals'[77] receiving 71 per cent of the CyberTipline referrals in 2005, and 84 per cent of the CyberTipline referrals from January to April 2006.[78]

Table 9.1 CyberTipline statistics

Year	Child Pornography Tips
1998	3,267
1999	7,736
2000	16,724
2001	21,611
2002	37,647
2003	76,204
2004	106,119
2005	64,250
2006	Not available

CyberTipLine claims success[79] as child pornography reports made to the hotline reached over 76,000 in 2003[80] and over 106,000 by December 2004 (see Table 9.1).[81] A total of 333,558 reports were made between 1998 and 2005, and by April

76 ICAC involves a network of co-ordinated regional task forces engaged in helping state and local law enforcement agencies to develop an effective response to cyber-enticement and child pornography cases.

77 US Department of Justice, Office of the Attorney General, *Project Safe Childhood: Protecting Children from Online Exploitation and Abuse*, May 2006, at <http://www.projectsafechildhood.gov/guide.htm>. See in particular Part II: The Need for a National Initiative to Protect Children, at <http://www.projectsafechildhood.gov/part2.pdf>.

78 Ibid.

79 See further, the CyberTipLine success stories pages at <http://www.missingkids.com/missingkids/servlet/PageServlet?LanguageCountry=en_US&PageId=376>.

80 See NCMEC press release, 'NCMEC announces dramatic increase in reports of child sexual exploitation', 4 February 2004, at <http://www.missingkids.com/missingkids/servlet/NewsEventServlet?LanguageCountry=en_US&PageId=1531>.

81 See <http://www.cybertipline.com/en_US/documents/CyberTiplineReportTotals.pdf>.

2007 CyberTipLine had received more than 422,000 reports.[82] These figures include reports made by members of the public as well as the mandated reports of child pornography from ISPs. However, according to a 2005 press release, 'only 142 of the more than 3,000 electronic communications service providers in the U.S comply with the federal law.'[83] The FBI has also reported success in terms of the number of child pornography websites and web hosts shut down following reports made to the CyberTipline. According to a Department of Justice paper, 2,638 US-based sites were shut down by the FBI during the 2004 Fiscal Year compared to 201 in the previous year.[84]

CYBERTIP.CA

It is also worth noting Canadian self-regulatory efforts through the establishment of Cybertip.ca,[85] the Canadian National Tipline for reporting the online sexual exploitation of children. Cybertip.ca was established as a two-year pilot project in September 2002 in response to the growing problem of child sexual exploitation on the Internet. Based on the success of a provincial pilot in Manitoba through Child Find Manitoba, Deputy Prime Minister Anne McLellan announced in May 2004 that Cybertip.ca would officially become a major component of Canada's child protection strategy. This led to the official launch of Cybertip.ca in January 2005. Cybertip.ca was created in partnership with the private and public sectors and law enforcement agencies to combat the online victimization of children. Cybertip.ca receives financial support from the Government of Canada and Bell Canada as well as Microsoft, TELUS, Shaw and Rogers.

In terms of its function, similarities exist with European hotlines such as the Internet Watch Foundation, but Cybertip.ca has a broader mandate which includes receiving reports from the public regarding not only child pornography but also luring (grooming), child sex tourism, and tips about children who are exploited through prostitution.

At the end of its first year of operation, Cybertip.ca reported that it had received 5,771 child sexual exploitation reports, and 2,258 of these reports were forwarded to law enforcement agencies.[86] Since it started as a pilot project in 2002, 9,145 public reports have been received resulting in 17 arrests and 972 websites being shut down.

82 See CyberTipLine PressKit, 6 November 2006, at <http://www.missingkids.com/en_US/documents/Presskit_CyberTipline.pdf>.

83 See National Center for Missing and Exploited Children (NCMEC) press release, 'Reports of Child Pornography to the National Center for Missing and Exploited Children continue to rise', 27 January 2005, at <http://www.missingkids.com/missingkids/servlet/NewsEventServlet?LanguageCountry=en_US&PageId=1865>.

84 See Department of Justice, *FY 2004 Performance and Accountability Report*, at <http://www.usdoj.gov/ag/annualreports/pr2004/P2/p04-13.pdf>.

85 See <http://www.cybertip.ca> for further information.

86 Cybertip.ca Press Release, 'Online child sexual abuse yips top 5,700 in first year', 23 February 2006, available through <http://www.cybertip.ca/en/cybertip/media_releases/>.

Cybertip.ca started using the CleanFeed system in Canada in November 2006,[87] and the hotline will create and maintain a regularly updated list of specific foreign-hosted Internet addresses associated with images of child sexual abuse and will provide that list in a secure manner to participating ISPs.[88] The hotline decided to block access to websites 'displaying images of prepubescent children being assaulted or who are posed deliberately in a sexualized manner',[89] rather than blocking access to all web based content displaying sexually explicit content involving children under the age of 18. The hotline provides an appeal process for unblocking legitimate websites which are 'inadvertently filtered' by the system 'modeled after the UK's Internet Watch Foundation system'.[90]

CRITICISM OF HOTLINES

The activities of hotlines have been the subject of debate and criticism. A French Council of State Report entitled *The Internet and Digital Networks*,[91] questioned the procedure of reporting and removing by private hotlines, stating that it could be accepted only for very specific subjects such as paedophilia and incitement to racial hatred. The report further notes:

> It is essential to know who is managing the [hot]line and in accordance with what criteria. In this connection, although it is seemingly effective, the British arrangements for handling unlawful messages has provoked a lot of criticism on the grounds that it gives the hotline very wide prerogatives both with regard to classifying the content of the sites and the possibility of cutting access to them. Has an association of access providers this right? Is there not a risk of censorship or of substitution for the court?[92]

This raises legitimate concerns about having an industry based system. It may be said that the hotline schemes reduce accountability and encourage 'vigilantism'.[93] Due process concepts are scarcely applied by the industry as there are no clear mechanisms for procedures for handling complaints.

---

87 Cybertip.ca press release, 'ISPs and Tipline step up battle against Internet child exploitation', 23 November 2006, at <http://www.cybertip.ca/PDFs/en/release_nov23.pdf>.

88 See the CleanFeed FAQ at <http://www.cybertip.ca/en/cybertip/cf_docs/>.

89 Ibid. See the Cleanfeed Appeal Process at <http://www.cybertip.ca/en/cybertip/cf_appeal>.

90 Ibid.

91 French Conseil d'État Report on *Internet et les réseaux numériques*, 8 September 1998 at <http://www.conseil-etat.fr/ce/rappor/index_ra_liau01.shtml>. An English version is available from the same web site (French Council of State Report: *The Internet and Digital Networks*).

92 Ibid. See also Cyber-Rights and Cyber-Liberties (UK) Report: 'Who Watches the Watchmen: Part II – Accountability and Effective Self-Regulation in the Information Age', September 1998 at <http://www.cyber-rights.org/watchmen-ii.htm>.

93 Per Professor Nadine Strossen, from an ACLU Press Release, 'ACLU oins International Protest Against Global Internet Censorship Plans', 9 September 1999, at <http://www.aclu.org/news/1999/n090999a.html>.

In March 1998 the DTI and the Home Office announced their intention to carry out a Review of the IWF. A report was published in February 1999[94] which was related to the structure of the IWF, and an assessment of its progress. It did not, for example, address concerns in relation to openness, transparency and accountability. Two *Who Watches the Watchmen* reports[95] by the non-profit organization Cyber-Rights and Cyber-Liberties (UK) have questioned the accountability of the IWF to the public and the openness and transparency of its procedures and decision-making process as a quasi-regulatory body.

The lack of transparency of the regulatory framework has also been emphasized by the Better Regulation Task Force's *Regulating Cyberspace – Better Regulation for E-Commerce* report,[96] published in December 2000. If bodies like the IWF are to exist, then they must be subjected to standards of constitutionality. Good governance needs to be kept at the same level of openness, transparency and accountability of other public bodies in order to maintain confidence. These bodies must also have greater regard to legal standards, especially those standards which serve to protect liberty. Decisions of the IWF affecting UK policy are potentially open to challenge under section 6 of the Human Rights Act 1998 as the IWF may be regarded as a 'public authority'[97] under section 6(3)(b) of the 1998 Act, which includes 'any person certain of whose functions are functions of a public nature' within that definition. The IWF recognized its public role in relation to the Human Rights Act 1998 in April 2001:

> The IWF accepts the principles of the European Convention on Human Rights and undertakes to be governed subject to the Human Rights Act on the basis that it should be treated as a public body.[98]

It is only by respecting such legal standards and observing such principles that a co-regulatory framework with an emphasis on industry self-regulation can hope to work effectively.

More fundamentally, it may be said that the monitoring of the Internet (or parts of it) at a national level is of limited value as the problems created by the Internet are

---

94 See 'Review of the Internet Watch Foundation: A report for the DTI and Home Office by KPMG and Denton Hall', February 1999.

95 Cyber-Rights and Cyber-Liberties (UK) Report, 'Who Watches the Watchmen: Internet Content Rating Systems, and Privatized Censorship', November 1997, at <http://www.cyber-rights.org/watchmen.htm> and Cyber-Rights and Cyber-Liberties (UK) Report: 'Who Watches the Watchmen: Part II – Accountability and Effective Self-Regulation in the Information Age', September 1998, at <http://www.cyber-rights.org/watchmen-ii.htm>.

96 Better Regulation Task Force's *Regulating Cyberspace – Better Regulation for E-Commerce*, December 2000, <at http://devtemp1/regulation/TaskForce/2001/BRTF-E-Commerce.pdf>.

97 Note the case of *Aston Cantlow and Wilmcote with Billesley Parochial Church Council v. Wallbank and another* (CA, Civil Division) [2001] EWCA Civ 713; [2001] 3 All ER 393 within this context. Note also the case of *Heather and others v. The Leonard Cheshire Foundation and another* (QBD) [2001] EWHC Admin 429, CO/4503/2000, CO/4727/00.

98 Minutes of Internet Watch Foundation Board Meeting, 25 April 2001, at <http://www.iwf.org.uk/about/bd4-01mins.rtf>.

global in scope and thus require global solutions. More practically, it could be argued that the formation of the IWF does not balance risk, cost and intended benefits to society.

It is not intended to suggest that the role played by hotlines or the co-regulatory approach adapted in this field should be dismissed, but serious concerns regarding what is essentially policing activity undertaken by such organizations remain. Hotlines have been developed in a number of countries and co-ordinated by the INHOPE network.[99] INHOPE is an organization which aims to facilitate and co-ordinate the work of Internet hotlines in responding to illegal use and content on the Internet. Currently it has 18 hotlines[100] as full members[101] and seven provisional members.[102] Such developments may be expedient, but privatized policing organizations are ill-equipped to judge the suitability or illegality of Internet content, and there is a serious risk of hotline operators acting as 'self-appointed judges'.[103] According to Nadine Strossen, 'these hotlines violate due process concepts that are also enshrined in international, regional, and national guarantees around the world.'[104] Similarly the Martabit report to the United Nations on combating racist content on the Internet stated that 'while encouraging these initiatives, States should ensure that the due process of law is respected and effective remedies remain available in relation to measures enforced.'[105]

It is submitted that a better approach would have been to introduce a confidential telephone hotline not run by the industry itself, but one which is similar to that run by the Metropolitan Police in London to combat terrorism or an initiative along the lines of US CyberTipline.[106] The agenda of the CyberTipline is wider than the IWF's and it encourages families to call its national toll-free hotline to report incidences involving child sexual exploitation, including not only information on the possession,

---

99 INHOPE – Internet Hotline Providers in Europe is a project under the EC Daphne Programme to encourage co-operation between European Internet Hotline providers to reduce the level of child pornography on the Internet. For details see <http://www.inhope.org/>.

100 Some but not all of the members of INHOPE deal with racist Internet content. See the hotlines from Austria, France, Germany, Greece, Ireland, UK and Spain in relation to reporting racist Internet content.

101 Full member hotlines are from Australia, Austria, Belgium, Denmark, Finland, France, Germany, Iceland, Ireland, Italy, Netherlands, South Korea, Spain, Taiwan, United Kingdom and the United States.

102 Provisional members are from Brazil, Canada, Cyprus, Greece, Hungary, Lithuania and Poland.

103 Per Professor Nadine Strossen, from an ACLU Press Release, 'ACLU Joins International Protest Against Global Internet Censorship Plans', 9 September 1999, at <http://www.aclu.org/news/1999/n090999a.html>.

104 Ibid.

105 Report of the Intergovernmental Working Group on the effective implementation of the Durban Declaration and Programme of Action on its fourth session (Chairperson-Rapporteur: Juan Martabit (Chile)), E/CN.4/2006/18, 20 March 2006, at <http://daccessdds.un.org/doc/UNDOC/GEN/G06/119/23/PDF/G0611923.pdf>, at para. 47.

106 National Council for Missing and Exploited Children (NCMEC), in partnership with the Federal Bureau of Investigation, U.S. Customs Service and the U.S. Postal Inspection Service, serves as the national CyberTipline and as the national Child Pornography Tipline.

manufacture or distribution of child pornography, but also information on online enticement of children for sexual acts, child prostitution and child-sex tourism.[107]

CONCLUSION

At a national level, it is now widely accepted that 'government cannot simply regulate to achieve its aims in this new global electronic environment',[108] and therefore a 'light regulatory touch' is preferred. There have been calls for a partnership between government and industry 'to get the right balance' in order to build confidence and protect consumers in the information age. If this is to be achieved this balance needs to reflect and respect the rights of individual Internet users as well as those of the business community, an issue often overlooked by regulators and industry. There is an urgent need for openness, accountability and transparency in relation to regulatory initiatives[109] aimed at Internet content at the national level. At the same time there are 'real and perceived doubts'[110] about the ability of professional and trade bodies as well as private hotlines such as the Internet Watch Foundation to 'both represent the interests of their members and aspire to a public interest role'.[111]

At the supranational level, the development of Europe-wide ISP codes of conduct has proved problematic as each country is liable to reach its own conclusion in defining the borderline between what is permissible (legal) and not permissible (illegal). The existence of such legitimate differences results in a fragmented market rather than a harmonized one in which Europe-wide codes of conduct can be developed. A European Commission analysis of work on notice and take down procedures published in 2003 claimed that 'though a consensus is still some way off, agreement would appear to have been reached among stake holders in regards to the essential elements which should be taken into consideration.'[112] However, there have been no further relevant developments to date.

---

107 See <http://www.missingkids.com/cybertip/>. Recently the US CyberTipline started to co-operate with INHOPE – Internet Hotline Providers in Europe Association (Formed in November 1999, currently six European hotlines are members of INHOPE. See further, <http://www.inhope.org/>) which exists to facilitate co-operation between European Internet Hotline providers.

108 Per Tony Blair, forward to the Cabinet Office Report, *e-commerce@its.best.uk*, September 1999.

109 Note also the Cyber-Rights and Cyber-Liberties (UK) Response to Better Regulation Task Force Review of E-Commerce, 12 October 2000, at <http://www.cyber-rights.org/reports/brtf.htm>, and the Task Force's report, Regulating Cyberspace: better regulation for e-commerce, 14 December 2000, at <http://www.cabinet-office.gov.uk/regulation/taskforce/ecommerce/default.htm>.

110 National Consumer Council report, *Models of Self-regulation: an overview of models in business and the professions*, November 2000 (reprinted with amendments from October 1999), at <http://www.ncc.org.uk/regulation/models_self_regulation.pdf>.

111 Ibid.

112 See Report from the Commission to the European Parliament, the Council and the European Economic and Social Committee (First report on the application of Directive

In the future it is possible that self-regulation will result in more technology-based solutions as witnessed by the development of the British Telecom (BT) CleanFeed Project[113] in the UK. ISPs may have no other alternative than implementing filtering and blocking systems to satisfy government demands. As with other initiatives discussed thus far, self- and co-regulatory measures have the potential to play an important role in the fight against Internet child pornography, but developments are still at a relatively emergent stage.

2000/31/EC on electronic commerce), COM(2003) 702 final, Brussels, 21 November 2003, at <http://europa.eu.int/eur-lex/en/com/rpt/2003/com2003_0702en01.pdf>, section 4.7.

113 IWF/BT Project CleanFeed, at <http://www.iwf.org.uk/media/news.archive-2004.39.htm>.

Chapter 10

Conclusion

The extent and nature of Internet child pornography has been the subject of much recent debate largely documented elsewhere.[1] Wider research into offending behaviour and offenders, as well as research into whether a causal link exists between the consumption of child pornography (possession) and the commission of sexual violent crimes is still ongoing.[2] This book has focused on legal and policy initiatives to address the problem, availability and distribution of child pornography through the Internet in recognition that governments have a compelling interest to protect children from sexual abuse and exploitation. A summary of main conclusions reached from legal and policy perspectives is set out below where remaining issues of concern are also highlighted.

LEGAL APPROACHES

The form and the application of laws dealing with child pornography within England and Wales, the United States and Canada have been reviewed in detail. This analysis has revealed that similarities exist in all three common law based jurisdictions where advancement in technology and Internet access and communications has had a significant impact upon the development of child pornography laws over the last 12 years. Although there are varied approaches in terms of what constitutes 'child pornography' in each jurisdiction, the creation and making, distribution and possession of child pornography are criminalized in all three jurisdictions. All three also criminalize child pornography involving real or non-real children, albeit with some noticeable differences in wording. Constitutional challenges were

1 See generally, Jenkins, P., *Beyond Tolerance: Child Pornography on the Internet*, New York: New York University Press, 2001; Taylor, M. and E. Quayle, *Child Pornography: An Internet Crime*, Hove: Brunner-Routledge, 2003; Quayle, E. and M. Taylor (eds), *Viewing Child Pornography on the Internet: Understanding the Offence, Managing the Offender, Helping the Victims*, Lyme Regis: Russell House, 2005.

2 Note generally Howitt, D. and G. Cumberbatch, *Pornography: Impacts and Influences*, London: HMSO, 1990; Seto M.C. and A.W. Eke, 'The Criminal Histories and Later Offending of Child Pornography Offenders' (2005), *Sexual Abuse: A Journal of Research and Treatment* 17, 201–10; Wolak, J., D. Finkelhor and K.J. Mitchell, *Child-Pornography Possessors Arrested in Internet-Related Crimes: Findings From the National Juvenile Online Victimization Study*, National Center for Missing and Exploited Children, 2005, at <http://www.missingkids.com/en_US/publications/NC144.pdf>.

resolved at the Supreme Court level in both the United States[3] and in Canada.[4] Both developments triggered the US and Canadian governments to introduce subsequent legislation to work around Supreme Court decisions. As far as non-photographic content is concerned, legal provisions in England and Wales and the United States deliberately exclude drawings, cartoons, paintings and sculptures. Conversely in Canada written material, as well as audio recordings, will be regarded as child pornography if the dominant characteristic of the content in question is the description, for a sexual purpose, of sexual activity with a person under the age of 18 years. Not surprisingly, definitional differences are also evident at an international level, and despite harmonization attempts, there remain different legal approaches in terms of the treatment of child pornography involving non-real children and content involving adults appearing to look like children. The Canadian policy with regards to drawings, cartoons, paintings and sculptures may not be so unique in the near future. Governments are anxious to further tighten child pornography laws, and the UK is currently considering whether to criminalize the possession of non-photographic graphic and explicit visual depictions of child sexual abuse in respect of cartoons, drawings, computer-generated images and other non-photographic representations.[5] A recent consultation paper argued that 'there is concern that such material reinforces inappropriate feelings towards children and that its circulation and possession should be prohibited.'[6] Many will no doubt welcome moves in this direction. Others are, however, beginning to question whether these laws go too far in curbing certain civil liberties in the name of child protection.[7] With the escalation of the crisis of child sexual abuse in society, Adler argues that 'the definition of what constitutes "child pornography" has also expanded dramatically, in a direction that makes it increasingly unrelated to the harm that the law was designed to combat.'[8] This assertion is evident in the Home Office proposals, and given the absence of evidence that such extreme content in the form of cartoons and drawings would 'poison the minds of its viewers',[9] or lead into the commission of sexual offences involving children, it can only be concluded that the consideration of criminalizing

---

3 *Ashcroft, Attorney General, et al. v. Free Speech Coalition et al.* (US Supreme Court, 2002) 535 U.S. 234, 198 F3d 1083, 16 April 2002, No. 00–795, Argued 30 October 2001, at <http://supct.law.cornell.edu/supct/html/00-795.ZS.html>.

4 *R v. Sharpe* (2001) SCC 2. File No. 27376, 26 January 2001.

5 Home Office, *Consultation On Possession Of Non-Photographic Visual Depictions Of Child Sexual Abuse*, April 2007, at <http://www.homeoffice.gov.uk/documents/cons-2007-depiction-sex-abuse>. UK also introduced various other statutory offences under the Sexual offences Act 2003 including the offences of causing child pornography, inciting child pornography, controlling a child involved in pornography, arranging child pornography and facilitating child pornography.

6 Ibid.

7 See Jenkins, P., *Beyond Tolerance: Child Pornography on the Internet*, New York: New York University Press, 2001, 218–21.

8 Adler, A., 'Inverting the First Amendment' (2001), 149 *U. Pa. L. Rev.* 921, at p. 941. See further, Adler, A., 'The Perverse Law of Child Pornography' (2001), 101 *Colum. L. Rev.* 209.

9 *Stanley v. Georgia* 394 U.S. 557 (1969).

the possession of non-photographic graphic and explicit visual depictions of child sexual abuse is based solely on moral and political grounds.

When it comes to sentencing, examination of a substantial number of cases reveals that despite the availability of serious sanctions, offenders are not immediately given the maximum penalties provided by law. This is evidently the case in relation to the treatment of offenders who commit possession offences in England and Wales and Canada, particularly in relation to first time offenders. US law has been amended with respect to child pornography cases and an offender's sentence may be increased or decreased in accordance with the Federal Sentencing Guidelines based on aggravating factors[10] and mitigating factors.[11] Similarly, in England and Wales the Court of Appeal in *R v. Oliver*[12] established detailed sentencing guidelines. The nature of the material based on the Oliver image description scale, the nature of the offender's activity including the defendant's proximity to the creation and circulation of the content in question, as well as mitigating circumstances are all relevant factors that are assessed when deciding the appropriate penalty for child pornography offenders.

STATISTICS

Detailed statistics on prosecutions and convictions involving child pornography cases are hard to obtain from government bodies, and publicly available data is limited and lacking in detail. Of the three individual jurisdictions examined in this book, the UK government is the only one which makes prosecution and conviction statistics publicly available. It was only possible to obtain detailed US statistics through the *Transactional Records Access Clearinghouse*,[13] a private organization

---

10 In terms of upward departure, note the case of *U.S. v. Schmeltzer*, 20 F3d 610 (5th Cir. 1994) which established that the commission of a similar offence in the past could result in an upward departure from the Federal Sentencing Guidelines and therefore in a more serious penalty. See Williams, E., 'Construction and Application of United States Sentencing Guideline § 2G2.1 et seq., Pertaining to Child Pornography', 145 *A.L.R. Fed.* 481. Note the following cases which involve constitutional challenges to sentencing guidelines involving child pornography cases. *U.S. v. Morell*, 429 F3d 1161 C.A.8 (Ark. 2005); *U.S. v. Detwiler,* 338 F.Supp.2d 1166 (D. Or. 2004).

11 In terms of downward departure, see United States Sentencing Commission, Report to the Congress: Downward Departures from the Federal Sentencing Guidelines (in response to section 401(m) of Public Law 108–21), October 2003. See section G of the report in relation to the Protect Act, and Williams, E., 'Construction and Application of United States Sentencing Guideline § 2G2.1 et seq., Pertaining to Child Pornography', 145 *A.L.R. Fed.* 481. Note the following cases which involve constitutional challenges to sentencing guidelines involving child pornography cases: *U.S. v. Morell*, 429 F3d 1161 C.A.8 (Ark.), 2005; *U.S. v. Detwiler*, 338 F.Supp.2d 1166 D. Or., 2004.

12 *R v. Oliver and others* [2002] EWCA Crim 2766; [2003] 2 Cr App R (S) 64; [2003] 1 Cr App R 28; [2003] 2 Cr App R (S.) 15; 2002 WL 31599711.

13 The Transactional Records Access Clearinghouse (TRAC) is a data gathering, data research and data distribution organization associated with Syracuse University. See <http://trac.syr.edu/>.

associated with Syracuse University. Canada, on the other hand, does not provide any prosecution and conviction statistics in relation to child pornography offences. Statistics help to shed light on the true nature of offending behaviour and the collection and publication of such data is crucial for researchers working in this field.

INTERNATIONAL HARMONIZATION

Another key factor to emerge from the foregoing analysis is the extent of duplication of efforts at supranational and international levels of policy making and governance. The problem of child pornography has been internationally recognized with G8 Ministers recently declaring that 'setting and agreeing to abide by international minimum standards is a critical step in developing a concerted global response to combat child pornography.'[14] To date, three substantial policy documents have been developed; namely, the European Union's Framework Decision on combating the sexual exploitation of children and child pornography,[15] the Council of Europe's Cybercrime Convention 2001,[16] and the United Nation's Optional Protocol to the Convention on the Rights of the Child on the Sale of Children, Child Prostitution and Child Pornography.[17]

All three were subject to major delays. It took almost ten years for the European Union to develop the Framework Decision and for its Member States to implement it. The Council of Europe's Cybercrime Convention took almost five years to develop and since it was opened to signature in late 2001 only 21 countries have ratified the Convention out of a potential 50 member states (including the various external supporters) at the time of writing. The UK and Canada are notably amongst these yet to ratify the Convention. To date, 115 countries[18] have signed and 119 member states have ratified the Optional Protocol[19] out of 192 UN member states.

---

14 G8 Ministers' Declaration, *Reinforcing the International Fight Against Child Pornography*, G-8 Justice and Home Affairs Ministers, 24 May 2007, at <http://www.g-8.de/Content/EN/__Anlagen/2007-05-24-g8-justiz-innen-start-erklaerung-en,property=publicationFile.pdf>. Note further Reuters, 'G8 needs private sector help to end child porn', 24 May 2007.

15 Council Framework Decision 2004/68/JHA of 22 December 2003 on combating the sexual exploitation of children and child pornography (see OJ L 013 2 January 2004, pp. 44–8), at <http://register.consilium.europa.eu/pdf/en/03/st10/st10748en03.pdf>. For a summary of the Framework Decision see <http://europa.eu/scadplus/leg/en/lvb/l33138.htm>.

16 Convention on Cybercrime, ETS No. 185, at <http://conventions.coe.int/Treaty/EN/Treaties/Html/185.htm>.

17 Optional Protocol to the Convention on the Rights of the Child on the Sale of Children, Child Prostitution and Child Pornography, New York, 25 May 2000, Fifty-fourth session (97th plenary meeting), Agenda item 116 (a), Distr. General A/RES/54/263, 26 June 2000.

18 See <http://www.unicef.org/crc/opsx-tableweb.htm>. See further, Special Rapporteur (Mr Juan Miguel Petit) Report of the Commission on Human Rights on the sale of children, child prostitution and child pornography, E/CN.4/2002/88, 4 February 2002, presented at the fifty-eighth session of the General Assembly of the United Nations, para. 57.

19 See generally, Office of the UN High Commissioner for Human Rights, Status of ratifications of the principal international human rights treaties, at <http://www.unhchr.ch/pdf/report.pdf>.

Ratification and state-level implementation of these treaties are also subject to various reservations by ratifying states with different approaches being adopted especially in relation to criminal provisions involving realistic images representing a minor engaged in sexually explicit conduct, as well as in relation to criminal provisions involving adults appearing to be minors engaged in sexually explicit conduct. While it is true that in most Western countries the making, distribution and possession of child pornography involving real children has been criminalized, countries need to adopt and effectively implement these treaties as a matter of priority. In the absence of wider harmonization, definitional and legal differences will continue to exist. International recognition of the problem of child pornography needs to translate into local action by individual states if it is to produce results. Unfortunately, in many countries the problem of paedophilia, sexual exploitation of children, and child pornography is not high on the political agenda.

DEFINING A 'CHILD'

The above-mentioned policy documents define a child as under the age of 18. Jenkins has criticized this approach arguing that '18 is too high a minimum age at which an individual can be depicted in sexual contexts, and 16 would be more sensible.'[20] It may be noted that in the UK, a child was defined as under the age of 16 under the Protection of Children Act 1978 until it was amended by the Sexual Offences Act 2003 to comply with the international requirements. In practice this may be an academic point as various studies conducted in this field, police and court reports indicate that child abuse images in circulation involve predominantly pre-teens rather than older teenagers. However, in many countries, the age of sexual consent[21] is lower than that used to define a child under child pornography laws. It is therefore possible that consensual legal sexual activity involving teenagers above the sexual consent age could be regarded as child pornography if that activity is photographed or filmed. As discussed in Chapter 2, policy makers in the UK have acknowledged this problem and provided an exception under the Sexual Offences Act 2003 for 'marriage and other relationships' in relation to images involving children aged 16 or 17.[22] This is a limited exception nonetheless, and there is a case for arguing that a child should be defined as under the age of 16 for the purposes of child pornography laws. Jenkins, for example, takes the view that '17 year olds are not children, and it is ludicrous to try to impose upon them the same limitations

---

20 Jenkins, P., *Beyond Tolerance: Child Pornography on the Internet*, New York: New York University Press, 2001, 219–20.

21 Bullough, V.L., 'Age of Consent A Historical Overview' (2006), *Journal of Psychology and Human Sexuality* 16(2–3), 25–42. See further, Levine, J., *Harmful to Minors: The Perils of Protecting Children from Sex*, New York: Thunder's Mouth Press, 2003.

22 See section 1A(1) of the Protection of Children Act 1978 as amended by the Sexual Offences Act 2003. See Explanatory Notes to Sexual Offences Act 2003, at <http://www.legislation.hmso.gov.uk/acts/en2003/2003en42.htm>, para. 73. See further, Gillespie, A., 'The Sexual Offences Act 2003: (3) Tinkering with "Child Pornography"' (2004), *Crim. L.R.*, May, 361–8.

that apply to seven year olds.'[23] There is at least a strong case for arguing that those who commit child pornography related offences in relation to 16- and 17-year-olds should ordinarily be treated leniently, especially at the sentencing stage, although this must of course depend upon the individual circumstances of any given case.

LAW ENFORCEMENT APPROACHES

Regardless of the disparities between legal systems, law enforcement operations targeting child pornography crimes and paedophile rings have been largely successful. There has been significant co-operation between national police forces at an international level to conduct operations to disrupt the trading of child pornography on computer networks dating back to 1993. *Operation Long Arm* conducted in that year was one of the earliest police operations involving the international distribution of child pornography via computer networks. US law enforcement officials, together with their Danish partners, tracked down the identity of users from the US who downloaded child pornography from a Danish computer bulletin board.[24] There have been a number of international police operations[25] since then including the British-police-led Operation Starburst,[26] the FBI's Operation Innocent Images,[27] and Operation Cathedral, involving the US-based paedophile

---

23 Jenkins, P., *Beyond Tolerance: Child Pornography on the Internet*, New York: New York University Press, 2001, at 220. See further, Graupner, H., 'The 17-Year-Old Child: An Absurdity of the Late 20th Century' (2006), *Journal of Psychology and Human Sexuality* 16(2–3), 7–24. Graupner argues that by defining a child as under the age of 18, 'these offences go far beyond combating child pornography and child prostitution, thus making a wide variety of adolescent sexual behaviour, hitherto completely legal in the overwhelming majority of jurisdictions in Europe, serious crimes.' Note also Hofmeister, L., '14 to 18 Year Olds as "Children" by Law: Reflections on Developments in National and European Law' (2006), *Journal of Psychology and Human Sexuality* 16(2–3), 63–70.

24 Several people were prosecuted as a result of this international co-operation. Reported in Cavazos, E.A. and G. Morin, *Cyberspace and the Law: Your Rights and Duties in the On-Line World*, Cambridge, MA: MIT Press, 1994.

25 See generally, Krone, T., 'International Police Operations against Online Child Pornography' (2005), *Trends and Issues in Crime and Criminal Justice* 296, Australian Institute of Criminology, at <http://www.aic.gov.au/publications/tandi2/tandi296t.html>.

26 See generally, Akdeniz, Y., 'The Regulation of Pornography and Child Pornography on the Internet' (1997), *The Journal of Information, Law and Technology* 1.

27 See CNN, 'FBI cracks down on child pornography on the Internet', 7 April 1997. See also 'Child Pornography', Statement of Louis J. Freeh, Director Federal Bureau of Investigation Before the Senate Appropriations Committee Subcommittee on the Departments of Commerce, Justice, and State, the Judiciary, and Related Agencies Committee on the Judiciary United States Senate, Washington, DC, 8 April 1997; 'Child Pornography on the Internet and the Sexual Exploitation of Children', Statement of Louis J. Freeh, Director Federal Bureau of Investigation Before the Senate Appropriations Subcommittee for the Departments of Commerce, Justice, and State, the Judiciary, and related Agencies, Washington, DC, 10 March 1998.

club known as 'W0nderland',[28] all of which could be cited as examples of success.[29] The biggest operation of recent times is Operation Ore,[30] which was launched in the UK after the FBI passed credit-card details of 7,250 alleged British subscribers to a pornography portal operated in Texas called Landslide,[31] which also provided access to child pornography sites.[32] As detailed in Chapter 2, question marks currently hang over this investigation as the reliability of evidence obtained from the US law enforcement agencies to prosecute alleged UK users of the Landslide website has been questioned[33] by a number of experts.[34]

These and other operations show that police forces around the globe are to some extent capable of adapting themselves to changes in criminal behaviour and activity even when this requires co-operation with international partners and the Internet industry. Whilst inadequate resources and lack of technical expertise can hinder policing operations, the main problem for law enforcement agencies regarding Internet related criminal activity remains the transnational nature of these crimes. Policing activity normally takes place within the borders of a nation-state in a localized form. The Internet is a global communications tool without any specific borders and boundaries, and crimes are not necessarily committed within a certain jurisdiction, or even local areas. Harmonization of child pornography laws as well as harmonization of procedural laws (for example, through the CoE Cybercrime Convention) could help to overcome some problems that are the result of the transnational nature of these crimes.[35] It is nevertheless desirable that existing and future policies respect

---

28 W0nderland's name stemmed from 'Alice in Wonderland' author Lewis Carroll's reputed penchant for photographing young girls. See Reuters, 'Police crack down on Net child porn', 2 September 1998; Lusher, A., 'Child sex victims' faces to be revealed', *Daily Telegraph*, 2 November 1998; 'Internet paedophiles jailed', *Guardian*, 13 February 2001; 'Dismay at paedophile sentences', *Guardian*, 14 February 2001.

29 See further, Krone, T., 'International Police Operations against Online Child Pornography' (2005), *Trends and Issues in Crime and Criminal Justice* 296, Australian Institute of Criminology, at <http://www.aic.gov.au/publications/tandi2/tandi296t.html>.

30 'FBI Investigation into child porn sites spans the world; Internet Crackdown: Dozens of British arrests have followed an international inquiry launched into three websites based in Houston', *Independent*, 14 September 2002.

31 Note *United States v. Reedy*, 119 Fed. Appx. 686; 2005 U.S. App. LEXIS 1474; *United States v. Reedy*, 304 F3d 358; 2002 U.S. App. LEXIS 17668 (5th Cir. Tex., 2002).

32 'Sex offenders slip the net: Thousands escape with cautions because police cannot cope with the flood of child porn offences', *Guardian*, 28 September 2003.

33 Campbell, D., 'Operation Ore Exposed', *PC Pro*, 1 July 2005; Campbell, D., 'Sex, Lies and the Missing Videotape', *PC Pro*, 1 April 2007. Note also Campbell, D., 'Operation Ore flawed by fraud', *Guardian*, 19 April 2007; Bates, J., *The Ore Reports*, at <http://www.computer-investigations.com/index3.html>. See further, Campbell, D., 'A flaw in the child porn witch-hunt', *Sunday Times*, 26 June 2005; and Leppard. D., 'Child porn suspects set to be cleared in evidence "shambles"', *Sunday Times*, 3 July 2005.

34 See Arthur, C., 'Is Operation Ore the UK's worst-ever policing scandal?', *Guardian*, 26 April 2007. See further, Operation Ore Exposed, at <http://www.ore-exposed.co.uk/>.

35 Note further International Centre for Missing and Exploited Children report, *Creating a Global Agenda to Combat Child Pornography*, 2003, at <http://www.icmec.org/en_X1/pdf/CreatingAGlobalAgenda.pdf>, p. 53.

fundamental human rights, and cross-border co-operation should be subject to principles of dual-criminality, privacy and data protection laws.[36]

On a wider note, criticism surrounding Operation Ore in England and Wales signals a need for reflection. Due to the great stigma attached to these crimes by society, any association with child pornography usually leads to terrifying social consequences for those who fall under suspicion.[37] An examination and evaluation of law enforcement operations and practices may be necessary to identify best practices in this field[38] and to avoid future potential mistakes in policing operations and evidence gathering.

ADDITIONAL METHODS OF REGULATION

As established in Part Three, it is often recognized that there should be co-operation with industry in the fight against Internet child pornography through the development of self-regulatory tools and practices. According to the UN Special Rapporteur on the sale of children, child prostitution and child pornography, this co-operation, which has so far predominantly involved Internet Service Providers, should extend to credit-card companies who could play a crucial role in stopping the commercial distribution of child pornography on the Internet. The Special Rapporteur, in a recent report, urged 'credit-card companies to make all possible efforts to avoid accepting payment for child pornography web sites',[39] and in March

---

36 Akdeniz, Y., *An Advocacy Handbook for the Non Governmental Organizations: The Council of Europe's Cybercrime Convention 2001 and the Aadditional Pprotocol on the Criminalisation of Acts of a Racist or Xenophobic Nature Committed through Computer Systems*, Cyber-Rights and Cyber-Liberties, December 2003 (revised and updated in February 2007), at <http://www.cyber-rights.org/cybercrime/coe_handbook_crcl.pdf>. Note further the EU Convention on Mutual Assistance in Criminal Matters between the Member States of the European Union, established by the Council in accordance with Article 34 of the Treaty on European Union. OJ C 197, 12 July 2000 pp. 3–23; CoE Recommendation No. R(87) 15 regulating the use of personal data in the police sector, 1987, at <http://www.coe.int/t/e/legal_affairs/legal_co-operation/combating_economic_crime/1_standard_settings/Rec_1987_15.pdf>; Third evaluation of Recommendation No. R (87) 15 regulating the use of personal data in the police sector (2002); CoE Recommendation 1181(1992) on police co-operation and protection of personal data in the police sector, and second evaluation report of the Recommendation adopted on 28 October 1999.

37 Campbell, D., 'A flaw in the child porn witch-hunt', *Sunday Times*, 26 June 2005; 'Navy man's death puts spotlight on child porn inquiry', *Daily Telegraph*, 12 January 2005.

38 Note Campbell, D., 'A flaw in the child porn witch-hunt', *Sunday Times*, 26 June 2005, which revealed flaws in relation to Operation Ore. Note also Leppard. D., 'Child porn suspects set to be cleared in evidence "shambles"', *Sunday Times*, 3 July 2005.

39 Special Rapporteur on the sale of children, child prostitution and child pornography, Thematic Report on child pornography on the Internet, E/CN.4/2005/78, Economic and Social Council, Commission on Human Rights, 23 December 2004, at <http://daccessdds.un.org/doc/UNDOC/GEN/G05/100/19/PDF/G0510019.pdf>.

2006 18 major organizations[40] responded by creating a Financial Coalition Ag Child Pornography with the aim of making it impossible for anyone to profit fro child pornography by 2008.

While many would consider these positive developments, there remain significant question marks over the effectiveness and efficacy of the various mechanisms and tools currently offered by the private sector. In terms of the work of hotlines to report child pornography, the removal or destruction of digital images does not necessarily mean that those images will no longer be available. As long as they are available in digital format, their re-circulation will always be a possibility. Consequently, 'judgements need to be made about the relative value of focussing on the disruption of trading activities (on the correct assumption that these both fuel and reflect demand for the production of images).'[41] The true nature of the success claimed by hotlines such as the Internet Watch Foundation should be subject to further scrutiny, given that serious concerns regarding the essentially policing role that is played by these organizations remain. Self- and co-regulatory measures may yet play an important role in the fight against Internet child pornography, but this will be dependent upon substantial improvement to existing systems, including various blocking tools developed and used by the industry, as well as a willingness to give due consideration to due process concerns that surround the use of such tools.

FUTURE DIRECTIONS

Governments, police forces and international organizations are reacting more positively against the dissemination of child pornography through the Internet, and there is generally more awareness of the nature of the problem with news items about Internet child pornography appearing in the media on a daily basis. However, as Adler argues, the 'peculiar nature of paedophilic desire itself may make the governance of child pornography an impossible task',[42] as certain paedophiles may prefer innocent looking images rather than abusive images. Work in this field is ongoing and there is more to be done to address effectively the twin goals of reducing the availability

---

40 Members of the Financial Coalition Against Child Pornography are: America Online, American Express Company, Authorize.Net, Bank of America, Chase, Citigroup, Discover Financial Services LLC, e-gold, First Data Corporation, First National Bank of Omaha, Google, MasterCard, Microsoft, North American Bancard, Nova Information Systems, PayPal, First PREMIER Bank/PREMIER Bankcard, Standard Chartered Bank, Visa, Wells Fargo and Yahoo! Inc. See NCMEC press release, 'Google joins industry-wide movement to combat child pornography', 23 August 2006. Note further BBC News, 'Sites selling child porn targeted', 16 March 2006, at <http://news.bbc.co.uk/1/hi/technology/4812962.stm>.

41 International Centre for Missing and Exploited Children report, *Creating a Global Agenda to Combat Child Pornography*, 2003, at <http://www.icmec.org/en_X1/pdf/CreatingAGlobalAgenda.pdf>, p. 58.

42 Adler, A., 'Child Pornography Law and the Proliferation of the Sexualized Child', in Atkins, R. and S. Mintcheva, *Censoring Culture: Contemporary Threats to Free Expression*, New York: The New Press, 2006, 228–42, at 234.

on the Internet and enhancing the protection of children from ıd abuse.[43]

research regarding the nature of the trade in child pornography is ording to a recent International Centre for Missing and Exploited tled *Creating a Global Agenda to Combat Child Pornography*, sting research in this field is evidenced in two ways:[44]

1. There is ... k of basic comparative knowledge about the nature of the trade in abuse images, the extent of material available, and the principle ways in which access to and possession of abuse images relates to contact offences against children. Concepts of dangerousness and risk assessment, for example, largely predate the advent of Internet child pornography.
2. This lack of basic information is reflected in the inadequate and largely nonexistent conceptual development in this area. For example, models of offending appropriate to pre-Internet days are applied to Internet related offences without any effort made to explore commonalities or differences in offending activities. The sense of the Internet itself being a factor seems to be largely ignored in many accounts of offending. Analyses of sex offending are not characterized by conceptual sophistication, which allied with the more fundamental lack of knowledge about the role of pornography in general in the offending process, has resulted in policy initiatives and operational police activity related to abuse images effectively developing in a conceptual vacuum.

There are also concerns that the problem of digital distribution may soon escalate to mobile phones,[45] and to public and private file sharing networks.[46] Further understanding of the nature of these crimes, and how individual offenders as well as paedophile networks operate, is essential to better address the problem.

Further research and investigative work is also required to assist in the identification of child victims who appear in abusive and sexually explicit images. There have been attempts to develop a global database of abusive images,[47] but there

---

43 See generally, Gallagher, B., C. Fraser, K. Christmann and B. Hodgson, *International and Internet Child Sexual Abuse and Exploitation* (2006), Research Report, Huddersfield: University of Huddersfield, at <http://www.hud.ac.uk/hhs/research/acs/staff/Inter_net_CSA.pdf>. See further, Chase, E. and J. Statham, 'Commercial and Sexual Exploitation of Children and Young People in the UK – A Review' (2005), *Child Abuse Review* 14, 4–25.

44 International Centre for Missing and Exploited Children report, *Creating a Global Agenda to Combat Child Pornography*, 2003, at <http://www.icmec.org/en_X1/pdf/CreatingAGlobalAgenda.pdf>, p. 55.

45 Palmer, T., *Just One Click: Sexual Abuse of Children and Young People through the Internet and Mobile Telephone Technology*, Barnardo's, 2004.

46 United States General Accounting Office, *File Sharing Programs: Users of Peer-to-Peer Networks can readily access child pornography*, Statement of Linda D. Koontz, Director, Information Management Issues, Testimony Before the Subcommittee on Commerce, Trade, and Consumer Protection, Committee on Energy and Commerce, House of Representatives, GAO-04-757T, May 2004.

47 International Centre for Missing and Exploited Children report, *Creating a Global Agenda to Combat Child Pornography*, 2003, at <http://www.icmec.org/en_X1/pdf/CreatingAGlobalAgenda.pdf>, p. 55.

has been little success and disturbingly few children are ever identified.[48] In 2001 Interpol established the International Child Sexual Exploitation Database which, as of May 2006, contains 'photographic evidence of more than 20,000 individual children who have been sexually abused for the production of child abuse images'.[49] The Interpol database was created with the intention of 'facilitating the sharing of images and information to help law enforcement agencies identify new victims'.[50] However, Save the Children claimed at the time that 'fewer than 500 of these victims had been identified and become subject to protection'.[51] Coordinated international efforts are needed to identify victims and prevent ongoing abuse. Rehabilitation and support programmes for children who have been saved from sexual exploitation and severe physical and psychological abuse are equally essential.

Policy makers need to gain a better understanding of the nature of offending and the nature of the offenders[52] and whether, for example, there are more offenders who sexually victimize children and at the same time commit child pornography related offences. Research into dual offending has been conducted in the United States,[53] but studies have yet to 'explain how possessing child pornography is related to child sexual victimization or whether it causes or encourages such victimization'.[54] Further research into convicted offenders could help to assess whether there are other types of offenders in addition to dual offenders, including whether some offenders are 'recreational users' who view and download child pornography out of curiosity or for a limited period of time rather than having a specific sexual interest in children.[55] The risk such offenders pose to children could then be more accurately assessed.

48 Taylor, M. and E. Quayle, *Child Pornography: An Internet Crime*, Hove: Brunner-Routledge, 2003, 19. See further, Holland, G., 'Identifying Children Who Are Victims of Child Abuse Images: An Analysis of Successful Identifications', in E. Quayle and M. Taylor (eds), *Viewing Child Pornography on the Internet: Understanding the Offence, Managing the Offender, Helping the Victims*, Lyme Regis: Russell House Publishing, 2005, 75–91.

49 Save the Children Europe, *Visible Evidence – Forgotten Children*, 2006, at <http://www.childcentre.info/projects/internet/abusiveimage/dbaFile13904.pdf>, p. 2.

50 Interpol, FactSheet: Crimes Against Children, COM/FS/2006-03/THB-03, at <http://www.interpol.int/Public/ICPO/FactSheets/THB03.pdf>. Similarly, the UK through the Child Exploitation and Online Protection Centre (CEOP, <http://www.ceop.gov.uk/>) developed a similar database called ChildBase.

51 Save the Children Europe, *Visible Evidence – Forgotten Children*, 2006, at <http://www.childcentre.info/projects/internet/abusiveimage/dbaFile13904.pdf>, p. 2.

52 Hood, R., S. Shute, M. Feilzer and A. Wilcox, 'Reconviction Rates of Serious Sex Offenders and Assessments of Their Risk', Findings No. 164, Home Office: Research, Development and Statistics Directorate, 2002.

53 See Wolak, J., D. Finkelhor and K.J. Mitchell, *Child-Pornography Possessors Arrested in Internet-Related Crimes: Findings From the National Juvenile Online Victimization Study*, National Center for Missing and Exploited Children, 2005, at <http://www.missingkids.com/en_US/publications/NC144.pdf>.

54 Ibid. Note further Seto M.C. and A.W. Eke, 'The Criminal Histories and Later Offending of Child Pornography Offenders' (2005), *Sexual Abuse: A Journal of Research and Treatment* 17, 201–10.

55 See generally, Wortley, R. and S. Smallbone, *Child Pornography on the Internet*, Problem Oriented Guides for Police Problem Specific Guides Series, No. 41, US Department

Other means to combat the problem of sexual exploitation and abuse include the education of children. As a recent UNICEF report observes, 'education and awareness-raising bring sexual abuse and exploitation of children out of the shadows. They uncover the many facets of the problem, including the attitudes that allow the sexual abuse of children to take place, and help create a culture that refuses to accept any form of violence against children.'[56] The report states, 'schools must educate children to recognize and avoid high-risk situations. In addition, societies must become open to recognizing and taking action against the exploitation of their children.'[57] Governments and international organizations, therefore, should dedicate more resources to empowering children in the fight against commercial sexual exploitation and abuse.

Finally, there needs to be more open, independent and informed debate about the nature of child pornography related crimes and offenders. Since the 1990s we have witnessed the 'unanimous moral condemnation of the threat posed to moral order'[58] by paedophilia and child pornography. Media,[59] government officials[60] and to some extent those working in the field of child protection often distort the meaning of 'paedophilia', and within the context of Internet crimes, those offenders who solely download or view child pornography are often tagged as predatory paedophiles[61] whose sexual appetite and 'assaults often escalate to murder',[62] even though the causal link between viewing and 'active molestation is tenuous and unproven'.[63] Garland argues, 'the risks they are perceived as posing, the anxieties they call forth, the sense of powerlessness that they engender, all work to reinforce the felt need for the imposition of order and the importance of a strong state response.'[64] Paedophiles,

---

of Justice, Office of Community Oriented Policing Services, May 2006, at <http://www.cops.usdoj.gov/mime/open.pdf?Item=1729>, 14–15. Note further Quayle, E., M. Taylor, L. Wright and M. Merooga, *Only Pictures? Therapeutic Work with Internet Sex Offenders*, Lyme Regis: Russell House, 2005.

56 UNICEF, *Profiting from Abuse*, 2001, at <http://www.unicef.org/publications/files/pub_profiting_en.pdf>.

57 Ibid.

58 Critcher, C., 'Media, Government and Moral Panic: The Politics of Paedophilia in Britain 2000–1' (2002), *Journalism Studies*, 3(4), 521–35, at 527.

59 Wilson, D. and I. Silverman, *Innocence Betrayed: Paedophilia, the Media and Society*, Cambridge: Polity Press, 2002.

60 Ashenden, S., 'Policing Perversion: The Contemporary Governance of Paedophilia (2002), *Cultural Values* 6(1–2), 197–222; Ashenden, S., *Governing Child Sexual Abuse*, London: Routledge, 2003.

61 Socarides, C. and L. Loeb (eds), *The Mind of the Paedophile: Psychoanalytic Perspectives*, London: Karnac Books, 2004.

62 Jenkins, P., 'Target the technical experts to suppress the child porn trade', *Guardian*, 23 January 2003. See further, Jenkins, P., *Intimate Enemies: Moral Panics in Contemporary Great Britain*, New Brunswick, NJ: AldineTransaction, 1992.

63 Ibid. See further, Seto, M.C., A. Maric and E.B. Howard, 'The Role of Pornography in the Etiology of Sexual Aggression' (2001), *Aggression and Violent Behavior* 6, 35–53.

64 Garland, D., *The Culture of Control: Crime and Social Order in Contemporary Society*, Oxford: Oxford University Press, 2001, 135–6.

therefore become a 'suitable enemy',[65] useful for a 'conservative social politics that stresses the need for authority, family values, and the resurrection of traditional morality.'[66] Their behaviour should neither be condoned nor tolerated, but at the same time moral panics[67] should be resisted. Society and the media demand swift justice and the punishment of those who commit child pornography related offences. This in turn leads to a panic-led 'disproportionate reaction to an exaggerated menace'.[68] Arguably, examples cited within this book include the pursuance of making (instead of possession) and incitement charges in the UK, the inclusion of written words and drawings within the definition of child pornography in Canada if they depict child sexual abuse,[69] and the extension of child pornography laws to children under the age of 18 rather than 16, all in the name of child protection. Mintcheva argues, 'the panic around child pornography has reached such proportions that the rationale for criminalizing it – that children are abused while producing the images – has been forgotten.'[70] This 'disproportionate share of official attention'[71] is arguably a small price to pay for the sake for the safety of children. However, despite all good intentions and a multi-agency, multi-actor effort to combat Internet child pornography, the question remains whether real children are actually better protected from the risk of sexual exploitation and abuse. Child pornography laws and the fight against child pornography have not always addressed this issue sufficiently closely. A majority of those prosecuted for child pornography related offences are not contact offenders, and there are different degrees of offensiveness as noted in previous chapters. Jenkins takes this point further, stating 'if we accept the myth that every casual child porn user is a potential Moors murderer, then we are going to squander a vast amount of official resources going after him, rather than doing something that might actually reduce the volume of child porn traffic. Focusing just on low-level consumers will do nothing to achieve this end, any more than trying to arrest everyone who has ever

65 Ibid., at 136.

66 Ibid.

67 Cohen, S., *Folk Devils and Moral Panics: Creation of Mods and Rockers*, London: Routledge: 30th Anniversary edition, 2002; Jenkins, P., *Moral Panic: Changing Concepts of the Child Molester in Modern America*, New Haven, CT: Yale University Press, 1998.

68 West, D., 'Paedophilia: Plague or Panic?' (2000), *Journal of Forensic Psychiatry* 11(3), 511–31, at 528.

69 A British Columbia Supreme Court judge who found the Canadian Criminal Code provisions unconstitutional during the *R v. Sharpe* trial was 'left with the stigma of having failed to defend children'. See Jenkins, P., *Moral Panic: Changing Concepts of the Child Molester in Modern America*, New Haven, CT: Yale University Press, 1998, 238. See further, Sauvageau, F., D. Schneiderman and D. Taras, *The Last Word: Media Coverage of the Supreme Court of Canada*, Vancouver: University of British Columbia Press, 2006.

70 Mintcheva, S., 'Protection or Politics? The Use and Abuse of Children', in R. Atkins and S. Mintcheva (eds), *Censoring Culture: Contemporary Threats to Free Expression*, New York: The New Press, 2006, 171.

71 Jenkins, P., *Moral Panic: Changing Concepts of the Child Molester in Modern America*, New Haven, CT: Yale University Press, 1998, 238.

taken an ecstasy pill will eliminate illicit drugs.'[72] Child pornography 'is only one element of the even more pervasive and deeply rooted problem of sexual abuse'.[73] An approach which takes the protection of children from sexual exploitation as its principal focus is accordingly preferable to policies which only target Internet child pornography. The chain of commercial sexual exploitation of children can be long[74] and complex, but the focus of any policy initiative in this field should be on those who fuel and financially profit from the market they have created and those who directly engage in the abuse of children.

72 Jenkins, P., 'Target the technical experts to suppress the child porn trade', *Guardian*, 23 January 2003.

73 Carol Bellamy, Executive Director, United Nations Children's Fund, UNICEF, *Profiting from Abuse*, 2001, at <http://www.unicef.org/publications/files/pub_profiting_en.pdf>, foreword.

74 UNICEF, *Profiting from Abuse*, 2001, at <http://www.unicef.org/publications/files/pub_profiting_en.pdf>.

Bibliography

Adelman, R.W., 'The Constitutionality of Congressional Efforts to Ban Computer-Generated Child Pornography: A First Amendment Assessment of S. 1237' (1996), *J. Marshall Journal of Computer and Information Law* 14 483–90.

Adler, A., 'Inverting the First Amendment' (2001), 149 *University of Pennsylvania Law Review* 921.

——, 'The Perverse Law of Child Pornography' (2001), 101 *Columbia. Law Review* 209.

——, 'Child Pornography Law and the Proliferation of the Sexualized Child', in R. Atkins and S. Mintcheva, *Censoring Culture: Contemporary Threats to Free Expression*, New York: New Press, 2006, 228–42.

Akdeniz, Y., 'Computer Pornography: A Comparative Study of the US and UK Obscenity Laws and Child Pornography Laws in Relation to the Internet' (1996), *International Review of Law, Computers and Technology* 10(2), 235–61.

——, 'Governance of Pornography and Child Pornography on the Global Internet: A Multi-Layered Approach', in L. Edwards and C. Waelde (eds), *Law and the Internet: Regulating Cyberspace*, Oxford: Hart, 1997, 223–41.

——, 'The Regulation of Pornography and Child Pornography on the Internet' (1997) (1), *The Journal of Information, Law and Technology*.

——, 'To Link or Not to Link: Problems with World Wide Web Links on the Internet' (1997), *International Review of Law, Computers and Technology* 11(2), 281–98.

——, 'The European Union and Illegal and Harmful Content on the Internet' (1998), *Journal of Civil Liberties* 3(1), March, 31–6.

——, 'Case Analysis: Laurence Godfrey v. Demon Internet Limited' (1999), *Journal of Civil Liberties*, 4(2), 260–67.

——, 'The Regulation of Internet Content in Europe: Governmental Control vs. Self-Responsibility' (1999), *Swiss Political Science Review*, 5(2), 123–31.

——, *Sex on the Net? The Dilemma of Policing Cyberspace*, Reading: South Street Press, 1999.

——, 'Anonymous Now', *Index on Censorship*, The Privacy Issue (2000) (3), June, 57–62.

——, 'Child Pornography', in Y. Akdeniz, C. Walker and D. Wall (eds), *The Internet, Law and Society*, Harlow: Addison Wesley Longman, 2000, 231–49.

——, 'Policing the Internet: Regulation and Censorship', in R. Gibson and S. Ward (eds), *Reinvigorating Democracy? British Politics and the Internet*, Aldershot: Ashgate, 2000, 169–88.

——, Case Review: League Against Racism and Antisemitism (LICRA), French Union of Jewish Students, v. Yahoo! Inc. (USA), Yahoo France (2001), *Electronic Business Law Reports*, 1(3), 110–20.

——, 'Governing Pornography and Child Pornography on the Internet: The UK Approach', in Cyber-Rights, Protection, and Markets: A Symposium (2001) 32, *University of West Los Angeles Law Review* 247–75.

——, 'Anonymity, Democracy, and Cyberspace', *Social Research* (2002) 69(1), Spring, 180–94.

——, Case Report: Court of Appeal Clarifies the Law on Downloading Child Pornography from the Web (2002), *Computer Law and Security Report*, 18(6), 433–5.

——, *Stocktaking on Efforts to Combat Racism on the Internet*, background report for the High Level Seminar on Racism and the Internet, Intergovernmental Working Group on the Effective Implementation of the Durban Declaration and Programme of Action, Fourth session, Geneva, 16–27 January 2006, E/CN.4/2006/WG.21/BP.1, published by the United Nations High Commissioner for Human Rights (UNHCHR) Office: Geneva, January 2006, at <http://www.ohchr.org/english/issues/racism/groups/docs/e_cn4_2006_wg21_bp1.doc> and <http://www.cyber-rights.org/reports/ya_un_paper_int_06.pdf>.

——, An Advocacy Handbook for the Non Governmental Organizations: The Council of Europe's Cybercrime Convention 2001 and the additional protocol on the criminalisation of acts of a racist or xenophobic nature committed through computer systems (Revised February 2007), online: Cyber-Rights and Cyber-Liberties <http://www.cyber-rights.org/cybercrime/coe_handbook_crcl.pdf>.

——, 'Governing Racist Content on the Internet: National and International Responses' (2007), *University of New Brunswick Law Journal* (Canada), 56, Spring, 103–61.

——, 'Possession and Dispossession: A Critical Assessment of Defences in Possession of Indecent Photographs of Children Cases' (2007), *Criminal Law Review*, April, 274–88.

—— and N. Bohm, 'Internet Privacy: New Concerns about Cybercrime and the Rule of Law' (1999), *Information Technology and Communications Law Journal* (5), 20–24.

Akdeniz, Y. and N. Strossen, 'Sexually Oriented Expression', in Y. Akdeniz, C. Walker and D. Wall (eds), *The Internet, Law and Society*, Harlow: Addison Wesley Longman, 2000, 207–31.

Akdeniz, Y., N. Taylor and C, Walker, Regulation of Investigatory Powers Act 2000 (1): Bigbrother.gov.uk: State surveillance in the age of information and rights (2001), *Criminal Law Review*, February, 73–90.

Akdeniz, Y. and W.R.H. Rogers, 'Defamation on the Internet', in Y. Akdeniz, C. Walker and D. Wall (eds), *The Internet, Law and Society*, Harlow: Addison Wesley Longman, 2000, 294–317.

Alexander, S., S. Meuwese and A. Wolthuis, 'Policies and Developments Relating to the Sexual Exploitation of Children: The Legacy of the Stockholm Conference' (2000), *European Journal on Criminal Policy and Research* (8), 479–501.

Arnaldo, C.A. (ed.), *Child Abuse on the Internet: Ending the Silence*, New York: Berghahn Books, Paris: UNESCO, 2001.

Ashenden, S., 'Policing Perversion: The Contemporary Governance of Paedophilia' (2002), *Cultural Values*, 6(1–2), 197–222.

——, *Governing Child Sexual Abuse*, London: Routledge, 2003.

Ashworth, A., 'Sentencing', in M. Maguire, R. Morgan and R. Reiner (eds), *The Oxford Handbook of Criminology*, Oxford University Press, 2002, 1076–112.

Aster, A.Z., 'New study examines risk factors for child sexual offences', CrossCurrents, The Centre for Addiction and Mental Health (CAMH), at <http://www.camh.net/Publications/Cross_Currents/Autumn_2005/sexualoffences_crcuautumn05.html>.

Atkins, R. and S. Mintcheva (eds), *Censoring Culture: Contemporary Threats to Free Expression*, New York: New Press, 2006.

Attorney General's Commission on Pornography: Final Report, 2 vols., Washington, DC: US Government Printing Office, July 1986.

AuCoin, K., *Children and Youth as Victims of Violent Crime*, Statistics Canada, Catalogue no. 85-002-XIE, 25(1) (April 2005) at <http://www.statcan.ca:8096/bsolc/english/bsolc?catno=85-002-XIE2005001>.

Bates, J., *The Ore Reports*, at <http://www.computer-investigations.com/index3.html>.

Bender, G., 'Bavaria v. Felix Somm: The Pornography Conviction of the Former CompuServe Manager', *International Journal of Communications Laws and Policy* (1) (Summer 1998), at <http://www.digital-law.net/IJCLP/1_1998/ijclp_webdoc_14_1_1998.html>.

Benedet, J., 'Children in Pornography after Sharpe' (2002), *43 C. de D.* 327.

Better Regulation Task Force (UK), interim report on *Self-Regulation*, October 1999.

——, *Alternatives to State Regulation*, July 2000, <http://www.cabinet-office.gov.uk/regulation/TaskForce/2000/StateRegulation.pdf>.

——, *Regulating Cyberspace – Better Regulation for E-Commerce*, December 2000, <http://devtemp1/regulation/TaskForce/2001/BRTF-E-Commerce.pdf>.

British Columbia Civil Liberties Association, 'Brief of the British Columbia Civil Liberties Association re Bill C-2', at <http://www.bccla.org/othercontent/05billc2.htm>.

Buckman, D.F., 'Validity, Construction, and Application of 18 U.S.C.A. § 2252A(a), Proscribing Certain Activities Relating to Material Constituting or Containing Child Pornography', 2 *A.L.R. Fed.* 2d 533.

Bullough, V.L., 'Age of Consent A Historical Overview' (2006), *Journal of Psychology and Human Sexuality*, 16(2–3), 25–42.

Cabinet Office, Prime Minister's Strategy Unit, *Connecting the UK: the Digital Strategy*, April 2005.

Campbell, D., 'A flaw in the child porn witch-hunt', *Sunday Times*, 26 June 2005.

——, 'Operation Ore Exposed', *PC Pro*, 1 July, 2005.

——, 'Sex, Lies and the Missing Videotape', *PC Pro*, 1 April 2007.

——, 'Operation Ore flawed by fraud', *Guardian*, 19 April 2007.

Casey, E., *Digital Evidence and Computer Crime*, London: Academic Press, 2004.

Cavazos, E.A. and G. Morin, *Cyberspace and the Law: Your Rights and Duties in the On-Line World*, Cambridge, MA: MIT Press, 1994.

Chase, E. and J. Statham, 'Commercial and Sexual Exploitation of Children and Young People in the UK – A Review' (2005), *Child Abuse Review*, 14, 4–25.

Children Europe, *Visible Evidence – Forgotten Children*, 2006, at <http://www.childcentre.info/projects/internet/abusiveimage/dbaFile13904.pdf>.

Clayton, R., 'Failures in a Hybrid Content Blocking System', research paper presented at the Workshop on Privacy Enhancing Technologies, Dubrovnik, Croatia, 30 May 2005 – 1 June 2005, at <http://www.cl.cam.ac.uk/~rnc1/cleanfeed.pdf>.

Cohen, S., *Folk Devils and Moral Panics: Creation of the Mods and Rockers*, London: Routledge, 30th Anniversary edition, 2002.

Conseil d'État Report (France) on *Internet et les réseaux numériques*, 8 September 1998, at <http://www.conseil-etat.fr/ce/rappor/index_ra_liau01.shtml>. An English version is also available from the same website (French Council of State Report: *The Internet and Digital Networks*).

Council of Europe, Additional Protocol concerning the Criminalisation of Acts of a Racist and Xenophobic Nature Committed Through Computer Systems.

——, Convention on Cybercrime, ETS No: 185, at <http://conventions.coe.int/Treaty/EN/Treaties/Html/185.htm>.

——, Committee of Experts on the protection of children against sexual exploitation and sexual abuse (PC-ES), Draft Convention on the protection of children against sexual exploitation and sexual abuse: Invitation to the Parliamentary Assembly to give an opinion, CM(2007)24, 14 February 2007, 989 Meeting, 14 March 2007.

——, European Committee On Crime Problems (CDPC), Explanatory Memorandum to the Convention on Cybercrime, document prepared by the Secretariat and former experts of the PC-CY Committee, Strasbourg, 14 February 2001, EXPC-CY (2001) 1, adopted on 8 November 2001.

——, European Committee on Crime Problems, Explanatory Memorandum related to the Cybercrime Convention, CDPC (2001) 17, Strasbourg, 29 June 2001, at <http://www.privacyinternational.org/issues/cybercrime/coe/cybercrimememo-final.html>.

——, Explanatory Report of the Council of Europe Cybercrime Convention, 2001, at <http://conventions.coe.int/treaty/en/Reports/Html/185.htm>.

——, Parliamentary Assembly, Report of debates of the Second Part of the 2001 Ordinary Session: *Draft convention against cyber crime*, Assembly Spring Session – 23–27 April 2001, 24 April 2001, at <http://www.cyber-rights.org/documents/coe_assembly.htm>.

——, Parliamentary Assembly Resolution 1307 (2002), *Sexual exploitation of children: zero tolerance*, text adopted by the Assembly on 27 September 2002 (32nd Sitting).

——, Recommendation 1065 (1987) of the Parliamentary Assembly of the Council of Europe on the traffic in children and other forms of child exploitation.

——, Recommendation No. R (91) 11 concerning sexual exploitation, pornography and prostitution of, and trafficking in, children and young adults.

——, Recommendation Rec(2001)8 on self-regulation concerning both illegal and harmful content.

——, Recommendation Rec(2001)16 on the protection of children against sexual exploitation.

——, Resolution No. 3 on sexual exploitation, pornography and prostitution of, and trafficking in, children and young adults of the 16th Conference of European Ministers of Justice (Lisbon, 1988).

Critcher, C., 'Media, Government and Moral Panic: The Politics of Paedophilia in Britain 2000–1' (2002), *Journalism Studies*, 3(4), 521–35.

Csonka, P. (Secretary to Committee PC-CY, Council of Europe), Contribution to the Conference on combating child pornography on the Internet, Vienna, 29 September – 1 October 1999, through <http://www.stop-childpornog.at/>.

Culture, Media and Sport Committee (HC, UK), *Second Report on the Communications White Paper*, Volume I HC 161-I, 15 March 2001.

Cyber-Rights and Cyber-Liberties (UK), Report, 'Who Watches the Watchmen: Internet Content Rating Systems, and Privatised Censorship', November 1997, <http://www.cyber-rights.org/watchmen.htm>.

——, Report, 'Who Watches the Watchmen: Part II – Accountability and Effective Self-Regulation in the Information Age', September 1998 at <http://www.cyber-rights.org/watchmen-ii.htm>.

Dardenne. S., *I Choose to Live*, London: Virago, 1996.

Davis, D., *The Internet Detective: An Investigator's Guide*, Police Research Group, Home Office, 1998.

Department for Trade and Industry (UK), 'Rating, Reporting, Responsibility, For Child Pornography and Illegal Material on the Internet', September 1996, at <http://www.mit.edu/activities/safe/labeling/r3.htm>.

Department of Justice Canada, *The Relationship between Child Pornography and the Commission of Sexual Offences against Children: A Review of the Literature*. Report prepared by L. Jill Rettinger, Ottawa: Research and Statistics Division, Department of Justice Canada, 2000, at <http://www.justice.gc.ca/en/ps/rs/rep/2000/rr00-5.html>.

——, Backgrounder: Key Highlights of Proposed Amendments to Protect Children and Other Vulnerable Persons, October 2004, at <http://www.justice.gc.ca/en/news/nr/2004/doc_31248.html>.

Department of Justice (US), *FY 2004 Performance and Accountability Report*, at <http://www.usdoj.gov/ag/annualreports/pr2004/P2/p04-13.pdf>.

Dowling, J., 'Noah v. AOL Time Warner: Are There Legitimate Barriers to Civil Rights Protection on the Internet?' (2004), 14 *Alb. L.J. Sci. and Tech.* 775.

Doyle, K. and D. Lacombe, 'Scapegoat in Risk Society: The Case of Pedophile/Child Pornographer Robin Sharpe' (2000), 20 *Studies in Law, Politics and Society* 183.

Drake, W.J. (ed.), *Reforming Internet Governance: Perspectives from the Working Group on Internet Governance*, November 2005, at <http://www.wgig.org/docs/book/WGIG_book.pdf>.

Dugan, K., 'Regulating What's Not Real: Federal Regulation in the Aftermath of Ashcroft v. Free Speech Coalition' (2004), 48 *Saint Louis University Law Journal* 1063 (Spring).

Dwyer, S., *The Problem of Pornography*, Belmont, CA: Wadsworth, 1995.

Eberwine, E.T., 'Note and Comment: Sound and Fury Signifying Nothing?: Jurgen Bussow's Battle against Hate-speech on the Internet' (2004), 49 *New York Law School Law Review* 353.

Edwards, S.M., 'Prosecuting "child pornography": Possession and Taking of Indecent Photographs' (2000), *Journal of Social Welfare and Family Law* 22(1), 1–21.

EU, Common Position on the CoE Convention, 27 May 1999. (OJ L 142, 05/06/1999 pp. 1–2.)

——, Council Decision of 29 May 2000 to combat child pornography on the Internet (2000/375/JHA), OJ L 138, 09/06/2000 p. 1.

——, Council Framework Decision 2004/68/JHA of 22 December 2003 on combating the sexual exploitation of children and child pornography (see OJ L 013 20 January 2004, pp. 44–8.

——, Council Recommendation of 24 September 1998 on the development of the competitiveness of the European audiovisual and information services industry by promoting national frameworks aimed at achieving a comparable and effective level of protection of minors and human dignity as published in the OJ L 270 of 7 October 1998, p. 48 (98/560/EC).

——, Decision No /98/EC of the European Parliament and of the Council of adopting a Multiannual Community Action Plan on promoting safer use of the Internet by combating illegal and harmful content on global networks, December 1998.

——, Decision No 276/1999/EC of the European Parliament and of the Council of 25 January 1999 adopting a Multiannual Community Action Plan on promoting safer use of the Internet by combating illegal and harmful content on global networks, OJ L 33, 6 February 1999.

——, Decision No 1151/2003/EC of the European Parliament and of the Council of 16 June 2003, amending Decision No 276/1999/EC adopting a Multiannual Community Action Plan on promoting safer use of the Internet by combating illegal and harmful content on global networks.

——, Decision No 854/2005/EC of the European Parliament and of the Council establishing a Multiannual Community Programme on promoting safer use of the Internet and new online technologies, PE-CONS 3688/1/04 REV1, Strasbourg, 11 May 2005.

——, Directive 2000/31/EC of the European Parliament and of the Council of 8 June 2000 on certain legal aspects of information society services, in particular electronic commerce, in the Internal Market ('Directive on electronic commerce') vol. 43, OJ L 178 17 July 2000 p. 1.

——, Directive 2002/58/ concerning the processing of personal data and the protection of privacy in the electronic communications sector (Directive on privacy and electronic communications) of 12 July 2002, *Official Journal of the European Communities*, 31 July 2002, L 201 pp. 37–47.

——, Directive 2006/24/EC of the European Parliament and of the Council of 15 March 2006 on the retention of data generated or processed in connection with the provision of publicly available electronic communications services or of public communications networks and amending Directive 2002/58/EC, L 105 13 April 2006, pp. 54–63.

——, Economic and Social Committee of the European Commission, *Opinion on the Proposal for a Council Decision adopting a Multiannual Community Action Plan on promoting safe use of the Internet* (*Official Journal of the European Communities*, 98/C 214/08, Brussels–Luxembourg, 10 July 1998) pp. 29–32.

——, Opinion of the Committee of the Regions on the 'Proposal for a Council Framework Decision on combating the sexual exploitation of children and child pornography', *Official Journal of the European Communities*, C 357/41-43, 14 December 2001.

——, Opinion of the Economic and Social Committee on 'eEurope 2002 An information society for all Draft Action Plan', OJ C 123, 25 April 2001 pp. 36–46, 25 April 2001.

——, Opinion of the Economic and Social Committee on 'A programme for child protection on the Internet' (2002/C 48/06), C 48/27-32 *Official Journal of the European Communities*, 21 February 2002.

——, Opinion of the Economic and Social Committee on the 'Proposal for a Council Recommendation concerning the protection of minors and human dignity in audiovisual and information services' (98/C 214/07), 10 July, 1998, EN C 214/25 *Official Journal of the European Communities*, C 214/25.

——, Report (Rapporteur: Timothy Kirkhope) of the Committee on Citizens' Freedoms and Rights, Justice and Home Affairs on the initiative of the Republic of Austria with a view to adopting a Council Decision to combat child pornography on the Internet (10317/1999 – C5-0318/1999 – 1999/0822(CNS)), A5-0090/2000, 28 March 2000.

European Commission, Amended proposal for a European Parliament and Council Directive on certain legal aspects of electronic commerce in the Internal Market (presented by the Commission pursuant to Article 250 (2) of the EC-Treaty), COM(1999)427 final, 98/0325 (COD).

——, Communication to the Council and European Parliament, *eEurope 2002 update* prepared by the European Commission for the European Council in Nice, 7–8 December 2000, COM/2000/0783 final.

——, Communication to the Council and the European Parliament COM(2000) 854 final 2, Brussels, 22 January, 2001.

——, Communication to the Council and the European Parliament on combating trafficking in human beings and combating the sexual exploitation of children and child pornography, COM(2000)854 final/2, Brussels, 22 January 2001.

——, Communication to the Council and the European Parliament on Creating a Safer Information Society by Improving the Security of Information Infrastructures and Combating Computer-related Crime, COM(2000) 890 final, Brussels, 26 January 2001.

——, Communication to the Council, the European Parliament, the Economic and Social Committee and the Committee of the Regions on Creating a Safer Information Society by Improving the Security of Information Infrastructures and Combating Computer-related Crime, COM(2000) 890 final, Brussels, 26 January 2001.

——, Communication to the Council and the European Parliament, *eEurope 2002: Impact and Priorities A communication to the Spring European Council in Stockholm*, 23–24 March 2001, COM/2001/0140 final.

——, Communication to the European Parliament, The Council, The Economic and Social Committee and the Committee of the Regions: Illegal and Harmful Content on the Internet, Com (96) 487, Brussels, 16 October 1996.

——, Communication to the European Parliament, the Council, the Economic and Social Committee and the Committee of the Regions Action Plan on promoting safe use of the Internet, November 1997.

——, Communication, *The Information Society and Development: the Role of the European Union* (COM(97) 351, Brussels–Luxembourg, 1997).

——, Communication, Follow-up to the Multiannual Community action plan on promoting safer use of the Internet by combating illegal and harmful content on global networks: Proposal for a decision of the European Parliament and of the Council amending Decision No 276/1999/EC adopting a Multiannual Community Action Plan on promoting safer use of the Internet by combating illegal and harmful content on global networks, COM 2002 152, Brussels, 22 March 2002, INFSO/D/5.

——, Communication on International Charter: The need for strengthened international co-ordination – Communication from the Commission to the European Parliament, the Council, the Economic and Social Committee and the Committee of the Regions (COM (98) 50, Brussels–Luxembourg).

——, *eEurope – An Information Society for all* – Progress report for the Special European Council on Employment, Economic reforms and social cohesion towards a Europe based on innovation and knowledge, Lisbon, 23 and 24 March 2000, COM/2000/0130 final, 8 March 2000.

——, *eEurope 2002 – An Information society for all – Draft Action Plan* prepared by the European Commission for the European Council in Feira – 19–20 June 2000, COM/2000/0330 final.

——, Evaluation Report from the Commission to the Council and the European Parliament on the application of Council Recommendation of 24 September 1998 concerning the protection of minors and human dignity, COM(2001) 106 final, Brussels, 27 February 2001.

——, Evaluation Report on the application of the recommendation concerning the protection of minors and human dignity (2001/C 213/03), 2001 OJ C 213, 31 July 2001.

——, *Green Paper on the Protection of Minors and Human Dignity in Audovisual and Information Services* (COM (96) 483 final, Brussels–Luxembourg, 16 October 1996).

——, 'Proposal for a European Parliament and Council Directive on certain legal aspects of electronic commerce in the internal market', COM(1998) 586 final, 98/0325 (COD), Brussels, 18 November 998.

——, Report to the European Parliament, the Council and the European Economic and Social Committee, *First report on the application of Directive 2000/31/EC on electronic commerce*, COM(2003) 702 final, Brussels, 21.11.2003, at <http://europa.eu.int/eur-lex/en/com/rpt/2003/com2003_0702en01.pdf>.

——, The second evaluation report to the Council and the European Parliament on the application of Council Recommendation of 24 September 1998 concerning the protection of minors and human dignity, COM(2003)776 final, adopted on 12 December 2003, at <http://eur-lex.europa.eu/LexUriServ/site/en/com/2003/com2003_0776en01.pdf>.

——, Staff Working paper, Ex Ante Evaluation: Safer Internet Plus, SEC(2004) 148, 12 March 2004, at <http://europa.eu.int/information_society/activities/sip/docs/pdf/si_plus/exante.pdf>.

——, Working Party Report, *Illegal and Harmful Content on the Internet*, 1996.

European Parliament, legislative resolution on the proposal for a Council Framework Decision on combating the sexual exploitation of children and child pornography (COM(2000) 854-C5-0043/2001–2001/0025(CNS)), 2002/C 53 E/108-113, vol. 45, 28 February 2002.

——, Recommendation on the Strategy for Creating a Safer Information Society by Improving the Security of Information Infrastructures and Combating Computer-related Crime (2001/2070(COS)), C 72 E/323-329, *Official Journal of the European Communities*, 21 March 2002.

——, report on Sexual exploitation of Children (A5-0206/2001).

——, Resolution of 24 October 1997 on the Commission Green Paper on the protection of minors and human dignity in audiovisual and information services (COM(96) 483).

——, Resolution on the Commission communication on illegal and harmful content on the Internet, 24 April 1997.

——, Strategy for Creating a Safer Information Society (A5-0284/2001), text adopted on 6 September, 2001.

European Parliament and Council, An amended proposal for a Recommendation on the Protection of Minors and Human Dignity and the Right of Reply in relation to the Competitiveness of the European Audiovisual and Information Services Industry on 20 January 2006, COM(2006)31final.

——, Recommendation on the protection of minors and human dignity and on the right of reply in relation to the competitiveness of the European audiovisual and online information services industry, 2004/0117 (COD), LEX 775, PE-CONS 3683/06, Brussels, 20 December 2006.

Feldmeier, J.P., 'Close Enough for Government Work: An Examination of Congressional Efforts to Reduce the Government's Burden of Proof in Child Pornography Cases' (2003), 30 *Northern Kentucky Law Review* 205, 220–23.

Frydman, B. and I. Rorive, 'Regulating Internet Content through Intermediaries in Europe and the USA' (2002), *Zeitschrift für Rechtssoziologie* 23(1), S. 41–59, Max Planck Institute, at <http://www.isys.ucl.ac.be/etudes/cours/linf2202/Frydman_&_Rorive_2002.pdf>.

Gallagher, B., C. Fraser, K. Christmann and B. Hodgson, *International and Internet Child Sexual Abuse and Exploitation* (2006) Research Report, Huddersfield: University of Huddersfield, at <http://www.hud.ac.uk/hhs/research/acs/staff/Inter_net_CSA.pdf>.

Garland, D., *The Culture of Control: Crime and Social Order in Contemporary Society*, Oxford University Press, 2001.

Gelbstein, E. and J. Kurbalija, *Internet Governance: Issues, Actors, and Divide*, DIPLO report, 2005, at <http://www.diplomacy.edu/isl/ig/>.

Gibbons, T., 'Computer Generated Pornography' (1995), *International Yearbook of Law Computers and Technology* (9), 83–95.

Gillespie, A., 'Sentences for Offences Involving Child Pornography' (2003), *Criminal Law Review* (February), 81–92.

——, 'The Sexual Offences Act 2003: (3) Tinkering with "Child Pornography"' (2004), *Criminal Law Review* (May), 361–8.

——, 'Child Pornography: Balancing Substantive and Evidential Law to Safeguard Children Effectively from Abuse' (2005), *International Journal of Evidence and Proof* 9(1), 29–50.

Gotell, L., 'Inverting Image and Reality: *R. v. Sharpe* and the Moral Panic Around Child Pornography' (2001/2002), 12 *Const. Forum Const.* 9.

Graupner, H., 'The 17-Year-Old Child an Absurdity of the Late 20th Century' (2006), *Journal of Psychology and Human Sexuality*, 16(2–3), 7–24.

Healy, M.A., 'Child Pornography: An International Perspective', paper presented at the World Congress against Commercial Sexual Exploitation of Children, Sweden: ECPAT, 1996, at <http://www.usis.usemb.se/children/csec/215e.htm>.

Hirst, P. and G. Thompson, 'Globalization and the Future of the Nation State' (1995), *Economy and Society* 24(3), 408–42.

Hofmeister, L., '14 to 18 Year Olds as "Children" by Law: Reflections on Developments in National and European Law' (2006), *Journal of Psychology and Human Sexuality*, 16(2–3), 63–70.

Holland, G., 'Identifying Children Who are Victims of Child Abuse Images: An Analysis of Successful Identifications', in E. Quayle and M. Taylor (eds), *Viewing Child Pornography on the Internet: Understanding the Offence, Managing the Offender, Helping the Victims*, Lyme Regis: Russell House Publishing, 2005, 75–91.

Home Office (UK), *Consultation Paper on Possession of Extreme Pornographic Material*, August 2005, at <http://www.scotland.gov.uk/Publications/2005/08/30112423/24254>.

——, *Consultation on the Possession of Extreme Pornographic Material: Summary of responses and next steps*, August 2006, at <http://www.homeoffice.gov.uk/documents/cons-extreme-porn-3008051/Gvt-response-extreme-porn.pdf>.

——, *Consultation on Possession of Non-Photographic Visual Depictions of Child Sexual Abuse*, April 2007, at <http://www.homeoffice.gov.uk/documents/cons-2007-depiction-sex-abuse>.

Hood, R., S. Shute, M. Feilzer and A. Wilcox, 'Reconviction rates of serious sex offenders and assessments of their risk', Findings No. 164, Home Office: Research, Development and Statistics Directorate, 2002.

House of Commons (England and Wales), Home Affairs Committee, First Report on Computer Pornography, London: HMSO, 1994.

House of Commons Canada, Standing Committee on Justice and Legal Affairs, 'Report on Pornography', No. 18–3 (22 March 1978) at 18:8 (Chairman: M. MacGuigan).

House of Lords (England and Wales), Select Committee on Science and Technology, *Information Society*, HL 77, HMSO, 1995–96.

Howitt, D. and G. Cumberbatch, *Pornography: Impacts and Influences*, HMSO, 1990.

Human Rights Watch 'Silencing The Net: The Threat to Freedom of Expression On-line' (1996), *Monitors: A Journal of Human Rights and Technology* 1, Special Release available at <http://www.cwrl.utexas.edu/~monitors/>.

Institute for Jewish Policy Research and American Jewish Committee, *Antisemitism World Report 1997*.

International Centre for Missing and Exploited Children research report, *Child Pornography: Model Legislation and Global Review*, 2006, at <http://www.icmec.org/en_X1/pdf/English_2nd_Edition.pdf>.

Internet Crime Forum IRC sub-group, *Chat Wise, Street Wise – Children and Internet Chat Services*, March 2001, at <http://www.internetcrimeforum.org.uk>.

Internet Watch Foundation, Annual Report 2004, January 2005, at <http://www.iwf.org.uk/documents/20050204_annual_report_2004.pdf>.

——, Annual Report 2005, at <http://www.iwf.org.uk/documents/20060306_iwf_annual_report_2005_-_high_res.pdf>.

——, Annual Report 2006, at <http://www.iwf.org.uk/documents/20070412_iwf_annual_report_2006_(web).pdf>.

Irish Department of Justice, Equality and Law Reform, *Illegal and Harmful Use of the Internet* (Pn.5231, Dublin, 1998).

Jenkins, P., *Intimate Enemies: Moral Panics in Contemporary Great Britain*, New Brunswick, NJ: AldineTransaction, 1992.

——, *Moral Panic: Changing Concepts of the Child Molester in Modern America*, New Haven, CT: Yale University Press, 1998.

——, *Beyond Tolerance: Child Pornography on the Internet*, New York: New York University Press, 2001.

——, 'Target the technical experts to suppress the child porn trade', *Guardian*, 23 January 2003.

Jones, T. and T. Newburn, *Private Security and Public Policing*, Oxford: Clarendon Press, 1998.

Klain, E.J., H.J. Davies and M.A. Hicks, *Child Pornography: The Criminal-Justice-System Response*, 2001, ICMEC, at <http://www.missingkids.com/en_US/publications/NC81.pdf>.

Kleinhans, C., 'Virtual Child Porn: The Law and the Semiotics of the Image' (2004), *Journal of Visual Culture* 3(1), 17–34.

Kong, R., H. Johnson, S. Beattie and A. Cardillo, *Sexual Offences in Canada*, 2003, Statistics Canada, Catalogue no. 85-002-XIE, vol. 23, no. 6, at http://www.statcan.ca/english/freepub/85-<002-XIE/0060385-002-XIE.pdf>.

Kreston, S.S., 'Defeating the Virtual Defense in Child Pornography Prosecutions' (2004), *J. High Tech. L.* 4(49), 60–61.

Krone, T., 'A typology of online child pornography offending' (2004), *Trends and Issues in Crime and Criminal Justice*, No. 279, Australian Institute of Criminology Canberra, at <http://www.aic.gov.au/publications/cfi/cfi084.html> and at <http://www.aic.gov.au/publications/tandi2/tandi279.html>.

——, 'International police operations against online child pornography' (2005), *Trends and Issues in Crime and Criminal Justice*, No. 296, Australian Institute of Criminology, at <http://www.aic.gov.au/publications/tandi2/tandi296t.html>.

Leong, G., 'Computer Child Pornography: The Liability of Distributors?' (1998), *Crim. L.R.*, Special Edition: Crime, Criminal Justice and the Internet, December 1998, 19–29.

Levine, J., *Harmful to Minors: The Perils of Protecting Children from Sex*, New York: Thunder's Mouth Press, 2003.

MacKay, R., Bill C-2: An Act To Amend The Criminal Code (Protection Of Children And Other Vulnerable Persons) And The Canada Evidence Act, Parliamentary Information and Research Centre, Library of Canadian Parliament, 13 October 2004, at <http://www.parl.gc.ca/38/1/parlbus/chambus/house/bills/summaries/c2-e.pdf>.

MacLean, D., *Internet Governance: A Grand Collaboration*, New York: United Nations ICT Task Force, 2004.

Malanczuk, P., *Akehurst's Modern Introduction to International Law*, 7th edn, London: Routledge, 1997.

Manchester, C., 'More About Computer Pornography' (1995), *Crim. L.R.*, 645.

Marcella, A.J., *Cyber Forensics: A Field Manual for Collecting, Examining and Preserving Evidence of Computer Crimes*, Boca Raton, FL: Auerbach, 2002.

Martin, R., 'Case Comment: *R. v. Sharpe*' (2001), 39 *Alberta Law Review* 585.

Menninger, L.A., II, 'Cyberporn: Transmission of Images by Computer as Obscene, Harmful to Minors or Child Pornography' (2007), 61 *AMJUR POF 3d* 51 (updated in January 2007).

Mota, S.A., 'The U.S. Supreme Court Addresses the Child Pornography Prevention Act and Child Online Protection Act in *Ashcroft v. Free Speech Coalition* and Ashcroft *v. American Civil Liberties Union*' (2002), *Federal Communications Law Journal* 55(1), 85–98.

Myers, D.A., 'Defamation and the Quiescent Anarchy of the Internet: A Case Study of Cyber Targeting' (2006), 110 *Penn State International Law Review* 667 (Winter).

National Consumer Council report, *Models of Self-regulation: An Overview of Models in Business and the Professions*, November 2000 (reprinted with amendments from October 1999), at <http://www.ncc.org.uk/pubs/pdf/models_self_regulation.pdf>.

National Criminal Intelligence Service, *Project Trawler: Crime on the Information Highways*, June 1999, at <http://www.cyber-rights.org/documents/trawler.htm>.

O'Brien, S., *Child Pornography*, 2nd edn, Dubuque, IA: Kendall Hunt, 1992.

ODIHR, *Background Paper on Human Rights Considerations in Combating Incitement to Terrorism and Related Offences* (2006), online: OSCE <http://www.osce.org/documents/ odihr/2006/10/21814_en.pdf>.

The Office of National Statistics, Internet Access: 2006 First Release, 23 August 2006, at <http://www.statistics.gov.uk/pdfdir/inta0806.pdf>.

Oftel consultation document, *Encouraging Self and Co-regulation in Telecoms to Benefit Consumers*, June 2000 at <http://www.oftel.gov.uk/publications/about_oftel/self0600.htm>.

Ormerod, D., 'Commentary on *R v. Porter*' (2006), *Crim. L.R.*, 748.

——, 'Case Commentary on *R v. Skinner*' (2006), *Criminal Law Review*, Jan, 56–60.

——, 'Case Comment on *R v. Smith (Graham Westgarth)*' (2002), *Criminal Law Review*, August, 659–63.

Ost, S., 'Children at Risk: Legal and Societal Perceptions of the Potential Threat that the Possession of Child Pornography Poses to Society' (2002), *Journal of Law and Society* 29(3), September, 436–60.

——, 'Getting to Grips with Sexual Grooming? The New Offence under the Sexual Offences Act 2003' (2004), *Journal of Social Welfare and Family Law* 26(2), 147–59.

Oswell, D., 'When Images Matter: Internet Child Pornography, Forms of Observation and an Ethics of the Virtual' (2006), *Information, Communication and Society* 9(2), 244–65(22).

Palmer, T., *Just One Click: Sexual Abuse of Children and Young People through the Internet and Mobile Telephone Technology*, Barnardo's, 2004.

Parker, LJ, 'Validity, Construction, and Application of Federal Enactments Proscribing Obscenity and Child Pornography or Access Thereto on the Internet' (2005), *7 A.L.R. Fed. 2d 1*.

Persky, S. and J. Dixon, *On Kiddie Porn: Sexual Representation, Free Speech and the Robin Sharpe Case*, Vancouver: New Star Books, 2001.

Petley, J., 'Press furore fuels knee-jerk response to "extreme" pornography' (2006), *Index on Censorship*, October, at <www.indexonline.org/en/news/articles/2006/3/britain-violent-porn-bill-addresses-public-a.shtml>.

Quayle, E. and M. Taylor (eds), *Viewing Child Pornography on the Internet: Understanding the Offence, Managing the Offender, Helping the Victims*, Lyme Regis: Russell House, 2005.

——, L. Wright and M. Merooga, *Only Pictures? Therapeutic Work with Internet Sex Offenders*, Lyme Regis: Russell House, 2005.

Quigley, J., 'Child Pornography and the Right to Privacy' (1991), 43 *Florida Law Review* 347.

Rees, T. and D. Ormerod, 'Possession of Indecent Pseudo-photograph of Children' (2004), *Criminal Law Review*, December, 1039–41.

Rose, N. and P. Miller, 'Political Power beyond the State' (1992), 43 *British Journal of Sociology* 173.

Ross, J., 'R. v. Sharpe and Private Possession of Child Pornography' (2000), *Constitutional Forum* (11) 50.

Rowbottom, J., 'Obscenity Laws and the Internet: Targeting the Supply and Demand' (2006), *Criminal Law Review*, February, 97–109.

Ryder, B., 'The Harms of Child Pornography Law' (2003), 36 *U.B.C. L. Rev.* 101 (Winter).

Sauvageau, F., D. Schneiderman and D. Taras, *The Last Word: Media Coverage of the Supreme Court of Canada*, Vancouver: University of British Columbia Press, 2006.

Save the Children Europe, *Visible Evidence – Forgotten Children*, 2006, at <http://www.childcentre.info/projects/internet/abusiveimage/dbaFile13904.pdf>.

Schauer, F., 'Codifying the First Amendment: *New York v. Ferber*' (1982), *Sup. Ct. Rev.* 285, 317.

Scheller, J.C., 'PC Peep Show: Computers, Privacy and Child Pornography' (1994), *John Marshall Law Review*, 27 (Summer), 989–1016.

Sentencing Advisory Panel, *Offences Involving Child Pornography*, August 2002, at, <http://www.sentencing-advisory-panel.gov.uk/c_and_a/advice/child_offences/page1.htm>, and <http://www.sentencing-advisory-panel.gov.uk/c_and_a/advice/child_offences/advice_child_porn.pdf>.

——, *Sexual Offences 2 Consultation Paper*, 22 April 2004, at <http://www.sentencing-guidelines.gov.uk/docs/consult_sexualoffences2.pdf>.
Seto, M.C., J.M. Cantor and R. Blanchard, 'Validation of Child Pornography Possession as a Diagnostic Indicator of Pedophilia' (2006), *Journal of Abnormal Psychology* 115, 610–15.
Seto M.C. and A.W. Eke, 'The Criminal Histories and Later Offending of Child Pornography Offenders' (2005), *Sexual Abuse: A Journal of Research and Treatment* 17, 201–10.
Seto, M.C., A. Maric and E.B. Howard, 'The Role of Pornography in the Etiology of Sexual Aggression' (2001), *Aggression and Violent Behavior* 6, 35–53.
Slocum, B.G., 'Virtual Child Pornography: Does It Mean the End of the Child Pornography Exception to the First Amendment?' (2004), 14 *Albany Law Journal of Science and Technology* 637.
Smith, L.S., 'Private Possession of Child Pornography: Narrowing At-Home Privacy Rights' (1991), *Ann. Surv. Am. L.* 1011.
Socarides, C. and L. Loeb (eds), *The Mind of the Paedophile: Psychoanalytic Perspectives*, London: Karnac Books, 2004.
Stone, R., 'Extending the Labyrinth: Part VII of the CJPOA 1994', [1995] *MLR* 58 (3) 389–94.
Strossen, N., *Defending Pornography: Free Speech, Sex and the Fight for Women's Rights*, New York: Abacus, 1996.
Sullivan, C., *Internet Traders of Child Pornography: Profiling Research*, Department of Internal Affairs, New Zealand, November 2005, at <http://www.dia.govt.nz/pubforms.nsf/URL/Profilingupdate2.pdf/$file/Profilingupdate2.pdf>.
Swire, P.P., 'Markets, Self-Regulation, and Government Enforcement in the Protection of Personal Information', <http://www.ntia.doc.gov/reports/privacy/selfreg1.htm>, in US Department of Commerce, *Privacy and Self-regulation in the Information Age*, Washington, D.C., June 1997, at <http://www.ntia.doc.gov/reports/privacy/privacy_rpt.htm>.
Tate, T., *Child Pornography: An Investigation*, London: Methuen, 1990.
Taylor, M. and E. Quayle, *Child Pornography: An Internet Crime*, Hove: Brunner-Routledge, 2003.
Thomas, D.A., 'Sentencing: Making Indecent Photographs or Pseudo Photographs of Children – Sentencing Guidelines' (2003), *Criminal Law Review*, February, 127–33.
——, 'Sample Counts and Specimen Charges' (2005), *Criminal Law Review*, 575–9.
UK White Paper, *A New Future for Communications*, December 2000, Cm 5010, at <http://www.communicationswhitepaper.gov.uk/>.
UN Commission on Human Rights, 'Rights of the Child: Report of the Special Rapporteur (Mrs Ofelia Calcetas-Santos) on the sale of children, child prostitution and child pornography', E/CN.4/1996/100, 17 January, 1996.
UN Committee on the Rights of the Child, Guidelines regarding initial reports to be submitted by States Parties under article 12 (1) of the Optional Protocol to the Convention on the Rights of the Child on the Sale of Children, Child Prostitution and Child Pornography (unedited version), CRC/OP/SA/1, adopted by the Committee at its 777th meeting (Twenty-ninth session) on 1 February 2002, at <http://www.unhchr.ch/html/menu2/6/crcart12(1)>.

UN Convention on the Rights of the Child Adopted and opened for signature, ratification and accession by General Assembly resolution 44/25 of 20 November 1989 entry into force 2 September 1990, in accordance with article 49.

UN Declaration of the Rights of the Child Proclaimed by General Assembly resolution 1386(XIV) of 20 November 1959.

UN Optional Protocol to the Convention on the Rights of the Child on the Sale of Children, Child Prostitution and Child Pornography, New York, 25 May 2000, Fifty-fourth session (97th plenary meeting), Agenda item 116 (a), Distr. General A/RES/54/263, 26 June 2000.

UN Special Rapporteur (Mr Vitit Muntarbhorn) Report of the Commission on Human Rights on the sale of children, child prostitution and child pornography, E/CN.4/1994/84, 14 January 1994, presented at the fiftieth session of the General Assembly of the United Nations.

—— (Ms Ofelia Calcetas-Santos) Report of the Commission on Human Rights on the sale of children, child prostitution and child pornography, A/50/456, 20 September 1995, presented at the fiftieth session of the General Assembly of the United Nations.

—— (Ms Ofelia Calcetas-Santos) Report of the Commission on Human Rights on the sale of children, child prostitution and child pornography, A/51/456, 7 October 1996, presented at the fifty-first session of the General Assembly of the United Nations.

—— (Ms Ofelia Calcetas-Santos) Report of the Commission on Human Rights on the sale of children, child prostitution and child pornography, A/52/482, 16 October 1997, presented at the fifty-second session of the General Assembly of the United Nations.

—— (Ms Ofelia Calcetas-Santos) Report of the Commission on Human Rights on the sale of children, child prostitution and child pornography, E/CN.4/1998/101, 13 January 1998, presented at the fifty fourth session of the General Assembly of the United Nations.

—— (Ms Ofelia Calcetas-Santos) Report of the Commission on Human Rights on the sale of children, child prostitution and child pornography, A/54/411, 29 September 1999, presented at the fifty-fourth session of the General Assembly of the United Nations.

—— (Ms Ofelia Calcetas-Santos) Report of the Commission on Human Rights on the sale of children, child prostitution and child pornography, E/CN.4/2001/78, 25 January 2001, presented at the fifty-seventh session of the General Assembly of the United Nations.

—— (Mr Juan Miguel Petit) Report of the Commission on Human Rights on the sale of children, child prostitution and child pornography, E/CN.4/2002/88, 4 February 2002, presented at the fifty-eighth session of the General Assembly of the United Nations.

—— on the sale of children, child prostitution and child pornography, Thematic Report on child pornography on the Internet, E/CN.4/2005/78, Economic and Social Council, Commission on Human Rights, 23 December 2004, at <http://daccessdds.un.org/doc/UNDOC/GEN/G05/100/19/PDF/G0510019.pdf>. Addendum: Communications sent to Governments and replies received, E/CN.4/2005/78/Add.3, 8 March 2005, at <http://daccessdds.un.org/doc/UNDOC/GEN/G05/127/92/PDF/G0512792.pdf>.

UN Report of the Intergovernmental Working Group on the effective implementation of the Durban Declaration and Programme of Action on its fourth session (Chairperson-Rapporteur: Juan Martabit (Chile)), E/CN.4/2006/18, 20 March 2006, at <http://daccessdds.un.org/doc/UNDOC/GEN/G06/119/23/PDF/G0611923.pdf>.

UN Note by the Secretary-General, *Promotion and Protection of the Rights of Children: Sale of children, child prostitution and child pornography*, A/52/482, 16 October, 1997.

UNICEF, *Profiting from Abuse*, 2001, at <http://www.unicef.org/publications/files/pub_profiting_en.pdf>.

US Department of Justice, Executive Office for U.S. ATT'y, Review of Child Pornography and Obscenity Crimes, Rep. No. I-2001-07, t.3 (2001), 19 July 2001, at <http://www.usdoj.gov/oig/inspection/plus/0107/>.

——, Fact Sheet: Preventing Child Pornography, A New Legislative Proposal, 1 May 2002.

——, Office of the Attorney General, *Project Safe Childhood: Protecting Children from Online Exploitation and Abuse*, May 2006, at <http://www.projectsafechildhood.gov/guide.htm>.

US General Accounting Office, *File Sharing Programs: Users of Peer-to-Peer Networks can readily access child pornography*, GAO-04-757T, May 2004.

US Senate, Permanent Subcommittee on Investigation, *Child Pornography and Paedophilia*, 99th Cong. 2d Sess. 10–12 (1986).

——, Committee on the Judiciary Report on the Child Pornography Prevention Act of 1995, 104th Congress Report, Senate 2d Session 104–358, August 27, 1996.

——, Report, The PROTECT Act of 2003, No: 19-010, 108-2, 1st Session, 11 February 2003 (Hatch Report).

US Sentencing Commission, Report to the Congress: Downward Departures from the Federal Sentencing Guidelines (in response to section 401(m) of Public Law 108-21), October 2003.

Van Blarcum, C.D., 'Internet Hate Speech: The European Framework and the Emerging American Haven' (2005), 62 *Washington and Lee Law Review* 781.

Walker, C. and Y. Akdeniz, 'The Governance of the Internet in Europe with Special Reference to Illegal and Harmful Content' (1998), *Criminal Law Review*, December Special Edition: *Crime, Criminal Justice and the Internet*, 5–19.

——, 'Anti-Terrorism Laws and Data Retention: War is Over?' (2003), *Northern Ireland Legal Quarterly*, 54(2), Summer, 159–82.

Walker, S., *Hate Speech: The History of an American Controversy*, University of Nebraska Press, 1994.

Wall, D., 'Policing and the Regulation of the Internet' (1998), *Criminal Law Review*, December Special Edition: *Crime, Criminal Justice and the Internet*, 79–91.

——, 'Insecurity and the Policing of Cyberspace', in A. Crawford (ed.), *Crime and Insecurity*, Cullompton: Willan, 2002, 186–209.

——, *Cybercrime: The Transformation of Crime in the Information Age*, Cambridge: Polity Press, 2007.

Wallace, J., 'Nameless in Cyberspace: Anonymity on the Internet', Cato Institute, December 1999, at <http://www.cato.org/pubs/briefs/bp-054es.html>.

West, D., 'Paedophilia: Plague or Panic?' (2000), *Journal of Forensic Psychiatry* 11(3), 511–31.

Williams, E., 'Construction and Application of United States Sentencing Guideline § 2G2.1 et seq., Pertaining to Child Pornography', 145 *A.L.R. Fed.* 481.

Williams, K.S., 'Child Pornography Law: Does It Protect Children?' (2004), *Journal of Social Welfare and Family Law* 26(3), 245–61.

Williams Committee Report, *Obscenity and Film Censorship*, Cmnd 7772, London: HMSO, 1979.

Wilson, D. and I. Silverman, *Innocence Betrayed: Paedophilia, the Media and Society*, Cambridge: Polity Press, 2002.

Wolak, J., D. Finkelhor, K.J. Mitchell, *Child-Pornography Possessors Arrested in Internet-Related Crimes: Findings From the National Juvenile Online Victimization Study*, National Center for Missing and Exploited Children, 2005, at <http://www.missingkids.com/en_US/publications/NC144.pdf>.

——, 'The Varieties of Child Pornography Production', in E. Quayle and M. Taylor (eds), *Viewing Child Pornography on the Internet: Understanding the Offence, Managing the Offender, Helping the Victims*, Lyme Regis: Russell House, 2005, 31–48.

The Working Group on Internet Governance, *Background Report*, July 2005, at <http://www.wgig.org/docs/WGIGREPORT.pdf>.

Wortley, R. and S. Smallbone, *Child Pornography on the Internet*, Problem Oriented Guides for Police Problem Specific Guides Series, No: 41, US Department of Justice, Office of Community Oriented Policing Services, May 2006, at <http://www.cops.usdoj.gov/mime/open.pdf?Item=1729>.

Zitter, J.M., 'Annotation: Liability of Internet Service Provider for Internet or E-Mail Defamation' (2000), *84 A.L.R. 5th 169*.

Index